Ordnance Survey

BRITAIN'S MOST COMPREHENSIVE REGIONAL ATLASES

STREET ATLASES

PHILIP'S

◆ **COUNTY-WIDE MAPPING**

Clear and accurate mapping covers each entire county at the detailed scale of 3½ inches to 1 mile (hardback, spiral and paperback atlases) and 2½ inches to 1 mile (pocket atlases).

◆ **DETAILED URBAN AND RURAL COVERAGE**

In towns, a wealth of useful information includes car parks, police and fire stations, post offices, railway stations and information centres. Schools and colleges, hospitals, public buildings and sports and leisure facilities are all marked or named. In rural areas, landscape features such as hills, woods and streams are marked and named where possible, as are farms and footpaths.

◆ **EVERY NAMED STREET IN TOWN AND COUNTRY**

All named streets and roads are featured, including private roads, tracks and footpaths. Principal routes are colour coded and road features are large, accurate and detailed.

◆ **COMPREHENSIVE INDEXES**

Each atlas is indexed by street, town and village names. Colour edition indexes contain postcodes for every street and highlight schools, hospitals and public amenities.

◆ **AVAILABLE IN THREE HANDY FORMATS**

Colour Editions

- Hardback (£10.99–£14.99)
- Spiral (£8.99–£9.99)
- Pocket (£3.99–£4.99)

Black/White Editions

- Hardback (£10.99–£12.99)
- Paperback (£9.99)
- Pocket (£4.99)

COLOUR EDITIONS

◆ Berkshire	◆ Hertfordshire	◆ Surrey
◆ Buckinghamshire	◆ East Kent	◆ East Sussex
◆ Durham	◆ West Kent	◆ West Sussex
◆ North Hampshire	◆ Lancashire	◆ Tyne and Wear
◆ South Hampshire	◆ Greater Manchester	◆ South Yorkshire
	◆ Merseyside	◆ West Yorkshire

BLACK/WHITE EDITIONS

◆ Bristol and Avon	◆ Edinburgh & East Central Scotland	◆ Nottinghamshire
◆ Cardiff, Swansea and Glamorgan	◆ East Essex	◆ Oxfordshire
◆ Cheshire	◆ West Essex	◆ Staffordshire
◆ Derbyshire	◆ Glasgow & West Central Scotland	◆ Warwickshire

---

The atlases are widely available from all good retailers including OS agents, bookstores, newsagents and garage forecourts.

Alternatively the atlases are available by mail order direct from the publisher by phoning our Customer Order Line on 01933 443863 or 01933 443849 during office hours 9am to 5pm. Or leave a message on the answering machine quoting your full name and address number plus expiry date and your full credit card

Knole
Sevenoaks, Kent TN15 0RP
☎ (01732) 450608/462100
℻ (01732) 465528 □ 23 L7

Knole is the largest private house in England and sits within a magnificent deer park owned by Lord Sackville. Dating from 1456, the house was enlarged and embellished in 1603 by Thomas Sackville, 1st Earl of Dorset, to whom it had been granted by Elizabeth I. The 13 state rooms open to the public contain a collection of historical portraits, including works by Van Dyck and Gainsborough and a room devoted to the works of Sir Joshua Reynolds. Silver, tapestries and a world-renowned collection of Stuart furniture and the prototype Knole Settee.

Lamb House (tenanted)
West Street, Rye, East Sussex TN31 7ES
☎ REGIONAL OFFICE (01892) 890651
□ 17 G3

Home of the writer Henry James from 1898 to 1916 where he wrote the best novels of his later period. The walled garden, staircase, hall and three rooms on the ground floor containing some of James' personal possessions are on view. Also once home to the author E.F. Benson.

Lavenham: The Guildhall of Corpus Christi
Market Place, Lavenham, Sudbury, Suffolk CO10 9QZ
☎ (01787) 247646 □ 36 E6

Early 16th-century timber-framed Tudor building, originally the hall of the Guild of Corpus Christi, overlooks and dominates the market place. Displays of local history, farming, industry and the development of the railway, and a unique exhibition of 700 years of the medieval woollen cloth trade. An unusual exhibit in the hall is a mummified cat found in the roof, where it had been placed to ward off evil spirits! There is a delightful walled garden with a 19th-century lock up and mortuary.

Lyveden New Bield
Nr Oundle, Peterborough, Northamptonshire PE8 5AT
☎ (01832) 205358 ℻ (01832) 205358
□ 34 D1

The shell of an uncompleted 'lodge' or garden house, begun c.1595 by Sir Thomas Tresham, and designed in the shape of a cross. The exterior incorporates friezes inscribed with religious quotations and signs of the Passion. Sir Thomas died before the building was completed and his son, Francis Tresham, was then imprisoned in connection with the Gunpowder Plot.

Melford Hall
Long Melford, Sudbury, Suffolk CO10 9AH
☎ (01787) 880286 □ 36 D5

A turreted brick Tudor mansion, little changed since 1578 with the original panelled banqueting hall, an 18th-century drawing room, a Regency library and a Victorian bedroom, showing fine furniture and Chinese porcelain. There is also a special Beatrix Potter display and a garden.

Mompesson House
The Close, Salisbury, Wiltshire SP1 2EL
☎ (01722) 335659 □ 12 D3

A perfect example of an 18th-century house, and one of the most distinguished in the Cathedral Close. Recently used as the location for Mrs Jennings' London residence in the film adaptation of Jane Austen's 'Sense and Sensibility'. The house holds the magnificent Turnbull collection of 18th-century drinking glasses. A peaceful garden enclosed on one side by the great wall of the Cathedral Close.

Monk's House (tenanted)
Rodmell, Lewes, East Sussex BN7 3HF
☎ REGIONAL OFFICE (01892) 890651
℻ (01892) 890110 □ 15 H5

A small village house and garden, and the home of Leonard and Virginia Woolf from 1919 until Leonard's death in 1969.

Mottisfont Abbey Garden
Mottisfont, nr Romsey, Hampshire SO51 0LP
☎ (01794) 340757
℻ (01794) 341492 □ 13 F3

The setting of this 12th-century Augustinian Priory is one of great beauty and tranquillity. A tributary of the River Test flows close to the Abbey and the grounds contain a magnificent collection of huge trees. The Priory became a house after the Dissolution of the Monasteries in the 16th century. The grounds also contain the spring or 'font' from which the place name is derived.

A drawing room decorated by Rex Whistler, and the cellarium of the old Priory.

The national collection of old-fashioned roses is housed in the walled garden.

The Needles Old Battery
West Highdown, Isle of Wight PO39 0JH
☎ (01983) 754772 DURING OPENING HOURS □ 7 H6

A Victorian coastal fort built in 1862, high above the sea. A tunnel leads to spectacular views of Needles Rocks, lighthouse and coastline. Two original gun barrels are mounted on carriages in the parade ground and the Laboratory, Searchlight Position and Poisition-Finding Cells have been restored.

Nymans Garden
Handcross, nr Haywards Heath, West Sussex RH17 6EB
☎ (01444) 400321/400777
℻ (01444) 400253 □ 15 F3

One of the great gardens of the Sussex Weald. Twelve hectares (30 acres) of rare and beautiful trees, shrubs and plants collected from across the world. Walled garden with Italian fountain, hidden sunken garden, laurel walk and ancient bank of bird cherries. The picturesque ruins of the house overlook the lawns. Across the road is the wild flower garden, formerly known as the Tasmania Garden, about 4 ha (10 acres).

Woodland Walks start from the Garden and include lakes and trees planted by the donor family.

Oakhurst Cottage
Hambledon, nr Godalming, Surrey GU8 4HF ☎ ℻ (01428) 683207
□ 14 C2

A very small 16th-century timber-framed cottage, restored and furnished as a simple cottager's dwelling. Delightful cottage garden with contemporary plant species.

Old Town Hall, Newtown
Contact Custodian, Ken Cottage, Upper Lane, Brighstone, Isle of Wight PO30 4AT
☎ (01983) 741052 □ 7 J5

A delightful, small 18th-century brick and stone building that was once the focal point of the 'rotten borough' of Newtown. Copies of ancient documents of the borough are on display with a facsimile of the mace from the hall. An exhibition depicts the history of the famous 'Ferguson's Gang'.

Osterley Park
Isleworth, Middlesex TW7 4RB
☎ (0181) 560 3918
℻ (0181) 758 2116 □ 23 G5

Osterley was completed in 1575 for Sir Thomas Gresham, founder of the Royal Exchange. Between 1760 and 1780 it was transformed into a neo-classical villa by Robert Adam for the wealthy London banker Robert Child. The superb interiors are one of the country's most complete examples of Robert Adam's work, and include plasterwork, carpets and furniture.

Owletts (tenanted)
The Street, Cobham, Gravesend, Kent DA12 3AP
☎ (01892) 890651 □ 24 C6

Red brick Charles II house best remembered as being the birthplace of architect Herbert Baker in 1862. The possessions he collected reflect his travelled past. Small pleasure and kitchen gardens.

Oxburgh Hall
Oxborough, King's Lynn, Norfolk PE33 9PS
☎ (01366) 328258
℻ (01366) 328066 □ 46 C6

The medieval gatehouse, a great battlemented edifice with large mullioned windows. Built in 1482 the rooms and their contents range from Tudor to Georgian and Victorian. Mary Queen of Scots embroidery, and a wonderful tapestry map of Oxfordshire and Berkshire.

Built on an island in the Fens, the land around is now drained and cultivated into a wonderful garden with delightful walks. Featured in BBC1's 'Love on a Branch Line' in June 1994.

Paycocke's (tenanted)
West Street, Coggeshall, Colchester, Essex CO6 1NS
☎ (01376) 561305 □ 36 D7

Delightful cameos frolic along the intricately decorated wooden beam spanning the whole width of this fine half-timbered merchant's house dating from 1500. Inside there is a display of the lace for which Coggeshall was famous. Pleasant garden.

Peckover House
North Brink, Wisbech, Cambridgeshire PE13 1JR
☎ (01945) 583463 ℻ (01945) 583463
□ 45 H6

Once a flourishing coastal port, fluctuations in the coastline have taken Wisbech far from the sea. Once owned by a prominent Quaker banking family, the classically plain exterior contrasts with the wealth of elaborate wood and plasterwork inside. Peckover recently came into the news when it was used as Montague Tigg's house in the BBC adaptation of the Dickensian classic 'Martin Chuzzlewit'. Visitors can play croquet in the 0.8 ha (2 acre) Victorian garden. Several summerhouses, a Victorian fernery and an orangery.

Petworth House & Park
Petworth, West Sussex GU28 0AE
☎ (01798) 342207
℻ (01798) 342963 □ 14 C3

More of a palace than a conventional country house, Petworth is set in 'Capability' Brown's famous 283-ha (700-acre) landscape park immortalised by Turner. Internationally known for its outstanding art collection, Petworth has over 300 paintings on display including works by Turner, Van Dyck, Titian, Gainsborough, Blake, Reynolds and Claude. The works of art are complemented by fine collections of ancient and neo-classical sculpture, furniture and wood carvings by Grinling Gibbons. These grand showrooms are joined by a suite of rooms in the servants' block on show for the first time.

Polesden Lacey
Nr Dorking, Surrey RH5 6BD
☎ (01372) 458203/452048
℻ (01372) 452023 □ 14 E1

Polesden Lacey is still a peaceful country estate, surrounded by trees and green pasture. The house, an elegant Regency 'villa', was luxuriously furnished in Edwardian times by society hostess, The Hon. Mrs Greville. Her collection of furniture, paintings, porcelain and silver is remarkable. King George VI and Queen Elizabeth (now the Queen Mother) chose this house for part of their honeymoon. Lovely walled garden and stunning walks through the North Downs.

Princes Risborough Manor House (tenanted)
Princes Risborough, Buckinghamshire HP17 9AW
☎ REGIONAL OFFICE (01494) 528051
□ 22 D2

A 17th-century red-brick house with Jacobean oak staircase. House and front garden by written arrangement only with tenant.

Quebec House
Westerham, Kent TN16 1TD
☎ REGIONAL OFFICE (01892) 890651
□ 23 K7

One of Britain's greatest military heroes, James Wolfe, spent the first eleven years of his life here. The 17th-century house is full of mementoes of his victory at Quebec when he defeated the French by scaling the Heights of Abraham above the town.

Rainham Hall (tenanted)
The Broadway, Rainham, Havering, Greater London RM13 9YN
☎ REGIONAL OFFICE (01494) 528051
□ 23 L4

Conveniently close to the Thames, this elegant Georgian house was completed in 1729 for prosperous merchant, John Harle. Built in the domestic Dutch style, with dormers in the hipped roof, the interior has hardly changed. Bookings by written application to the Tenant.

Runnymede
Egham, Surrey
☎ (01784) 432891
℻ (01784) 470194 □ 22 F5

76 ha (188 acres) of historic meadows where King John sealed the Magna Carta in 1215; 44.5 ha (110 acres) of wooded slopes on Cooper's Hill overlook the meadows. Memorials dedicated to the Magna Carta, John F. Kennedy and the Air Forces.

St John's Jerusalem
Sutton-at-Hone, Dartford, Kent DA4 9HQ
☎ REGIONAL OFFICE (01892) 890651
□ 23 L5

A large garden, moated by the River Darent. The house is the former chapel of a Knight's Hospitallers' Commandery, since converted into a private residence.The east end of the chapel was retained for family worship, but later was converted into a billiard room.

Sandham Memorial Chapel
Burghclere, nr Newbury, Hampshire RG15 9JT
☎ ℻ (01635) 278394 □ 21 J6

Sandham Memorial Chapel houses the largest collection of paintings by a single artist and is one of the most unique and intriguing properties of the National Trust. The walls of this First World War memorial built in the 1920s are entirely covered with murals by Stanley Spencer. This astonishing project, executed between 1926–32 and illustrating the artist's experiences during the war, is considered to be his greatest achievement.

As there is no lighting in the Chapel it is advisable to view the paintings on a bright day.

Scotney Castle Garden
Lamberhurst, Tunbridge Wells, Kent TN3 8JN
☎ (01892) 891081 ℻ (01892) 890110
□ 16 D2

Often described as the most romantic garden in England, the ruins of the small 14th-century castle are reflected in its moat, forming the backdrop to a garden of breathtaking beauty and considerable importance to the garden-historian. Rhododendrons and azaleas in season and specimen trees offer picturesque views from all angles; truly an enchanted place.

Shaw's Corner
Ayot St Lawrence, nr Welwyn, Hertfordshire AL6 9BX
☎ (01438) 820307 □ 23 G1

An early 20th-century house, and the home of George Bernard Shaw from 1906 until his death in 1950. Many literary and personal relics are shown in the downstairs rooms, which remain as in his lifetime. Shaw's bedroom and bathroom are also on view, and there is a display room upstairs.

Sheffield Park Garden
Uckfield, East Sussex TN22 3QX
☎ (01825) 790231
℻ (01825) 791264 □ 15 H3

A highly impressive 40-ha (100-acre) garden, with five lakes, laid out in the 18th century by 'Capability' Brown. In early summer the 'Stream Garden' is particularly attractive and in the autumn hundreds of trees and shrubs, planted specially for their autumn colour, are a spectacular display.

Sissinghurst Castle Garden
Sissinghurst, nr Cranbrook, Kent TN17 2AB
☎ (01580) 715330
℻ (01580) 713911 □ 16 E2

Of international acclaim, this connoisseur's garden was created by the late Vita Sackville-West and her husband, Sir Harold Nicolson, between the surviving parts of an Elizabethan mansion. A series of small enclosed romantic gardens or 'outdoor rooms' are the spring garden, orchard, white garden and herb garden. Also the study where Vita Sackville-West worked, and the Long Library.

Smallhythe Place
Smallhythe, Tenterden, Kent TN30 7NG
☎ (01580) 762334 □ 17 F2

Legendary actress Dame Ellen Terry lived here for nearly 30 years, from 1899 until her death in July 1928. The house is a museum of the great actress's career and includes many personal and theatrical mementoes from the greats of Victorian drama. A charming cottage garden includes Ellen Terry's rose garden.

South Foreland Lighthouse
St Margaret's-at-Cliffe, Dover, Kent
☎ REGIONAL OFFICE (01892) 890651
℻ (01892) 890110 □ 17 L1

A distinctive landmark on the White Cliffs of Dover with views to France. The lighthouse was built in 1843 and used by Marconi for the first radio communications as an aid to navigation in 1898. The tower and information room are open (the cottage is tenanted) and you can climb the spiral stairs to the balcony around the light.

Sprivers Garden (tenanted)
Horsmonden, Kent TN12 8DR
☎ REGIONAL OFFICE (01892) 890651
□ 16 D2

This garden includes flowering and foliage shrubs, herbaceous borders, old walls and spring and summer bedding.

Standen
East Grinstead, West Sussex RH19 4NE
☎ (01342) 323029
℻ (01342) 316424 □ 15 G2

Built in the 1890s by the architect Philip Webb, whose friendship with William Morris led to the house being decorated with many of the famous designer's textiles and wallpapers. These have been carefully restored and the house is full of light and colour. There is also a good collection of contemporary furniture, pottery and pictures, as well as the original electric light fittings. A beautiful hillside garden and woodland walk.

Stoneacre (tenanted)
Otham, Maidstone, Kent ME15 8RS
☎ (01622) 862871 □ 24 D7

A half-timbered mainly late 15th-century yeoman's house, with great hall and crowpost, and newly restored cottage-style garden.

Sutton House
2 & 4 Homerton High Street, Hackney, London E9 6JQ
☎ (0181) 986 2264 □ 23 J4

A rare example of a Tudor red-brick house in London's East End. Built in 1535 by Sir Rafe Sadleir, Principal Secretary of State for Henry VIII. Recent restoration revealed many 16th-century details which are now displayed when 'secret' panels are opened. Erroneously named after Thomas Sutton, sometime steward to the Earl of Warwick, who, in fact, lived next door.

Tattershall Castle
Tattershall, Lincolnshire LN4 4LR
☎ (01526) 342543 □ 45 F1

A magnificent example of medieval brick architecture, with walls 14 ft (4.5 m) thick at the base, it rises through four floors to a roof-top courtyard and battlement walkway.

Each floor contains a single enormous state room and many smaller rooms within the thickness of the walls. Surrounding the castle is a double moat.

Theatre Royal
Westgate Street, Bury St Edmunds, Suffolk IP33 1QR
☎ (01284) 755127
℻ (01284) 706035 □ 36 D3

Built in 1819 by William Wilkins, a rare example of a late Georgian playhouse with fine pit, boxes and gallery. A working theatre presenting a year-round programme of professional drama, comedy, dance, music, mime, pantomime and amateur work. It boasts a national reputation and attracts the best touring companies in the country.

Uppark
South Harting, Petersfield, Hampshire GU31 5QR
☎ (01730) 825415
℻ (01730) 825873 □ 14 A4

A fine late 17th-century house, recently re-opened after major restoration following the fire in 1989. Situated high on the South Downs, there are magnificent views towards the Solent. There is also an important collection of paintings formed by members of the Fetherstonhaugh family. Below stairs attractions include extensive servants' rooms where the mother of H.G. Wells worked as housekeeper.

The garden has been replanned and replanted.

The Vyne
Sherborne St John, Basingstoke, Hampshire RG24 9HL
☎ (01256) 881337
℻ (01256) 881720 □ 22 B7

A house of comfortable charm drawing the visitor back to the time of Henry VIII. Now set in fine parkland dating from the mid 18th-century.

The pillared portico, added to in the 1650s, is the first to be built onto an English country house.

A remarkable staircase, rich Tudor panelling and excellent 18th-century furnishings.

The house will be closed throughout 1997 to allow essential services and restoration work to begin and will re-open mid 1998. The grounds are planned to remain open.

Waddesdon Manor
Waddesdon, nr Aylesbury, Buckinghamshire HP18 0JH
☎ (01296) 651282
℻ (01296) 651293 □ 22 C1

Waddesdon Manor, designed in the style of a French Renaissance château, was built in the 1870s by Baron Ferdinand de Rothschild from the Austrian branch of the famous Rothschild banking family. The interior evokes 18th-century France and is furnished with panelling, furniture, carpets and porcelain, many of which have a royal French provenance. There is an important collection of English 18th-century portraits by Gainsborough and Reynolds and of 17th-century Old Masters. There are rooms devoted to Sèvres porcelain and Baron Ferdinand's 18th-century panelling. In the garden a rococo-style aviary houses exotic birds. The garden includes the formal parterre, with lavish 19th-century planting scheme.

Wakehurst Place
Ardingly, nr Haywards Heath, West Sussex RH17 6TN
☎ (01444) 894066 ℻ (01444) 894069
□ 15 G3

This magnificent garden is leased to the Royal Botanic Gardens, Kew who manage and fund it. With over 70 ha (170 acres), Wakehurst Place offers a unique blend of education, conservation and science. Here you can see four comprehensive National Collections – birch, hypericum, southern beech and skimmia, and compare the many different species. Temperate trees from across the continents and several lakes and ponds. An Elizabethan mansion built in 1590 houses an exhibition of the work of the Royal Botanic Gardens, Kew. Please note – only a small section of the mansion is open to the public.

West Wycombe Park
West Wycombe, Buckinghamshire HP14 3AJ
☎ (01628) 488675 □ 22 D3

A Palladian house with frescos and painted ceilings, fashioned for Sir Francis Dashwood in the mid-18th century. Dashwood is now chiefly remembered for his connection with the notorious Hellfire Club which met in caves on the estate. The landscape garden and lake were laid out at the same time as the house, with various classical temples. Guided tours of house on weekdays. Guided tours of the grounds by written arrangement.

West Wycombe Village & Hill
□ 22 D3

For six centuries, the principal route from London to Oxford, the Midlands and Wales, passed through West Wycombe, nurturing the creation of this Chilterns village. There are fine examples of buildings from the 16th to 18th centuries. The hill is part of the 18th-century landscape of West Wycombe Park. It is surmounted by an Iron Age hill fort, now the site of the church and Dashwood mausoleum, and commands fine views.

Wimpole Hall and Wimpole Home Farm
Arrington, Royston, Cambridgeshire SG8 0BW
☎ (01223) 207257
℻ (01223) 207838 □ 35 G4

In 1936 Rudyard Kipling's daughter started the stunning restoration of the largest house in Cambridgeshire. The façades date from the first half of the 18th century when visitors included Swift and Pope.

An impressive library designed by James Gibbs. There is also a Chapel with painted decorations by James Thornhill. Parkland designed by 'Capability' Brown among others.

Home Farm presents a living museum of agriculture with ancient farm implements and many rare breeds, all housed in Sir John Soane's thatched farm buildings.

Winkworth Arboretum
Hascombe Road, Godalming, Surrey GU8 4AD
☎ (01483) 208477 □ 14 C1

Winkworth Arboretum was planned and planted as a woodland in the 1930s and every effort is made to preserve that special character. It covers over 40.5 ha (100 acres), has two lakes and many rare trees and shrubs. The Arboretum is worth a visit at any time of the year. It is open from dawn to dusk daily. Wildlife abounds and there is an impressive show of butterflies and moths.

The West Country

Antony
Torpoint, Plymouth, Cornwall PL11 2QA
☎ (01752) 812191 □ 4 E4

One of Cornwall's finest early 18th-century houses faced in the lustrous silvery-grey Pentewan stone, offset by colonnaded wings of red brick and set within extensive grounds. The fine garden contains a national collection of day lilies, magnolias and summer borders. Also of note is an 18th-century dovecote and the 1789 Bath Pond House. Antony has been the home of the Carew family for almost 600 years.

Arlington Court
Arlington, nr Barnstaple, Devon EX31 4LP
☎ (01271) 850296
℻ (01271) 850711 □ 9 G1

A house full of collections, a stable block with horses and one of the finest carriage collections in the country. Walks through colourful gardens, grounds and woods, all set in miles of beautiful North Devon countryside.

The air in North Devon being so pure, the property has more lichens and mosses to be seen than almost any other in the country.

Avebury
Nr Marlborough, Wiltshire SN8 1RF
☎ ANSWERPHONE (01672) 539250
□ 20 E6

One of the most important Megalithic monuments in Europe, this site with stone circles enclosed by a ditch and external bank is approached by an avenue of stones. Includes the Alexander Keiller Museum and the Wiltshire Life Society's display of Wiltshire rural life in the Great Barn. The National Trust also owns 626 ha (1,546 acres) which provide the setting for the stone circle. Museum collection on loan to the National Trust.

Avebury Manor & Garden
Nr Marlborough, Wiltshire SN8 1RF
☎ (01672) 539250 □ 20 E6

A regularly altered house of monastic origin, the present buildings date from the early 16th century, with notable Queen Anne alterations and Edwardian renovations by Colonel Jenner. The topiary and flower gardens contain medieval walls, ancient box and numerous compartments. Parts of the house are open to view.

Barrington Court
Nr Ilminster, Somerset TA19 0NQ
☎ (01460) 241938 □ 10 E4

A particularly fine garden laid out in a series of 'rooms' with a working kitchen garden.

The Tudor manor house was restored in the 1920s by the Lyle family. It is now let to Stuart Interiors, the furniture reproducers, and is open to National Trust visitors at the same time as the garden.

Bradley
Newton Abbot, Devon TQ12 6BN
☎ (01626) 54513 □ 5 J2

A small 15th-century medieval manor house with original decoration set in woodland and meadows. Bradley is a tenanted property.

Buckland Abbey
Yelverton, Devon PL20 6EY
☎ (01822) 853607
℻ (01822) 855448 □ 4 F3

In its own secluded valley on the edge of Dartmoor, above the River Tavy, Buckland Abbey holds the secret to over 700 years of history. Medieval monks established a Cistercian monastery. Sir Richard Grenville converted the Abbey into a dwelling place. Later, Sir Francis Drake lived at Buckland during the turbulent period of the Armada.

Walks through the estate farm and woodlands. The location for BBC Television's 'The Vet' series.

The Courts
Holt, nr Trowbridge, Wiltshire BA14 6RR
☎ (01225) 782340 □ 20 C6

2.8-ha (7-acre) garden of mystery flanking an 18th-century house (not open to the public), with an ornamental façade.

Castle Drogo
Drewsteignton, nr Exeter, Devon EX6 6PB
☎ (01647) 433306
℻ (01647) 433186 □ 9 H6

The last castle to be built in Britain, this 20th-century home designed by Sir Edwin Lutyens incorporates modern conveniences with a medieval atmosphere. The garden is colourful from spring to autumn. A huge, circular croquet lawn is available for visitors. Castle Drogo is superbly situated on a Dartmoor crag, with magnificent views and walks into the wooded gorge of the River Teign.

Chedworth Roman Villa

Yanworth, nr Cheltenham, Gloucestershire GL54 3LJ
☎ (01242) 890256
Fax (01242) 890544 20 E1

One of the best exposed Romano-British villas in Britain, the remains are those of the luxurious 4th-century house. The rooms are arranged in three wings around a large courtyard, and features include several 4th-century mosaics, two bath-houses and a water shrine with running spring. A small museum houses a fine selection of objects illustrating all aspects of life in Roman times. The site is situated in a beautiful wooded combe in quiet countryside. Conservation and archaeological fieldwork can be seen in operation.

Clevedon Court

Tickenham Road, Clevedon, N.W. Somerset BS21 6QU
☎ (01275) 872257 19 J5

Clevedon Court is the manor house of Clevedon. It was built about 1320 by Sir John de Clevedon and is one of the very few complete houses of its time that has survived. The property was bought in 1709 by Abraham Elton who became 1st Baronet, and has been in continuous occupation by the Elton family up to the present day. The house contains a number of family collections and Monuments of Engineering: part of a collection made by Sir Arthur Elton, 10th Baronet, which illustrates aspects of the Industrial Revolution.

Coleridge Cottage

35 Lime Street, Nether Stowey, Bridgwater, Somerset TA5 1NQ
☎ (01278) 732662 10 C2

Coleridge's home for three years from 1797. It was here that he wrote 'The Rime of the Ancient Mariner', part of 'Christabel and Frost at Midnight'. The parlour and reading room only are open to the public.

Coleton Fishacre Garden

Coleton, Kingswear, Dartmouth, Devon TQ6 0EQ
☎ (01803) 752466 5 J4

This 8-hectare (20-acre) garden, developed by Lady Dorothy D'Oyly Carte, lies in a stream fed valley amid the spectacular scenery of this National Trust Coast. The subtropical climate and sheltered location provides a superb setting for the large collection of tender and exotic plants, started in the 1920s and is continually being developed by the National Trust today and also provides a sanctuary for a wide range of birds and wild animals. Minimum tour time 1 to 2 hours, more for those with special horticultural interest. Guided walks by special arrangement.

Compton Castle

Marldon, Paignton, Devon TQ3 1TA
☎ (01803) 872112 5 J3

A fortified manor house with curtain wall, built at three periods: 1340, 1450, 1520, by the Gilbert family. It was the home of Sir Humphrey Gilbert (1539–83), coloniser of Newfoundland and half-brother of Sir Walter Raleigh: the family still lives here.

Corfe Castle

Wareham, Dorset BH20 5EZ
☎ (01929) 481294
Fax (01929) 481294 6 D6

The magnificent ruins of this 1000-year-old castle dominate the Isle of Purbeck. The ruins of the castle have many fine medieval defensive features and the Gloriette features some of the best early Gothic architecture in England.

For more information on Living History weekends and medieval and civil war re-enactments, please contact the Property Manager on the above number.

Cornish Engines

Pool, nr Redruth, Cornwall
☎ (01209) 216657 2 E5

The key to the growth of the Cornish mining industry was the expiry of the patent on the Boulton and Watt steam engine in 1800. With restrictions removed, Cornish engineers set about producing more efficient engines. The Trust owns several survivals from this great chapter in Cornish history. At the East Pool and Agar mine is the largest of the great beam engines left in Cornwall, commissioned from Harvey's in 1891 and put to work in 1925.

Cotehele

St Dominick, nr Saltash, Cornwall PL12 6TA
☎ (01579) 351346 4 E3

Built 1485–1627, and home of the Edgcumbe family for centuries, the house contains original furniture, armour and a remarkable set of tapestries and other textiles. There is a series of formal gardens near the house and a richly planted valley garden including a medieval dovecote, stewpond and Victorian summerhouse as well as an 18th-century tower with fine views. Cotehele Mill has been restored to working condition, with adjoining workshops. Also of interest is Cotehele Quay, on the River Tamar. There are woodland walks throughout the estate.

Dunster Castle

Dunster, nr Minehead, Somerset TA24 6SL
☎ (01643) 821314 10 A1

600 years of Luttrell family residence has groomed and moulded the property from coastal fortress to a secluded county seat. The house and medieval ruins are magically framed with sub-tropical plants including the famous Dunster Lemon; the National Collection of Arbutus; palm trees and Kiwi fruit. Each winding path reveals a new secret, whether a rare shrub or a glimpse of the sea with the Welsh mountains beyond.

Dunster Working Water Mill

Mill Lane, Dunster, nr Minehead, Somerset TA24 6SW
☎ (01643) 821759 10 A1

Built on the site of a mill mentioned in the Domesday Survey of 1086, the present mill dates from the 18th century and was restored to working order in 1979.

Dyrham Park

Nr Chippenham, Wiltshire SN14 8ER
☎ (0117) 9372501 20 B5

The mansion at Dyrham Park lies at the foot of an ancient parkland situated at the end of the Cotswold Scarp. The deer park has been here since Saxon times.

The present house dates from the time of William and Mary: much of the content of the house reflects that period. A magnificent collection of Delft, paintings by Dutch masters and intricate furniture.

The formal garden with two lakes which is all that remains of a splendid water garden. The Park and the exterior of the house were used in the making of the film 'The Remains of the Day'.

Finch Foundry

Sticklepath, Okehampton, Devon EX20 2NW
☎ (01837) 840046 9 G6

Fascinating 19th-century forge, powered by three water wheels. The forge produced sickles, scythes and shovels for both agriculture and mining. The forge is in the centre of the picturesque village of Sticklepath with countryside and river walks adjoining.

Glendurgan Garden

Mawnan Smith, nr Falmouth, Cornwall TR11 5JZ
☎ (01208) 74281 OR (01326) 250906 (OPENING HOURS ONLY) 2 F7

Set in a wooded valley rich in fine trees and rare and exotic plants, Glendurgan is one of the great sub-tropical gardens of the South West. The 1833 laurel maze, recently restored, and the 'Giant's Stride' (a pole with ropes to swing from) are unusual and popular features. The garden runs down to the tiny village of Durgan and its beach. The house is privately occupied.

Great Chalfield Manor

Nr Melksham, Wiltshire SN12 8NJ
☎ (01985) 843600 20 D6

Dating from 1480, the manor house is set across a moat between parish church and stables. Restored early this century by Major R. Fuller, whose family still lives here. No free-flow; guided tours only.

Hardy's Cottage

Higher Bockhampton, nr Dorchester, Dorset DT2 8QJ
☎ (01305) 262366 11 H6

A small thatched cottage where the novelist and poet Thomas Hardy was born in 1840. It was built by his great grandfather and little altered; furnished by the Trust. The interior can be viewed by appointment with the Custodian. Exterior from end of garden. See also Max Gate.

Killerton

Broadclyst, Exeter, Devon EX5 3LE
☎ (01392) 881345 10 A6

The spectacular hillside garden is beautiful throughout the year. The grounds are surrounded by parkland and woods through which a number of specially designed circular walks have been created.

The house, built in 1778, is furnished as a comfortable family home and includes a music room where the piano and organ can be played by visitors. Upstairs, the Paulise de Bush collection of costumes from the 18th century to the present day is displayed in a series of period rooms.

Knightshayes Court

Bolham, Tiverton, Devon EX16 7RQ
☎ (01884) 254665
Fax (01884) 243050 9 K4

Designed by William Burges and built in 1869, a rare example of the architect's High Victorian Gothic style. Of equal beauty and fascination is the 20 ha (50 acre) garden. Originally designed by Edward Kemp, this glorious garden owes much to the late Sir John and Joyce, Lady Amory who devoted themselves to its development.

The Levant Steam Engine

Trewellard, Pendeen, nr St Just, Cornwall ☎ (01209) 216657 2 B6

Harvey's of Hayle built the machinery in 1840 for the Levant mine which visitors will discover just north of St Just, spectacularly housed in a building set on the edge of the cliffs. After 60 idle years, the famous engine is steaming again.

Lanhydrock

Bodmin, Cornwall PL30 5AD
☎ (01208) 73320
Fax (01208) 74084 3 J3

Superbly positioned above the River Fowey and enfolded in its wooded parkland estate. One of the most beautiful houses in Cornwall, and the most complete house on show in the British Isles. A blend of High Victorian splendour and elements from the original house, almost destroyed by fire in 1881. Beautiful Victorian garden.

Lacock Abbey

Lacock, nr Chippenham, Wiltshire, SN15 2LG
☎ (01249) 730227
Fax (01249) 730501 20 D6

The abbey was founded in 1232, and was converted into a country house in the mid 16th century. Home of the Talbot family, the Fox Talbot Museum of Photography at the entrance gates is a museum of early photography. The abbey is in the village of Lacock, a medieval wool village also in the care of the National Trust.

Lundy Island

Devon EX39 2LY
☎ (01237) 431831
Fax (01237) 431832 8 B1

An unspoilt island, with rocky headlands and fascinating animal and bird life, with no cars to disrupt the peace. The small island community includes a church, tavern and castle. There is a steep climb to the village from the landing beach. Lundy is financed, administered and maintained by the Landmark Trust.

Lydford Gorge

The Stables, Lydford Gorge, Lydford, nr Okehampton, Devon EX20 4BH
☎ (01822) 820441/820320 8 F7

The Gorge is perhaps best known for its spectacular White Lady Waterfall, a 90 ft (27.5 metre) cascade of water which falls through trees and rocks into the river below. A circular walk through the Gorge takes you to the Devil's Cauldron, a whirlpool of water where the River Lyd rushes through a series of potholes. You can watch this fascinating sight from the safety of a specially constructed walkway. Lydford is an important site for wildlife.

Lytes Cary Manor

Charlton Mackrell, Somerton, Somerset TA11 7HU
☎ REGIONAL OFFICE (01985) 843600 11 G3

A manor house with a 14th-century chapel, 15th-century hall and 16th-century great chamber. The home of Henry Lyte, translator of 'Niewe Herball' (1578).

Max Gate (tenanted)

Alington Avenue, Dorchester, Dorset DT1 2AA
☎ (01305) 262538 11 H6

Designed by Poet and novelist Thomas Hardy who lived here from 1885 until his death in 1928. The house is leased to tenants and only the Garden and Drawing Room are open. Unfortunately no Hardy memorabilia remains.

Montacute House

Montacute, Somerset TA15 6XP
☎ (01935) 823289 11 F4

Built between 1558 and 1601 by Sir Edward Phelips, this is a magnificent Elizabethan mansion in the tranquil setting of Montacute village. In the Gallery, the longest in England, there are portraits on loan from the National Portrait Gallery of Elizabethan and Jacobean courtiers. The Garden includes colourful mixed borders and formal landscapes.

Overbecks

Sharpitor, Salcombe, Devon TQ8 8LW
☎ (01548) 842893 5 H6

A beautiful 2.5-ha (6-acre) garden with many rare plants, shrubs and trees from around the world and with spectacular views over the Salcombe Estuary. The elegant Edwardian house contains collections of local photographs taken at the end of the last century and inventions by its former owner, Otto Overbeck. There is a secret room for children with toys, dolls and Fred the friendly ghost to find!

St Michael's Mount

Marazion, nr Penzance, Cornwall TR17 0EF
☎ (01736) 710507
Fax (01736) 711544 2 D6

The spectacular castle on top of this famous rocky island dates from the 14th century. Approached by a causeway at low tide, the castle has magnificent views towards Land's End. Fascinating early rooms, armoury, a rococo Gothic drawing room and, at the highest point, a 14th century church.

Saltram

Plympton, Plymouth, Devon PL7 3UH
☎ (01752) 336546
Fax (01752) 336474 4 F4

Stunning state rooms designed by Robert Adam, furniture by Chippendale and family portraits by Sir Joshua Reynolds. The Great Kitchen is possibly England's most complete survival of a large country house kitchen.

Set in 5.5 ha (13 acres) of romantic gardens that contain a wealth of follies while the whole is set in 202 ha (500 acres) of undulating parkland, laid out by Richmond. Featured as the setting for Norland Park in the film of Jane Austen's 'Sense and Sensibility'.

Shute Barton

Shute, nr Axminster, Devon EX13 7PT
☎ (01297) 34692 10 D6

One of the most important surviving non-fortified manor houses of the Middle Ages. Begun in 1380 and completed in the late 16th century, then partly demolished in the late 18th century, the house has battlemented turrets, late Gothic windows and a Tudor gatehouse. This property is tenanted. Access to most parts of the interior for conducted tours only.

Stourhead

The Estate Office, Stourton, Warminster, Wiltshire BA12 6QD
☎ (01747) 841152 11 J2

Stourhead is one of the most famous examples of the early 18th-century English landscape movement. Sheets of water reflecting splendid mature trees, several temples, a classical bridge, a grotto and rustic buildings in the best 18th-century tradition. The house contains a wealth of Grand Tour paintings and works of art, together with furniture designed by Chippendale the Younger.

Stembridge Tower Mill

High Ham, Somerset TA10 9DJ
☎ (01458) 250818 11 F2

The last thatched windmill in England, dating from 1822 and in use until 1910.

Tintagel Old Post Office

Tintagel, Cornwall PL34 0DB
☎ (01840) 770024 DURING OPENING HOURS ONLY. 8 A7

One of the most distinctive buildings in Cornwall, and a house of great antiquity, this small 14th-century manor is full of charm and interest. Restored in the fashion of the Post Office it was for nearly 50 years.

Tintinhull House Garden

Farm Street, Tintinhull, Yeovil, Somerset BA22 9PZ
☎ (01935) 822545 11 F4

Tintinhull House Garden, largely the inspiration of Mrs Phyllis Reiss who moved to Tintinhull in 1933, is a delightful walled garden divided into separate areas by clipped hedges. Closer to the house stands the impressive cedar court. Ingenious planting provides interest for visitors throughout the open season.

Treasurer's House

Martock, Somerset TA12 6JL
☎ REGIONAL OFFICE (01985) 843600 11 F4

A small house dating from the 13th and 14th centuries, with a medieval hall and kitchen, recently refurbished by the Trust.

Trelissick Garden

Feock, nr Truro, Cornwall TR3 6QL
☎ (01872) 862090 Fax (01872) 865808 3 G6

10-ha (The 25-acre) garden set in rolling parkland has exotic flora in the summer. The park itself, with its walks beside the River Fal and views down to Falmouth and the open sea, is never closed.

Stables, harness room, converted barn restaurant and fairy-tale water tower and a new orchard featuring many old varieties of Cornish apples.

Trengwainton

Nr Penzance, Cornwall TR20 8RZ
☎ (01736) 63021 OR 68410 (DURING OPENING HOURS) 2 C6

The garden of mainland Britain perhaps most favoured for the cultivation of exotic trees and shrubs. The walled garden shelters many tender plants.

Trerice

Nr Newquay, Cornwall TR8 4PG
☎ (01637) 875404
Fax (01637) 879300 3 G3

A delightful, secluded Elizabethan manor house, built in 1571 with an early gabled façade, containing fine fireplaces, good plaster ceilings, oak and walnut furniture, and clocks. A small museum in the barn traces the development of the lawn mower. The summer garden has some unusual plants and there is also an orchard of old varieties of fruit trees.

Westbury Court Garden

Westbury-on-Severn, Gloucestershire GL14 1PD
☎ (01452) 760461 20 B1

A formal water garden with canals and yew hedges, laid out between 1696 and 1705. It is the earliest of its kind remaining in England, restored in 1971 and planted with species dating from pre-1700, including apple, pear and plum trees.

Westwood Manor (tenanted)

Bradford-on-Avon, Whitchurch BA15 2AF
☎ (01225) 863374 20 C6

A 15th-century stone manor house, altered in the late 16th century, with late Gothic and Jacobean windows and Jacobean plasterwork. There is a modern topiary garden.

Wales

Aberconwy House

Conwy, N Wales LL32 8AY
☎ (01492) 592246 49 G3

Dating from the 14th-century, Aberconwy House is the last remaining medieval merchant's house in the old walled town of Conwy. Recently restored, each room showing a different moment in time, reflecting the taste and character of some of the families who lived there.

Aberdulais Falls

Aberdulais, nr Neath, S Wales SA10 8EU
☎ (01639) 636674
Fax (01639) 645069 18 B3

For over 300 years this famous waterfall has provided the energy for industry from the first manufacture of copper in 1584 to present day remains of the Tinplate works. Today the Turbine House provides access to an interactive computer, fish pass and display panels. A lift has been installed to allow disabled visitors access to roof level, with excellent views of the falls and new water-wheel which makes Aberdulais Falls self-sufficient in environmentally friendly energy.

Bodnant Garden

Tal-y-Cafn, Colwyn Bay, N Wales LL28 5RE
☎ (01492) 650460
Fax (01492) 650448 49 G3

Bodnant covers nearly 100 acres (40.5 ha) on a slope looking down to the River Conwy and across to Snowdonia. Above are a series of five Italianate-style terraces and formal lawns whilst below, in a wooded valley, a stream runs through the secluded wild garden. Magnificent 200-year-old native trees. Bodnant holds the National Collections of Rhododendrons, Magnolias and Eucryphias.

One of the finest gardens in Europe.

Chirk Castle

Chirk, Wrexham, N Wales LL14 5AF
☎ (01691) 777701
Fax (01691) 774706 40 D3

A magnificent, furnished marcher fortress now 700-years-old. A dramatic dungeon deep under the west range contrasts with the elegant State Rooms which contain elaborate plasterwork, superb furniture, tapestries and portraits. A beautiful and fragrant garden.

Colby Woodland Gardens

Stepaside, Narberth, Pembrokeshire SA67 8PP
☎ (01834) 811885 26 F6

8 acres (3 ha) of woodland garden set in a tranquil and secluded valley. Gentle strolls or extensive walks to explore the estate. A haven for bird watchers and gardeners alike.

Video and interpretation centre to tell the history of this mining valley.

Conwy Suspension Bridge

Conwy, N Wales LL32 8LD
☎ (01492) 573282 49 G3

Designed and built by Thomas Telford, the famous engineer, this elegant suspension bridge was completed in 1826, replacing the ferry. The left side springing from the rocky crag crowned with Conwy Castle. The original Toll House has recently been restored to show how it was, when last occupied in 1891.

Dinefwr Park

Llandeilo, Dyfed, Carmarthenshire SA19 6RT
☎ (01558) 823902
Fax (01558) 822036 27 L4

A 450-acre (182 ha) landscaped park attributed to 'Capability' Brown. The Deer park has also been home to the ancient White Park Cattle since the 9th-century. The 12th-century Castle of Dinefwr, the home of the Princes of Deheubarth, and Newton House will be open during the 1996 season.

Dolaucothi Gold Mines

Pumsaint, Llanwrda, Carmarthenshire SA19 8RR
☎ (01558) 650359 27 L2

These unique Roman goldmines are set amid wooded hillsides overlooking the beautiful Cothi Valley on the Dolaucothi Estate. The Trust's Exhibition Centre and Miners' Way vividly illustrate the ancient and modern mine workings. Guided underground tours in mid-summer with miners' helmets and lamps.

Erddig

Nr Wrexham, N Wales LL13 0YT
☎ (01978) 355314
Fax (01978) 313333 40 E1

The most evocative 'upstairs-downstairs' house in Britain. The authentic kitchen, bakehouse, coach-house, smithy and joiners' shop show how 18th-and 19th-century servants lived and worked. Upstairs the State Rooms display the exquisite furniture and textiles made for the house in the 1720s. Around the canal, the formal early 18th-century garden has been fully restored and also contains the National Ivy Collection.

Llanerchaeron

Nr Aberaeron, Ceredigion SA48 8DG
☎ (01545) 570200
Fax (01545) 571759 28 B3

A rare survivor of a Welsh gentry estate acquired by the Trust in 1994. The core area includes a principal house designed and built by John Nash in 1794–96, service wing and courtyard; model home farm, kennels and stables. All set in 80 acres (32.5 ha) of pleasure grounds and parkland. The house is not yet open to the public.

Penrhyn Castle

Nr Bangor, Gwynedd LL57 4HN
☎ (01248) 353084
Fax (01248) 371281 48 E3

A massive neo-Norman castle commanding superb views of Snowdonia and the Menai Strait. It houses an important collection of old master paintings and much of the furniture, designed by the architect Thomas Hopper and built between 1820 and 1845.

New interactive exhibition of the National Trust's work on the estate.

The castle is surrounded by gardens created by the Victorian gardener Walter Speed which includes the Walled Garden.

Plas Newydd

Llanfairpwll, Anglesey LL61 6DQ
☎ (01248) 714795
Fax (01248) 713673 48 E3

Impressive 18th-century house by James Wyatt in unspoilt surroundings on the Menai Strait, with magnificent views of Snowdonia. The house contains Rex Whistler's largest wall painting and an exhibition devoted to his work. In the military museum are campaign relics of the Ist Marquess of Anglesey who commanded the Cavalry at Waterloo.

The garden displays exotic shrubs and mature woodland.

Plas Yn Rhiw

Rhiw, Pwllheli, Gwynedd LL53 8AB
☎ (01758) 780219 38 B4

A small manor house with garden and woodlands, overlooking the west shore of Porth Neigwl (Hell's Mouth Bay) on the Llŷn peninsula. The house is part medieval with Tudor and Georgian additions, with ornamental gardens.

Powis Castle

Welshpool, Powys SY21 8RF
☎ (01938) 554338
Fax (01938) 554336 40 D6

Perched dramatically above the late 17th-century garden terraces, Powis Castle is one of the finest country houses in Wales. Established in 1987, the Clive Museum, shows the treasures brought from India by Clive and his son. Built c.1200. The world-famous garden shelters rare and tender plants.

Tudor Merchant's House

Quay Hill, Tenby, Pembrokeshire SA70 7BX
☎ (01834) 842279 26 F6

A late 15th-century example of domestic town architecture, characteristic of the stone building tradition found in south west Wales. Furnishings and fittings recreate the atmosphere of the house when a Tudor family was in residence.

Tŷ Mawr Wybrnant

Penmachno, Betws-y-coed, N Wales LL25 0HJ
☎ (01690) 760213 39 G1

Situated in the beautiful and secluded Wybrnant Valley, Tŷ Mawr was the birthplace of Bishop William Morgan (1545–1604), first translator of the entire Bible into Welsh. The house has been restored to its probable 16th-/17th-century appearance, with a display of Welsh Bibles.

Ty'n-y-coed uchaf

Penmachno, Betws-y-coed, N Wales LL24 0PS
☎ (01690) 760229 39 G1

A smallholding with 19th-century farmhouse and outbuildings which provide a record of the Welsh traditional way of life.

The Midlands

Attingham Park

Shrewsbury, Shropshire SY4 4TP
☎ (01743) 709203
Fax (01743) 709352 41 G6

Designed in 1782 by the innovative Scottish architect George Steuart. The rich collections of furniture, paintings and silver represent the taste of two brothers, the 2nd and 3rd Lords Berwick, and together form one of the most complete representations of Regency taste. The top-lit picture gallery and circular painted boudoir are among the most important country house interiors to survive unaltered.

Baddesley Clinton

Rising Lane, Baddesley Clinton Village, Knowle, Solihull, Warwickshire B93 0DQ
☎ (01564) 783294 32 D2

A romantically-sited intimate medieval moated manor house dating from the 14th-century, and little changed since 1634. The contents owe much to Elizabethan antiquary Henry Ferrers. He introduced the rich oak panelling and highly decorated overmantels in many of the rooms. This remote house became a haven for Catholics in the late 16th-century. Visitors can still see the hiding place. There is also a garden, ponds and lake walk.

Belton House

Grantham, Lincolnshire NG32 2LS
☎ (01476) 566116
Fax (01476) 579071 44 C3

The serenity of Belton House has made it a favourite for royal visitors. Edward VIII often stayed here during his short reign and nearly 250 years earlier, William III visited. Built late in Charles II's reign, the interiors are exuberantly baroque, with a stunning collection of Old Masters. Formal gardens, orangery and magnificent landscaped park.

Belton House was recently used by the BBC as the setting for Rosings, the home of Lady Catherine De Burgh in the classic serial 'Pride and Prejudice'.

Benthall Hall (tenanted)

Broseley, Shropshire TF12 5RX
☎ (01952) 882159 □ 41 H6

Seat of the Benthall family, whose origins stretch back to Anglo Saxon times, the exterior of Benthall Hall has changed little since it was built in the 16th century. The early 17th-century interior includes an intricately carved oak staircase, decorated plaster ceilings and oak panelling. Rococo chimney pieces were added by T. F. Pritchard, architect of the Iron Bridge spanning the River Severn. The intimate garden, sheltered and enclosed by trees, is largely the work of Robert Bateman, son of James Bateman who created Biddulph Grange Garden.

Berrington Hall

Nr Leominster,
Herefordshire HR6 0DW
☎ (01568) 615721 □ 31 G3

This elegant, compact house was designed by Henry Holland (later architect to the Prince Regent) and built between 1778 and 1783 for the Rt Hon. Thomas Harley. There is much fine furniture on show, including the Digby Collection of French Regency furniture. The gardens immediately surrounding the house contain many interesting and exotic plants and there is a Victorian walled garden containing the national collection of historic Hereford and March apples. Lancelot 'Capability' Brown, Holland's father-in-law, laid out the extensive park in the 1780s.

Bredon Barn

Bredon, nr Tewkesbury,
Worcestershire
☎ REGIONAL OFFICE (01684) 850051
□ 32 A6

A 14th-century barn, 132 ft (40 metres) long, with fine porches, one of which has unusual stone chimney cowling. The barn was restored with traditional materials after a fire in 1980.

Calke Abbey

Ticknall, Derbyshire DE73 1LE
☎ (01332) 863822
℻ (01332) 865272 □ 43 F4

Present house built in 1701–3 for Sir John Harpur, set in a 303.5-ha (750-acre) park with ponds and oak woodland. Within the house is a magnificent 18th-century staircase and good examples of 18th- and 19th-century interiors, notably in the Caricature and Drawing Rooms. Fascinating collections amidst the more familiar furniture, portraits and books create Calke's unique atmosphere. Pleasure grounds and attractive walled gardens with an 18th-century Orangery at their centre.

Canons Ashby House

Canons Ashby, Daventry,
Northamptonshire NN11 3SD
☎ (01327) 860044
℻ (01327) 860168 □ 33 H4

Canons Ashby House, a country house that is one of Northamptonshire's historic gems. Built in the 1550s by John Dryden and occupied by his descendants for over 400 years. Formal gardens, created by Edward Dryden, are now almost completely restored to reflect the taste of the early 18th-century, providing panoramic views of the surrounding parkland and the church 'of almost cathedral proportions'.

Claydon House

Middle Claydon, nr Buckingham,
Buckinghamshire MK18 2EY
☎ (01296) 730349
℻ (01296) 738511 □ 33 K7

Mementoes of Florence Nightingale, who often visited her sister Parthenope here, are displayed in a room adjoining the one where she always slept at this elegant manor house that remains the most perfect expression of rococo decoration in England. Ralph, the 2nd Lord Verney, inherited the estate in 1752 and set about reconstructing his father's old Jacobean manor house. Within the grounds there is a peaceful little church, and a garden walk with views across the three lakes in the park.

Coughton Court

Nr Alcester, Warwickshire B49 5JA
☎ (01789) 762435
℻ (01789) 765544 □ 32 C4

An impressive central gatehouse dating from 1530 with Elizabethan half-timbered courtyard. During the Civil War this mainly Elizabethan house was attacked by both Parliamentary and Royalist forces. It has important connections with the Gunpowder Plot and contains priests' hiding places. Some notable furniture, porcelain and portraits. There are two churches, a tranquil lake, riverside walk and newly created formal gardens. There are Gunpowder Plot and children's clothes exhibitions. Coughton Court is managed by the Throckmorton family who have lived here since 1409.

Croft Castle

Nr Leominster, Herefordshire HR6 9PW
☎ (01568) 780246 □ 31 F3

Croft Castle, set in the beautiful countryside of north Herefordshire, with superb views southwards and westwards to the Brecon Beacons, has been the property of the Croft family since Domesday (with an intermission of 170 years). The house retains its ancient walls and corner towers although was modified over the centuries when the fine ceilings and Gothic staircase were installed. Avenues and landscape lakes embellish one of the best surviving Herefordshire parks.

Dudmaston

Quatt, nr Bridgnorth,
Shropshire WV15 6QN
☎ (01746) 780866
℻ (01746) 780744 □ 31 J1

Home of Sir George and Lady Labouchere, this late 17th-century house of mellow red brick contains collections of modern art and sculpture. Many of the contents reflect the history of this notable family. The house is surrounded by an extensive and impressive lakeside garden with a colourful rockery and woodland walks.

Farnborough Hall (tenanted)

Banbury, Warwickshire OX17 1DU
☎ (01295) 690002

A classical, mid 18th-century stone house, home of the Holbech family for 300 years. The entrance hall, staircase and 2 principal rooms are shown; the plasterwork is particularly notable. The grounds contain charming 18th-century temples, a terrace walk and obelisk.

Hanbury Hall

Droitwich, Worcestershire WR9 7EA
☎ (01527) 821214
℻ (01527) 821251 □ 32 A3

Hanbury Hall is every Englishman's idea of a substantial squire's house, tucked away in 162 ha (400 acres) of parkland. The home of the Vernon family for more than three centuries, it was entirely remodelled by 1701.

Ten showrooms are open to the public with paintings by Sir James Thornhill, whose work can also be seen in St Paul's Cathedral, and the collection of fine porcelain and Dutch flower paintings given to the house by Mr R. S. Watney. Principle elements of the formal gardens designed by George London are re-created. The orangery and ice house are later mid-century additions that are also on show.

Hidcote Manor Garden

Hidcote Bartrim, nr Chipping Campden,
Gloucestershire GL55 6LR
☎ (01386) 438333 □ 32 D5

4-hectare (ten-acre) Arts and Crafts garden on a hilltop. One of the most delightful gardens in England created this century by the great horticulturist Major Lawrence Johnston. A series of small gardens within the whole, separated by walls and hedges of different species. Hidcote is famous for rare shrubs, trees, herbaceous borders, 'old' roses and interesting plant species.

Kedleston Hall

Derby, Derbyshire DE22 5JH
☎ (01332) 842191
℻ (01332) 841972 □ 43 F3

Built between 1759 and 1765 for the Curzon family and little altered since. Robert Adam designed the South front and the decoration of the magnificent State Rooms.

The rooms remain adorned with the important portrait, landscape and history painting which it was built to display. Includes an Indian Museum.

The garden is being restored in part to an 18th-century pleasure ground. The park contains several original Adam buildings including a bridge and fishing pavilion and fine lakes with cascades.

Lower Brockhampton

Bringsty, Worcestershire WR6 5UH
☎ (01885) 488099 □ 31 H4

A late 14th-century moated manor house, with an attractive detached half-timbered 15th-century gatehouse, a rare example of this type of structure. Also the ruins of a 12th-century chapel.

Moseley Old Hall

Moseley Old Hall Lane,
Fordhouses, Wolverhampton,
Staffordshire WV10 7HY
☎ (01902) 782808
℻ (01902) 782808 □ 42 B6

An Elizabethan house with later alterations. Charles II hid here after the Battle of Worcester and the bed in which he slept is on view, as well as the ingenious hiding place he used. A new, special exhibition in the barn tells the story of the King's escape. The small garden has been reconstructed in 17th-century style with formal box parterre; 17th-century plants only are grown.

Packwood House

Lapworth, Solihull,
Warwickshire B94 6AT
☎ (01564) 782024 □ 32 D2

Dating from the 16th-century, Packwood House has been extended and much changed over the years. Constructed by John Fetherston at the end of the 16th-century, this fascinating timber-framed house contains a wealth of fine tapestries and furniture. Cromwell's general, Henry Ireton, slept here the night before the Battle of Edgehill in 1642. The superb gardens are noted mainly for their yew topiary and Carolean Garden and the renowned herbaceous borders attract many visitors.

Shugborough Estate

Milford, nr Stafford,
Staffordshire ST17 0XB
☎ (01889) 881388
℻ (01889) 881323 □ 42 B4

Shugborough is the magnificent 364-hectare (900-acre) estate of the Earls of Lichfield, testament to the efforts of two people – Thomas Anson (1695–1773) and his brother George.

Visit the servants' quarters and the restored working brew-house, the impressive collection of horse-drawn vehicles and the authentic Victorian schoolroom.

The Park Farm – designed by Wyatt in 1805 – houses a Rare Breeds Approved Centre and working corn mill; there is a 7.5-ha (18-acre) Grade 1 historic garden and a unique collection of neo-classical monuments by James Stuart.

Shugborough is financed and administered by Staffordshire County Council.

Snowshill Manor

Snowshill, nr Broadway,
Worcestershire WR12 7JU
☎ (01386) 852410 □ 32 C6

Snowshill Manor is no ordinary Cotswold manor house but the setting for Charles Paget Wade's 'Collection of Craftsmanship.' You will see English, European and Oriental furniture, musical instruments, clocks and model ships and other collections in nearly all the 21 rooms. Visitors can also see Wade's inventively equipped cottage where he lived, and the delightful garden he created. The garden is now organically managed.

Staunton Harold Church

Ashby-de-la-Zouch, Leicestershire
☎ (01332) 863822 □ 43 F4

Built by Sir Robert Shirley in an open act of defiance to Oliver Cromwell's Puritan regime, leading to death in the Tower of London at 27 years of age. The church survives, little changed.

A voluntary vehicle charge may be requested on busy summer Sundays and Bank Holidays at which time a one-way system will be in operation on the estate.

Stowe Landscape Garden

Buckingham,
Buckinghamshire MK18 5EH
☎ (01280) 822850
℻ (01280) 822437 □ 33 J6

One of the supreme creations of the Georgian era. The first formal layout was adorned with many buildings by Vanbrugh, Kent and Gibbs. One of the earliest examples of the reaction against formality leading to the evolution of the Landscape Garden. Miraculously, this beautiful garden survives; its sheer scale must make it Britain's largest work of art. The House (not NT) has been owned and occupied by Stowe School since 1923. The State Rooms and Marble Hall may be visited and the view from the South Portico should not be missed.

Sudbury Hall

Sudbury, Derbyshire DE6 5HT
☎ (01283) 585305
℻ (01283) 585139 □ 42 D3

A most individual Charles II house. The great staircase under the dome is the finest of its kind in an English house, and the long gallery is notable for the period. The interior of the house features in the TV series 'Pride and Prejudice' as Pemberley, Mr Darcy's home. The National Trust Museum of Childhood in the old servants' wing houses the Betty Cadbury collection of playthings past.

The Fleece Inn

Bretforton, nr Evesham, Worcestershire WR11 5JE
☎ (01386) 831173 □ 32 C5

A medieval farmhouse in the centre of the village, containing family collection of furniture. It became a licensed house in 1848 and remains largely unaltered. It recently featured as Mrs Lupin's pub 'The Dragon Inn' in the BBC's adaptation of the Dickensian classic, 'Martin Chuzzlewit'.

The Greyfriars

Friar Street, Worcester, Worcestershire WR1 2LZ
☎ (01905) 23571 □ 32 A4

Built in 1480 for a Worcester brewer on a site next to a Franciscan monastery. The Greyfriars remains a good example of a wealthy merchant's home of the late Middle Ages with early 17th- and late 18th-century additions. Interesting textiles and furnishings add character to the panelled rooms. An archway leads through to a delightful garden.

The Weir

Swainshill, nr Hereford, Herefordshire
☎ REGIONAL OFFICE (01684) 850051
□ 31 F5

Delightful riverside garden particularly spectacular in early spring, with fine views over the River Wye and Black Mountains.

Upton House

Nr Banbury, Oxfordshire OX15 6HT
☎ (01295) 670266 □ 33 G5

The house, built of a mellow local stone, dates from 1695, but the outstanding collections it contains are the chief attraction. Assembled this century by the 2nd Viscount Bearsted, son of Marcus Samuel, the founder of petroleum and manufacturing giant Royal Dutch Shell, they include paintings by Old Masters, Brussels tapestries, Sèvres porcelain, Chelsea figures and 18th-century furniture. The garden is also of great interest, with the national collection of asters, a large kitchen garden, a water garden laid out in the 1930s and pools with ornamental fish.

Wightwick Manor

Wightwick Bank, Wolverhampton,
West Midlands WV6 8EE
☎ (01902) 761108
℻ (01902) 764663 □ 42 B7

Begun in 1887, the house is a notable example of the influence of William Morris, with many original Morris wallpapers and fabrics. Also of interest are Pre-Raphaelite pictures, Kempe glass and de Morgan ware. The Victorian/Edwardian garden has yew hedges and topiary, terraces and two pools. Unsuitable for large groups.

Woolsthorpe Manor

23 Newton Way,
Woolsthorpe-by-Colsterworth,
Lincolnshire NG33 5NR
☎ (01476) 860338
℻ (01476) 860338
□ 44 C4

Sir Isaac Newton grew up here (returning when plague closed Cambridge University in 1665).

Upstairs is his study, hung with prints of other famous scientists of the day, many of whom fell out with their brilliant but difficult peer. It is furnished with an upright desk, reflecting the 17th-century fashion for writing while standing up. In the orchard is a descendant of the famous apple tree.

Northern England

Acorn Bank Garden

Temple Sowerby, nr Penrith,
Cumbria CA10 1SP
☎ (017683) 61893 □ 64 D5

Set below the bleak moors of the Pennines, this is the largest culinary and medical herb collection in the north of England. The garden is laid out around an old manor house – now a Sue Ryder home – and at its heart is a 17th-century walled garden, now an orchard.

Beatrix Potter Gallery

Main Street, Hawkshead,
Cumbria LA22 0NS
☎ (015394) 36355 □ 63 J8

Once the office of her husband and her solicitor, William Heelis, this largely unchanged interior now houses an annually changing exhibition of Beatrix Potter's original water-colour illustrations from her captivating children's story books. Corners of Hawkshead and views of the surrounding countryside can be seen throughout the drawings and stories.

The gallery complements a visit to Hill Top, Beatrix Potter's house.

Beningbrough Hall

Shipton-by-Beningbrough, York,
North Yorkshire YO6 1DD
☎ (01904) 470666
℻ (01904) 470002 □ 60 C5

John Bourchier completed the building of this imposing country house in 1716. Set on a slight rise above the water meadows of the River Ouse, this beautifully restored country house, set in 148 ha (365 acres), has exquisite woodcarvings and an impressive cantilevered oak staircase, furniture and porcelain. The Great Hall, which is two storeys high, has one of the most impressive Baroque interiors in England. Although the house has none of its original contents, it is furnished in period style and now also displays over one hundred 18th-century portraits on loan from the National Portrait Gallery.

Other attractions include a Victorian potting shed, wilderness play area, 3-ha (7-acre) garden, pike ponds walk and monthly exhibitions.

Cherryburn

Station Bank, Mickley, nr Stocksfield,
Northumberland NE43 7DB
☎ (01661) 843276 □ 65 H1

Visitors are welcomed with Northumbrian pipe music in the farmhouse which houses an exhibition on the wood engraver Thomas Bewick's life and works. You will find a roaring fire in the old kitchen range and there are demonstrations of wood engraving and printing in the press room. Across the cobbled farmyard is the cottage where Bewick was born in 1753. The farmyard is still home to a number of animals including donkeys, pigs, sheep, poultry and doves.

Clumber Park

Worksop, Nottinghamshire S80 3AZ
☎ (01909) 476592
℻ (01909) 500721 □ 53 H6

With a vast 1538 hectares (3800 acres), Clumber Park is a unique mosaic of grassland, heath, woodland and 35-ha (87-acre) lake. A memorable entrance of almost 3km (2 miles) can be made down the longest lime tree avenue in Europe, and although the mansion was demolished in 1938, many features of the Estate survive, namely the Victorian chapel, a Gothic revival mini cathedral, the stableyard and garages, and ornate park entrance lodges.

Superb 19th-century glasshouses, Victorian apiary and walled kitchen garden.

Cragside House & Gardens

Rothbury, Morpeth,
Northumberland NE65 7PX
☎ (01669) 620333/620266
℻ (01669) 620150 □ 75 G4

Described by contemporaries as 'the palace of a modern magician', Cragside was the first house in the world to be lit by hydro-electric power, with state-of-the-art hydraulics powering both the revolutionary new lift systems and internal telephones which so mesmerised the guests of William Armstrong. Today you can visit the Armstrong Energy Centre or take a walk past the restored Ram and Power Houses with their hydraulic and hydro-electric machinery. The formal Victorian Garden is a short walk from the house. It is also accessible by road to a car park at the rear of the garden.

Dunham Massey

Altrincham, Cheshire WA14 4SJ
☎ (0161) 941 1025
℻ (0161) 929 7508 □ 51 G5

Georgian house with Edwardian additions set in a wooded deer park. Built in 1732 for George Booth, the 2nd Earl of Warrington. Over 30 rooms are open, with fine furniture, paintings and outstanding Huguenot silver. The moat provides power for a working Jacobean mill. The large garden contains an 18th-century Orangery, a Victorian bark house and well house. A collection of rare, late-flowering azaleas.

East Riddlesden Hall

Bradford Road, Keighley,
West Yorkshire BD20 5EL
☎ (01535) 607075 ℻ (01535) 691462
□ 59 F6

A charming 17th-century West Yorkshire manor house with embroideries, pewter and a fine collection of Yorkshire oak furniture. The tranquil walled garden overlooking a grass maze has now been restored to its original design. There is also an impressive Great Barn which houses a collection of traditional farm implements.

Farne Islands

Seahouses Information Centre,
Northumberland
☎ (01665) 721099
WARDEN (01665) 720651 □ 83 L8

The islands provide a summer home for over 17 different species of seabirds including Puffin, Kittiwake, Eider duck, Guillemot, Fulmar, Tern. Large colony of grey seals. St Cuthbert died on Inner Farne in 687 and there is a chapel built to his memory in the 14th-century and restored in 1845.

Fountains Abbey and Studley Royal Water Garden

Fountains, Ripon,
North Yorkshire HG4 3DY
☎ (01765) 601005
℻ (01765) 601002 □ 59 H4

Sheltered in a North Yorkshire valley lies one of the most remarkable sites in Europe. The 32-ha (800-acre) World Heritage Site. The dramatic remains of Fountains Abbey, the largest monastic ruin in Europe, elegant ornamental lakes. A Medieval deer park, Victorian church and remarkable Jacobean mansion transport the visitor through 900 years of history. Studley Royal is one of the few surviving examples of a Georgian green garden. A popular venue for filming; 'The Secret Garden' was filmed here.

Gawthorpe Hall

Padiham, nr Burnley, Lancashire
BB12 8UA
☎ (01282) 771004
℻ (01282) 770178 □ 58 D7

Built between 1600 and 1605, and restored by Sir Charles Barry in the 1850s; Barry's designs have been re-created in the principal rooms. Gawthorpe was the home of the Shuttleworth family, and the Rachel Kay-Shuttleworth textile collections are on display in the house; private study by arrangement. Collection of portraits on loan from the National Portrait Gallery.

George Stephenson's Birthplace

Wylam, Northumberland NE41 8BP
☎ (01661) 853457 □ 65 J1

A small stone tenement built in 1760 to accommodate four pitmen's families. The furnishings are circa 1781, when George Stephenson was born. The room in which he was born is open to visitors.

Gibside

Nr Rowlands Gill, Burnopfield,
Newcastle-upon-Tyne, Gateshead
NE16 6BG
☎ (01207) 542255 □ 66 B2

This atmospheric property in the leafy Derwent valley is haunted by the ghosts of Gibside's previous owners, the Bowes-Lyons.

There is much to explore in this historic estate, along forest paths and above the river. The Palladian interior of the chapel is dominated by a rare triple-decker mahogany pulpit. The remains of the Orangery lie within the sight of a great avenue of ancient oaks: the remnants of one of the greatest 18th-century landscape designs.

Gunby Hall (tenanted)

Gunby, nr Spilsby,
Lincolnshire PE23 5SS
☎ REGIONAL OFFICE (01909) 486411
℻ (01909) 486377 □ 55 J7

A red-brick house with stone dressings, built in 1700 and extended in the 1870s. Within the house, there is a good early 18th-century wainscoting and a fine oak staircase, also English furniture and portraits by Reynolds. Contemporary stable block, a walled garden, sweeping lawns and borders. Gunby was reputedly Tennyson's 'haunt of ancient peace'.

Hardwick Hall

Doe Lea, Chesterfield,
Derbyshire S44 5QJ
☎ (01246) 850430
℻ (01246) 854200 □ 53 F6

A spectacular Elizabethan house built for the ambitious and formidable Bess of Hardwick – the richest woman in England after the queen. Elizabethan and later furniture, tapestries, needlework and a dramatic frieze in the High Great Chamber. Walled courtyards enclose fine gardens, orchards and a herb garden. Historic parkland with Longhorn cattle and ponds.

Hill Top

Nr Sawrey, Ambleside, Cumbria
LA22 0LF
☎ (015394) 36269 □ 57 G1

Beatrix Potter wrote many famous stories in this little 17th-century farmhouse, which she bought in 1905. When she left Hill Top to the Trust in 1944, Beatrix stipulated that the rooms and furnishings should be kept in their present condition and left a detailed list of where each item should stand.

Hill Top is a very small house and a maximum of 300 visitors can be admitted in any one day.

Lindisfarne Castle

Holy Island, Berwick-upon-Tweed
Northumberland TD15 2SH
☎ (01289) 389244. □ 83 K7

Built in the 1540s as a defence against border raids by the Scots, Lindisfarne lost its military importance after the unification of England and Scotland under James I. It was in ruins by 1901 when Edward Hudson, founder and proprietor of the magazine 'Country Life', bought it in 1902 and immediately commissioned Edwin Lutyens to restore it as a summer retreat. The small walled garden was designed by Gertrude Jekyll.

Little Moreton Hall

Congleton, Cheshire CW12 4SD
☎ (01260) 272018 □ 51 H7

Regarded as the most perfect example of a timber-framed manor house in the country, Little Moreton Hall remains exceptional among half-timbered houses of its time and has been the star of a thousand chocolate boxes and jigsaw puzzles.

Built by the prosperous Moreton farming family, they extended the original two-storey home between 1570 and 1580, adding the long gallery that gives the house its curious top-heavy look.

Lyme Park

Disley, Stockport,
Cheshire SK12 2NX
☎ (01663) 762023/766492
℻ (01663) 765035 □ 51 J5

The exterior of Lyme Hall, one of the largest houses in Cheshire, is a splendid example of Palladian architecture containing Mortlake tapestries, Grinling Gibbons carvings and a unique collection of English clocks.

The 7-ha (17-acre) garden encompasses a sunken 'Dutch' garden, Victorian-style formal bedding, a lake, lawns, 'secret' paths, herbaceous border and rhododendron walk.

Dramatic views of the Pennine Hills and Cheshire Plains and Lyme's deer park, as seen in the BBC's production of 'Pride and Prejudice'.

Nostell Priory

Doncaster Road, Nostell, nr Wakefield,
West Yorkshire WF4 1QE
☎ (01924) 863892
℻ (01924) 865282 □ 53 F2

A fine Palladian house, built for the Winn family in the 18th century. An additional wing and many of the state rooms were designed by Adam. Fine collection of Chippendale furniture specially made for the house. There are also delightful lakeside walks through the grounds.

Nunnington Hall

Nr Helmsley,
North Yorkshire YO6 5UY
☎ (01439) 748283
℻ (01439) 748284 □ 60 D3

A delightful, mainly 17th-century, manor house on the banks of the River Rye. A magnificent panelled hall with a fine carved chimneypiece; also, fine tapestries, china and the Carlisle Collection of Miniature Rooms. Parliamentarian troops left their sword marks on the window frames. A series of changing exhibitions is also held each year.

The delightful walled garden is a rare survival from the 17th-century which still bears traces of the original formal layout.

Ormesby Hall

Ormesby, Middlesbrough TS7 9AS
☎ (01642) 324188
🖷 (01642) 300937 📖 67 F6

Sir James Pennyman, 6th Baronet, ran through the fortune he inherited by enlarging Ormesby estate only to be forced to hand it over to the bailiffs on completion.

Probably completed by 1743, in Palladian style, then popular in north Yorkshire. A developing model railway exhibition in the Old Wing. The stable block, attributed to Carr of York, is a particularly fine late 18th-century building with an attractive courtyard leased to the Mounted Police.

Quarry Bank Mill

Wilmslow, Cheshire SK9 4LA
☎ (01625) 527468
🖷 (01625) 539267 📖 51 H5

Set in a country park with riverside and woodland walks, Quarry Bank Mill is a Georgian cotton mill, built in 1784 by Samuel Greg, and restored as Europe's largest working textile museum. Its garden is a fascinating example of a Victorian utilitarian garden, growing fruits, vegetables and herbs using the same methods as 150 years ago. The nearby, picturesque village of Styal, built to house the mill workers, with its shop, school and chapels, completes this uniquely preserved 18th-century factory colony.

Rievaulx Terrace & Temples

Nr Helmsley, North Yorkshire YO6 5LJ
☎ (01439) 798340
🖷 (01439) 748284 📖 60 C2

Like Fountains Abbey the Cistercian abbey of Rievaulx was established in a secluded valley. Overlooking the ruins (owned by English Heritage), there is a fascinating 1 km (0.5 mile) long, grass-covered terrace and two mid-18th century temples. This Italianate vision was the creation of Thomas Duncombe III who inherited Rievaulx in 1746. There is a permanent exhibition in the basement relating to 18th-century English landscape design.

Rufford Old Hall

Rufford, nr Ormskirk,
Lancashire L40 1SG
☎ (01704) 821254🖷 (01704) 821254
📖 50 D2

There is a legend that William Shakespeare performed here for owner Sir Thomas Hesketh in the Great Hall of this, one of the finest 16th-century buildings in Lancashire. Built in 1530, it established the Hesketh family's seat for the next 250 years. In the Carolean Wing, altered in 1821, there are fine collections of 16th- and 17th-century oak furniture, arms, armour and tapestries.

Sizergh Castle

Nr Kendal, Cumbria LA8 8AE
☎ (015395) 60070 📖 57 J1

Sizergh was built 750 years ago to withstand Scottish attack in the frequent border raids which troubled the region for centuries. Once moated, and rising almost 60 ft (18 m), its limestone rubble walls are still formidable. A number of Stuart portraits advertise another colourful chapter in the Strickland family history. Following the Glorious Revolution in 1688, Sir Thomas Strickland and his family – all fervent Jacobites – refused to desert James II and fled with him to exile in France.

Souter Lighthouse

Coast Road, Whitburn,
Sunderland SR6 7NR
☎ (0191) 529 3161 📖 66 E1

Built after a disastrous year in 1869, when no fewer than 20 vessels came to grief between South Shields and Sunderland, Souter was purchased in 1990 as part of the Trust's Enterprise Neptune campaign. Climb 76 steps up to the 76 foot (23 metre) high tower and see the automatic radio beacon and the light which shines out, 150 ft (46 m) above sea level – the original lighthouse was the first ever to be powered by an electric current.

Speke Hall

The Walk, Liverpool,
Merseyside L24 1XD
☎ (0151) 427 7231
INFOLINE (LOCAL RATE) 0345 585702
🖷 (0151) 427 9860 📖 50 D5

Henry Norris inherited Speke Hall from his father in 1490, and continued the building work he started. His son, Sir William Norris, made room for his 19 children with considerable additions in the mid-16th century and merchant Richard Watt bought Speke Hall in 1795. One of the most famous half-timbered houses in the country, its Elizabethan stone bridge still spans the now grassy moat. William Morris wallpapers, Jacobean plasterwork, as well as a fully-equipped Victorian kitchen and servants' hall.

Steam Yacht Gondola

National Trust (Enterprises) Ltd,
Gondola Bookings, Pier Cottage,
Coniston, Cumbria LA21 8AJ
☎ (015394) 41288 📖 63 J8

Steam Yacht Gondola, first launched in 1859, and now completely renovated by the Trust, provides a steam-powered passenger service, carrying 86 passengers in opulently upholstered saloons. Travelling aboard the Gondola is an experience in its own right, and a superb way to see Coniston's scenery.

Mr Straw's House

7 Blyth Grove, Worksop,
Nottinghamshire S81 0JG
☎ (01909) 482380 📖 53 H6

A semi-detached house built at the turn of the century, belonging to William Straw and his brother, Walter. The interior has been preserved since the death of their parents in the 1930s with 1920s wallpaper, furnishings and local furniture. Museum room contains displays of family memorabilia, and there is a suburban garden.

Tatton Park

Knutsford, Cheshire WA16 6QN
☎ (01565) 654822
☎ INFOLINE (01565) 750250
🖷 (01565) 650179 📖 51 G6

One of the most complete historic estates open to visitors in England. The 19th-century Wyatt house, set in an extensive deer park, contains the Egerton family collections and specially commissioned Gillow furniture; servants' rooms and cellars. The 24 ha (60 acres) of gardens contain authentic Japanese and Italian gardens. Also, a medieval hall and 18th-century farm – working as in the 1930s – and many varieties of wildfowl. New outdoor and sailing centre for pre-booked groups.

Townend

Troutbeck, Windermere,
Cumbria LA23 1LB
☎ (015394) 32628 📖 63 K7

Townend is one of the finest examples of vernacular domestic Lake District architecture, lived in by the same family for over 400 years. Its contents reflect a fascinating accumulation by a sheep-farming family gradually rising in society. In the unique little library are first editions of Milton and throughout the house an impressive range of heavy oak furniture.

Treasurer's House

Chapter House Street, York,
North Yorkshire YO1 2JD
☎ (01904) 624247 📖 60 C5

In the shade of York Minster this elegant 17th-/18th-century town house, the site of the former residence of the Treasurers of the Minster, is set in a peaceful garden. It has a medieval-style hall with a half-timbered gallery, fine Georgian features with handsomely decorated plasterwork, panelling and elaborate fireplaces, and an excellent collection of furniture. A private home until 1930, it is renowned for being the home of the oldest ghost in England!

Wallington

Cambo, Morpeth,
Northumberland NE61 4AR
☎ (01670) 774283 📖 75 G6

In 1728 Sir Walter Calverley Blackett inherited the estate which he transformed, laying out the park and gardens. He also turned the house, as Arthur Young the agriculturalist wrote after his visit in 1766, into a 'piece of magnificence that cannot be too much praised'.

In the writing room there stands the desk at which George Trevelyan, Lord Macauley, wrote his monumental history of England. Other things to see include the wonderful dolls' house collection, 19th-century gentleman's bathroom and coaches and carriages in the coach house.

Washington Old Hall

The Avenue, Washington Village,
Tyne & Wear NE38 7LE
☎ (0191) 416 6879 📖 66 D2

From 1183 this house was the home of George Washington's direct ancestors who took their surname from the surrounding village of Washington. In 1613 it was purchased by William James, Bishop of Durham. Intriguing arched doorways and a 17th-century staircase, lifted from the White Hart Hotel in Guildford, take the visitor past a fan given to Martha Washington by General Lafayette. The Jacobean garden filled with Old English flowers and herbs with a pair of 18th-century gates, a gift from the Colonial Dames of America.

Wordsworth House

Main Street, Cockermouth,
Cumbria CA13 9RX
☎ (01900) 824805 📖 63 G4

Built in 1745 for the Sheriff of Cumberland, the house is now famous as the birthplace of the poet Wordsworth. This Georgian house is preserved in an 18th-century style, and stands a stone's throw from one of Wordsworth's favourite subjects, the ruined castle of Cockermouth. The house includes many personal effects. The garden referred to in 'The Prelude' is a blend of North Country cottage planting and Georgian town garden, with a terrace walk overlooking the River Derwent.

NATIONAL TRUST FOR SCOTLAND

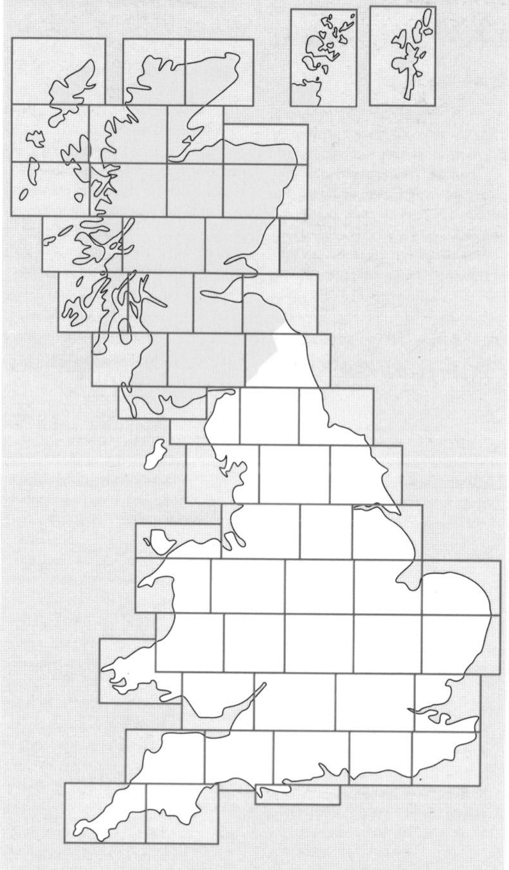

THE FOLLOWING DIRECTORY LISTS PROPERTIES OWNED AND MANAGED BY THE NATIONAL TRUST FOR SCOTLAND THAT ARE OPEN TO THE PUBLIC

📖 Atlas page and grid references are shown in blue

How to join The National Trust for Scotland

For immediate membership you can join at almost all of the trust's properties or shops. Alternatively contact:
The National Trust for Scotland
5 Charlotte Square,
Edinburgh EH2 4DU
☎ 0131 226 5922 🖷 0131 243 9501

Alloa Tower

On A907 in Alloa, Clackmannanshire
Alloa Park, Alloa, Clackmannanshire
FK10 1PP 📖 80 E2

Beautifully restored by the Alloa Tower Building Preservation Trust and Clackmannanshire Council, the Tower, built c. 1467, is the only remaining part of the ancestral home of the Earls of Mar. It was splendidly remodelled by the 6th Earl and partially completed before he was sent into excile after the 1715 Jacobite uprising. The building retains rare Medieval features, notably the complete timber roof structure and groin vaulting. A superb collection of portraits and chattels of the Erskine family includes paintings by Jamesone and Raeburn.

Angus Folk Museum

Angus. Off A94, in Glamis, 8 km (5 miles) SW of Forfar.
Kirkwynd, Glamis, Forfar,
Angus DD8 1RT 📖 89 F4

The Angus Folk Collection was made by Jean, Lady Maitland. Housed in Kirkwynd Cottages, a row of 6 early 19th-century cottages with stone-slabbed roofs, restored and adapted by the Trust in 1957. Reconstructed Angus steading, where life on the farm is displayed.

Arduaine Garden

Argyll & Bute. A816, 32 km (20 miles) S of Oban and 18 miles (30 km) N of Lochgilphead.
Arduaine, nr Oban, Argyll PA34 4XQ
📖 85 J7

Outstanding 8 ha (20-acre) garden on a promontory bounded by Loch Melfort and the Sound of Jura, climatically favoured by the Gulf Stream. Nationally noted for rhododendrons, azaleas, magnolias and other rare trees and shrubs.

Bachelors' Club

South Ayrshire. In Tarbolton, B744, 12 km (7.5 miles) NE of Ayr, off B743.
Sandgate Street, Tarbolton
KA5 5RB 📖 71 K2

In this 17th-century thatched house, Robert Burns and friends formed a debating club in 1780. Burns attended dancing lessons, and was initiated into Freemasonry here, in 1781.

Balmacara Estate and Lochalsh Woodland Garden

Highland. A87, 4 km (3 miles) E of Kyle of Lochalsh.
Lochalsh House (NTS), Balmacara,
Kyle IV40 8DN 📖 92 E3

An extensive crofting estate with outstanding views and access to Skye and Applecross. Traditional crofting is still carried out at Drumbuie and Duirinish, and Plockton is an Outstanding Conservation Area. Ranger service guided walks in season. Lochalsh Woodland Garden provides pleasant sheltered walks beside the shores of Loch Alsh.

Balmerino Abbey

Fife. Off A914, in Balmerino, 8 km (5 miles) SW of Newport-on-Tay.
📖 89 F6

Ruins of a Cistercian monastery, founded in 1229. Visitors may not enter the buildings but can view them from the grounds, which contain an ancient Spanish Chestnut tree, one of the oldest in the country.

Bannockburn

Off M80/M9 at junction 9, 3 km (2 miles) S of Stirling.
Glasgow Road, Stirling FK7 0LJ
📖 80 D2

The Bannockburn Heritage Centre is situated at one of the most important historic sites in Scotland. On the battlefield nearby, in June 1314, King Robert the Bruce routed the forces of King Edward II to win freedom for the Scots from English domination.The Centre provides an exhibition – The Kingdom of the Scots – opened in 1987 and an audio-visual presentation of the Battle of Bannockburn (French and German versions available for groups).

Barrie's Birthplace

Angus, A90/A926, in Kirriemuir, 9 km (6 miles) NW of Forfar.
9 Brechin Road, Kirriemuir,
Angus DD8 4BX 📖 89 F3

In this two-storeyed house J M Barrie (1860–1937) was born. The upper floors are furnished as they may have been when Barrie lived there. The adjacent house, No 11, houses an exhibition – The Genius of J M Barrie – about Barrie's literary and theatrical works. The outside wash-house is said to have been his first theatre.

Barry Mill

Angus. N of Barry village between A92 and A930, 3 km (2 miles) W of Carnoustie.
Barry, Carnoustie,
Angus DD7 7RJ 📖 89 H5

This 19th-century meal mill works on a demonstration basis. Records show that a mill has occupied the site since at least 1539. The present building was rebuilt in 1814 and was the last water-powered meal mill to work in Angus, until 1982. Now the original machinery is fully restored and turning again.

Ben Lawers

Perth & Kinross. Off A827, 8 km (6 miles) NE of Killin, N of Loch Tay.
NTS Office, Fagus, Manse Road,
Killin FK21 8UY 📖 87 J4

Perthshire's highest mountain, with views from the Atlantic to the North Sea. In the Trust's care are 3,452 ha (8,530 acres) of the southern slopes of the Lawers range, and (3,230) of the Ptarnigan range, noted for a rich variety of mountain plants. Birds include raven, ring-ouzel, red grouse, ptarmigan, dipper and curlew. Nature Trail and audio-visual programmes. Ranger service. Dogs must be kept on leads at all times.

Ben Lomond

B837, at Rowardennan, 17 km (11 miles) beyond Drymen off A811.
Ardess Lodge, Rowardennan, by
Drymen, Glasgow G63 0AR 📖 79 F1

Probably Scotland's most beloved mountain. Rising from the east shore of Loch Lomond to 974 m (3194 ft), the Ben offers exhilarating walking and spectacular views all round. The hills are used for sheep-farming. Dogs must be kept on a lead at all times.

Blackhill

South Lanarkshire. Off B7018 between Kirkfieldbank and Lesmahagow, 5 km (3 miles) W of Lanark. 📖 80 D7

Site of Iron-Age hill fort and outlook point over the Clyde valley. 2 ha (5 acres).

Boath Doocot

Highland. Off A96, in Auldearn, 3 km (2 miles) E of Nairn. 📖 103 H7

A 17th-century doocot on the site of an ancient motte. Montrose defeated the Covenanters nearby on 9 May 1645; battle-plan on display.

Branklyn Garden

Perth & Kinross. A85, Perth.
116 Dundee Road,
Perth PH2 7BB 📖 88 D6

This attractive little garden in Perth was once described as 'the finest two acres of private garden in the country'. In 1922, on the site of a former orchard, Mr and Mrs John T Renton began to establish an outstanding collection of plants that attract gardeners and botanists from all over the world.

Brodick Castle, Garden and Country Park

Isle of Arran. Ferry from Ardrossan (55 mins) to Brodick. Connecting bus from ferry to castle. Isle of Arran KA27 8HY
📖 78 C8

Even in Viking times the site on which Brodick Castle now stands was a fortress. Part dates from the 13th century with extensions of 1652 and 1844. This ancient seat of the Dukes of Hamilton was more recently the home of the late Mary, Duchess of Montrose. The contents include superb silver, porcelain and paintings. The woodland garden, started in 1923 by the Duchess, ranks as one of Europe's finest rhododendron gardens; the formal garden, dating from 1710, has been restored as a Victorian garden.

Goatfell

Isle of Arran 📖 78 B7

Goatfell is the highest peak on the Isle of Arran, with impressive views. Trust property includes part of Glen Rosa and Cir Mhòr; fine rock-climbing and ridge-walking.

Brodie Castle

Moray. Off A96, 7 km (4.5 miles) W of Forres and 38 km (24 miles) E of Inverness.
Brodie, Forres IV36 0TE 📖 103 H7

Set in parkland, Brodie Castle is old but the family association with the area is even older. The Brodies were first endowed with their lands by Malcolm IV in 1160. Damaged in 1645 during the Montrose campaigns, the oldest part is 16th-century 'Z' plan, with additions made in the 17th and 19th centuries. The house contains fine French furniture, English, Continental and Chinese porcelain, and a major collection of paintings. A woodland walk with access to wildlife observation hides and wild garden.

Broughton House & Garden

Dumfries & Galloway. High Street, Kirkcudbright, off A711/A755.
12 High Street, Kirkcudbright
DG6 4JX 📖 69 H5

18th-century town house of the Murrays of Broughton to which the artist E A Hornel of 'Glasgow Boys' renown added between 1901 and 1933 an art gallery, an extensive library, a studio and a sheltered garden with a Japanese-style feature near the house.

Bruce's Stone

Dumfries & Galloway. By A712, 9 km (6 miles) W of New Galloway.
📖 72 A7

This granite boulder on Moss Raploch marks the spot where Bruce defeated the English in 1307.

Bucinch & Ceardach

In Loch Lomond.
📖 79 F2

These two small, uninhabited islands in the loch, between Luss and Balmaha, were presented by Col Charles L Spencer of Warmanbie, Dumfries, in 1943.

Burg

Isle of Mull, Argyll & Bute. By footpath, 8 km (5 miles) W of Tiroran, off B8035 on N shore of Loch Scridain.
📖 85 F6

These 569 ha (1405 acres) of Mull, with high cliffs known as 'The Wilderness', were bequeathed by Mr A Campbell Blair of Dolgelly in 1932. MacCulloch's Fossil Tree, possibly 50 million years old, is beyond Burg Farm and can be reached at low water with difficulty. A 9 km (5.5-mile) walk on a path which becomes very rough and precipitous culminates in a steep descent to the beach by an iron ladder. Dogs must be kept on a lead at all times.

Caiy Stone

Edinburgh. In Caiystone View, off B701, Oxgangs Road.
📖 81 H5

This 3 m (9 ft) tall prehistoric cup-marked stone, also known as General Kay's Monument, or the Kel Stone, traditionally marks the site of an ancient battle between the Picts and the Romans.

Cameronians' Regimental Memorial

South Lanarkshire. Off A70, in Douglas 3 km (2 miles) W of M74.
📖 72 D1

Statue of the Earl of Angus who was the first Colonel of the Cameronian Regiment which was raised at Douglas in 1689. The statue is situated at north edge of village.

Canna

Highland. Cruises from Mallaig and Arisaig.
📖 91 H5

The most westerly of the Small Isles, Canna is 8 km (5 miles) long and 2 km (1.25 miles) wide and is one of the most interesting islands in the Hebrides for scenic, agricultural, scientific and historical reasons.

Carlyle's Birthplace

Dumfries & Galloway. Off M74, on A74, in Ecclefechan, 9 km (5.5 miles) SE of Lockerbie.
The Arched House, Ecclefechan,
Lockerbie DG11 3DG 📖 73 G7

The arched house in which Thomas Carlyle was born in 1795 contains a collection of his belongings and manuscript letters. Built by his father and uncle in about 1791, the house is representative of the local artisan dwelling of that period.

Castle Fraser

Aberdeenshire. Off A944, 6 km (4 miles) N of Dunecht and 26 km (16 miles) W of Aberdeen.
Sauchen, Inverurie AB51 7LD 📖 97 G4

This magnificent castle, one of the Castles of Mar, was begun about 1575 by the 6th Laird, Michael Fraser, and incorporates earlier building. Two great families of master masons, Bel and Leiper, took part in the work which was completed in 1636. The most sophisticated example of this indigenous style owned by the Trust. The interior was remodelled in 1838 and decoration and furnishings of that period survive in some of the rooms. A formal garden has been created in the old walled garden.

Corrieshalloch Gorge National Nature Reserve

Highland. A835 at Braemore, 19 km (12 miles) SSE of Ullapool.

This spectacular gorge, one of the finest examples in Britain of a box canyon, is 60 m (200 ft) deep. The river which carved this channel through hard metamorphic rock, plunges over the Falls of Measach. The suspension bridge, downstream from the falls, was built by John Fowler, joint designer of the Forth Railway Bridge, who bought the estate of Braemore in 1867.

Craigower

Perth & Kinross. Off A924 at Moulin, 2 km (1.5 miles) N of Pitlochry.
📖 88 B3

An 4 ha (11-acre) beacon hill with splendid views. The path from the small car park to the summit has been extended to form the Dunmore Trail in memory of John, Earl of Dunmore (1939–80), and of his father, the Viscount Fincastle, killed in action in 1940.

Crathes Castle, Garden and Estate

Aberdeenshire. On A93, 5 km (3 miles) E of Banchory and 24 km (15 miles) W of Aberdeen.
Banchory AB31 3QJ □ 97 G6

Royal historic associations date from 1323, when the lands of Leys were granted to the Burnett family by King Robert the Bruce. Built during the second half of the 16th century, has remarkable late 16th-century painted ceilings and collections of family portraits and vernacular furniture, some of it contemporary with the building of the castle. The walled garden is a composite of eight separate gardens, which include fascinating examples of the art of topiary, dating from 1702. The grounds are ideal for nature study and there are six trails.

Culloden

Highland. B9006, 8 km (5 miles) E of Inverness.
NTS Visitor Centre, Culloden Moor, Inverness IV1 2ED □ 103 F8

Scene of the last major battle fought on mainland Britain. The final Jacobite uprising ended here on 16 April, 1746, when the army of Prince Charles Edward Stuart was crushed by the Government forces, led by the Duke of Cumberland. Turf and stone dykes which played a crucial part in the battle are have been reconstructed on their original 18th-century site as part of a longterm strategy to return the battlefield to its original 1746 state. The adjacent Old Leanach Cottage, which survived the battle being fought around it, is open to the public. Also in the Trust's care are the Graves of the Clans, the Well of the Dead, the Memorial Cairn, the Cumberland Stone and the Field of the English.

Culross

Fife. Off A985, 19 km (12 miles) W of Forth Road Bridge.
□ 80 E3

This small, royal burgh on the north shore of the Forth provides a striking introduction to Scottish domestic life in the 16th and 17th centuries. The Palace was built between 1597 and 1611 for Sir George Bruce and features decorative painted woodwork and original interiors. A model 17th-century garden has been built to the rear of the Palace. The Town House and The Study are both open to the public, while The Ark, Bishop Leighton's House, The Nunnery and other restored houses may only be viewed from the outside.

Culzean Castle & Country Park

South Ayrshire. 19 km (12 miles) S of Ayr, on A719, 6 km (4 miles) W of Maybole, off A77.
Maybole KA19 8LE □ 71 H4

Culzean Castle and Country Park is the Trust's most visited property and one of the major tourist attractions in Scotland. Robert Adam's castle, built 1772–90 for David, 10th Earl of Cassillis on a cliff-top site associated with the Kennedy family since the late 14th century, is notable for the Oval Staircase and Circular Saloon. Scotland's first Country Park, created in 1969 and consisting of 906 ha (563 acres), from shoreline through the Deer Park, Swan Pond to mature parklands, gardens, woodland walks and adventure playground.

Cunninghame Graham Memorial

Stirling. Off A81, in Gartmore, 4 km (2.5 miles) SW of Aberfoyle.
□ 79 H2

Cairn to the memory of R B Cunninghame Graham of Ardoch, distinguished Scottish author; erected in 1937, a year after his death, at Castlehill, Dumbarton. Moved to Gartmore in 1981.

Dollar Glen

Clackmannanshire. Off A91, N of Dollar. □ 80 E2

This wooded glen provides a spectacular walk to Castle Campbell. 22 ha (54 acres). Waymarked walks. During or after rain the path can be dangerous. Dogs must be kept strictly under control and on leads during lambing season.

Drum Castle

Aberdeenshire. Off A93, 5 km (3 miles) W of Peterculter, 16 km (10 miles) W of Aberdeen and 13 km (8 miles) E of Banchory.
Drumoak, nr Banchory AB31 3EY
□ 97 G5

The great, square tower of Drum Castle is one of the three oldest tower houses in Scotland. It was the work of Richard Cementarius, first Provost of Aberdeen and King's Master Mason, in the late 13th century. Additions were made in 1619 and during the reign of Queen Victoria to the very fine Jacobean mansion house. The house contains a collection of portraits and good Georgian furniture. The grounds contain the 40 ha (100-acre) Old Wood of Drum – a natural oakwood – and Garden of Historic Roses.

Dunkeld

Perth & Kinross. Off A9, 15 miles N of Perth.
Ell Shop, The Cross,
Dunkeld PH8 0AN □ 88 C4

The Trust owns 20 houses (not open to the public) in Cathedral and High Streets; most date from the rebuilding of the town after the Battle of Dunkeld in 1689. Restored by the Trust, the houses provide homes of modern standards while retaining the charm of their period exteriors. Trust shop opened in restored Ell House in 1982. Tourist Information Centre, information provided by the local Tourist Association. The south banks of the River Tay and the River Braan, form part of the Birnam Circular Walk.

Fair Isle

Accessible in summer by regular sailings of the mail boat from Grutness, on Shetland or Loganair flights from Tingwall (Lerwick) airport and Kirkwall, Orkney
□ 112 N1

One of the most isolated inhabited islands in Britain. The Fair Isle Knitting Co-operative sells island knitwear world-wide. Important for the study of birds, flora and fauna, for its traditional crofting practices and for conservation of the environment. Additional crafts now include traditional wooden boat-building, fiddle making and the manufacture of stained glass windows.

Falkland Palace

Garden & Old Burgh Fife. A912, 16 km (10 miles) from M90/junction 8, 18 km (11 miles) N of Kirkcaldy.
Falkland, Cupar,
Fife KY15 7BU □ 88 E8

The Royal Palace of Falkland was the country residence of the Stewart kings and queens when they hunted deer and wild boar in the Fife forest. Mary, Queen of Scots spent some of the happiest days of her tragic life here. The Palace was built between 1501 and 1541 by James IV and James V, replacing earlier castle and palace buildings dating from the 12th century. The Keeper's Apartments in the Gatehouse are now also on display. The garden was designed and built by Percy Cane between 1947 and 1952. The original Royal Tennis Court – the oldest in Britain – was built in 1539. The palace still belongs to Her Majesty the Queen but is maintained and managed by the Trust.

Falls of Glomach

Highland. NE of A87, 29 km (18 miles) E of Kyle of Lochalsh.
□ 93 G3

One of the highest waterfalls in Britain, set in a steep narrow cleft in remote country. The best approach is from the Dorusduain car park, 4 km (2.5 miles) off the north section of the loop in the old A87. By path 8 km (5 miles), allow 5 hours for round trip, or, for the very fit only, leave car by the Ling bridge, N end Loch Long, for a long walk along Glen Elchaig before making a steep climb to the Falls, 11 km (7 miles) allow 8 hours.

Finavon Doocot

Angus. Off A94 9 km (6 miles) N of Forfar.
□ 89 G3

Largest doocot in Scotland, with 2400 nesting boxes. Believed to have been built by the Earl of Crawford in the 16th century.

Fyvie Castle

Aberdeenshire. Off A947, 13 km (8 miles) SE of Turriff and 40 km (25 miles) NW of Aberdeen.
Fyvie, Turriff AB53 8JS □ 97 G2

The five towers of Fyvie Castle enshrine five centuries of Scottish history, the oldest part dating from the 13th century. The castle is now probably the grandest example of Scottish baronial architecture. A great wheel-stair, the finest in Scotland and 17th-century morning room with contemporary panelling and plaster ceiling. Exceptionally important collection of portraits, arms, armour and 17th-century tapestries.

The grounds and Fyvie Loch were designed as a landscaped parkland around the beginning of the 18th century. Restored racquets court, ice house and bird hide.

Gatehouse of Fleet

Dumfries & Galloway. Off A75.
□ 69 H5

Venniehill: a field with hilltop viewpoint at the west end of the main street. The Murray Isles: two small uninhabited islands in the Islands of Fleet, Wigtown Bay, off Carrick Point.

The Georgian House and Charlotte Square

Edinburgh. Charlotte Square, 2 mins from west end of Princes Street.
7 Charlotte Square,
Edinburgh EH2 4DR □ 81 H4

The Georgian House: the rooms are furnished as they might have been by the first owners, reflecting the social conditions of that age. A fine example of New Town architecture of the 18th century.

Gladstone's Land

Edinburgh. Lawnmarket (part of The Royal Mile), 5 mins walk from Princes Street via The Mound.
477B Lawnmarket,
Edinburgh EH1 2NT □ 81 H4

A typical example of the 17th-century tenement building of the overcrowded Old Town which grew up along the ridge between Edinburgh Castle and the Palace of Holyroodhouse – the Royal Mile. Its site and the extent of its accommodation mark its prestige in terms of mercantile dignity. Completed in 1620, the six-storey building contains remarkable painted ceilings. Originally the home of an Edinburgh burgess, Thomas Gledstanes.

Glencoe & Dalness

Highland. A82, 27 km (17 miles) S of Fort William.
NTS Visitor Centre, Glencoe,
Ballachulish PA39 4HX □ 86 D3

The A82 Glasgow to Fort William road runs through this dramatic and historic glen and the Visitor Centre is a perfect stopping-place for the traveller going north or south. Some of the finest climbing and walking country in the Highlands within the 5,670 ha (14,010 acres). Ossian's Cave, associated with legends of the ancient Scottish bard. The Glencoe hills are internationally important as a geological site which demonstrates the phenomenon of a volcano collapsing in on itself during a series of violent eruptions.

Glenfinnan Monument

Highland. A830, 30 km (18.5 miles) W of Fort William.
NTS Information Centre,
Glenfinnan PH37 4LT □ 93 F7

Set amid superb Highland scenery at the head of Loch Shiel, was erected in 1815 by Alexander Macdonald of Glenaladale in tribute to the clansmen who fought and died in the cause of Prince Charles Edward Stuart. In the Visitor Centre there are displays and an audio programme, with commentary in four languages, of the Prince's campaign from Glenfinnan to Derby and back to the final defeat at Culloden.

Greenbank Garden

East Renfrewshire. Flenders Road off Mearns Road, 1.6 km (1 miles) S of Clarkston Toll off A726, 9 km (6 miles) S of Glasgow city centre, off A77.
Flenders Road, Clarkston,
Glasgow G76 8RB □ 79 H6

Large walled garden and 5 ha (13 acres) of policies surround the elegant Georgian house, built in 1764 for a Glasgow merchant. The attractive garden indicates how wide a range of ornamental plants, annuals, perennials, shrubs and trees can be grown in the area and is especially relevant to owners of small gardens.

Grey Mare's Tail

Dumfries & Galloway. Adjacent to A708, 16 km (10 miles) NE of Moffat.
□ 73 G3

Spectacular 60 m (200 ft) waterfall. Area rich in wild flowers and geological interest; herd of wild goats. The hinterland has changed little since the days when the Covenanters sought sanctuary there.

Haddo House

Aberdeenshire. Off B999, 6 km (4 miles) N of Pitmedden, 30 km (19 miles) N of Aberdeen and 16 km (10 miles) NW of Ellon.
Ellon AB41 0ER □ 97 H2

Designed in 1731 by William Adam, a pupil of Sir William Bruce and father of the Adam brothers, for William, 2nd Earl of Aberdeen. Much of the interior is 'Adam Revival' carried out about 1880 for John, 7th Earl and 1st Marquess of Aberdeen and his Countess, Ishbel.

The Hermitage

Perth & Kinross. Off A9, 3 km (2 miles) W of Dunkeld. □ 88 C4

Particularly interesting mixed conifer and deciduous woodlands with very tall Douglas fir trees. There is a picturesque folly built in 1758 above the wooded gorge of the River Braan, restored in 1952 with further work carried out in 1986.

The Hill House

Upper Colquhoun Street, Helensburgh. Off B832, between A82 and A814, 37 km (23 miles) NW of Glasgow.
Upper Colquhoun Street,
Helensburgh G84 9AJ □ 78 E3

The house stands high above the River Clyde at Helensburgh and is probably Charles Rennie Mackintosh's finest domestic creation. The commission of Walter Blackie, the Glasgow publisher, included furniture, fittings and decorative schemes. Mackintosh's wife, Margaret MacDonald, contributed fabric designs and a unique gesso panel. The overall effect is as modern today as it must have been in 1904 when the Blackie family moved in. The gardens are being restored to their former glory. The original kitchen has been restored and now houses a small tearoom.

Hill of Tarvit Mansionhouse & Garden

Fife. Off A916, 4 km (2.5 miles) S of Cupar.
Cupar, Fife KY15 5PB □ 89 F7

The present house was virtually rebuilt in 1906 by Sir Robert Lorimer for Mr F B Sharp to form a suitable setting for his notable collection which includes French, Chippendale and vernacular furniture, Dutch paintings and pictures by Raeburn and Ramsay, Flemish tapestries and Chinese porcelain and bronzes. Lorimer also designed the formal garden. Restored Edwardian laundry. Regular exhibitions of local artists' work.

House of the Binns

West Lothian. Off A904, 24 km (15 miles) W of Edinburgh.
Linlithgow, West
Lothian EH49 7NA □ 80 F4

The historic home of the Dalyells, among them General Tam Dalyell who raised the Royal Scots Greys here in 1681. Parts of the present house date from the time of General Tam's father (1612–30). It reflects the early 17th-century transition in Scottish architecture from fortified stronghold to more spacious mansion. An excellent run of family portraits and an interesting collection of china. Woodland walk to panoramic viewpoint over Firth of Forth.

House of Dun

Angus. On A935, 5 km (3 miles) W of Montrose.
Montrose, Angus DD10 9LQ □ 89 J3

Georgian house overlooking the Montrose Basin, designed and built by William Adam in 1730 for David Erskine, Lord Dun. Superb contemporary plasterwork by Joseph Enzer. Contains royal mementos of that period and many examples of Lady Augusta's woolwork and embroidery. Family collection of portraits, furniture and porcelain. Small walled garden, largely restored to a late Victorian period and includes a range of plants typical of the 1880s.

Hugh Miller's Cottage

Highland. Via Kessock Bridge and A832, in Cromarty, 13 km (22 miles) NE of Inverness.
Cromarty IV11 8XA □ 103 F6

Hugh Miller was born here in 1802 – stonemason, eminent geologist, editor and writer. Furnished thatched cottage, built c. 1698 by his great-grandfather, contains an exhibition on his life and work.

Hutchesons' Hall

Glasgow. Ingram Street, near SE corner of George Square.
158 Ingram Street,
Glasgow G1 1EJ
□ 79 H5

One of the most elegant buildings in Glasgow's city centre, Hutchesons' Hall was built in 1802–5 to a design by David Hamilton. A major reconstruction in 1876 by John Baird heightened the Hall to its present proportions and provided an impressive staircase.

Inveresk Lodge Garden

East Lothian. A6124, S of Musselburgh, 9 km (6 miles) E of Edinburgh.
24 Inveresk Village, Musselburgh,
East Lothian EH21 7TE □ 81 J4

This attractive terraced garden and 17th-century lodge (which is not open to the public) were presented to the Trust in 1959 by Mrs Helen E Brunton.

Inverewe Garden

Highland. On A832, by Poolewe, 9 km (6 miles) NE of Gairloch.
Poolewe IV22 2LQ □ 100 E4

This outstanding climatically-favoured garden is impressively set on a peninsula on the shores of Loch Ewe. It is an oasis of colour and fertility where exotic plants from many countries flourish in the Gulf Stream which brings warm currents to the shores of the sea-loch.

Iona

Argyll and Bute. By ferry from Fionnphort, Isle of Mull (A 849).
□ 84 D6

In AD 563 Columba and his followers arrived here from Ireland to extend in Scotland and the north of England the gospel which had first been introduced by St Ninian at Whithorn in AD 397.

Kellie Castle & Garden

Fife. On B9171, 5 km (3 miles) NNW of Pittenweem.
Pittenweem, Fife KY10 2RF □ 82 D1

A very fine example of the domestic architecture of Lowland Scotland. The oldest part is believed to date from 1360, but the building in its present form was completed in about 1606. Sympathetically restored by the Lorimer family around 1878, it contains magnificent plaster ceilings, painted panelling and furniture designed by Sir Robert Lorimer. The layout of the organic walled garden is late Victorian.

Killiecrankie

Perth & Kinross. B8079 (old A9), 5 km (3 miles) N of Pitlochry.
NTS Visitor Centre, Killiecrankie,
Pitlochry PH16 5LG □ 88 B2

The first shots in the Jacobite cause were fired in 1689 at the Battle of Killiecrankie about one mile from the Trust's property. One government soldier evaded capture by making a spectacular jump across the river at Soldier's Leap. The wooded gorge was admired by Queen Victoria.

Kintail & Morvich

Highland. N of A87, 26 km (16 miles) E of Kyle of Lochalsh.
□ 93 F3

A magnificent stretch of West Highland scenery, the 7050 ha (17,422-acre) estate includes the Falls of Glomach and the Five Sisters of Kintail. Site of Battle of Glen Shiel (1719).

Leith Hall & Garden

Aberdeenshire. On B9002, 1.6 km (1 mile) W of Kennethmont and 55 km (34 miles) NW of Aberdeen.
Huntly AB54 4NQ □ 96 E3

Leith Hall is at the centre of a 115 ha (286-acre) estate which was the home of the head of the Leith family from 1650. The house contains personal possessions of successive lairds, most of whom followed a tradition of military service. The garden features extensive herbaceous borders and a fine collection of alpines and primulas. There are two ponds, a bird observation hide and three countryside walks.

Linn of Tummel

Perth & Kinross. B8019, 4 km (2.5 miles) NW of Pitlochry.
□ 88 B3

Characteristic of the beauty of the Perthshire Highlands, the Linn of Tummel comprises 23 ha (56 acres) by the banks of the Rivers Tummel and Garry and is adjacent to the Trust's Killiecrankie property. A path through mixed woodland leads to the Linn of Tummel.

Malleny Garden

In Balerno, near Edinburgh, off Lanark Road (A70).
Balerno EH14 7AF □ 81 G5

The 17th-century house (not open to the public) was built for Sir James Murray of Kilbaberton about 1635, with two Georgian reception rooms added in 1823. The walled garden is dominated by four 400-year-old clipped yew trees and a large collection of old-fashioned roses. National Bonsai Collection for Scotland. Extensive woodland.

Mar Lodge Estate

Aberdeenshire. 8 km (5 miles) W of Braemar. Access from A93 via an unclassified road.
Braemar, Ballater,
Aberdeenshire AB35 5YJ □ 95 K6

The 31,364 ha (77,500-acre) estate is part of the core area of the Cairngorm Mountains, internationally recognised as the most important nature conservation landscape in the British Isles. The estate contains four of the ten highest mountains in the UK and includes a remnant Caledonian pine forest of national importance. Large parts of the estate are designated as Sites of Special Scientific Interest and the majority of it is within National Scenic Areas. Outstanding wildlife and birdlife.

Moirlanich Longhouse

Stirling. Off A827, 1m NW of Killin.
NTS Office, Fagus, Manse Road,
Killin FK21 8UY □ 87 H5

An outstanding example of traditional cruck frame cottage and byre, dating from the mid-19th century. Little altered and retaining many original features such as the box beds. A small adjacent shed displays a rare collection of working clothes found in the Longhouse, and an exhibition interprets the history and restoration of the building.

Pitmedden Garden

Aberdeenshire. On A920, 1.6 km (1 mile) W of Pitmedden village and 22 km (14 miles) N of Aberdeen.
Ellon AB41 0PD □ 97 H3

The centrepiece of this property is the Great Garden, originally laid out in 1675 by Sir Alexander Seton, 1st Baronet of Pitmedden. In the 1950s, the elaborate floral designs were re-created under the guidance of the late Dr James Richardson. On the 40 ha (100-acre) estate is a woodland walk, Museum of Farming Life, herb garden and wildlife garden.

Preston Mill & Phantassie Doocot

East Lothian. Off A1, in East Linton, 37 km (23 miles) E of Edinburgh.
East Linton, East Lothian EH40 3DS
□ 82 E4

There has been a mill on the site for centuries, and the present stone buildings date from the 18th century. The water-wheel and the grain milling machinery it powers are relatively modern and the mill continued in commercial use until 1957. The conical-roofed kiln, red pantiles and groupings of the buildings are popular with artists.

Priorwood Garden & Dried Flower Shop

Borders. Off A6091, in Melrose, adjacent to Abbey.
Melrose TD6 9PX □ 74 B1

Priorwood is a unique garden, organised with volunteer help, where the majority of plants grown are suitable for drying. In the adjacent orchard, many varieties of historic apple trees grow.

Rockcliffe

Dumfries & Galloway. Off A710, 11 km (7 miles) S of Dalbeattie.
□ 69 K5

The Trust owns several properties in this area. Mote of Mark, site of an ancient hill-fort, and Rough Island, 8 ha (20-acre) bird sanctuary. Owing to the sensitivity of ground-nesting birds, the public are requested not to visit the island during May and June. Muckle Lands and Jubilee Path, 20 ha (51.5 acres) of rough coastline between Rockcliffe and Kippford.

St Abb's Head National Nature Reserve

Borders. Off A1107, 3 km (2 miles) N of Coldingham.
□ 83 H5

National Nature Reserve, managed jointly with the Scottish Wildlife Trust. A spectacular headland with 90 m (300 ft) cliffs. The most important location for cliff-nesting seabirds in SE Scotland. The offshore waters are part of Scotland's first voluntary marine nature reserve, declared in 1984. No vehicles allowed on road to lighthouse. Dogs must be kept on leash.

St Kilda National Nature Reserve

Western Isles. Remote and spectacular, the St Kilda archipelago lies 177 km (110 miles) out in the Atlantic.

Its main island of Hirta maintained its population until 1930, when the islanders were evacuated at their own request. Each year, Trust working parties using volunteer labour conserve and repair buildings and carry out archaeological work.

Shieldaig Island

Highland. In Loch Torridon, off Shieldaig, A896.
□ 100 E7

This 13 ha (32-acre) island is almost entirely covered in Scots pine which once formed vast forests covering much of the Scottish Highlands.

Robert Smail's Printing Works

Borders. High Street, Innerleithen, 48 km (30 miles) S of Edinburgh.
7/9 High Street, Innerleithen
EH44 6HA □ 81 J8

These buildings contain an office, a paper store with reconstructed water-wheel, composing and press rooms. Necessary but sympathetic restoration, included bringing all machinery to full working order, now enables visitors to try their own hand at setting type manually. The Victorian office contains many historic items.

Souter Johnnie's Cottage

South Ayrshire. On A77, in Kirkoswald, 6 km (4 miles) SW of Maybole (car park at S end of village).
Main Road, Kirkoswald
KA19 8HY □ 71 H4

The home of John Davidson, village souter (cobbler), who was the original Souter Johnnie of Robert Burns' Tam o' Shanter. Life-sized stone figures of the Souter, Tam, the innkeeper and his wife are in the restored ale house in the cottage garden. The thatched cottage contains Burns relics and the souter's work-shop.

Staffa

Argyll & Bute. 9 km (6 miles) NE of Iona.
□ 84 E5

Romantic and uninhabited island, famous for its basaltic formations, the best known of which is Fingal's Cave. Immortalised by Mendelssohn in his celebrated Hebrides overture, its cluster columns and seemingly man-made symmetry give the cave a cathedral-like majesty. Visitors include the artist J M W Turner, and poets and writers Keats, Wordsworth, Tennyson and Sir Walter Scott.

Strome Castle

Highland. Off A896, 7 km (4.5 miles) SW of Lochcarron.
□ 92 E2

Ruined castle, romantically situated on a rocky promontory jutting into Loch Carron. First recorded in 1472 when it was a stronghold of the Lords of the Isles, it later belonged to the MacDonnells of Glengarry. Following a quarrel with Kenneth MacKenzie, Lord of Kintail, it fell in 1602 after a long seige and was blown up. The tower remains a heap of rubble but substantial sections of the enclosing wall still stand.

The Tenement House

Glasgow. Buccleuch Street, Garnethill, three streets N of Sauchiehall Street, nr Charing Cross. Restricted parking.
145 Buccleuch Street, Glasgow
G3 6QN □ 79 H5

Built in 1892 when Garnethill was established as a superior residential district in Glasgow's west end, the Tenement House illustrates the inherent character given to Glasgow by its Victorian tenement buildings. All original box-beds, closed kitchen range, sink and coal-bunker, furnishings and domestic items from the family who lived there for more than 50 years.

Threave Garden & Estate

Dumfries & Galloway. Off A75, 1.6 km (1 mile) W of Castle Douglas.
Castle Douglas DG7 1RX □ 69 J4

The extensive garden provides interest throughout the year and 200 varieties of daffodil in Spring. Victorian house (not open to the public), home to the Trust's School of Practical Gardening. Threave Estate: includes farmland, woodland, a 3 km (2-mile) stretch of the River Dee and wetland important for its plants, and wildfowl. Five bird hides, marked walks and trail (open May–Sep).

Tighnabruaich Viewpoint

Argyll & Bute. On A8003, NE of Tighnabruaich.
□ 78 B4

The indicators, attributed to the Trust and the Scottish Civic Trust, were erected by a Trust supporter in memory of two brothers, who gave generously of their time to the work of the Trust.

Torridon

Highland. N of A896, 14 km (9 miles) SW of Kinlochewe.
□ 101 F7

A 6,515-ha (16,100-acre) estate including some of Scotland's finest mountain scenery which has seven tops, and Beinn Alligin. Liathach is of Torridonian sandstone, some 750 million years old; the tops, of white quartzite some 150 million years younger. A Trust Countryside Centre, with interpretive display and an audio-visual presentation on wildlife, is at the junction of A896 and the Diabaig road. Deer Museum located 550 m on, down the gravel road leading to The Mains.

Weaver's Cottage

Renfrewshire. Off A740 and A737, at The Cross, Kilbarchan, 19 km (12 miles) SW of Glasgow.
The Cross, Kilbarchan
PA10 2JG □ 79 G5

This typical cottage of an 18th-century handloom weaver contains looms, weaving equipment and domestic utensils. Displays of local historical and weaving items. Attractive cottage garden.

West Affric

Highland. Park cars either at Kintail or at the Forest Enterprise car park near Affric Lodge (OS map 25 ref 200 235), reached from Cannich on the A831.
□ 93 J3

The Trust bought this important area in 1993 to protect its wild land character, restore its natural flora and secure one of the most popular east/west paths in the Highlands. The path, now only used by walkers, was once part of the drove road from Skye to Dingwall.

ENGLISH HERITAGE PROPERTIES

THIS DIRECTORY OF ENGLISH HERITAGE PROPERTIES IS DIVIDED INTO THE SIX AREAS SHOWN ON THE KEY MAP BELOW.

The properties are classified to make it easier to choose those of particular interest. Most categories are self-explanatory. Others include *Humps and Bumps* which are archaeological remains (many still remarkably intact), *Pot luck*, which can be anything from a medieval bridge to a Georgian deer shelter, and *Far from the crowd*, remote sites that are mostly free but tend to be less easily accessible. Opening times vary so please telephone before visiting to avoid disappointment

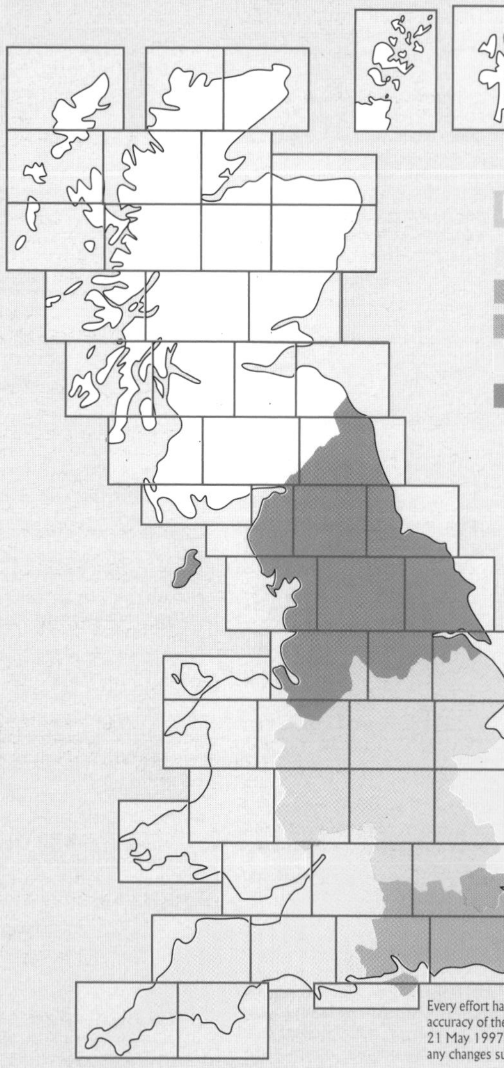

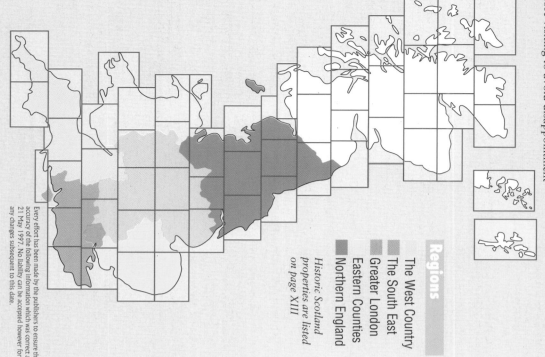

Regions

- The West Country
- The South East
- Greater London
- Eastern Counties
- Northern England

Historic Scotland properties are listed on page XIII

Every effort has been made by the publishers to ensure the accuracy of the following information which was correct at 21 May 1997. No liability can be accepted however for any changes subsequent to this date.

Key to symbols

- Christian heritage
- Castle / fort
- Historic house
- Romantic ruin
- Humps and bumps
- Roman
- Garden / park
- Industrial monument
- Pot luck
- Far from the crowd
- Great antiquity

Listed in blue are: atlas page numbers and grid squares; OS Landranger 1: 50 000 sheet map numbers and OS National Grid references. These can be used to precisely locate the site in this atlas or on any Ordnance Survey sheet map (see page 123 for details of the National Grid)

The West Country

Abbotsbury Abbey Remains
Dorset
The remains of a cloister building of this Benedictine abbey, founded in 1044.
In Abbotsbury, off B3157, near churchyard.
11 G7; Landranger 194; SY 578852

Avebury
Wiltshire
See also Silbury Hill, The Sanctuary, West Kennet Avenue, West Kennet Long Barrow and Windmill Hill.

Avebury Museum
Wiltshire
The investigation of Avebury Stone Circles was largely the work of Alexander Keiller in the 1930s. He put together one of the most important prehistoric archaeological collections in Britain, and this can be seen in the Avebury Museum. ☎01672 539250
In Avebury 7m W of Marlborough.
20 E6; Landranger 173; SU 100700

Avebury Stone Circles
Wiltshire
Complex, gigantic and mysterious, the Circles were constructed 4,000 years ago, originally comprising more than 180 stones. The remains of the Circles still surround the later village of Avebury. In Avebury 7m W of Marlborough.
20 F5; Landranger 173; SU 103700

Ballowall Barrow
St Just, Cornwall
In a spectacular position, this is an unusual Bronze Age chambered tomb with a complex layout. 1m W of St Just, near Carn Gloose.
2 B6; Landranger 203; SW 354313

Bant's Carn Burial Chamber and Halangy Down Ancient Village
St Mary's, Isles of Scilly
In a wonderful scenic location, on a hill above the site of the ancient Iron Age village, lies this Bronze Age burial mound with entrance passage and chamber. 1m N of Hugh Town.
2 P2; Landranger 203; SV 911124

Bayard's Cove Fort
Dartmouth, Devon
A small artillery fort built before 1534 to defend the harbour entrance. In Dartmouth, on riverfront.
5 J4; Landranger 202; SX 879510

Belas Knap Long Barrow
Gloucestershire
A good example of a Neolithic long barrow, with the mound still intact and surrounded by a stone wall. The chamber tombs, where the remains of 31 people were found, have been opened up so that visitors can see inside.
2m S of Winchcombe, near Charlton Abbots, ½ mile on Cotswold Way.
32 C7; Landranger 163; SP 021254

Berry Pomeroy Castle
Devon
A romantic late-medieval castle, unusual in combining the remains of a large castle with a flamboyant courtier's mansion. It is reputed to be haunted. ☎01803 866618 2½m E of Totnes off A385.
5 J3; Landranger 202; SX 839623

Blackbury Camp
Devon
An Iron Age hillfort, defended by a bank and ditch. 1½m SW of Southleigh off B3174 / A3052.
10 C6; Landranger 192; SY 188924

Blackfriars
Gloucester, Gloucestershire
A small Dominican priory church. Most of the original 13th-century church remains, including a rare scissor-braced roof.
☎0117 975 0700). In Ladybellegate Street off Southgate Street and Blackfriars Walk.
20 C1; Landranger 162; SO 830186

Bowhill
Exeter, Devon
A mansion of considerable status built c.1500 by a member of the Holland family. The impressive Great Hall has been carefully restored by English Heritage craftsmen using traditional materials and techniques. ☎ 0117 975 0700). 1½m SW of Exeter on B3212.
73 K2; Landranger 192; SX 906916

Bradford-on-Avon Tithe Barn
Wiltshire
A medieval stone-built barn with slate roof and wooden beamed interior. ¼m S of town centre, off B3109.
20 C6; Landranger 173; ST 824604

Bratton Camp and White Horse
Wiltshire
A large Iron Age hill fort. 2m E of Westbury off B3098, 1m SW of Bratton.
20 D7; Landranger 184; ST 900516

Butter Cross
Dunster, Somerset
A medieval stone cross. Beside minor road to Alcombe, 350m (400 yds) NW of Dunster parish church.
10 A1; Landranger 181; SS 988439

Carn Euny Ancient Village
Cornwall
The remains of an Iron Age settlement, with foundations of stone huts and an intriguing curved underground passage, or *fogou*.
1¼m SW of Sancreed off A30.
2 C7; Landranger 203; SW 402289

Chisbury Chapel
Wiltshire
A thatched 13th-century chapel rescued from use as a farm building. On unclassified road ¼m E of Chisbury off A4 6m E of Marlborough.
21 G6; Landranger 174; SU 280658

Christchurch Castle and Norman House
Dorset
Early 12th-century Norman keep, and Constable's house, built c.1160. In Christchurch, near Priory.
12 D6; Landranger 195; SZ 160927

Chysauster Ancient Village
Cornwall
A deserted Romano-Cornish village with a 'street' of eight well-preserved houses, each comprising a number of rooms around an open court. ☎0831 757934 for details. 2½m NW of Gulval off B3311.
2 C6; Landranger 203; SW 473350

Cirencester Amphitheatre
Gloucestershire
A large well-preserved Roman amphitheatre. Next to bypass W of town – access from town or along Chesterton Lane from W end of bypass onto Cotswold Ave. Park next to obelisk.
20 E2; Landranger 163; SP 020014

Cleeve Abbey
Somerset
One of the few 13th-century monastic sites where you will see such a complete set of cloister buildings, including the refectory with its magnificent timber roof. ☎01984 640377
In Washford, ¼m S of A39.
10 B1; Landranger 181; ST 047407

Cromwell's Castle
Tresco, Isles of Scilly
Standing on a promontory guarding the lovely anchorage between Bryher and Tresco, this 17th-century round tower was built to command the haven of New Grimsby.
On shoreline, ¾m NW of New Grimsby.
2 N2; Landranger 203; SV 882159

Dartmouth Castle
Devon
This brilliantly positioned defensive castle juts out into the narrow entrance to the Dart estuary, with the sea lapping at its foot. It was one of the first castles constructed with artillery in mind and has seen 450 years of fortification and preparation for war.
☎01803 833588 1m SE of Dartmouth off B3205, narrow approach road.
5 J4; Landranger 202; SX 887503

Daws Castle
Somerset
The site where the people of the Saxon town of Watchet sought refuge against the threat of Viking attack. ½m W of Watchet off B3191 on cliff top.
10 B1; Landranger 181; ST 062432

Dupath Well
Callington, Cornwall
A charming granite-built well house set over a holy well of c.1500 and almost complete.
1m E of Callington off A388.
4 D3; Landranger 201; SX 374693

Farleigh Hungerford Castle
Somerset
Ruins of a 14th-century castle with a chapel containing wall paintings, stained glass and the fine tomb of Sir Thomas Hungerford, the builder of the castle. ☎01225 754026
In Farleigh Hungerford 3½m W of Trowbridge on A366.
20 B7; Landranger 173; ST 801577

Fiddleford Manor
Dorset
Part of a medieval manor house, with a remarkable interior. The splendid roof structures in the hall and upper living room are the best in Dorset. 1m E of Sturminster Newton off A357.
11 K4; Landranger 194; ST 801136

Gallox Bridge
Dunster, Somerset
A stone packhorse bridge with two ribbed arches which spans the old mill stream.
Off A396 at S end of Dunster.
10 A1; Landranger 181; SS 990432

Garrison Walls
St Mary's, Isles of Scilly
You can take a pleasant walk along the ramparts of these well-preserved walls and earthworks, built as part of the island's defences. Around the headland W of Hugh Town.
2 P2; Landranger 203; SV 898104

Glastonbury Tribunal
Somerset
A well-preserved medieval town house, reputedly once used as the courthouse of Glastonbury Abbey. ☎01458 832954
In Glastonbury High St.
11 F2; Landranger 182; ST 499390

Great Witcombe Roman Villa
Gloucestershire
The remains of a large villa. Built around three sides of a courtyard, it had a luxurious bath-house complex. ☎ 0117 975 0700).
5m SE of Gloucester, off A417, ½m S of reservoir in Witcombe Park.
20 D1; Landranger 163; SO 899144

Greyfriars
Gloucester, Gloucestershire
Remains of a late 15th- early 16th-century Franciscan friary church. On Greyfriars Walk, behind Eastgate Market off Southgate St.
20 C1; Landranger 162; SO 830186

Grimspound
Dartmoor, Devon
This late Bronze Age settlement displays the remains of 24 huts in an area of four acres enclosed by a stone wall. 6m SW of Moretonhampstead off B3212.
9 H7; Landranger 191; SX 701809

Hailes Abbey
Gloucestershire
13th-century Cistercian abbey, set in wooded pastureland, with examples of high quality sculpture in the site museum.
☎01242 602398 2m NE of Winchcombe off B4632.
32 C7; Landranger 150; SP 050300

Halliggye Fogou
Cornwall
One of several strange underground tunnels, associated with Iron Age villages, which are unique to Cornwall. 5m SE of Helston off B3293 E of Garras on Trelowarren estate.
2 F7; Landranger 203; SW 714239

Harry's Walls
St Mary's, Isles of Scilly
An uncompleted 16th-century fort intended to command the harbour of St Mary's Pool.
¼m NE of Hugh Town.
2 F2; Landranger 203; SV 910110

Hatfield Earthworks
Wiltshire
Part of a Neolithic enclosure complex 3,500 years old, formerly with a Bronze Age barrow in its centre. 5½m SE of Devizes off A342 NE of village of Marden.
20 F7; Landranger 173; SU 091583 or SU 092583

Hound Tor Deserted Medieval Village
Dartmoor, Devon
Remains of three or four medieval farmsteads, first occupied in the Bronze Age.
1½m S of Manaton off The Ashburton Road. Park in Hound Tor car park, ½m walk.
5 H1; Landranger 191; SX 746788.

Hurlers Stone Circles
Cornwall
These three Bronze Age stone circles in a line are some of the best examples of ceremonial standing stones in the South West. ½m NW of Minions off B3254.
4 C2; Landranger 201; SX 258714

Innisidgen Lower and Upper Burial Chambers
St Mary's, Isles of Scilly
Two Bronze Age cairns, about 30 metres (200 feet) apart, with stunning views towards St Martins. 1¾m NE of Hugh Town.
2 P2; Landranger 203; SV 921127

Jordan Hill Roman Temple
Weymouth, Dorset
Foundations of a Romano-Celtic temple enclosing an area of about 22 square metres (240 square feet). 2m NE of Weymouth off A353.
11 H7; Landranger 194; SY 698821

King Charles's Castle
Tresco, Isles of Scilly
At the end of a bracing coastal walk to the northern end of Tresco you will find the remains of this castle built for coastal defence. ¾ m NW of New Grimsby.
2 N2; Landranger 203; SV 882161

King Doniert's Stone
St Cleer, Cornwall
Two decorated pieces of a 9th-century cross with an inscription believed to commemorate Durngarth, King of Cornwall, who drowned c.875. 1m NW of St Cleer off B3254.
4 C3; Landranger 201; SX 236688

Kingston Russell Stone Circle
Dorset
A Bronze Age stone circle of 18 stones.
2m N of Abbotsbury, 1m along footpath off minor road to Hardy Monument.
11 G7; Landranger 194; SY 577878

Kingswood Abbey Gatehouse
Gloucestershire
The 16th-century gatehouse, with a richly carved mullioned window, is all that remains of the Cistercian abbey In Kingswood off B4060 1m SW of Wotton-under-Edge.
20 B3; Landranger 162; ST 748919

Kirkham House
Paignton, Devon
A well preserved, medieval stone house, much restored and repaired, which gives a fascinating insight into life in a town residence in the 15th century.
☎ 0117 975 0700. In Kirkham St, off Cecil Rd, Paignton.
5 J3; Landranger 202; SX 885610

Knowlton Church and Earthworks
Dorset
The ruins of this Norman church stand in the middle of Neolithic earthworks, symbolizing the transition from pagan to Christian worship. 3m SW of Cranborne on B3078.
12 C4; Landranger 195; SU 024100

Launceston Castle
Cornwall
Set on the motte of a Norman castle and commanding the town and surrounding countryside, this medieval castle controlled the main route into Cornwall. The shell keep and tower survive. ☎01566 772365
In Launceston.
8 D7; Landranger 201; SX 330846

Leigh Barton
Devon
A small late-medieval domestic complex with a fine gatehouse and three ranges around a galleried courtyard.
☎ 0117 975 0700. 2m NW of Kingsbridge at Leigh on unclassified road off B3194.
5 H5; Landranger 202; SX 721467

Ludgershall Castle and Cross
Wiltshire
Ruins of an early 12th-century royal hunting palace and a late-medieval cross. On N side of Ludgershall off A342.
12 E1; Landranger 184; SU 264513

Lulworth Castle
Dorset
An early 17th-century romantic hunting lodge, Lulworth Castle became a fashionable country house set in beautiful parkland during the 18th century. Gutted by fire in 1929, the exterior is now being restored by English Heritage. ☎01929 400510 In east Lulworth off B3070, 3 miles NE of Lulworth Cove.
11 K7; Landranger 194; SY 853822

Lydford Castles and Saxon Town
Devon
Standing above the gorge of the River Lyd, this 12th-century tower was notorious as a prison. The earthworks of the original Norman fort are to the south In Lydford off A386 8m S of Okehampton.
8 F7; Landranger 191; Castle SX 510848, Fort SX 509847

Maiden Castle
Dorset
This is the finest Iron Age hill fort in Britain. The earthworks are enormous, with a series of ramparts and complicated entrances, but they could not prevent the castle's capture by the Romans c. AD 43. 2m S of Dorchester. Access off A354, N of bypass.
11 H7; Landranger 194; SY 670885

Meare Fish House
Somerset
A simple, well-preserved stone dwelling.
In Meare village on B3151.
11 F1; Landranger 182; ST 458418

Merrivale Prehistoric Settlement
Dartmoor, Devon
Two rows of standing stones stretching up to 263 metres (864 feet) across the moors, together with the remains of an early Bronze Age village. 1m E of Merrivale.
4 F2; Landranger 191; SX 553746

Muchelney Abbey
Somerset
The well-preserved remains of the cloisters and abbot's lodging of this Benedictine abbey
☎01458 250664 In Muchelney 2m S of Langport.
11 F3; Landranger 193; ST 428248

Netheravon Dovecote
Wiltshire
A charming 18th-century brick dovecote, standing in a pleasant orchard, with most of its 700 or more nesting boxes still present.
In Netheravon, 4½m N of Amesbury on A345.
12 D1; Landranger 184; SU 146485

The Nine Stones
Winterbourne Abbas, Dorset
Remains of a prehistoric circle of nine standing stones constructed about 4,000 years ago. ½ m W of Winterbourne Abbas, on A35.
11 H6; Landranger 194; SY 611904

Notgrove Long Barrow
Gloucestershire
A Neolithic burial mound with chambers for human remains opening from a stone-built central passage. 1½m NW of Notgrove on A436.
32 C7; Landranger 163; SP 096211

Nunney Castle
Somerset
A small 14th-century moated castle which is distinctly French in style. In Nunney 3½m SW of Frome, off A361 (no coach access).
11 J1; Landranger 183; ST 737457

Nympsfield Long Barrow
Gloucestershire
A chambered Neolithic long barrow 30 metres (90 feet) in length. 1m NW of Nympsfield on B4066.
20 B2; Landranger 162; SO 795014

Odda's Chapel
Deerhurst, Gloucestershire
A rare Anglo-Saxon chapel attached, unusually, to a half-timbered farmhouse
In Deerhurst (off B4213) at Abbots Court SW of parish church.
32 A7; Landranger 150; SO 869298

Offa's Dyke
Gloucestershire
Three-mile section of the great earthwork built by Offa, King of Mercia 757–96, from the Severn estuary to the Welsh coast as a defensive boundary to his kingdom.
3m NE of Chepstow off B4228. Access via Forestry Commission Tidenham car park. 1m walk (way marked) down to Devil's Pulpit on Offa's Dyke. (Access suitable only for those wearing proper walking shoes; not suitable for very young, old or infirm).
19 K3; Landranger 162; SO 545005–549977

Okehampton Castle
Devon
The ruins of the largest castle in Devon include the Norman motte and the keep's jagged remains. There is a picnic area and there are also lovely woodland walks.
☎01837 52844 1m SW of Okehampton town centre.
9 F6; Landranger 191; SX 584942

Old Blockhouse
Tresco, Isles of Scilly
The remains of a small 16th-century gun tower overlooking the white sandy bay at Old Grimsby. On Blockhouse Point, at S end of Old Grimsby harbour.
2 P2; Landranger 203; SV 898155

Old Sarum
Wiltshire
This great earthwork with its huge banks and ditch lies near Salisbury, on the edge of the Wiltshire chalk plains. It was built by Iron Age peoples around 500 BC and was taken over by succeeding settlers and conquerors.
☎01722 335398 2m N of Salisbury, Wiltshire off A345.
12 D2; Landranger 184; SU 138327.

Old Wardour Castle
Wiltshire
The unusual hexagonal ruins of this 14th-century castle are on the edge of a beautiful lake, surrounded by landscaped grounds, which include an elaborate rockwork grotto.
☎01747 870487 Off A30 2m SW of Tisbury.
12 B3; Landranger 184; ST 939263

Over Bridge ◉
Gloucestershire
A single-arch masonry bridge spanning the River Severn, built by Thomas Telford 1825–27. ➲ 1m NW of Gloucester city centre at junction of A40 (Ross) & A419 (Ledbury).
☐ 20 C1; Landranger 162; SO 817196

Pendennis Castle ♜
Cornwall
Pendennis and its neighbour St Mawes Castle face each other across the mouth of the estuary of the River Fal. They are the Cornish end of a chain of castles built by Henry VIII along England's south coast from 1539–45 as protection against the threat of attack and invasion from France. Many of these castles are in the care of English Heritage. ✆ 01326 316594 ➲ On Pendennis Head, Cornwall, 1m SE of Falmouth.
☐ 3 G6; Landranger 204; SW 824318.

Penhallam ◉
Cornwall
Ruins of a medieval manor house surrounded by a protective moat. ➲ 1m NW of Week St Mary, off minor road off A39 from Treskinnick Cross (10 minute walk from car park).
☐ 8 C6; Landranger 190; SX 224974

Porth Hellick Down Burial Chamber ◉▲
St Mary's, Isles of Scilly
Probably the best-preserved Bronze Age burial mound on the Islands, with an entrance passage and chamber.
➲ 1½ m E of Hugh Town.
☐ 2 P2; Landranger 203; SV 929108

Portland Castle ♜
Dorset
One of the best preserved of Henry VIII's coastal forts, built of white Portland stone. It was originally intended to repel the Spanish and French, and changed hands several times during the Civil War. ✆ 01305 820539
➲ Overlooking Portland harbour adjacent to RN helicopter base.
☐ 6 A7; Landranger 194; SY 684743

Ratfyn Barrows ▲
Wiltshire
Part of Bronze Age cemetery containing burial mounds of different styles
✆ 0117 975 0700 ➲ 1½ m E of Amesbury on both sides of A303. Barrows can be seen from A303 (no stopping).
☐ 12 D1; Landranger 184; SU 180417

Restormel Castle ♜
Cornwall
Perched on a high mound, surrounded by a deep moat, the huge circular keep of this splendid Norman castle survives in remarkably good condition. It offers splendid views over the surrounding countryside. ✆ 01208 872687 ➲ 1½m N of Lostwithiel off A390.
☐ 7 K3; Landranger 200; SX 104614

Royal Citadel ◉
Plymouth, Devon
A dramatic 17th-century fortress, with walls up to 21 metres (70 feet) high, built to defend the coastline from the Dutch, and still in use today. ✆ 01752 775841 ➲ At E end of Plymouth Hoe.
☐ 4 E4; Landranger 201; SX 480538

St Breock Downs Monolith ▲◉
Cornwall
A prehistoric standing stone, originally about 5 metres (16 feet) high, set in beautiful countryside. ➲ On St Breock Downs, 3¾ m SW of Wadebridge off unclassified road to Rosenannon.
☐ 3 H2; Landranger 200; SW 968683

St Briavel's Castle ◉
Gloucestershire
A splendid 12th-century castle now used as a youth hostel, which is appropriate for a building set in such marvellous walking country. ➲ In St Briavel's, 7m NE of Chepstow off B4228.
☐ 19 K2; Landranger 162; SO 559046.

St Catherine's Castle ♜
Fowey, Cornwall
A small fort built by Henry VIII to defend Fowey Harbour. ➲ ¾ m SW of Fowey along footpath off A3082.
☐ 3 K4; Landranger 200; SX 118508.

St Catherine's Chapel ✝
Abbotsbury, Dorset
A small stone chapel, set on a hilltop, with an unusual roof and small turret used as a lighthouse. ➲ ½m S of Abbotsbury by pedestrian track from village off B3157.
☐ 11 G7; Landranger 194; SY 572848.

St Mary's Church ✝
Kempley, Gloucestershire
A Norman church with superb wall paintings from the 12th–14th centuries. ➲ 1m N of Kempley off B4024, 6m NE of Ross-on-Wye.
☐ 31 H6; Landranger 149; SO 670313.

St Mawes Castle ♜⚙
Cornwall
Together with Pendennis, St Mawes Castle was built by Henry VIII to guard the entrance to safe anchorage in the Carrick Roads. Its three huge circular bastions with gun ports were formidable defences indeed. Today the castle stands in delightful sub-tropical gardens featuring plants from around the world.
Some of the finest views of the surrounding coastline can be enjoyed from here.
✆ 01326 270526 ➲ In St Mawes on A3078.
☐ 3 G6; Landranger 204; SW 842328.

The Sanctuary ▲
Wiltshire
Possibly 5,000 years old, The Sanctuary consists of two concentric circles of stones and six of timber uprights indicated by concrete posts. The Sanctuary is connected to Avebury by the West Kennet Avenue of standing stones. ➲ Beside A4, ½m E of West Kennet.
☐ 20 F6; Landranger 173; SU 118679.

Sherborne Old Castle ◉♜
Dorset
The ruins of this early 12th-century castle are a testament to the 16 days Cromwell took to capture it during the Civil War. It was then abandoned. ✆ 01935 812730 ➲ ½m E of Sherborne off B3145.
☐ 11 H4; Landranger 183; ST 647167.

Silbury Hill ⓘ
Wiltshire
An extraordinary artificial prehistoric mound, the largest Neolithic construction of its type in Europe.
➲ 1m W of West Kennet on A4.
☐ 20 F6; Landranger 173; SU 100685

Sir Bevil Grenville's Monument ◉
Lansdown, Bath & N.E. Somerset
Commemorates the heroism of a Royalist commander and his Cornish pikemen at the Battle of Lansdown. ➲ 4m NW of Bath, on N edge of Lansdown Hill, near road to Wick.
☐ 20 B5; Landranger 172; ST 721703

Stanton Drew Circles and Cove ▲
Bath & NE Somerset
A fascinating assembly of three stone circles, two avenues and a burial chamber makes this one of the finest Neolithic religious sites in the country. ✆ 0117 975 0700 for details.
➲ Circles: E of Stanton Drew village; Cove: in garden of Druid's Arms.
☐ 19 L6; Landranger 172; Circles ST 601634, Cove ST 598633

Stonehenge ⓘ
Wiltshire
The great and ancient stone circle of Stonehenge is one of the wonders of the world, as old as many of the great temples and pyramids of Egypt, as old as Troy. Stonehenge is not an isolated monument, however. Although visitors over the centuries have tended to focus on the massive stones, these stand at the centre of an extensive prehistoric landscape filled with the remains of ceremonial and domestic structures. Some are older than the great monument itself. Many of these features – earthworks, burial mounds, and other circular 'henge' monuments – are accessible by road or public footpath. Now a World Heritage Site, Stonehenge and its surroundings remain powerful witnesses to the once great civilization of the Stone and Bronze Ages, between 5000 and 3000 years ago.
✆ 01980 624715 ➲ 2m W of Amesbury, Wiltshire on junction A303 and A344/A360.
☐ 12 D1; Landranger 184; SU 123422.

Stoney Littleton Long Barrow ▲
Bath & NE Somerset
This Neolithic burial mound is about 30 metres (100 feet) long and has chambers where human remains once lay. ➲ 1m S of Wellow off A367.
☐ 20 B7; Landranger 172; ST 735573

Temple Church ✝
Bristol
The handsome tower and walls of this 15th-century church defied the bombs of World War II. The graveyard is now a pleasant public garden. ➲ In Temple St off Victoria St.
☐ 19 K5; Landranger 172; ST 593727

Tintagel Castle ♜♡
Cornwall
With its specacular location on one of England's most dramatic coastlines, Tintagel Castle is a place of legends. Joined to the mainland by a narrow neck of land, Tintagel Island faces the full force of the Atlantic. On the mainland itself, the remains of the medieval castle, thought to date from the second quarter of the 13th century, represent only one phase in a long history of occupation. Even before Richard, Earl of Cornwall, built the castle, Tintagel had become associated with King Arthur as his birthplace and the legend, depicted in Geoffrey of Monmouth's *History of the Kings of Britain* (c. 1139), has lived on. Today fact and fiction lie intertwined but we know for sure that Tintagel remains one of the most awe-inspiring and romantic spots in Britain. ✆ 01840 770328 ➲ On Tintagel Head ½m along uneven track from Tintagel, no vehicles.
☐ 8 A7; Landranger 200; SX 048891.

Totnes Castle ♜♡
Devon
A superb motte and bailey castle, with splendid views to the River Dart – a fine example of Norman fortification.
✆ 01803 864406 ➲ In Totnes, on hill overlooking town.
☐ 5 H3; Landranger 202; SX 800605

Tregiffian Burial Chamber ▲
St Buryan, Cornwall
A Neolithic or early Bronze Age chambered tomb by the side of a country road.
➲ 2m SE of St Buryan on B3315.
☐ 2 C7; Landranger 203; SW 430245

Trethevy Quoit ▲
St Cleer, Cornwall
An ancient Neolithic burial chamber, standing 2.7 metres (9 feet) high and consisting of five standing stones surmounted by a huge capstone. ➲ 1m NE of St Cleer near Darite off B3254.
☐ 4 C3; Landranger 201; SX 259688

Uley Long Barrow (Hetty Pegler's Tump) ▲
Gloucestershire
Dating from around 3000 BC, this 55 metre-(180 foot-) long Neolithic chambered burial mound is unusual in that its mound is still intact. ➲ 3½m NE of Dursley on B4066.
☐ 20 B2; Landranger 162; SO 790000.

Upper Plym Valley ▲
Dartmoor, Devon
Scores of prehistoric and medieval sites covering six square miles of ancient landscape ➲ 4m E of Yelverton.
☐ 4 F3; Landranger 202

West Kennet Avenue ▲
Avebury, Wiltshire
An avenue of standing stones, which ran in a curve from Avebury Stone Circles to The Sanctuary, probably dating from the late Neolithic Age. ➲ Runs alongside B4003.
☐ 20 F5; Landranger 173; SU 105695

West Kennet Long Barrow ▲
Wiltshire
A Neolithic chambered tomb, consisting of a long earthen mound containing a passage with side chambers, and with the entrance guarded by a large stone. ➲ ¾m SW of West Kennet along footpath off A4.
☐ 20 F6; Landranger 173; SU 104677

Windmill Hill ▲
Wiltshire
Neolithic remains of three concentric rings of ditches, enclosing an area of 21 acres.
➲ 1½m NW of Avebury.
☐ 20 E6; Landranger 173; SU 086714

Winterbourne Poor Lot Barrows ▲
Dorset
Part of an extensive 4,000-year-old Bronze Age cemetery. ➲ 2m W of Winterbourne Abbas, S of junction of A35 with minor road to Compton Valence. Access via Wellbottom Lodge – 180 metres (200 yards) E along A35 from junction.
☐ 11 G6; Landranger 194; SY 590906

Woodhenge ▲
Wiltshire
Neolithic ceremonial monument of c. 2300 BC, consisting of a bank and ditch and six concentric rings of timber posts, now shown by concrete markers. The entrance and long axis of the oval rings points to the rising sun on Midsummer Day. ➲ 1½m N of Amesbury, off A345 just S of Durrington.
☐ 12 D1; Landranger 184; SU 151434

Yarn Market ◉
Dunster, Somerset
A 17th-century octagonal market hall. ➲ In Dunster High St.
☐ 10 A1; Landranger 181; SS 992437

The South East

Appuldurcombe House ♡◉
Isle of Wight
Although now mainly a shell, Appuldurcombe was once the grandest house on the Isle of Wight. The fine 18th-century baroque-style house retains its elegant east front and stands in its own ornamental grounds, designed by 'Capability' Brown. ✆ 01983 852484 ➲ ½ m W of Wroxall off B3327.
☐ 7 K7; Landranger 196; SZ 543800

Battle Abbey and Battlefield ✝
Sussex
The one date in English history that everyone can remember is 1066: the Battle of Hastings, when the conquering Normans vanquished the Anglo-Saxons on 14 October. There is just as much myth surrounding the conflict as known fact. The two armies did not even fight at Hastings, but at the place which became the town of Battle, 6 miles inland. ✆ 01424 773792 ➲ In Battle, East Sussex, at S end of High St.
☐ 16 E4; Landranger 199; TQ 749157

Bayham Old Abbey ✝
Sussex
Ruins of a house of 'white' canons, founded in c.1208, in an 18th-century landscaped setting. The Georgian House (Dower House) is also open to the public. ✆ 01892 890381 ➲ 1¾ m W of Lamberhurst off B2169.
☐ 16 D2; Landranger 188; TQ 651366

Bishop's Waltham Palace ✝
Hampshire
This medieval seat of the Bishops of Winchester once stood in an enormous park. Wooded grounds still surround the mainly 12th- and 14th-century remains, including the Great Hall and three-storey tower, as well as the moat which once enclosed the palace. Much was destroyed in a fire by Parliamentarians in the Civil War after the Battle of Cheriton in 1644, but the ground floor of the Dower House is intact and furnished as a 19th-century farmhouse, with an exhibition on the powerful Winchester Bishops on the first floor. ✆ 01489 892460 ➲ In Bishop's Waltham 5m from junction 8 of M27.
☐ 13 H4; Landranger 185; SU 552173 -

Boxgrove Priory ✝
Sussex
Remains of the Guest House, Chapter House and church of a 12th century priory. ➲ N of Boxgrove, 4m E of Chichester on minor road off A27.
☐ 14 C5; Landranger 197; SU 909076

Bramber Castle ◉
Sussex
The remains of a Norman castle gatehouse, walls and earthworks. ➲ On W side of Bramber village off A283.
☐ 15 F4; Landranger 198; TQ 187107

Calshot Castle ♜
Hampshire
This century, the fort has been part of both an RN and an RAF base. Spectacular views of the Solent can be seen from the roof. Henry VIII built this coastal fort to command the sea passage to Southampton. The barrack room has been restored to its pre-World War I artillery garrison appearance, complete with bunks and uniform. ✆ 01703 892023 ➲ On spit 2m SE of Fawley off B3053.
☐ 13 G5; Landranger 196; SU 488025

Camber Castle ♜
Sussex
A rare example of an Henrician fort surviving in its original plan. ✆ 01797 223862 for further information. (Site managed by Rye Harbour Nature Reserve.) ➲ Access by a delightful 1m walk across fields, off the A259, 1m S of Rye off harbour road.
☐ 17 G4; Landranger 189; TQ 922185

Carisbrooke Castle ♜
Isle of Wight
From time immemorial, whosoever controlled Carisbrooke controlled the Isle of Wight. The castle sits at the very heart of the island, and has been a fixture since its foundation as a Saxon camp during the 8th century. Carisbrooke's royal connections date from the end of the 13th century when it was purchased from the Redvers family by Edward I. For a brief period the castle occupied the centre of the national and political stage when Charles I was imprisoned there from 1647 to 1648, before being taken for trial and execution in London. His story is commemorated in the Charles I rooms and in the many exhibits relating to his imprisonment. ✆ 01983 522107 ➲ 1¼m SW of Newport, Isle of Wight.
☐ 7 J6; Landranger 196; SZ 486877.

Conduit House ◉
Canterbury, Kent
The Conduit House is the monastic waterworks which supplied nearby St Augustine's Abbey. ➲ Approximately 5–10 minutes' walk from St Augustine's Abbey. Situated within the new St Martin's Heights housing estate, St Martin's Avenue, Canterbury.
☐ 25 H7; Landranger 179; TR 159585

Deal Castle ♜
Kent
Crouching low and menacing, the huge, rounded bastions of this austere fort, built by Henry VIII, once carried 119 guns. It is a fascinating castle to explore, with long, dark passages, battlements, and a huge basement with an exhibition on England's coastal defences. ✆ 01304 372762 ➲ SW of Deal town centre.
☐ 25 K7; Landranger 179; TR 378521

Donnington Castle ♜
Berkshire
Built in the late 14th century, the twin towered gatehouse of this castle survives amidst some impressive earthworks.
➲ 1m N of Newbury off B4494.
☐ 21 J6; Landranger 174; SU 461694

Dover Castle ♜
Kent
The white cliffs of Dover are among England's most celebrated sights, yet hidden underground is a fascinating and secret world. On top of the cliffs stands the ancient and mighty fortress of Dover Castle but below, running deep into the ground, are miles of tunnels. First used during the Napoleonic wars, their greatest moment came nearly 150 years later when they became a nerve centre in World War II and were the headquarters from which the Dunkirk evacuation was masterminded. ✆ 01304 201628 ➲ On E side of Dover.
☐ 17 L1; Landranger 179; TR 326416.

Down House ⊕
Kent
Charles Darwin was perhaps the most influential scientist of the 19th century. It was from his study at Down House that he worked on the scientific theories that first scandalized and then revolutionized the Victorian world, culminating in the publication of the most significant book of the century, *On the Origin of Species by means of Natural Selection*, in 1859. His home for forty years, Down House was the centre of his intellectual world and even now his study remains full of his notebooks and journals, and mementoes from his epic voyage of discovery that took him most famously to the Galapagos Islands. The house is currently being restored so that by the summer of 1997 you can visit Darwin's much-loved family home in the tranquil Kent countryside. Visitors can wander in the gardens along the 'Sandwalk', as Darwin did every morning to compose his thoughts before beginning his scientific studies.
✆ 0171 973 3479 or Customer Services
✆ 0171 973 3434. ➲ In Luxted Road, Downe, Kent, off A21 near Biggin Hill.
☐ 23 K6

Dymchurch Martello Tower ◉
Kent
One of many artillery towers which formed part of a chain of strongholds intended to resist invasion by Napoleon. It is fully restored, with a 24-pounder gun on the roof.
➲ Access from High Street, not from seafront.
☐ 17 J3; Landranger 189; TR 102294

Eynsford Castle ◉
Kent
One of the first stone castles built by the Normans. The moat and remains of the curtain wall and hall can still be seen.
➲ In Eynsford off A225.
☐ 23 L6; Landranger 177; TQ 542658

Farnham Castle Keep ◉
Surrey
A motte and bailey castle, once one of the seats of the Bishop of Winchester, which has been in continuous occupation since the 12th century. ✆ 01252 713393 ➲ ½m N of Farnham town centre on A287.
☐ 14 B1; Landranger 186; SU 839474

Faversham: Stone Chapel ✝
Kent
The remains of a small medieval church incorporating part of a 4th-century Romano-British pagan mausoleum. ➲ 1¼m W of Faversham on A2.
☐ 25 F6; Landranger 178; TQ 992614

Flowerdown Barrows ▲
Hampshire
Round barrows of a Bronze Age burial site which were once part of a larger group.
➲ In Littleton, 2½m NW of Winchester off A272.
☐ 13 G2; Landranger 185; SU 459320

Fort Brockhurst ♜
Hampshire
This was a new type of fort, built in the 19th century to protect Portsmouth with formidable fire-power. Largely unaltered, the parade ground, gun ramps and moated keep can all be viewed. An exhibition illustrates the history of Portsmouth's defences.
✆ 01705 581059 ➲ Off A32, in Gunner's Way, Elson, on N side of Gosport.
☐ 13 J5; Landranger 196; SU 596020

Fort Cumberland ♜
Hampshire
Constructed in the shape of a wide pentagon by the Duke of Cumberland in 1746. The fort was occupied by the Royal Marines until 1973 and is perhaps the most impressive piece of 18th-century defensive architecture remaining in England. ➲ In the Eastney district of Portsmouth on the estuary approach via Henderson Road, a turning off Eastney Road, or from the Esplanade.
☐ 13 J6; Landranger 196; SZ 682992

Horne's Place Chapel ✝
Appledore, Kent
This 14th-century domestic chapel was once attached to the manor house. The house and chapel are privately owned. ✆ 01304 211067.
➲ 1½m N of Appledore.
☐ 17 G2; Landranger 189; TQ 957307

Hurst Castle ♜
Hampshire
This was one of the most sophisticated fortresses built by Henry VIII, and later strengthened in the 19th and 20th centuries, to command the narrow entrance to the Solent. There are two exhibitions in the castle, and two huge 38-ton guns from the fort's armaments. ✆ 01590 642344
➲ On Pebble Spit S of Keyhaven. Best approached by ferry from Keyhaven, telephone 01590 642500 (June–Sept. 9am– 2pm) or answerphone
01425 610784, for ferry details.
☐ 13 F7; Landranger 196; SZ 319898

King James's and Landport Gates ◉
Portsmouth, Hampshire
These gates were once part of the 17th-century defences of Portsmouth
➲ King James's Gate: forms entrance to United Services Recreation Ground (officers) on Park Rd; Landport Gate: as above, men's entrance on St George's Rd.
☐ 13 J6; Landranger 196; King James's Gate ref SU 638000, Landport Gate SU 634998.

Kit's Coty House and Little Kit's Coty House ▲
Kent
Ruins of two prehistoric burial chambers, taking their name from the Celtic phrase for 'tomb in the woods' ➲ W of A229 2m N of Maidstone.
☐ 24 D7; Landranger 188; TQ 745608 & TQ 745604

Knights Templar Church ✝
Dover, Kent
Standing across the valley from Dover Castle are the foundations of a small circular 12th-century church. ➲ On the Western Heights above Dover.
☐ 17 L1; Landranger 179; TR 313408

Lullingstone Roman Villa ◉
Kent
The villa, discovered in 1939, was one of the most exciting finds of the century. Dating from c.100 AD, but extended during 300 years of Roman occupation, much is visible today. ✆ 01322 863467 ➲ ½m SW of Eynsford off A225 off junction 3 of M25. Follow A20 towards Brands Hatch.
☐ 23 L6; Landranger 177; TQ 529651

Maison Dieu ◉
Ospringe, Kent
Part of a medieval complex of Royal lodge, almshouses and hospital, it is much as it was 400 years ago, with a crown-post roof and a decorative 16th-century ceiling. It contains an exhibition about Ospringe in Roman times. ➲ In Ospringe on A2. ½m W of Faversham.
☐ 25 F6; Landranger 178; TR 002608

Medieval Merchant's House ⊕
Southampton, Hampshire
Life in the Middle Ages is vividly evoked by the brightly painted cabinets and colourful wall hangings authentically re-created for this 13th-century town house, originally built as shop and home for a prosperous wine merchant. ✆ 01703 221503 ➲ 58 French Street, ¼m S of city centre just off Castle Way (between High St and Bugle St).
☐ 13 G4; Landranger 196; SU 419112

Milton Chantry ✝
Gravesend, Kent
A small 14th-century building which housed the chapel of a leper hospital and a family chantry. It later became a tavern and, in 1780, part of a fort. ➲ In New Tavern Fort Gardens E of central Gravesend off A226.
☐ 24 C6; Landranger 177; TQ 652743

Netley Abbey ✝
Hampshire
A 13th-century Cistercian abbey converted in Tudor times for use as a house. Watch out for ghostly figures drifting amongst the ruins.
✆ 01705 378291 ➲ In Netley, 4m SE of Southampton, facing Southampton Water.
☐ 13 G5; Landranger 196; SU 453089

Northington Grange ♡◉
Hampshire
Magnificent neoclassical country house, built at the beginning of the 18th century. ➲ 4m N of New Alresford off B3046.
☐ 13 H2; Landranger 185; SU 562362

Old Soar Manor ◉
Plaxtol, Kent
The remains of a late 13th-century knight's manor house, comprising the two-storey solar and chapel. There is an exhibition to visit. ✆ 01732 810378 ➲ 1m E of Plaxtol.
☐ 24 C7; Landranger 188; TQ 619541

Osborne House ⊕⚙
Isle of Wight
Osborne House was 'a place of one's own, quiet and retired', for Queen Victoria and Prince Albert. They found tranquillity on the Isle of Wight, far from the formality of court life at Buckingham Palace and Windsor Castle. The house they built was set among terraced gardens and filled with treasured mementoes. Victoria died at Osborne in 1901, still mourning her beloved Albert, who had died in middle age. ✆ 01983 200022 ➲ 1m SE of East Cowes, Isle of Wight.
☐ 7 K5; Landranger 196; SZ 516948.

Pevensey Castle ♜
East Sussex
William the Conqueror landed at Pevensey on September 28, 1066. He may have used the Roman Shore Fort as a shelter for his troops. Today you can see the ruins of the medieval castle including remains of an unusual keep enclosed within its walls, originally dating back to the 4th-century Roman fort Anderida. ✆ 01323 762604 ➲ In Pevensey off A259.
☐ 16 D5; Landranger 199; TQ 645048

Portchester Castle ♜
Hampshire
A residence for kings and a rallying point for troops, this grand castle has a history stretching back nearly 2,000 years. There are Roman walls, the most complete in Europe, substantial remains of the castle and an exhibition telling the story of Portchester.
✆ 01705 378291 ➲ On S side of Portchester off A27. Junction 11 on M27.
☐ 13 J5; Landranger 196; ref SU 625046

Reculver Towers and Roman Fort ◉
Kent
Standing in a country park, a 12th-century landmark of twin towers and the walls of a Roman fort. ✆ 01227 366444
➲ At Reculver 3m E of Herne Bay.
☐ 25 J6; Landranger 179; TR 228694

Richborough Castle, Roman Fort ◉◉
Kent
This fort and township date back to the Roman landing in AD 43. The fortified walls and the massive foundations of a triumphal arch which stood 25 m (80 ft) high still survive. ✆ 01304 612013 ➲ 1½m N of Sandwich off A257.
☐ 25 K6; Landranger 179; TR 324602

Richborough Roman Amphitheatre ◉◉
Kent
Ditch associated with the nearby 3rd-century castle. ✆ 01304 612013) for details.
➲ 1¼m N of Sandwich off A257, Junction 7 of M2, onto A2.
☐ 25 K7; Landranger 179; TR 321598

Rochester Castle ♜
Kent
Built on the Roman city wall, this Norman bishop's castle was a vital royal stronghold.
✆ 01634 402276 ➲ By Rochester Bridge (A2). Junction 1 of M2 and Junction 2 of M25.
☐ 24 D6; Landranger 178; TQ 742686

Royal Garrison Church ✝
Portsmouth, Hampshire
Originally a hospice for pilgrims, this 16th-century chapel became the Garrison Church after the Dissolution. Expertly restored in the 1860s but fire-bombed in 1941, the chancel survived and there is still plenty to see.
✆ 01705 378291 ➲ On Grand Parade S of Portsmouth High St.
☐ 13 J6; Landranger 196; SU 633992

St Augustine's Abbey ✝
Canterbury, Kent
This great shrine, which was built the year after he arrived, became the centre of the English Christian movement. It is the burial place of the early Archbishops of Canterbury, as well as of St Augustine himself.
Along with the Cathedral, the Abbey is part of the Canterbury World Heritage site. Its foundation represented the most important change in English life since Roman times.
✆ 01227 767345 ➲ In Longport ¼m E of Cathedral Close.
☐ 25 H7; Landranger 179; TR 154578.

St Augustine's Cross ✝
Ebbsfleet, Kent
19th-century cross, in Celtic design, marking the traditional site of St Augustine's landing in 597. ➲ 2m E of Minster off B29048.
☐ 25 K6; Landranger 179; TR 340641

St Catherine's Oratory ◉◉
Isle of Wight
Affectionately known as the Pepperpot, this 14th-century lighthouse, erected following the wreck of the wine ship St Marie, stands on the highest point of the island. ➲ ¾m NW of Niton.
☐ 7 J7; Landranger 196; SZ 494773

St John's Commandery ✝
Swingfield, Kent
A medieval chapel, converted into a farmhouse in the 16th century. It has a fine moulded plaster ceiling and a remarkable timber roof. ✆ 01304 211067 for details.
➲ 2m NE of Densole off A260.
☐ 17 K1; Landranger 179; TR 232440

St Leonard's Tower ✝
West Malling, Kent
An early and particularly fine example of a Norman tower keep, built c.1080 by Gundulf, Bishop of Rochester. ✆ 01732 870872. ➲ On unclassified road W of A228.
☐ 24 C7; Landranger 188; TQ 675570

Silchester Roman City Walls and Amphitheatre ◉◉
Hampshire
The best preserved Roman town walls in Britain, almost one-and-a-half miles around, with an impressive, recently restored amphitheatre. ➲ On minor road 1m E of Silchester.
☐ 22 B6; Landranger 175; SU 643624

Stone Chapel
See Faversham: Stone Chapel

Sutton Valence Castle
Kent
The ruins of a 12th-century stone keep built to monitor the important medieval route across the Weald from Rye to Maidstone.
5m SE of Maidstone in Sutton Valence village on A274.
16 F1; Landranger 188; TR 815491

Temple Manor
Rochester, Kent
The 13th-century manor house of the Knights Templar. In Strood (Rochester) off A228.
24 D6; Landranger 178; TQ 733686

Titchfield Abbey
Hampshire
Remains of a 13th-century abbey overshadowed by a grand Tudor gatehouse.
½m N of Titchfield off A27.
13 H5; Landranger 196; SU 541067

Upnor Castle
Kent
Well preserved 16th-century gun fort, built to protect Queen Elizabeth I's warships. However in 1667 it failed to resist the Dutch navy, which stormed up the Medway destroying half the English fleet.
01634 718742 At Upnor, on unclassified road off A228.
24 D5; Landranger 178; TQ 758706

Walmer Castle and Gardens
Kent
Walmer Castle was among the first of a new breed of castle. It was one of the many forts built along the south coast by Henry VIII in the early 16th century, that were specially designed to defend against the new threat of attack by gunpowder. The castle was later transformed into an elegant stately home that serves as a residence of the Lords Warden of the Cinque Ports. 01304 364288 On coast S of Walmer, Kent, on A258. Junction 13 off M20 or from M2 to Deal.
25 K7; Landranger 179; TR 378501.

Waverley Abbey
Surrey
First Cistercian house in England, founded in 1128. The remaining ruins date from the 13th century. 2m SE of Farnham off B3001 and off junction 10 of M25.
14 B1; Landranger 186; SU 868453.

Western Heights
Dover, Kent
Parts of moat of 19th-century fort built to fend off a French attack. Now part of the White Cliffs Countryside Project.
01304 241806 Above Dover town on W side of Harbour.
17 L1; Landranger 179; TR 312408.

Wolvesey Castle (Old Bishop's Palace)
Winchester, Hampshire
One of the greatest medieval buildings in England, the Palace was the chief residence of the Bishops of Winchester. Its extensive ruins still reflect their importance and wealth. The last great occasion was on 25th July, 1554 when Queen Mary and Philip of Spain held their wedding breakfast in the East Hall.
01962 854766 (01732 778030 in winter)
¼m SE of Winchester Cathedral, next to the Bishop's Palace; access from College St.
13 G3; Landranger 185; SU 484291.

Yarmouth Castle
Isle of Wight
This last addition to Henry VIII's coastal defences was completed in 1547. It houses exhibitions of paintings of the Isle of Wight and photographs of old Yarmouth.
01983 760678 In Yarmouth adjacent to car ferry terminal.
13 F7; Landranger 196; SZ 354898.

Greater London

Albert Memorial
Kensington, Greater London
An elaborate national memorial by George Gilbert Scott to commemorate the Prince Consort. Finally completed in 1876, the figure of the Consort sits on a pyramid of 868 brick arches and has above it a lofty Gothic canopy supported by granite columns. The memorial is undergoing extensive conservation by English Heritage, explained in an exhibition and video in the Visitor Centre. 0171 225 1059
23 H5

Chapter House, Pyx Chamber and Abbey Museum
Westminster Abbey, Greater London
The Chapter House, built by the royal masons in 1250, contains some of the finest medieval English sculpture to be seen. The building is octagonal, with a central column, and still has its original floor of glazed tiles. The 11th-century Pyx Chamber now houses the Abbey treasures. The Abbey museum contains medieval royal effigies. 0171 222 5897
Approach either through the Abbey or through Dean's Yard and the cloister.
23 F5

Chiswick House
Chiswick, Greater London
Close to the centre of London lies one of the first and finest English Palladian villas, surrounded by beautiful gardens. It was designed by the third Earl of Burlington who sought to create the kind of house and garden found in the suburbs of ancient Rome. He was one of the foremost architects of his generation and a great promoter of the Palladian style first pioneered in England by Inigo Jones. He designed the villa to serve as a fitting showcase for his large collection of art and books. Today you can enjoy the house and its lavish interiors before stepping outside into the classical gardens – a perfect complement to the house itself.
0181 995 0508 Burlington Lane, London W4. Tube: Turnham Green
23 G5

Coombe Conduit
Kingston-Upon-Thames, Greater London
Built by Henry VIII to supply water to Hampton Court Palace, three miles away, Coombe Conduit consists of two small buildings (one now a ruin) connected by an underground passage. 0181 892 5115
23 G6

Eltham Palace
Eltham, Greater London
A fascinating blend of a medieval royal palace and a 1930's Art Deco country house. Step from the 15th-century Great Hall, straight into the lost pre-War world with a suite of striking Modernist interiors. 0181 294 2548
¾m N of A20 off Court Yard, SE9.
23 K5

Jewel Tower
Westminster, Greater London
One of two surviving buildings of the original Palace of Westminster, the Jewel Tower was built c.1365 to house the personal treasure of Edward III. It was subsequently used as a storehouse and government office. The exhibition, 'Parliament Past and Present', shows how Parliament works and a new touch-screen computer gives a virtual reality tour of both Houses of Parliament.
0171 222 2219 Opposite S end of Houses of Parliament (Victoria Tower).
23 H5

Kenwood
Hampstead, Greater London
Standing in splendid, landscaped grounds on the edge of Hampstead Heath, Kenwood contains the most important private collection of paintings ever given to the nation, the Iveagh Bequest. Among the finest is the 'Self-Portrait' by Rembrandt and 'The Guitar Player' by Vermeer, and also other works by such eminent British artists as Gainsborough, Turner and Reynolds. The outstanding neoclassical house was remodelled by Robert Adam, 1764–79 and English Heritage has restored his original colour scheme in the Entrance Hall. Outside, the landscaped park forms the perfect setting for the concerts that are held here in summer.
0181 348 1286 Hampstead Lane, London, NW3.
23 H4

London Wall
Tower Hill, Greater London
The best preserved piece of the Roman Wall, heightened in the Middle Ages, which formed part of the eastern defences of the City of London. Near Tower Hill Underground station EC3
23 J4

Marble Hill House
Twickenham, Greater London
A magnificent Thames-side Palladian villa built 1724–29 for Henrietta Howard, Countess of Suffolk, set in 66 acres of parkland. The Great Room has lavish gilded decoration and architectural paintings by Panini. The house also contains an important collection of early Georgian furniture, the Lazenby Bequest Chinoiserie collection and an 18th-century lacquer screen. There is a display on the ground floor with an introductory film about the house, grounds, and the life and times of Henrietta Howard.
0181 892 5115 Richmond Road, Twickenham.
23 G5

Ranger's House
Blackheath, Greater London
A handsome red brick villa built c.1700, on the edge of Greenwich Park, with a splendid bow-windowed gallery. The Architectural Study Collection is displayed in the Coach House, showing interesting domestic architectural features from London dwellings of the 18th–19th centuries. 0181 853 0035
Chesterfield Walk, Blackheath, SE10.
23 J5

Winchester Palace
Southwark, Greater London
The west gable end, with its unusual round window, is the prominent feature of the remains of the Great Hall of this 13th-century town house of the Bishops of Winchester, damaged by fire in 1814. Near Southwark Cathedral, at corner of Clink St & Storey St, SE1.
23 J5

Eastern Counties

Audley End House and Park
Essex
Audley End was one of the great wonders of the nation when it was built by the first Earl of Suffolk, Lord Treasurer to James I. It was on the scale of a great royal palace, and soon became one after Charles II bought it in 1668 for £50,000 using it as a base when he attended the nearby Newmarket races. Returned to the Suffolks after his death, substantial parts of the house were demolished. Even so, what remains is one of the most significant Jacobean houses in England. Successive owners have since placed their stylistic imprint both within the graceful exterior and in the surrounding parkland. As we see it now, Audley End's interior with its historic picture collection and furniture is largely the product of its owner in the mid-19th century, the third Lord Braybrooke. The challenge for the visitor today is to piece together the many changes over time that have created such a harmonious whole.
01799 522399 (information line) 1m W of Saffron Walden, Essex on B1383 (M11 exits 8, 9 Northbound only, & 10).
35 J6; Landranger 154; TL 525382.

Baconsthorpe Castle
Norfolk
Remains of the gatehouses of a large 15th-century fortified manor house, partly surrounded by a moat. ¾m N of village of Baconsthorpe off unclassified road 3m E of Holt.
47 G3; Landranger 133; TG 122382

Berney Arms Windmill
Norfolk
A wonderfully situated marsh mill, one of the best and largest remaining in Norfolk, with seven floors, making it a landmark for miles around. Built to grind a constituent of cement, it was in use until 1951, ending its days pumping water to drain surrounding marshes. 01493 700605 3½m NE of Reedham on N bank of River Yare. Accessible by boat, or by footpath from Halvergate (3½m).
47 K6; Landranger 134; TG 465051.

Binham Priory
Norfolk
Extensive remains of a Benedictine priory, of which the original nave of the church still continues in use as the parish church. ¼m NW of village of Binham-on-Wells on road off B1388.
46 E3; Landranger 132; TF 982399

Binham Wayside Cross
Norfolk
Medieval cross marking the site of an annual fair held from the reign of Henry I until the 1950s. On village green adjacent to Priory.
46 E3; Landranger 132; TF 982399

Blakeney Guildhall
Norfolk
The surviving basement, most likely used for storage, of a large 14th-century building, probably a merchant's house. In Blakeney off A149.
46 F2; Landranger 133; TG 030441

Burgh Castle
Norfolk
Impressive walls, with projecting bastions, of a Roman fort built in the late 3rd century as one of a chain to defend the coast against Saxon raiders. At far W end of Breydon Water, on unclassified road 3m W of Great Yarmouth.
47 K6; Landranger134; TG 475046.

Bury St Edmunds Abbey
Suffolk
A Norman tower and 14th-century gatehouse of a ruined Benedictine abbey, church and precinct. The visitor centre has interactive displays. E end of town centre.
36 D3; Landranger 155; TL 858642

Caister Roman Site
Norfolk
The remains of a Roman site, possibly a fort, including part of a defensive wall, a gateway and buildings along a main street. Near Caister-on-Sea, 3m N of Great Yarmouth.
47 L5; Landranger 134; TG 518125

Castle Acre: Bailey Gate
Norfolk
The north gateway to the medieval planned town of Acre with flint towers. In Castle Acre, at E end of Stocks Green, 5m N of Swaffham.
46 D5; Landranger 132; TF 817152

Castle Acre Castle
Norfolk
The remains of a Norman manor house, which became a castle with earthworks, set by the side of the village. At E end of Castle Acre, 5m N of Swaffham.
46 D5; Landranger 132; TF 819152

Castle Acre Priory
Norfolk
The great west front of the 12th-century church of this Cluniac priory still rises to its full height and is elaborately decorated, whilst the prior's lodgings and porch retain their roofs. The delightful herb garden, re-created to show herbs used in medieval times for both culinary and medicinal purposes, should not be missed. 01760 755394 ¼m W of village of Castle Acre, 5m N of Swaffham.
46 D5; Landranger 132; TF 814148

Castle Rising Castle
Norfolk
A fine mid 12th-century domestic keep, set in the centre of massive defensive earthworks, once palace and prison to Isabella, 'She-Wolf' dowager Queen of England. The keep walls stand to their original height and many of the fortifications are intact.
01553 631330 4m NE of King's Lynn off A149.
46 B4; Landranger 132; TF 666246

Church of the Holy Sepulchre
Thetford, Norfolk
The ruined nave of a priory church of the Canons of the Holy Sepulchre, the only surviving remains in England of a house of this order. On W side of Thetford off B1107.
36 D1; Landranger 144; TL 865831

Cow Tower
Norwich, Norfolk
A circular brick tower, which once formed part of the 14th-century city defences. In Norwich, near cathedral.
47 H6; Landranger 134; TG 240091

Creake Abbey
Norfolk
The ruins of the church of an Augustinian abbey. 1m N of North Creake off B1355.
46 D3; Landranger 132; TF 856395

Denny Abbey
Cambridgeshire
What at first appears to be an attractive stone-built farmhouse is actually the remains of a 12th-century Benedictine abbey founded by the Countess of Pembroke which, at different times, also housed the Knights Templar and Franciscan nuns.
01223 860489 6m N of Cambridge on A10.
35 H3; Landranger 154; TL 495684

Duxford Chapel
Cambridgeshire
A medieval chapel once part of the Hospital of St John. Adjacent to Whittlesford station off A505.
35 H5; Landranger 154; TL 486472

Framlingham Castle
Suffolk
A superb 12th-century castle which, from the outside, looks almost the same as when it was built. From the continuous curtain wall, linking 13 towers, there are excellent views over Framlingham and the charming reed-fringed mere. At different times, the castle has been a fortress, an Elizabethan prison, a poor house and a school. 01724 724189
In Framlingham on B1116.
37 H3; Landranger 156; TM 287637

Grime's Graves
Norfolk
These remarkable Neolithic flint mines, unique in England, comprise over 300 pits and shafts. The visitor can descend some 10m (30ft) by ladder into one excavated shaft, and look along the radiating galleries, where the flint for making axes and knives was extracted. 01842 810656 7m NW of Thetford off A134.
36 D1; Landranger 144; TL 818898

Hadleigh Castle
Essex
The curtain wall and two towers of this 13th-century castle survive almost to their full height and overlook the Essex marshes and Thames estuary. 01760 755161
¾m S of A13 at Hadleigh.
24 E4; Landranger 178; TQ 810860

Hill Hall
Essex
This fine Elizabethan mansion has some of the earliest Renaissance decoration in the country. Rare wall paintings of mythological and biblical subjects date from the same period. The house is surrounded by parkland landscaped by Repton. 01992 561657
3m E of Epping on unclassified road to Theydon Mount. From M11 – Junction 7, S on B1393 to Epping, then as above.
23 K3; Landranger 167; TQ 489994

Isleham Priory Church
Cambridgeshire
Rare example of an early Norman church. It has survived little altered, despite being later converted to a barn. In Isleham, 16m NE of Cambridge on B1104.
35 J3; Landranger 143; TL 642744.

Landguard Fort
Felixstowe, Suffolk
An 18th-century fort, with later additions. There is a museum featuring displays of local history. 01394 286403 (evenings) 1m S of Felixstowe near docks.
37 H6; Landranger 169; TM 284318

Leiston Abbey
Suffolk
The remains of this abbey for Premonstratensian canons include a restored chapel. 1m N of Leiston off B1069.
37 K3; Landranger 156; TM 445642

Lexden Earthworks and Bluebottle Grove
Colchester, Essex
Parts of a series of earthworks, once encompassing 12 square miles, which protected Iron Age Colchester and were subsequently added to by the conquering Romans. 2m W of Colchester off A604.
36 E7; Landranger 168; TL 965246 (Lexden Earthworks) and TL 975245 (Bluebottle Grove).

Longthorpe Tower
Cambridgeshire
The finest example of 14th-century domestic wall paintings in northern Europe. They show many secular and sacred objects, including the Wheel of Life, the Labors of the Months, the Nativity and King David. The tower, with the Great Chamber that contains the paintings, is part of a fortified manor house. Closed 1–2pm. 01733 268482
2m W of Peterborough on A47.
44 E7; Landranger 142; TL 163983

Mistley Towers
Essex
The remains of a church designed by Robert Adam and built in 1776. It was unusual in having towers at both the east and west ends. 01206 393884. (Site managed by Mistley Thorn Residents Association.) On B1352, 1½m E of A137 at Lawford, 9m E of Colchester.
37 G6; Landranger 169; TM 116320.

Moulton Packhorse Bridge
Suffolk
Medieval four-arched bridge spanning the River Kennett. In Moulton off B1085, 4m E of Newmarket.
36 B3; Landranger 154; TL 698645.

North Elmham Chapel
Norfolk
Remains of a Norman chapel converted into a fortified dwelling and enclosed by earthworks in the late 14th century by the notorious Bishop of Norwich, Hugh le Despencer.
6m N of East Dereham on B1110.
46 E4; Landranger 132; TF 988217.

Old Merchant's House, Row 111 House and Greyfriars' Cloisters
Great Yarmouth, Norfolk
Two 17th-century Row Houses, a type of building unique to Great Yarmouth, containing original fixtures and displays of local architectural fittings salvaged from bombing in 1942–43. Nearby are the remains of a Franciscan friary, with rare early wall paintings, accidentally discovered during bomb damage repairs. 01493 857900
Great Yarmouth, make for South Quay along riverside and dock, ½m inland from beach. Follow signs to dock and south quay.
47 L6; Landranger 134; TG 525072 (Houses) and TG 525073 (Cloisters).

Orford Castle
Suffolk
A royal castle built for coastal defence in the 12th century. A magnificent keep survives almost intact with three immense towers reaching to 30m (90 feet). Inside a spiral stair leads to a maze of rooms and passageways. 01394 450472 In Orford on B1084 20m NE of Ipswich. 37 K5; Landranger 169; TM 419499.

Prior's Hall Barn
Widdington, Essex
One of the finest surviving medieval barns in south-east England and representative of the aisled barns of north-west Essex.
In Widdington, on unclassified road 2m SE of Newport, off B1383. 01799 522842
35 J6; Landranger 167; TL 538319.

St Botolph's Priory
Colchester, Essex
The nave, with an impressive arcaded west end, of the first Augustinian priory in England. Colchester, near Colchester Town station.
36 F7; Landranger 168; TL 999249.

St James's Chapel
Lindsey, Suffolk
A little 13th-century chapel with thatched roof and lancet windows. On unclassified road ½m E of Rose Green, 8m E of Sudbury.
36 E5; Landranger 155; TL 978443

St John's Abbey Gate
Colchester, Essex
This fine abbey gatehouse, in East Anglian flintwork, survives from the Benedictine abbey of St John. On S side of central Colchester.
36 F7; Landranger 168; TL 998248

St Olave's Priory
Norfolk
Remains of an Augustinian priory founded nearly 200 years after the death in 1030 of the patron saint of Norway, after whom it is named. 5½m SW of Great Yarmouth on A143.
47 K7; Landranger 134; TM 459996

Saxtead Green Post Mill
Suffolk
A fine example of a post mill, where the superstructure turns on a great post to face the wind. The mill, which ceased production in 1947, is still in working order and you can climb the wooden stairs to the various floors, which are full of fascinating mill machinery.
01728 685789 2½m NW of Framlingham on A1120.
37 H3; Landranger 156; TM 253645

Thetford Priory
Norfolk
The 14th-century gatehouse is the best preserved part of this Cluniac priory built in 1103. The extensive remains include the plan of the cloisters On W side of Thetford near station.
36 D1; Landranger 144; TL 865836

Thetford Warren Lodge
Norfolk
The ruins of a small, two-storeyed medieval house, set in pleasant woods, which was probably the home of the priory's gamekeeper. 2m W of Thetford off B1107.
36 D1; Landranger 144; TL 839841

Tilbury Fort
Essex
The largest and best preserved example of 17th-century military engineering in England, commanding the Thames and showing the development of fortifications over the following 200 years. Exhibitions, the powder magazine and the bunker-like 'casemates' demonstrate how the fort protected London from seaborne attack – there's even a chance to fire an anti-aircraft gun! 01375 858489
½m E of Tilbury off A126.
24 C5; Landranger 177; TQ 651754

Waltham Abbey Gatehouse and Bridge
Essex
A late 14th-century abbey gatehouse, part of the cloister and 'Harold's Bridge'.
In Waltham Abbey off A112.
23 J2; Landranger 166; TL 381008

Weeting Castle
Norfolk
The ruins of an early medieval manor house within a shallow rectangular moat. 2m N of Brandon off B1106.
36 C1; Landranger 144; TL 778891

The Midlands

Abingdon County Hall
Oxfordshire
A grand centrepiece for the market place at Abingdon, this 17th-century public building was built to house the Assize Courts.
01235 523703 In Abingdon, 7m S of Oxford in Market Place.
21 J3; Landranger 164; SU 497971

Acton Burnell Castle
Shropshire
The warm red sandstone shell of a fortified 13th-century manor house. In Acton Burnell, on unclassified road 8m S of Shrewsbury.
41 G6; Landranger 126; SJ 534019

Arbor Low Stone Circle and Gib Hill Barrow
Derbyshire
A fine Neolithic monument, this 'Stonehenge of Derbyshire' comprises many slabs of limestone, surrounded by an unusually large ditch. ½m W of A515 2m S of Monyash.
52 D7; Landranger 119; SK 161636

Arthur's Stone
Dorstone, Hereford & Worcester
Impressive prehistoric burial chamber formed of large blocks of stone. 7m E of Hay-on-Wye off B4348 near Dorstone.
30 E5; Landranger 148; SO 319431

Ashby de la Zouch Castle
Leicestershire
The impressive ruins of this late-medieval castle are dominated by a magnificent 24-metre (80-foot) high tower, split in two during the Civil War, from which there are panoramic views of the surrounding countryside. 01530 413343 In Ashby de la Zouch, 12m S of Derby on A50.
43 F5; Landranger 128; SK 363167

Berkhamsted Castle
Hertfordshire
The extensive remains of a large 11th-century motte and bailey castle. 01442 871737
By Berkhamsted station.
22 E2; Landranger 165; SP 996083

Bolingbroke Castle
Lincolnshire
Remains of a 13th-century hexagonal castle, birthplace of Henry IV in 1367 and besieged by Parliamentary forces in 1643. In Old Bolingbroke, 16m N of Boston off A16.
55 H7; Landranger 122; TF 349649

Bolsover Castle
Derbyshire
An enchanting and romantic spectacle, situated high on a wooded hilltop dominating the surrounding landscape. Built on the site of a Norman castle, this is largely an early 17th-century mansion. Explore the 'Little Castle' or 'keep', a unique celebration of Jacobean romanticism with its elaborate fireplaces, panelling and wall paintings. There is also an impressive 17th-century indoor Riding School, built by the Duke of Newcastle, and ruins of great state apartments. 01246 822844 or 823349
Off M1 at junction 29, 6m from Mansfield. In Bolsover, 6m E of Chesterfield on A632.
53 G6; Landranger 120; SK 471707

Boscobel House and the Royal Oak
Shropshire
Fully refurnished and restored, the panelled rooms, secret hiding places and pretty gardens lend this 17th-century timber-framed hunting lodge a truly romantic character. King Charles II hid in the house and the nearby Royal Oak after the Battle of Worcester in 1651 to avoid detection by Cromwell's troops. Today there is a farmhouse with dairy, farmyard and smithy, and an exhibition in the house.
01902 850244 On minor road from A41 to A5, 8m NW of Wolverhampton.
42 A6; Landranger 127; SJ 837083

Buildwas Abbey
Shropshire
Set beside the River Severn, against a backdrop of wooded grounds, are extensive remains of this Cistercian abbey begun in 1135. On S bank of River Severn on B4378, 2m W of Iron Bridge.
41 H6; Landranger 127; SJ 642044

Bushmead Priory
Bedfordshire
A rare survival of the medieval refectory of an Augustinian priory. Its original timber-framed roof is almost intact and contains interesting wall paintings and stained glass.
01234 376614 On classified road near Colmworth, 2m E of B660.
34 E3; Landranger 153; TL 115607

Cantlop Bridge
Shropshire
Single-span cast-iron road bridge over the Cound Brook, designed by the great engineer Thomas Telford. ¾m SW of Berrington on unclassified road off A458.
41 G6; Landranger 126; SJ 517062

Chichele College
Northamptonshire
Parts of a quadrangle remain of this college for secular canons, founded in 1422.
01933 317182. (Site managed by East Northamptonshire District Council.)
In Higham Ferrers, on A6.
34 C3; Landranger 153; SP 960687

Clun Castle
Shropshire
The remains of a four-storey keep and other buildings of this border castle. In Clun, off A488, 18m W of Ludlow.
30 D1; Landranger 137; SO 299809

Croxden Abbey
Staffordshire
Remains of a Cistercian abbey founded in 1176. 5m NW of Uttoxeter off A522.
42 C3; Landranger 128; SK 065397

De Grey Mausoleum
Flitton, Bedfordshire
A remarkable treasure-house of sculpted tombs and monuments from the 16th to 19th centuries, dedicated to the de Grey family of Wrest Park. 01525 860094. Access through Flitton Church. 01799 522842 Flitton, attached to church, on unclassified road 1½m W of A6 at Silsoe.
34 D6; Landranger 153; TL 059359

Deddington Castle
Oxfordshire
Extensive earthworks conceal the remains of a 12th-century castle. S of B4031 on E side of Deddington, 17m N of Oxford on A423.
33 G6; Landranger 151; SP 471316

Edvin Loach Old Church
Hereford & Worcester
Peaceful and isolated 11th-century church remains. 4m N of Bromyard on unclassified road off B4203.
31 H4; Landranger 149; SO 663585

Eleanor Cross
Geddington, Northamptonshire
One of a series of famous crosses erected by Edward I to mark the resting places of the body of his wife, Eleanor, when brought for burial from Harby in Nottinghamshire to Westminster Abbey. In Geddington, off A43 between Kettering and Corby.
34 B1; Landranger 141; SP 896830

Gainsborough Old Hall
Lincolnshire
A large medieval house with a magnificent Great Hall and suites of rooms. A collection of historic furniture and a re-created medieval kitchen are on display.
01427 612669 In Gainsborough, opposite the Library.
54 C5; Landranger 121; SK 815895.

Geddington, Eleanor Cross
See Eleanor Cross.

Goodrich Castle
Hereford & Worcester
Remarkably complete, magnificent red sandstone castle with 12th-century keep and extensive remains from the 13th and 14th centuries. 01600 890538 5m S of Ross-on-Wye off A40.
31 G7; Landranger 162; SO 579199

Halesowen Abbey
West Midlands
Remains of an abbey founded by King John in the 13th century, now incorporated into a 19th-century farm. Off A456 Kidderminster road, 6m W of Birmingham city centre.
32 B1; Landranger 139; SO 975828

Hardwick Old Hall
Derbyshire
This large ruined house, finished in 1591, still displays Bess of Hardwick's innovative planning and interesting decorative plasterwork. The views from the top floor over the country park and 'New' Hall are spectacular. 01246 850431 9½m SE of Chesterfield, off A6175, from J 29 of M1.
53 G7; Landranger 120; SK 463638

Haughmond Abbey
Shropshire
The extensive remains of this 12th-century Augustinian abbey include the Chapter House, which retains its late-medieval timber ceiling, and some fine medieval sculpture.
01743 709661 3m NE of Shrewsbury off B5062.
41 G5; Landranger 126; SJ 542152

Hob Hurst's House
Derbyshire
A square prehistoric burial mound with an earthwork ditch and outer bank. ➲ From unclassified road off B5057, 9m W of Chesterfield.
52 E7; Landranger 119; SK 287692

Houghton House
Bedfordshire
Reputedly the inspiration for 'House Beautiful' in Bunyan's Pilgrim's Progress, the remains of this early 17th-century mansion still convey elements that justify the description, including work attributed to Inigo Jones. ➲ 1m NE of Ampthill off A421, 8m S of Bedford.
34 D6; Landranger 153; TL 039394

Iron Bridge
Shropshire
The world's first iron bridge and Britain's best-known industrial monument. Cast in Coalbrookdale by local ironmaster Abraham Darby, it was erected across the River Severn in 1779. ➲ In Ironbridge, adjacent to A4169.
41 H6; Landranger 127; SJ 672034

Jewry Wall
Leicester, Leicestershire
One of the largest surviving lengths of Roman wall in the country. Over 9 metres (30 ft) high, it formed one side of the civic baths' exercise hall. ➲ In St Nicholas St W of Church of St Nicholas.
43 H6; Landranger 140; SK 583044

Kenilworth Castle
Warwickshire
Queen Elizabeth I did sleep here. The massive, red sandstone castle, which seems positively to glow in the early morning and evening light, was the Warwickshire power base of the best beloved of all her courtiers, Robert Dudley, Earl of Leicester. Today, with some of its Tudor gardens, its impressive Norman 'keep' and John of Gaunt's Great Hall, it is the largest castle ruin in England. ✆01926 852078 ➲ In Kenilworth, Warwickshire
32 E2; Landranger 140; SP 278723

Kirby Hall
Northamptonshire
Outstanding example of a large, stone-built Elizabethan mansion, begun in 1570 with 17th-century alterations. The fine gardens, currently being restored, are home to beautiful peacocks. ✆01536 203230
➲ On unclassified road off A43 4m NE of Corby.
44 C7; Landranger 141; SP 926927

Kirby Muxloe Castle
Leicestershire
Picturesque, moated, brick-built castle begun in 1480 by William, Lord Hastings. ➲ 4m W of Leicester off B5380.
43 H6; Landranger 140; SK 524046

Langley Chapel
Shropshire
This small chapel, standing alone in a field, contains a complete set of early 17th-century wooden fittings and furniture. ➲ 1½m S of Acton Burnell, on unclassified road off A49, 9½m S of Shrewsbury.
41 G6; Landranger 126; SJ 538001

Leicester Jewry Wall
See Jewry Wall.

Leigh Court Barn
Hereford & Worcester
Magnificent 14th-century timber-framed barn, built for the monks of Pershore Abbey. It is the largest of its kind in Britain. ➲ 5m W of Worcester on unclassified road off A4103.
31 J4; Landranger 150; 784534.

Lilleshall Abbey
Shropshire
Extensive and evocative ruins of an abbey of Augustinian canons, including remains of the 12th- and 13th-century church and the cloister buildings, surrounded by green lawns and ancient yew trees. ➲ On unclassified road off A518, 4m N of Oakengates.
41 J5; Landranger 127; SJ 738142

Lincoln Bishop's Old Palace
Lincoln, Lincolnshire
The remains of this medieval palace of the Bishops of Lincoln are in the shadow of Lincoln Cathedral. You can climb the stairs to the Alnwick Tower, explore the undercroft and see the recently established vineyard, which is one of the most northerly in Europe. ✆01522 527468 ➲ S side of Lincoln Cathedral.
54 D6; Landranger 121; SK 981717

Longtown Castle
Hereford & Worcester
An unusual cylindrical keep built c.1200, with walls 4.5 metres (15 feet) thick. There are magnificent views to the Black Mountains. ➲ 4m WSW of Abbey Dore.
30 E7; Landranger 161; SO 321291

Lyddington Bede House
Leicestershire
Set among picturesque golden stone cottages, beside the handsome parish church of St Andrew, the Bede House (house of prayer) was originally a medieval palace of the Bishops of Lincoln. It was later converted into an almshouse. ✆01572 822438 ➲ In Lyddington, 6m N of Corby, 1m E of A6003.
44 B7; Landranger 141; SP 875970

Mattersey Priory
Nottinghamshire
Remains of a small Gilbertine monastery founded in 1185. ➲ Rough access down drive ¾m long, 1m E of Mattersey off B6045, 7m N of East Retford.
53 K5; Landranger 112; SK 704896

Minster Lovell Hall and Dovecote
Oxfordshire
The handsome ruins of Lord Lovell's 15th-century manor house stand in a lovely setting on the banks of the River Windrush.
➲ Adjacent to Minster Lovell church, 3m W of Witney off A40.
21 H1; Landranger 164; SP 324114

Mitchell's Fold Stone Circle
Shropshire
An air of mystery surrounds this Bronze Age stone circle, set on dramatic moorland and consisting of some 30 stones of which 15 are visible. ➲ 16m SW of Shrewsbury W of A488.
30 E1; Landranger 137; SO 306984

Moreton Corbet Castle
Shropshire
A ruined medieval castle with the substantial remains of a splendid Elizabethan mansion.
➲ In Moreton Corbet off B5063, 7m NE of Shrewsbury.
41 G4; Landranger 126; SJ 562232

Mortimer's Cross Water Mill
Hereford & Worcester
Intriguing 18th-century mill, still in working order, showing the process of corn milling. ✆01568 708820 ➲ 7m NW of Leominster on B4362.
31 F3; Landranger 148; SO 426637.

Nine Ladies Stone Circle
Stanton Moor, Derbyshire
Once part of the burial site for 300–400 people, this Early Bronze Age circle is 15 metres (50 feet) across. ➲ From unclassified road off A6, 5m SE of Bakewell.
52 E7; Landranger 119; SK 253635.

North Hinksey Conduit House
Oxfordshire
Roofed reservoir for Oxford's first water mains, built in the early 17th century. ➲ In North Hinksey off A34, 2½m W of Oxford. Located off track leading from Harcourt Hill; use footpath from Ferry Hinksey Lane (near station).
21 J2; Landranger 164; SP 494049.

North Leigh Roman Villa
Oxfordshire
The remains of a large and well-built Roman courtyard villa. The most important feature is an almost complete mosaic tile floor, intricately patterned in reds and browns.
➲ 2m N of North Leigh, 10m W of Oxford off A4095. 21 J1; Landranger 164; SP 397154.

Old Gorhambury House
Hertfordshire
The remains of this Elizabethan mansion illustrate the impact of the Renaissance on English architecture.
✆01604 730320 for more information.
➲ ¼m W of Gorhambury House and accessible only through private drive from A4147 at St Albans (2m).
23 G2; Landranger 166; TL 110077.

Old Oswestry Hill Fort
Shropshire
An impressive Iron Age fort of 68 acres defended by a series of five ramparts, with an elaborate western entrance and unusual earthwork cisterns. ➲ 1m N of Oswestry, accessible from unclassified road off A483.
40 D3; Landranger 126; SJ 295310.

Peveril Castle
Derbyshire
There are breathtaking views of the Peak District from this castle, perched high above the pretty village of Castleton. The great square tower stands almost to its original height. ✆01433 620613 ➲ On S side of Castleton, 15m W of Sheffield on A625.
52 D5; Landranger 110; SK 150827.

Rollright Stones
Oxfordshire
Three groups of stones, known as 'The King's Men', 'The Whispering Knights' and 'The King Stone', spanning nearly 2,000 years of the Neolithic and Bronze Ages. ➲ Off unclassified road between A44 and A3400, 2m NW of Chipping Norton near villages of Little Rollright and Long Compton.
32 E6; Landranger 185; SP 297308.

Roman Wall
St Albans, Hertfordshire
Several hundred yards of the wall, built c. AD 200, which enclosed the Roman city of Verulamium. The remains of towers and foundations of a gateway can still be seen.
➲ On S side of St Albans, ½m from centre off A4147.
23 G2; Landranger 166; TL 135067.

Rotherwas Chapel
Hereford & Worcester
This Roman Catholic chapel dates from the 14th and 16th centuries and features an interesting mid-Victorian side chapel and High Altar. ➲ 1½m SE of Hereford on B4399.
31 G6; Landranger 149; SO 537383.

Rufford Abbey
Nottinghamshire
The remains of a 17th-century country house, built on the foundations of a 12th-century Cistercian abbey, set in the Rufford Country Park. ✆01623 823148 ➲ 2m S of Ollerton off A614.
53 J7; Landranger 120; SK 645646.

Rushton Triangular Lodge
Northamptonshire
Extraordinary building built by the Catholic Sir Thomas Tresham on his return from imprisonment for his religious beliefs. Completed in 1597, it symbolizes the Holy Trinity – it has three sides, three floors, trefoil windows and three triangular gables on each side. ✆01536 710761 ➲ 1m W of Rushton, on unclassified road 3m from Desborough on A6.
34 B1; Landranger 141; SP 830831.

Rycote Chapel
Oxfordshire
This lovely 15th-century chapel, with exquisitely carved and painted woodwork, has many intriguing features, including two roofed pews and a musicians' gallery.
➲ 3m SW of Thame off A329.
22 B2; Landranger 165; SP 667046.

Sibsey Trader Windmill
Lincolnshire
An impressive tower mill built in 1877, with its machinery and six sails intact. Flour milled on the spot can be bought there.
✆01205 820065 ➲ ½m W of village of Sibsey, off A16 5m N of Boston.
45 G1; Landranger 122; TF 345511.

St Albans Roman Wall
See Roman Wall.

Stokesay Castle
Shropshire
The finest medieval manor house in England, situated in peaceful countryside. The castle now stands in a picturesque group with its own splendid timber-framed Jacobean gatehouse and the parish church.
✆01588 672544 ➲ 7m NW of Ludlow off A49.
31 F1; Landranger 137; SO 436817.

Sutton Scarsdale Hall
Derbyshire
The dramatic hilltop shell of a great early 18th-century baroque mansion. ➲ Between Chesterfield and Bolsover, 1½m S of Arkwright Town.
53 G7; Landranger 120; SK 441690

Tattershall College
Lincolnshire
Remains of a grammar school for church choristers, built in the mid-15th century by Ralph, Lord Cromwell, the builder of nearby Tattershall Castle ➲ In Tattershall (off Market Place) 14m NE of Sleaford on A153.
45 F1; Landranger 122; TF 213577

Uffington Castle, White Horse and Dragon Hill
Oxfordshire
A group of sites lying along the Ridegway, an old prehistoric route. There is a large Iron Age camp enclosed within ramparts, a natural mound known as Dragon Hill and the spectacular White Horse, cut from turf to reveal chalk. ➲ S of B4507, 7m W of Wantage.
21 G4; Landranger 174; SU 301866

Wall Roman Site (Letocetum)
Staffordshire
The remains of a staging post, alongside Watling Street. Foundations of an inn and bath-house can be seen, and there is a display of finds in the site museum ✆01543 480768
➲ Off A5 at Wall near Lichfield.
42 D6; Landranger 139; SK 099067

Wayland's Smithy
Oxfordshire
Near to the Uffington White Horse lies this evocative Neolithic burial site, surrounded by a small circle of trees. It is an unusual site in that two grave types lie one upon the other
➲ On the Ridgeway ¾m NE of B4000 Ashbury–Lambourn road.
21 G4; Landranger 174; SU 281854

Wenlock Priory
Shropshire
The ruins of a large Cluniac priory in an attractive garden setting featuring delightful topiary. There are substantial remains of the early 13th-century church and Norman chapter house ✆01952 727466 ➲ In Much Wenlock.
41 H6; Landranger 127; SJ 625001

White Ladies Priory
Shropshire
The ruins of the late 12th-century church of a small priory of Augustinian canonesses.
➲ 1m SW of Boscobel House off unclassified road between A41 and A5, 8m NW of Wolverhampton.
42 A6; Landranger 127; SJ 826076

Wigmore Castle
Hereford & Worcester
Fortified since the 1060s, the present ruins date from the 13th and 14th centuries. The castle was dismantled during the Civil War, and remains very much as it was left then.
➲ 11m NW of Leominster, 14m SW of Ludlow off W side of A4110.
31 F3; Landranger 137; SO 408693

Wingfield Manor
Derbyshire
Huge, ruined, country mansion built in mid-15th century. Mary Queen of Scots was imprisoned here in 1569. Though unoccupied since the 1770s, the late-Gothic Great Hall and the 'High Tower' are fine testaments to Wingfield in its heyday. The manor has been used as a film location for *Peak Practice* and Zeffirelli's *Jane Eyre*.
✆01773 832060 ➲ 17m N of Derby, 11m S of Chesterfield on B5035 ½m S of South Wingfield. From M1 – Junc. 28, W on A38, A615 (Matlock Road) at Alfreton and turn onto B5035 after 1½m.
43 F1; Landranger 119; SK 374548

Witley Court
Hereford & Worcester
Spectacular ruins of a once great house. An earlier Jacobean manor house was converted in the 19th century into a vast Italianate mansion with porticoes by John Nash. The adjoining church, by James Gibbs, has a remarkable 18th-century baroque interior. The gardens were equally elaborate (William Nesfield's 'Monster Work') and contained immense stone fountains, which still survive. The largest, the Poseidon Fountain, is being restored to working order. ✆01299 896636
31 J3; Landranger 150; 769649

Wrest Park Gardens
Bedfordshire
Over 90 acres of wonderful gardens originally laid out in the early 18th century, including the Great Garden, with charming buildings and ornaments, and the delightfully intricate French Garden, with statues and fountain. The house, once the home of the de Grey family whose Mausoleum at Flitton is nearby, was inspired by 18th-century French chateaux. ✆01525 860152 ➲ ¾m E of Silsoe off A6, 10m S of Bedford.
34 D6; Landranger 153; TL 093356

Wroxeter Roman City
Shropshire
The excavated centre of the fourth largest city in Roman Britain, with impressive remains of the 2nd-century municipal baths.
✆01743 761330 ➲ At Wroxeter, 5m E of Shrewsbury on B4380.
41 G6; Landranger 126; SJ 568088

Northern England

Aldborough Roman Town
North Yorkshire
The principal town of the Brigantes, the largest tribe in Roman Britain. The delightfully located remains include parts of the Roman defences and two mosaic pavements. A museum displays Roman mosaic designs. ✆01423 322768 ➲ ¾m SE of Boroughbridge, on minor road off B6265 within 1m of junction of A1 and A6055.
59 K4; Landranger 99; SE 405661

Ambleside Roman Fort
Cumbria
The remains of this 1st- and 2nd-century fort were built to guard the Roman road from Brougham to Ravenglass. ➲ 200 yds W of Waterhead car park, Ambleside.
63 J7; Landranger 90; NY 376033

Arthur's Round Table
Cumbria
A prehistoric circular earthwork bounded by a ditch and an outer bank. ➲ At Eamont Bridge, 1m S of Penrith.
64 C5; Landranger 90; NY 523284

Auckland Castle Deer House
Bishop Auckland, County Durham
A charming building erected in 1760 in the park of the Bishops of Durham so that deer could shelter and find food. ➲ In Auckland Park, Bishop Auckland, N of town centre on A688.
66 C4; Landranger 93; NZ 216305

Aydon Castle
Northumberland
One of the finest fortified manor houses in England, built in the late 13th century. Situated in a position of great natural beauty, its remarkably intact state is due to its conversion to a farmhouse in the 17th century. ✆01434 632450 ➲ 1m NE of Corbridge, on minor road off B6321 or A68.
65 H1; Landranger 87; NZ 002663

Baguley Hall
Greater Manchester
A medieval timber-framed hall house dating from the 14th century, with 18th- and 19th-century additions. An extensive programme of repair is being carried out, with access on advertised open days only.
➲ 6m S of Manchester, in Hall Lane, Baguley, near Wythenshawe (E of junction 3 of M56, off A560).
51 H4; Landranger 109; SJ 815893

Barnard Castle
County Durham
The substantial remains of this large castle stand on a rugged escarpment overlooking the River Tees. You can still see parts of the 14th-century Great Hall and the cylindrical 12th-century tower. ✆01833 638212
65 H6; Landranger 92; NZ 049165

Beeston Castle
Cheshire
Standing majestically on sheer, rocky crags which fall sharply away from the castle walls, Beeston has possibly the most stunning views of the surrounding countryside of any castle in England and the rock has a history which stretches back over 2,500 years.
✆01829 260464 ➲ 11m SE of Chester on minor road off A49 or A41.
50 E8; Landranger 117; SJ 537593

Belsay Hall, Castle and Gardens
The beautiful honey-coloured stone from which Belsay Hall is built came from its own quarries in the grounds. Those quarries have since become the unusual setting for one of a series of spectacular gardens. They are the property's finest feature, deservedly listed Grade I in the Register of Gardens. The house itself was innovative, when built between 1810 and 1817 in a style derived directly from Ancient Greece. ✆01661 881636
➲ In Belsay, Northumberland, 14m NW of Newcastle on A696.
75 G7; Landranger 88; NZ 088785

Berwick-upon-Tweed Barracks
Northumberland
Among the earliest purpose-built barracks, these have changed very little since 1717. The barracks house 'By Beat of Drum', an exhibition which re-creates scenes such as a British infantryman's life in a barrack room, the Museum of the King's Own Scottish Borderers, the Borough Museum with its imaginative exhibitions and part of the Burrell Collection. ✆01289 304493 ➲ On the Parade, off Church St, Berwick town centre.
83 H6; Landranger 75; NT 994535

Berwick-upon-Tweed Castle
Northumberland
Remains of 12th-century castle ➲ Adjacent to Berwick railway station, W of town centre, accessible also from river bank.
83 J6; Landranger 75; NT 994535

Berwick-upon-Tweed Main Guard
Northumberland
Georgian Guard House near the quay. An exhibition celebrates the 150th anniversary of the railway coming to Berwick-upon Tweed. The Story of a Border Garrison Town is a permanent display of the history of the town and its fortifications. ➲ Surrounding Berwick town centre on N bank of River Tweed.
83 H6; Landranger 75; NT 994535

Berwick-upon-Tweed Ramparts
Northumberland
Remarkably complete, 16th-century town fortifications, with gateways and projecting bastions. ➲ Surrounding Berwick town centre on N bank of River Tweed.
83 H6; Landranger 75; NT 994535

Bessie Surtees House
Tyne & Wear
Two 16th- and 17th-century merchants' houses. One is a remarkable and rare example of Jacobean domestic architecture. An exhibition about these buildings is on the first floor. ✆0191 261 1585 ➲ 41–44 Sandhill, Newcastle.
66 C1; Landranger 88; NZ 252639

Bishop Auckland Deer House
See Auckland Castle Deer House.

Black Middens Bastle House
Northumberland
A 16th-century two-storey defended farmhouse, set in splendid walking country.
➲ 200yds N of minor road 7m NW of Bellingham; access also along minor road from A688.
74 D6; Landranger 80; NY 774900

Bow Bridge
Barrow-in-Furness, Cumbria
Late medieval stone bridge across Mill Beck, carrying a route to nearby Furness Abbey.
➲ ½m N of Barrow-in-Furness, on minor road off A590 near Furness Abbey.
57 F3; Landranger 96; SD 224715

Bowes Castle
County Durham
Massive ruins of Henry II's tower keep, three storeys high and set within the earthworks of a Roman fort. ➲ In Bowes Village just off A66, 4m W of Barnard Castle.
65 G6; Landranger 92; NY 992135

Brinkburn Priory
Northumberland
This late 12th-century church is a fine example of early Gothic architecture, almost perfectly preserved, and is set in a lovely spot beside the River Coquet. ✆01665 570628
➲ 4½m SE of Rothbury off B6344.
75 H5; Landranger 81; NZ 116984

Brodsworth Hall
South Yorkshire
One of England's most beautiful Victorian country houses, Brodsworth Hall has survived almost completely intact since the 1860s – an extraordinary time warp of richly marbled walls, Axminster carpets and family portraits. Opened for the first time in 1995, Brodsworth Hall and gardens offer visitors a breathtaking journey through the passage of time. When bequeathed to English Heritage, conservation policy was aimed at preserving the Hall's faded grandeur. In the long-abandoned kitchen, visitors can readily picture how meals were really made in the age of Mrs Beeton. And deep in the cluttered remains of the servants' wing, it is easy to imagine life below stairs, with all the benefits and drawbacks that such an insular Victorian existence brought. ✆01302 722598 ➲ In Brodsworth, South Yorkshire, off A635 Barnsley Road, from junction 37 of A1(M).
53 H3; Landranger 111; SE 507071.

Brough Castle
Cumbria
Dating from Roman times, the 12th-century keep replaced an earlier stronghold destroyed by the Scots in 1174. It was restored by Lady Anne Clifford in the 17th century. ➲ 8m SE of Appleby S of A66.
64 E6; Landranger 91; NY 791141

Brougham Castle
Cumbria
These impressive ruins on the banks of the River Eamont include an early 13th-century keep and later buildings. Its one-time owner Lady Anne Clifford restored the castle in the 17th century. There is an exhibition of Roman tombstones from the nearby fort. ✆01768 862488 ➲ 1½m SE of Penrith on minor road off A66.
64 C5; Landranger 90; NY 537290

Burton Agnes Manor House
East Riding of Yorkshire
Rare example of a Norman house, altered and encased in brick in the 17th and 18th centuries. ➲ In Burton Agnes village, 5m SW of Bridlington on A166.
61 H4; Landranger 101; TA 103633

Byland Abbey
North Yorkshire
A hauntingly lovely ruin set in peaceful meadows in the shadow of the Hambleton Hills. It illustrates the later development of Cistercian churches, including the beautiful floor tiles. ✆01347 868614 ➲ 2m S of A170 between Thirsk and Helmsley, near Coxwold village.
59 L3; Landranger 100; SE 549789

Carlisle Castle
Cumbria
Sitting proudly on the highest point above the River Eden, Carlisle Castle has guarded the western end of the Anglo-Scottish border for over nine centuries. It was first built after William II relieved Carlisle of two centuries of Scottish domination in 1092. Since then it has often been the scene of turbulent conflict between the two nations, being fought over fairly constantly until the union of the crowns in 1603. It then fell into Scottish hands again during the Civil War and the Jacobite Rising 100 years later. ✆01228 591922 ➲ In Carlisle, Cumbria
63 J2; Landranger; NY 397563.

Castlerigg Stone Circle
Cumbria
Possibly one of the earliest Neolithic stone circles in Britain, its 33 stones stand in a beautiful setting. ➲ 1½m E of Keswick.
63 J5; Landranger 90; NY 293236

Chester Castle: Agricola Tower and Castle Walls
Cheshire
Set in the angle of the city walls, this 12th-century tower contains a fine vaulted chapel. ➲ Access via Assizes Court car park on Grosvenor St.
50 D7; Landranger 117; SJ 405658

Chester Roman Amphitheatre
Cheshire
The largest Roman amphitheatre in Britain, partially excavated. Used for entertainment and military training by the 20th Legion, based at the fortress of Deva. ➲ On Vicars Lane beyond Newgate, Chester.
50 D7; Landranger 117; SJ 404660

Clifford's Tower
Standing high on its mound in the city of York, Clifford's Tower is one of the few vestiges of the pair of castles built by William the Conqueror after his victory in 1066. ✆01904 646940 ➲ In Tower St.
60 D5; Landranger 105; SE 605515.

Clifton Hall
Cumbria
The surviving tower block of a 15th-century manor house. ➲ In Clifton next to Clifton Hall Farm, 2m S of Penrith on A6.
64 C5; Landranger 90; NY 530271

Conisbrough Castle
South Yorkshire
The spectacular white circular keep of a 12th-century castle. It is the oldest circular keep in England and one of the finest medieval buildings. An exciting audio-visual presentation evokes a dramatic episode in the castle's history. There is also a visitor centre and exhibition. ✆01709 863329 ➲ NE of Conisbrough town centre off A630, 4½m SW of Doncaster.
53 H4; Landranger 111; SK 515989

Countess Pillar
Brougham, Cumbria
An unusual monument, bearing sundials and family crests, erected in 1656 by Lady Anne Clifford to commemorate her parting with her mother in 1616. ➲ 1m SE of Brougham on A66
63 L5; Landranger 90; NY 546289

Derwentcote Steel Furnace
County Durham
Built in the 18th century, the earliest and most complete steel-making furnace to have survived. Closed in the 1870s, it has now been restored and opened to the public. ✆01207 562573 ➲ 10m SW of Newcastle on A694 between Rowland's Gill and Hamsterley.
66 B2; Landranger 88; NZ 131566

Dunstanburgh Castle
Northumberland
An easy coastal walk leads to the eerie skeleton of this wonderful 14th-century castle, which is sited on a basalt crag more than 30 metres (100 feet) high. Dunstanburgh is noted for its seabirds, wildlife and flowers. The surviving ruins include the large gatehouse, which later became the keep, and curtain walls. ✆01665 576231 ➲ 8m NE of Alnwick, on footpaths from Craster or Embleton.
75 J2; Landranger 75; NU 258220

Easby Abbey
North Yorkshire
Substantial remains of the medieval abbey buildings stand in a beautiful setting by the River Swale near Richmond. The abbey can be reached by a pleasant riverside walk from Richmond Castle. ➲ 1m SE of Richmond off B6271.
66 B7; Landranger 92; NZ 185003

Edlingham Castle
Northumberland
Set in a beautiful valley, this complex ruin has defensive features spanning the 13th–15th centuries. ➲ At E end of Edlingham village, on minor road off B6341 6m SW of Alnwick.
75 H4; Landranger 81; NU 115092

Egglestone Abbey
County Durham
Picturesque remains of a 12th- century abbey. Substantial parts of the church and abbey buildings remain. ➲ 1m S of Barnard Castle on minor road off B6277.
65 H6; Landranger 92; NZ 062151

Etal Castle
Northumberland
A 14th-century border castle located in the picturesque village of Etal. There is a major award-winning exhibition about the castle, border warfare and the Battle of Flodden, which took place nearby in 1513. ✆01890 820332 ➲ In Etal village, 10m SW of Berwick.
83 H8; Landranger 75; NT 925394

Finchale Priory
County Durham
These beautiful priory ruins, dating from the 13th century, are in a wooded setting beside the River Wear. ✆0191 386 3828 ➲ 3m NE of Durham, on minor road off A167.
66 C3; Landranger 88; NZ 29471

Furness Abbey
Cumbria
In a peaceful valley, the red sandstone remains of a wealthy abbey founded in 1123 by Stephen, later King of England, are at the end of an ancient route from Bow Bridge. There is an exhibition and a museum contains fine stone carvings. ✆01229 823420 ➲ 1½m N of Barrow-in-Furness, on minor road off A590.
57 F3; Landranger 96; SD 218717

Gainsthorpe Medieval Village
North Lincolnshire
Originally discovered and still best seen from the air, this hidden village comprises earthworks of peasant houses, gardens and streets. ➲ On minor road W of A15 S of Hibaldstow 5m SW of Brigg (no signs).
54 D3; Landranger 112; SK 955012

Guisborough Priory
Redcar & Cleveland
An Augustinian priory. The remains also include the gatehouse and the east end of an early 14th-century church. ✆01287 633801
➲ In Guisborough town, next to parish church.
67 G6; Landranger 94; NZ 618163

Goodshaw Chapel
Lancashire
A recently restored 18th-century Baptist chapel with all its furnishings complete.
✆0191 261 1585 for details.
➲ In Crawshawbooth, 2m N of Rawtenstall, in Goodshaw Avenue off A682.
51 H1; Landranger 103; SD 815263

Hadrian's Wall
Cumbria, Northumberland
Stretching across northern England from the Solway Firth in the west to the Tyne in the east, Hadrian's Wall divided the 'civilized' world of the Romans, from the northern tribes beyond. Emperor Hadrian, who came to Britain in 122, was unusual in that he believed consolidation to be more glorious than new conquest. The Wall was the physical manifestation of his strategy, a defensive barrier linking the existing system of forts and watchtowers along the Stanegate road.
➲ West of Hexham, the Wall runs roughly parallel to the A69 Carlisle– Newcastle-upon-Tyne road, lying between 1–4 miles North of it, close to the B6318.

ENGLISH HERITAGE PROPERTIES

Banks East Turret
A well-preserved turret with adjoining stretches of Wall and fine views.
3¼m NE of Lanercost, off minor road E of Banks village. On minor road E of Brampton.
64 C1. Landranger 86, NY 575647.

Benwell Roman Temple
Remains of small temple, surrounded by modern housing in Broomridge Ave.
At Benwell in Broomridge Ave.
75 H8. Landranger 88, NZ 217546.

Benwell Vallum Crossing
The sole remaining example of an original stone-built causeway across the ditch of the Vallum earthwork that ran parallel to the Wall, which is among the best-preserved on the Wall.
At Benwell, immediately S of A69 at Denton Bank on minor road off B6318.
64 D1. Landranger 88, NZ 217546.

Birdoswald Fort
Almost on the edge of the trifling escarpment, there is a commanding position and visible evidence of the fort, the west gate and, most importantly the east gate, which is among the best-preserved.
2m W of Chollerford on B6318.
64 C1. Landranger 86, NY 615663.

Black Carts Turret
A 460 metre (500 yard) length of Wall and turret foundations, with a 20 metre (70 yard) stretch to the north.
9m S of Low Brunton on A6079.
74 E7. Landranger 87, NY 884712.

Brunton Turret
Well-preserved turret on minor road to the north.
¼m N of Chollerford on B6318.
74 E7. Landranger 87, NY 922698.

Cawfields Roman Wall
A concentration of Roman sites – camps, turrets, a fortlet, and Milecastle 42 – along Hadrian's Wall across the North Tyne are visible on both banks. The most impressive remains are at the east side.
2m N of Haltwhistle off B6318.
74 D8. Landranger 87, NY 716667.

Chesters Bridge
Fragments of the bridge that carried Hadrian's Wall across the North Tyne.
¼m S of Chollerford on B6318.
74 F7. Landranger 87, NY 913701.

Chesters Roman Fort
Throughout the Empire, Roman forts were built to a very similar pattern. Chesters, located between the 27th and 28th milecastles, is one of the best-preserved example.
¼m W of Chollerford on B6318.
74 E7. Landranger 87, NY 913701.

Corbridge Roman Site
Originally the site of a fort on the former patrol road, Corbridge evolved into a principal town in the 5th century. There with their ingenious ventilation systems, are among its most impressive remains. Corbridge has an excellent starting point to explore the Wall.
½m NW of Corbridge on minor road, signed Corbridge Roman Site.
64 E1. Landranger 87, NZ 983649.

Denton Hall Turret
Foundations of a turret (70 yard) section of Wall, and 65 metre stretch of the Wall, snaking over the crags to the turret on its summit.
64 D1 on minor road ½m W of Gilsland.
75 H8. Landranger 88, NZ 195656.

Corbridge Roman Site

Hare Hill
A short length of wall standing nine feet high.
¾m NE of Lanercost, off minor road E of Banks village. On minor road E of Brampton.
64 C1. Landranger 86, NY 562646.

Harrow's Scar Milecastle
64 C1. Landranger 87, NY 745676.

Heddon-on-the-Wall
A fine stretch of the Wall up to three metres (ten feet) thick, near the remains of a medieval kiln near the west end.
Immediately E of Heddon village, S of A69.
64 D1. Landranger 88, NZ 136669.

Housesteads Roman Fort
One of the twelve permanent forts built by Hadrian c. 124, between milecastles 36 and 37, Housesteads is the most complete example of a Roman fort to be seen in Britain. Spectacular earthworks surround a great ruined Roman fort. There is an exhibition on the history of the site.
2¾m NE of Bardon Mill on B6318.
60 D2. Landranger 100, SE 611836.

Hardknott Roman Fort
Very rugged section of wall, including the highest point at Winshields Crag. W of Steel Rigg car park, on minor road off B6318.
64 E1. Landranger 87, NY 745676.

Winshields Wall
Set on a wooded hillside overlooking the River Tyne are the extensive remains of a 12th-century castle, with gatehouse.
W of Prudhoe, off minor road off A695.
65 H1. Landranger 88, NZ 092634.

Helmsley Castle
This powerful castle lies close to the market square, with a view of the town, enclosing a school great. The ruined Norman keep, with a fine market square, with a view of the town.
North Yorkshire
At Helmsley. Landranger 100, SE 611836.

Howden Minster
The remains of this church, cathedral-like keep-gatehouse, with a fine display of medieval heraldry adorning the chapter house as well as the remains of the 14th-century chancel and octagonal chapter house.
North Yorkshire
At Howden, 25m SE of York near junction of A63 & A614.
60 E4. Landranger 106, SE 748283.

Marmion Tower
Set on a wooded hillside overlooking the River Tyne are the extensive remains of a 12th-century castle, with gatehouse.
North Yorkshire
¼m S of Ripon off A6108 in West Tanfield.
59 H3. Landranger 99, SE 267787.

Mayburgh Earthwork
An impressive prehistoric circular earthwork, with banks up to 4.5 metres (15 feet) high, enclosing a central area of one acre containing a single large stone.
Cumbria
At Eamont Bridge, 1m S of Penrith off A6.
64 C5. Landranger 90, NY 519285.

Middleham Castle
This childhood home of Richard III stands controlling the river that winds through Wensleydale. There is a massive 12th-century keep with splendid views of the surrounding countryside.
North Yorkshire
At Middleham, 2m S of Leyburn on A6108.
60 D2. Landranger 99, SE 128675.

Monk Bretton Priory
The remains of a Cluniac monastery. Sandstone ruins of a Cluniac monastery, which was built in the 12th century.
South Yorkshire
1m E of Barnsley town centre off A633.
66 B7. Landranger 111, SE 373085.

Mount Grace Priory
Mount Grace Priory is the best-preserved of the ten Carthusian monasteries in Britain.
North Yorkshire
12m NE of Thirsk, 7m NE of Northallerton on A19.
66 E8. Landranger 99, SE 453982.

Rievaulx Abbey
Everywhere peace, everywhere serenity, and a marvellous freedom from the tumult of the world.' Those words could easily be taken to describe Rievaulx today, one of the most atmospheric of all the monastic ruins of the North.
North Yorkshire
2¼m W of Helmsley on minor road off B1257.
66 B7. Landranger 100, SE 577644.

Richmond Castle
North Yorkshire
In Richmond. Landranger 92, NZ 174006.

Ravenglass Roman Bath House
Cumbria
At Ravenglass, off minor road leading to A595.
56 D1. Landranger 96, NY 088961.

Scarborough Castle
North Yorkshire
At Scarborough. Landranger 101, TA 050893.

Sandbach Crosses
Cheshire
Market square, Sandbach.
51 G1. Landranger 118, SJ 758686.

Shap Abbey
Cumbria
At Shap. Landranger 90, NY 548153.

Skipsea Castle
East Riding of Yorkshire
8m S of Bridlington, W of Skipsea village.
61 J5. Landranger 107, TA 163551.

Spofforth Castle
North Yorkshire
At Spofforth, 3½m SE of Harrogate, off A661.
59 J5. Landranger 104, SE 360511.

Stanwick Iron Age Fortifications
North Yorkshire
60 F4. Landranger 100, SE 180114.

Steeton Hall Gateway
North Yorkshire
4m NE of Castleford, on minor road off A162 at South Milford.
66 B6. Landranger 105, SE 484314.

Wheeldale Roman Road
North Yorkshire
57 KG. Landranger 94, SE 904115.

Prudhoe Castle
Northumberland
W of Prudhoe, off minor road off A695.
65 H1. Landranger 88, NZ 092634.

Sailey Abbey
Lancashire
Barton-upon-Humber, North Lincolnshire
58 D6. Landranger 103, SD 776464.

St Peter's Church
North Lincolnshire
At Barton-upon-Humber.
54 E1. Landranger 112, TA 034220.

Thornton Abbey and Gatehouse
North Lincolnshire
7m SE of Humber Bridge on minor road off A160.
54 F2. Landranger 113, TA 115190.

HISTORIC
ROYAL PALACES

The Banqueting House
The Banqueting House was built between 1619 and 1622 during the reign of James I. Designed by Inigo Jones, it is the only surviving building of the vast rambling Whitehall Palace, destroyed by fire nearly 300 years ago.

How to get there
Underground Westminster (District and Circle lines), Embankment (Bakerloo, Northern, District and Circle Lines)
Rail Charing Cross

Hampton Court Palace

With its 500 years of royal history, Hampton Court Palace has something to offer everyone. Set in sixty acres of world-famous gardens, the Palace is a living tapestry of history.

How to get there
Car M3 and several exits off the M25
Bus 111, 411, R68, 501, 440, 415, 513, 726, 267 (Sundays)
Green Line coach 415 and 718
Rail Hampton Court station, 32 minutes from Waterloo via Clapham Junction
Underground Wimbledon (District Line) for connecting train from Waterloo to Hampton Court or Richmond (District Line) then R68
River launch From Westminster, Richmond or Kingston upon Thames

HM Tower of London

A palace and fortress for over 900 years, the Tower's bloody legends and its sinister reputation draw visitors from all over the world.

How to get there
Underground Tower Hill station
Bus 15, x15, 25, 42, 78, 100, D1, D9, D11
Docklands Light Railway (DLR) Tower Gateway station
Rail Fenchurch Street station, London Bridge

Kensington Palace State Apartments

How to get there
Underground Queensway (Central Line), Notting Hill Gate (Central, District and Circle Lines), High Street Kensington (District and Circle Lines)
Bus 9, 10, 33, 49, 52, 70, C1

Kew Palace and Queen Charlotte's Cottage

How to get there
Underground Kew Gardens (District Line)

The Council for British Archaeology

Further information about Britain's historic environment, as well as archaeological projects and events, is available from the Council for British Archaeology.

For details of special membership terms for users of this atlas, please contact:
The Membership Secretary
The Council for British Archaeology
Bowes Morrell House
111 Walmgate
York YO1 2UA
☎ 01904 671417
📠 01904 671384
e-mail: archaeology@compuserve.com

HISTORIC SCOTLAND PROPERTIES

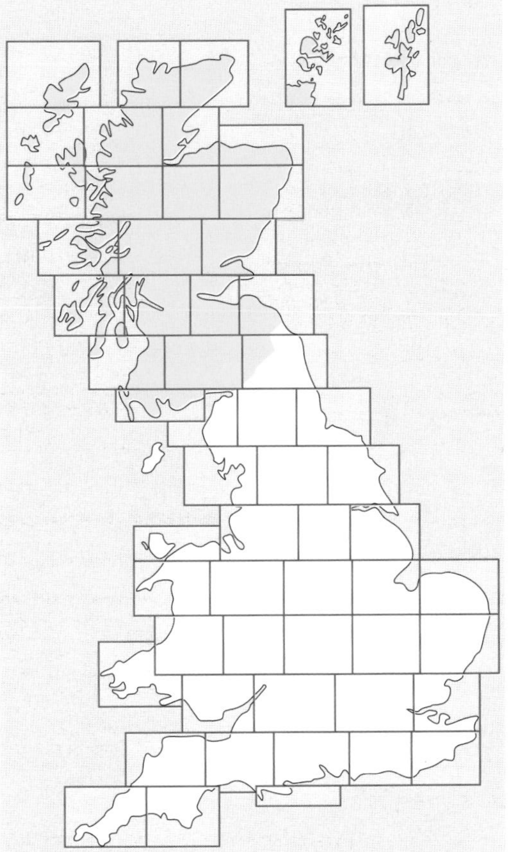

THE FOLLOWING DIRECTORY LISTS PROPERTIES OWNED AND MANAGED BY HISTORIC SCOTLAND THAT ARE OPEN TO THE PUBLIC. OPENING TIMES VARY SO PLEASE TELEPHONE IN ADVANCE TO AVOID DISAPPOINTMENT.

□ Atlas page and grid references are shown in blue

For further information contact:
Historic Scotland
Longmore House
Salisbury Place
Edinburgh EH9 1SH
☎ *0131 668 8800*

Aberdour Castle
Fife
A 14th-century castle, extended in the 16th and 17th centuries with splendid residential accommodation and a terraced garden and bowling green. There is a fine circular dovecote. ✆01383 860519. ➲ In Aberdour.
□ 81 G3

Arbroath Abbey
Angus
The substantial ruins of a Tironensian monastery, founded by William the Lion in 1178. Parts of the abbey church and domestic buildings remain. This was the scene of the Declaration of Arbroath of 1320, which asserted Scotland's Independence from England.
✆01241 878756. ➲ In Arbroath.
□ 89 J4

Balvenie Castle
Moray
A castle of enclosure first owned by the Comyns with a curtain wall of 13th-century date. Added to in the 15th and 16th centuries and visited by Mary Queen of Scots in 1562. ✆01340 820121 ➲ At Dufftown.
□ 96 C1

Bishop's and Earl's Palaces
Orkney
The Bishop's palace is a 12th-century hall-house, later much altered, with a round tower begun by Bishop Reid in 1541. A later addition was made by the notorious Patrick Stewart, Earl of Orkney, who built the adjacent Earl's Palace between 1600 and 1607 in a splendid Renaissance style.
✆01856 875461. ➲ In Kirkwall.
□ 112 C4

Black House
Western Isles
A traditional Lewis thatched house, with byre, attached barn and stackyard, complete and furnished.
✆01851 710395. ➲ In Arnol village, Lewis.
□ 107 H4

Blackness Castle
Falkirk
Built in the 1440s, and massively strengthened in the 16th century as an artillery fortress, Blackness was an ammunition depot in the 1870s. It was restored by the Office of Works in the 1920s. ✆01506 834807. ➲ 4m N of Linlithgow, on a promontory in the Forth estuary.
□ 81 F3

Bonawe Iron Furnace
Argyll & Bute
Founded in 1753 by a Lake District partnership, this is the most complete charcoal-fuelled ironworks in Britain. Displays illustrate how iron was made here. ✆01866 822432. ➲ Close to the village of Taynuilt.
□ 86 C5

Bothwell Castle
South Lanarkshire
The largest and finest 13th- century stone castle in Scotland, much fought over during the Wars of Independence. Part of the original circular keep survives, but most of the castle dates from the 14th and 15th centuries. ✆01698 816894. ➲ In Bothwell, approached from Uddingston, off the B7071.
□ 80 B6

Broch of Gurness
Orkney
Protected by three lines of ditch and rampart, the base of the broch is surrounded by a warren of Iron Age buildings.
✆01831 579478. ➲ At Aikerness, about 14m NW of Kirkwall.
□ 112 C2

Caerlaverock Castle
Dumfries & Galloway
One of the finest castles in Scotland, on a triangular site surrounded by moats. Its special features are the twin-towered gatehouse and the Nithsdale Lodging, a Renaissance range dating from 1638.
✆01387 770244. ➲ 8m SE of Dumfries.
□ 73 F8

Cardoness Castle
Dumfries & Galloway
The well-preserved ruin of a tower house of 15th-century date, the ancient home of the McCullochs. ✆01557 814427. ➲ 1m SW of Gatehouse of Fleet.
□ 69 G5

Castle Campbell
Clackmannanshire
Traditionally known as the 'Castle of Gloom'. The oldest part is a well-preserved 15th-century tower, around which other buildings were constructed, including an unusual loggia.
✆01259 742408. ➲ At the head of Dollar Glen.
□ 80 E2

Corgarff Castle
Aberdeenshire
A 16th-century tower house converted into a barracks for Hanoverian troops in 1748. Its last military use was to control the smuggling of illicit whisky between 1827 and 1831. Still complete and with star-shaped fortification.
✆01975 651460. ➲ 8m W of Strathdon village.
□ 96 B5

Craigmillar Castle
City of Edinburgh
Built round an L-plan tower house of the early 15th century, Craigmillar was much expanded in the 15th and 16th centuries. It is a handsome ruin, and includes a range of private rooms. ✆0131 661 4445. ➲ 2½ m SE of central Edinburgh, to E of Edinburgh–Dalkeith Road.
□ 81 H4

Craignethan Castle
South Lanarkshire
The oldest part is a tower house built by Sir James Hamilton of Finnart in the 16th century, defended by an outer wall pierced by gun ports, and by a wide and deep ditch with a most unusual 'caponier' – a stone vaulted chamber for artillery.
✆01555 860364. ✆5½m NW of Lanark.
□ 80 D7

Crichton Castle
Midlothian
A large and sophisticated castle, of which the most spectacular part is the range erected by the Earl of Bothwell between 1581 and 1591.
✆01875 320017. ➲ 2½ m SW of Pathhead.
□ 81 J5

Crossraguel Abbey
South Ayrshire
The 13th-century remains, which are remarkably complete and of high quality, include the church, cloister, chapter house and much of the domestic premises.
✆01655 883113. ➲ 2m S of Maybole.
□ 71 H4

Dallas Dhu Distillery and Visitor Centre
Moray
A perfectly preserved time capsule of the distiller's art. Built in 1898 to supply malt whisky for Wright and Greig's 'Roderick Dhu' blend. Video presentation and a glass of whisky to end your visit. ✆01309 676548.
➲ About 1m S of Forres off the Grantown Road.
□ 103 J7

Dirleton Castle and Gardens
East Lothian
The oldest part of this romantic castle dates from the 13th century. It was rebuilt in the 14th century and extended in the 16th century, when the gardens were established.
✆01620 850330. ➲ In the village of Dirleton.
□ 82 D3

Doune Castle
Stirling
A late 14th-century courtyard castle built for the Regent Albany. Its most striking feature is the combination of keep, gatehouse and hall, with its kitchen in a massive frontal block.
✆01786 841742. ➲ In Doune.
□ 80 C1

Dryburgh Abbey
Scottish Borders
Both beautifully situated and of intrinsic quality, the ruins of Dryburgh Abbey are remarkably complete. Much of the work is of the 12th and 13th century. Sir Walter Scott and Field Marshal Earl Haig are buried in the abbey. ✆01835 822381. ➲ 5m SE of Melrose, near St Boswells.
□ 74 B1

Dumbarton Castle
West Dunbartonshire
Spectacularly sited on a volcanic rock, this was the site of the ancient capital of Strathclyde. The most interesting features are the 18th-century artillery fortifications, with 19th-century guns.
✆01389 732167. ➲ At Dumbarton.
□ 79 F4

Dundonald Castle
South Ayrshire
A fine 13th-century tower built by Robert II incorporating part of an earlier building. The king used the castle as a summer residence until his death in 1390. ✆01563 850201.
➲ In Dundonald, off the A759.
□ 71 J1

Dundrennan Abbey
Dumfries & Galloway
The beautiful ruins of a Cistercian abbey founded by David I. Mary Queen of Scots spent her last night on Scottish soil here.
✆01557 500262. ➲ 6½m SE of Kirkcudbright.
□ 69 J6

Dunfermline Abbey and Palace
Fife
The remains of a Benedictine abbey which was founded by Queen Margaret in the 11th century. The foundations of her church are under the superb, Romanesque nave, built in the 12th century. Robert the Bruce was buried in the choir, now the site of the present parish church. ✆01383 739026.
➲ In Dunfermline.
□ 81 F3

Dunstaffnage Castle and Chapel
Argyll & Bute
A very fine 13th-century castle enclosure, built on a rock, with nearby ruins of a chapel of exceptional architectural refinement.
✆01631 562465. ➲ By Loch Etive, 3½m from Oban.
□ 85 K5

Edinburgh Castle
City of Edinburgh
The most famous of Scottish castles has a complex history. The oldest part dates from the Norman period; there is a Great Hall built by the James IV; the Half Moon battery was built by Regent Morton in the late 16th century; the Scottish National War Memorial was formed after World War I. The castle also houses the crown jewels (Honours) of Scotland, the history of which is described in a new exhibition. Also see the famous 15th-century gun, Mons Meg. Attractive restaurant with spectacular views over the city. ✆0131 225 9846. ➲ In the centre of Edinburgh.
□ 81 H4

Edzell Castle and Garden
Angus
Very beautiful complex with a late-medieval tower house incorporated into a 16th-century courtyard mansion. The carved decoration of the garden walls is unique in Britain. ✆01356 648631. ➲ At Edzell, 6m N of Brechin.
□ 89 H2

Elgin Cathedral
Moray
The superb ruin of what many think was Scotland's most beautiful cathedral. Much of the work is in a rich late 13th century style, much modified after the burning of the church by the Wolf of Badenoch in 1390. The octagonal chapter house is the finest in Scotland. ✆01343 547171. ➲ In Elgin.
□ 104 B2

Fort George
Highland
A vast site and one of the most outstanding artillery fortifications in Europe. It was planned in 1747 as a base for George II's army, and was completed in 1769. Since then it has served as a barracks. There are reconstructions of barrack rooms in different periods and a display of muskets and pikes.
✆01667 462777. ➲ 11m NE of Inverness, by the village of Ardersier.
□ 103 F7

Glenluce Abbey
Dumfries & Galloway
Cistercian abbey founded in 1192. The remains include a handsome early 16th-century chapter house. ✆01581 300541.
➲ 2m N of Glenluce village.
□ 68 C5

Hermitage Castle
Scottish Borders
A vast and eerie ruin in a lonely situation, of the 14th and 15th centuries. Mary Queen of Scots made her famous ride there to meet the Earl of Bothwell. ✆013873 76222. ➲ In Liddesdale, 5½m NE of Newcastleton, off the B6399.
□ 74 A5

Huntingtower Castle
Perth & Kinross
Two fine and complete towers, of the 15th and 16th centuries, now linked by a 17th-century range. There are fine painted ceilings.
✆01738 627231. ➲ 2m W of Perth.
□ 88 C6

Huntly Castle
Aberdeenshire
A magnificent ruin consisting mainly of a palace block erected in the 16th and 17th centuries by the Gordon family.
✆01466 793191. ➲ In Huntly.
□ 96 E1

Inchcolm Abbey
Fife
The best-preserved group of monastic buildings in Scotland, founded in about 1123, and including a 13th-century octagonal chapter house. ✆0131 331 4857.
➲ On an island on the Firth of Forth, opposite Aberdour. Ferries from South Queensferry and North Queensferry.
□ 81 G3

Inchmahome Priory
Stirling
A beautifully situated Augustinian monastery founded in 1238, with much of the original 13th-century building surviving. ✆01877 385294. ➲ On an island in the Lake of Menteith, approached by boat from Port of Menteith.
□ 79 H1

Jarlshof Prehistoric and Norse Settlement
Shetland
An very important site with a complex of ancient settlements within three acres. The oldest is a Bronze Age village of oval stone huts. There is an Iron Age broch and an entire Viking settlement. The visitor centre has new displays on Iron Age life and a history of the site. ✆01950 460112. ➲ At Sumburgh Head, about 22m S of Lerwick.
□ 113 D6

Jedburgh Abbey and Visitor Centre
Scottish Borders
One of the abbeys founded by David I and the Bishop of Glasgow in about 1138 for Augustinian canons. The church is mostly in Romanesque and early Gothic styles and is remarkably complete.
✆01835 863925. ➲ In Jedburgh.
□ 74 C2

Kildrummy Castle
Aberdeenshire
Though ruined, the best example in Scotland of a 13th-century castle, with a curtain wall, four round towers, hall and chapel. The seat of the Earls of Mar, it was dismantled after the 1715 Jacobite Rising. ✆01975 571331.
➲ 10m W of Alford.
□ 96 D4

Kinnaird Head Lighthouse
Aberdeenshire
Built in 1787 within a 16th-century tower house, Kinnaird Head was the first lighthouse built by the Northern Lighthouse Company.
✆01346 511022. ➲ On a promontory in Fraserburgh.
□ 105 K2

Linlithgow Palace
West Lothian
Magnificent ruin of a great royal palace, set in its own park. All the Stewart kings lived here, and work commissioned by James I, III, IV, V and VI can be seen. The great hall and the chapel are particularly fine. ✆01506 842896.
➲ In Linlithgow.
□ 80 F4

Lochleven Castle
Fife
Late 14th-century tower on one side of an irregular courtyard. Mary Queen of Scots was imprisoned here in 1567 and escaped in 1568. ✆01786 450000. ➲ On an island in Loch Leven, accessible by boat from Kinross.
□ 81 G1

MacLellan's Castle
Dumfries & Galloway
A castellated town house built by the then provost of Kirkcudbright from 1577, with particularly good architectural details.
✆01557 331856. ➲ In the centre of Kirkcudbright.
□ 69 H5

Maes Howe Chambered Cairn
Orkney
The finest megalithic tomb in the British Isles, with a large mound covering a stone-built passage and a large burial chamber with cells in the walls. Of Neolithic date, broken into during Viking times, with Viking runes carved on the walls. ✆01856 761606. ➲ About 9m W of Kirkwall.
□ 112 B4

Meigle Sculptured Stone Museum
Perth & Kinross
A magnificent collection of 25 sculptured monuments of the Celtic Christian period, one of the finest collections of Dark Age sculpture in Western Europe.
✆01828 640612. ➲ In Meigle.
□ 88 E4

Melrose Abbey
Scottish Borders
Probably the most famous ruin in Scotland, founded around 1136 as a Cistercian abbey by David I, and repeatedly wrecked in the Wars of Independence. The surviving remains of the church are 15th century and of an elegance unique in Scotland. The Commendator's house contains displays relating to the abbey's history and to the Roman fort at Newstead. ✆01896 822562.
➲ In Melrose.
□ 74 B1

New Abbey Corn Mill
Dumfries & Galloway
A carefully renovated water-powered oatmeal mill, in working order, and demonstrated regularly to visitors in the summer.
✆01387 850260. ➲ In New Abbey village.
□ 72 E8

Newark Castle
Inverclyde
The oldest part of the castle is a tower built soon after 1478, with a detached gatehouse. The main part was added in 1597–9 by Patrick Maxwell. ✆01475 741858. ➲ In Port Glasgow.
□ 79 F4

Rothesay Castle
Argyll & Bute
A remarkable 13th-century, circular castle of enclosure. A favourite residence of the Stewart kings. ✆01700 502691. ➲ In Rothesay, Isle of Bute.
□ 78 C5

St Andrews Castle and Visitor Centre
Fife
Ruins of the castle of the Archbishops of St Andrews, dating in part from the 13th century. Features include a 'bottle dungeon', and mine and counter-mine tunnelled during the siege that followed the murder of Cardinal Beaton in 1546. Visitor Centre with shop and major exhibition depicting the history of the castle and cathedral. ✆01334 477196.
➲ In St Andrews.
□ 89 H7

St Andrews Cathedral
Fife
Remains of the largest cathedral in Scotland, and of the priory's domestic ranges. The precinct walls are particularly well-preserved.
✆01334 472563. ➲ In St Andrews.
□ 89 H7

Seton Collegiate Church
East Lothian
The chancel and apse of this lovely building date from the 15th century, and the transepts and steeple were built by the widow of Lord Seton, who was killed at Flodden in 1513.
✆01875 813334. ➲ 1m SE of Cockenzie off Edinburgh–North Berwick Road.
□ 82 C4

Skara Brae Prehistoric Village
Orkney
The best-preserved group of Stone Age houses in Western Europe. The houses contain hearths, stone furniture and drains, and give a remarkable picture of life in Neolithic times. ✆01856 841815.
➲ 19m NW of Kirkwall.
□ 112 B4

Smailholm Tower
Scottish Borders
A simple rectangular tower in a good state of preservation. It houses costume figures and tapestries relating to Sir Walter Scott's 'Minstrelsy of the Scottish Borders'.
✆01573 460365. ➲ Near Smailholm village, 6m NW of Kelso.
□ 74 C1

Spynie Palace
Moray
Residence of the Bishops of Moray from the 14th century to 1686. The site is dominated by the massive tower built by Bishop David Stewart (1461–77). ✆01343 546358.
➲ 2m N of Elgin, off the A941.
□ 104 B2

Stirling Castle
Stirling
The grandest of all Scottish castles. The Great Hall and the Gatehouse of James IV, the marvellous Palace of James V, the Chapel Royal remodelled by James VI, and the artillery fortifications of the 16th and 18th centuries, are all of outstanding interest. Medieval kitchens and introductory display now open. ✆01786 450000. ➲ In Stirling.
□ 80 C2

Sweetheart Abbey
Dumfries & Galloway
Splendid ruin of a late 13th- and early 14th-century Cistercian abbey founded by Dervorgilla, Lady of Galloway. ✆01387 850397. ➲ In New Abbey village, 7m S of Dumfries.
□ 72 E8

Tantallon Castle
East Lothian
Remarkable fortification with earthwork defences, and a massive 14th-century curtain wall with towers. Interpretive displays include replica guns. ✆01620 892727. ➲ 3m E of North Berwick.
□ 82 D3

Threave Castle
Dumfries & Galloway
Massive tower built in the late 14th century. Round its base is an artillery fortification built before 1455, when the castle was besieged by James II. It is on an island, approached by boat, followed by a long walk. ✆0831 168512.
➲ 3m W of Castle Douglas.
□ 69 J4

Tolquhon Castle
Aberdeenshire
Built for the Forbes family, Tolquhon has an early 15th-century tower. It is noted for its highly ornamented gatehouse. ✆01651 851286. ➲ 15m from Aberdeen off the Pitmedden–Tarves Road.
□ 97 H3

Urquhart Castle
Highland
Standing above Loch Ness, this was one of the largest castles in Scotland, having fallen into decay after 1689. Most of the existing buildings date from after the 16th century.
✆01456 450551. ➲ On Loch Ness, near Drumnadrochit.
□ 94 D3

Whithorn Priory and Museum
Dumfries & Galloway
Site of the first Christian church in Scotland, founded as 'Candida Casa' by St Ninian in the early 5th century. The priory was built over the church for remonstratensian canons in the 12th century and became the cathedral church of Galloway. In the museum is a fine collection of early Christian stones.
✆01988 500508. ➲ In Whithorn.
□ 68 F6

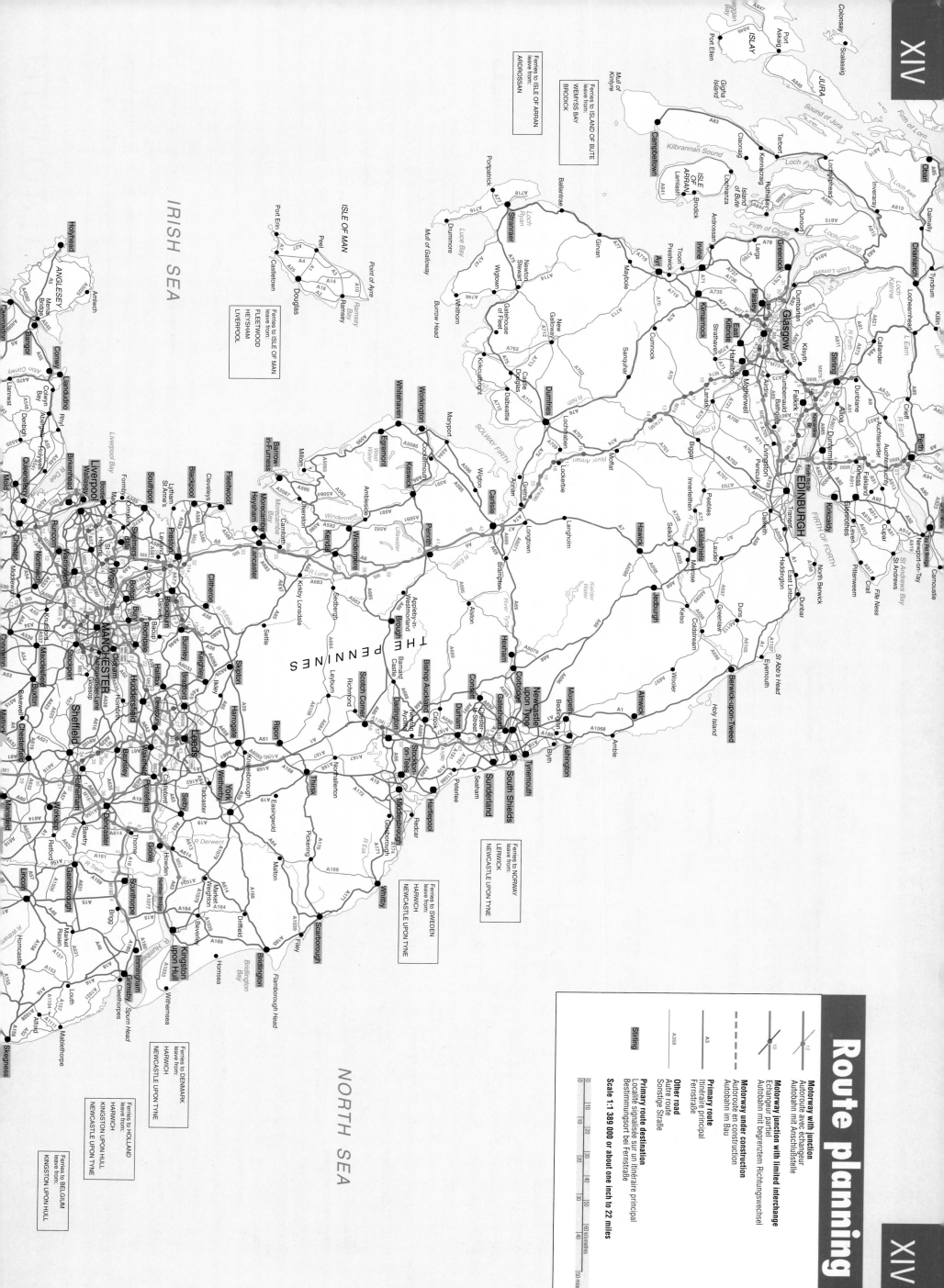

Route planning

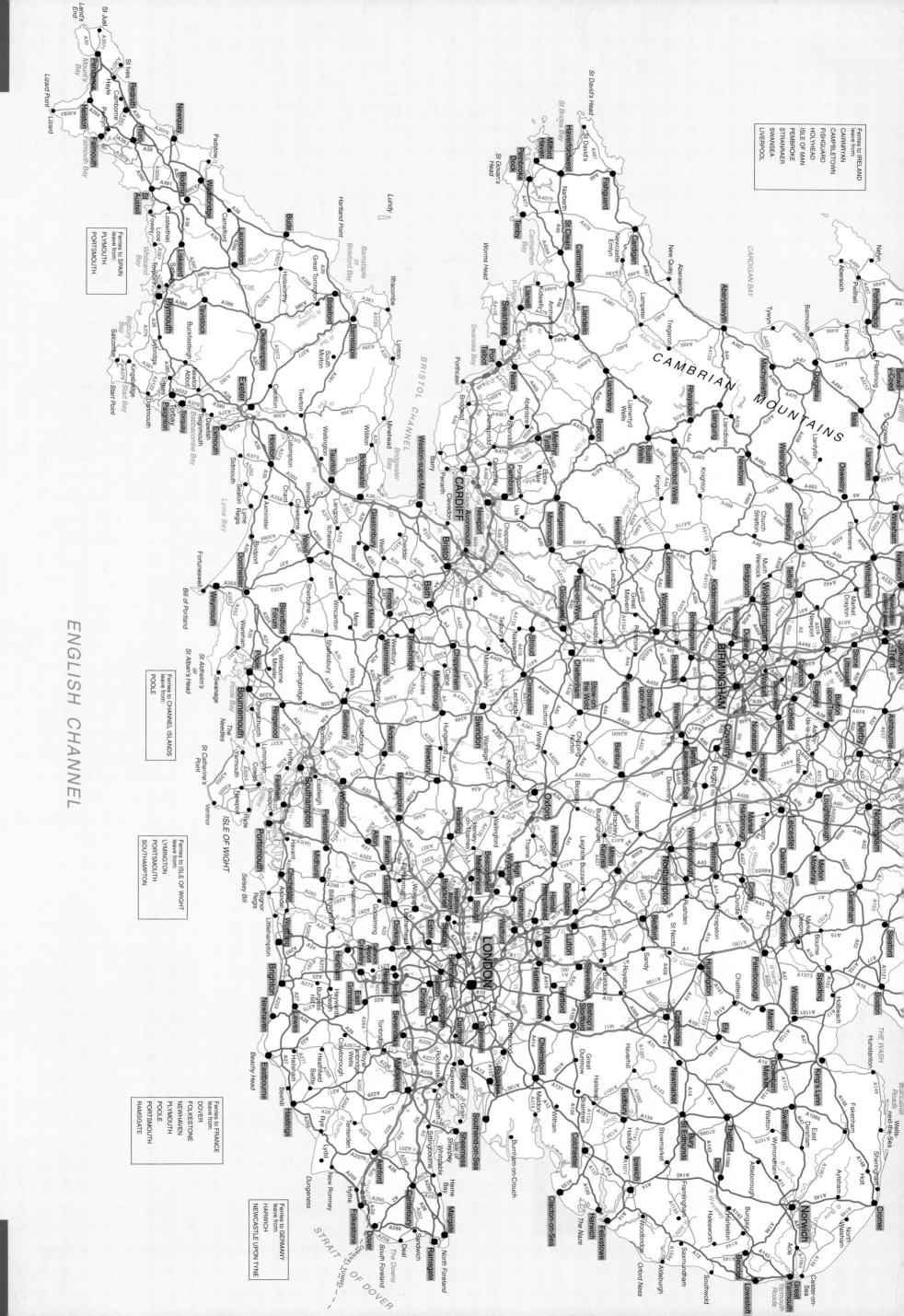

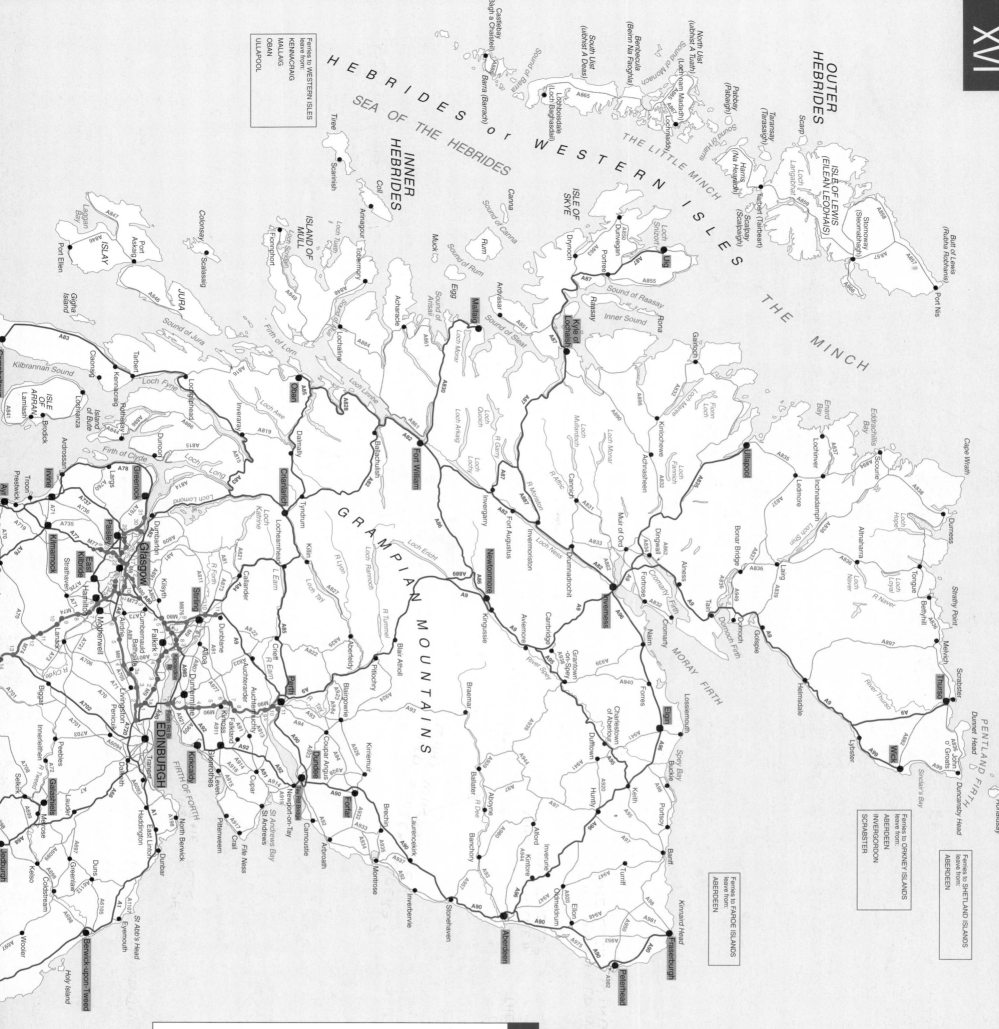

NORTH SEA

Primary routes

These form a national network of recommended through routes which complement the motorway system.

Selected places of major traffic importance are known as Primary Route Destinations and are shown on this map, thus **Stirling**. Distances and directions to such destinations are repeated on traffic signs which, on primary routes, have a green background or, on motorways, have a blue background.

To continue on a primary route through or past a place which has appeared as a destination on previous signs, follow the directions to the next primary destination shown on the green-backed signs.

Signs on Primary Routes

A 38
Tamworth
(A 4091)

Sutton C'field

At the junction

Ring road

R Route confirmatory sign after junction

A 46

On approaches to junctions

Birmingham
M 10 (M 1)

Watford
A 405

St Albans
A 5

Radlett A 5

On approaches to junctions (The blue panel indicates that the motorway commences from the junction ahead. The motorway shown in brackets can also be reached by proceeding in that direction)

→ Scarborough A 64
← Pickering A 169
↓ York A 64

A 46
Lincoln 12
Newark 28
(Nottingham 48)
Leicester 63

Route confirmatory sign after junction

Ferries to WESTERN ISLES leave from:
KENNACRAIG
MALLAIG
OBAN
ULLAPOOL

Ferries to ORKNEY ISLANDS leave from:
ABERDEEN
INVERGORDON
SCRABSTER

Ferries to SHETLAND ISLANDS leave from:
ABERDEEN

Ferries to FAROE ISLANDS leave from:
ABERDEEN

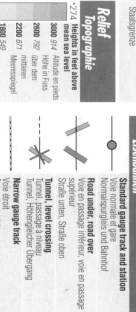

Legend to main mapping

Straßen

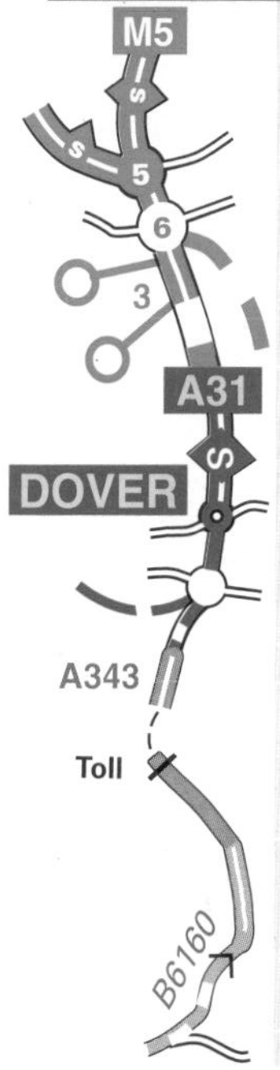
M5
A31
DOVER
A343
Toll
B6160

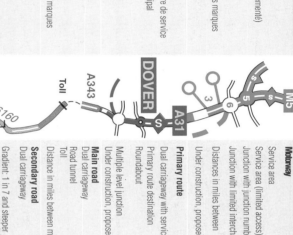

Autobahn
Servicestation
Servicestation (mit begrenztem Zugang)
Anschlußstelle mit Nummer
Teilanschlußstelle
Entfernung in Meilen
Im Bau, Geplant

Fernverkehrsstraße
Zweibahnige Straße mit Servicestation
Bestimmungsort bei Fernverkehrsstraße
Kreisverkehr
Anschlußstelle
Im Bau, Geplant

Hauptstraße
Zweibahnige Straße
Straßentunnel
Straßenbenutzungsgebühr
Entfernung in Meilen

Nebenstraße
Zweibahnige Straße
Steigungen: 14% und mehr
Enge Straße mit Ausweichstelle
Sonstige Straße

Routes

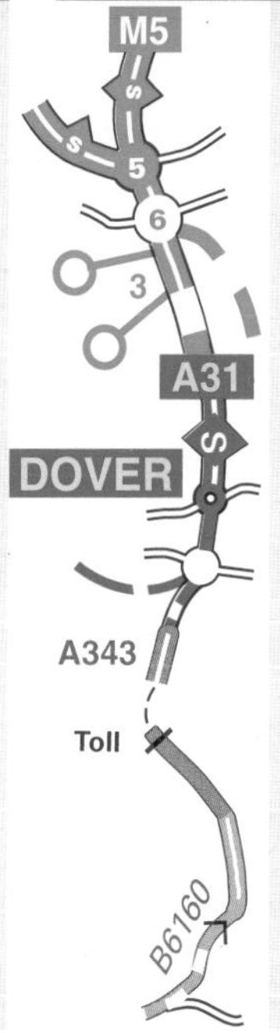
M5
A31
DOVER
A343
Toll
B6160

Autoroute
Aire de service
Aire de service (accès réglementé)
Echangeur numéroté
Echangeur partiel
Distances en miles entre les marques
En construction, en projet

Itinéraire principal
Chaussée séparées avec aire de service
Destination d'itinéraire principal
Rond-point
Giratoire ou échangeur
En construction, en projet

Route principale
Chaussée séparées
Tunnel routier
Péage
Distance en miles entre les marques

Route secondaire
Chaussée séparées
Pente: de14% et plus
Route étroite aires voies de dépassement et de croisement
Autre route

Roads

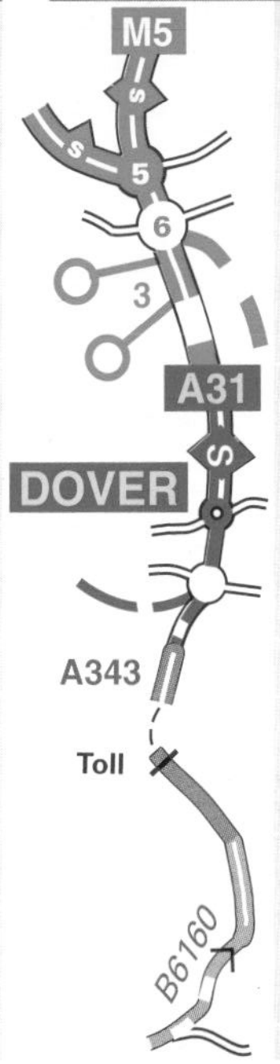
M5
A31
DOVER
A343
Toll
B6160

Motorway
Service area
Service area (limited access)
Junction with junction number
Junction with limited interchange
Distances in miles between
Under construction, proposed

Primary route
Dual carriageway with service area
Primary route destination
Roundabout
Multiple level junction
Under construction, proposed

Main road
Dual carriageway
Road tunnel
Toll
Distance in miles between markers

Secondary road
Dual carriageway
Gradient: 1 in 7 and steeper
Narrow road with passing places
Minor road

Tourist Information   Renseignements Touristiques   Touristeninformation

Abbey, Cathedral, Priory
Abbaye, Cathédrale, Prieuré
Abtei, Kathedrale, Priorei

Aquarium
Aquarium
Aquarium

Camp site
Terrain de camping
Campingplatz

Caravan site
Terrain pour caravanes
Wohnwagenplatz

Castle
Château
Schloß, Burg

Cave
Caverne
Höhle

Country park
Parc naturel
Landschaftspark

Craft centre
Centre artisanal
Zentrum für Kunsthandwerk

Garden
Jardin
Garten

Golf course or links
Terrain de golf
Golfplatz

Historic house
Manoir, Palais
Historisches Gebäude

Information centre
Office de tourisme
Informationsbüro

Information centre
Office de tourisme, ouvert en saison
Informationsbüro, saisonal

Motor racing
Courses automobiles
Autorennen

Museum
Musée
Museum

Nature reserve
Réserve naturelle
Naturschutzgebiet

Other tourist feature
Autre site intéressant
Sonstige Sehenswurdigkeit

Picnic site
Emplacement de pique-nique
Picknickplatz

Preserved railway
Chemin de fer touristique
Museumseisenbahn

Racecourse
Hippodrome
Pferderennbahn

Skiing
Piste de ski
Skilaufen

Viewpoint
Point de vue
Aussichtspunkt

Wildlife park
Parc animalier
Wildpark

Zoo
Zoo
Tiergarten

Wolds Way **National trail-Long Distance Route**
Sentier de randonnée national
Itinéraire de grande randonnée
Nationaler Wanderweg-Fernverkehrsstraße

National Park, New Forest and Broads (England and Wales)
Forest Parks (Scotland)
Parc National, New Forest et Broads (Angleterre et Galles)
Parc Forestier (Ecosse)
Nationalpark, New Forest und Broads (England und Wales)
Waldparks (Schottland)

Antiquities   Antiquités   Altertümer

Ancient monument open to the public
Monument historique ouvert au public
Kulturdenkmal, der Öfentlichkeit zugängig

Native fortress
Forteresse pré-romaine
Einheimische Festung

Castle **Other antiquities**
Autres antiquités
Sonstige Altertümer

ROMAN CAMP **Roman antiquity**
Antiquité romaine
Altertümer ans Römischer Zeit

Roman road (course of)
Route romaine (course de)
Römerstraße (Verlauf)

1066 **Site of battle (with date)**
Champ de bataille historique (avec date)
Schlachtfeld (mit Datum)

Boundaries   Limites   Grenzen

National
Limite d'Etat
Staatsgrenze

Water features   Aspects Hydrologiques   Gewässer

Ferry routes for vehicles (Boat / Hovercraft / Catamaran). Times are approximate
Bac pour véhicules (par bateau / par aéroglisseur / catamaran). Les horaires sont approximatifs
Kurzer Fähreweg für Fahrzeuge (Schiff / Luftkissenfahrzeug / Katamaran). Die Zieten sind Richtwerte

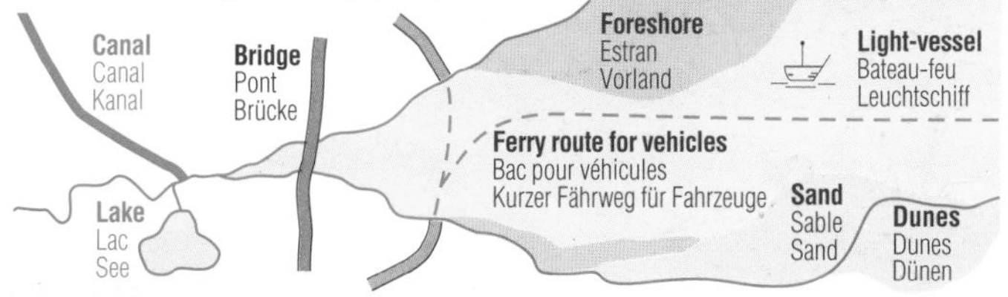
Canal
Canal
Kanal
Bridge
Pont
Brücke
Lake
Lac
See
Foreshore
Estran
Vorland
Light-vessel
Bateau-feu
Leuchtschiff
Ferry route for vehicles
Bac pour véhicules
Kurzer Fährweg für Fahrzeuge
Sand
Sable
Sand
Dunes
Dunes
Dünen

Relief   Topographie

·274 **Heights in feet above mean sea level**
Altitude en pieds
Höhe in Fuss über dem mittleren Meeresspiegel

3000 *914*
2600 *792*
2200 *671*
1800 *549*
1400 *427*
1000 *305*
0 feet / pieds / fuß
0 metres / mètres / meter

General Features   Aspects généraux   Allgemeine Merkmale

Airfield with / without customs facilities
Aérodrome avec / sans poste de douane
Flugplatz mit / ohne Zollabfertigung

Buildings
Bâtiments
Gebäude

Heliport
Héliport
Hubschrauber - Landeplatz

Lighthouse in use / disused
Phare en usage / désaffecté
Leuchtturm in Betrieb / außer Betrieb

Motoring organisation telephone
Téléphone d'associations automobiles
Automobilklub - Telefon

Public telephone
Téléphone public
Öffentliches Telefon

Radio or TV mast
Pylône de radio / TV
Radio oder Fernseh - Antennemast

Windgenerator
Eolienne
Windkraftgenerator

Windmill
Moulin à vent
Windmühle

Wood
Bois
Wald

Youth hostel
Auberge de jeunesse
Jugendherberge

Railways   Chemins de Fer   Eisenbahnen

Standard gauge track and station
Voie normale et gare
Normalspurgleis und Bahnhof

Road under, road over
Voie en passage inférieur, voie en passage supérieur
Straße unten, Straße oben

Tunnel, level crossing
Tunnel, passage à niveau
Tunnel, Höhengleicher Übergang

Narrow gauge track
Voie étroit
Schmalspurgleis

Scale 1:136 898 or about 2 miles to 1 inch

0 Kilometres	2.5	5	7.5
0 Miles 1	2	3	4	5

Restricted motorway junctions

M1	Southbound	Northbound
46	No access	
45	No exit	No access
44	No access	No exit
35A	No exit	No access
34 (North)	No access	No exit
34 (South)	No exit	No access
23A	No exit to A453	No access from A453
21A	No exit	No access
19	No access from A14	No exit to A14
17	No exit	No access
7	No access	No exit
6A	No access from M25	No exit to M25
4	No access	No exit
2	No access	No exit

M2	Eastbound	Westbound
1	No access from A2 westbound	No exit to A2 eastbound

M3	Eastbound	Westbound
8	No exit; access from A303 only	Exit to A303 only; no access
10	No access	No exit
14	No exit	No access

M4	Eastbound	Westbound
46	No exit	No access
39	No access; no exit	No exit
38		No access
29	No exit	No access from A48(M)
25a	No exit	No access
23	No access; exit to M48 eastbound	No exit: access from M48 westbound
21	No exit; access from M48 eastbound	No access; exit to M48 westbound
2	No exit or access from A4 westbound	No exit or access from A4 eastbound
1	No exit to A4 westbound	No access from A4 eastbound

M5	Southbound	Northbound
10	No access	No exit
11A	No exit to A417 westbound	No access from A417 eastbound
12	No exit	No access
L	No access	No exit
18	No exit	No access
18a	No access	
L	No access	
29	No exit	No access

M6	Southbound	Northbound
30	No access	No exit
25	No exit	No access
24	No access	No exit
20		No exit
31A	No exit	No access
10A	No exit	No access
5	No exit	No access
4A	No access; exit to M42 only	No exit; access from M42 southbound only

M11	Southbound	Northbound
14	No access from A1307 or A45 eastbound	No exit to A1307 or A45 westbound
13	No exit	No access
9	No exit	No access
5	No exit	No access
4	No exit to A1400	No access from A1400

M20	Eastbound	Westbound
2 (North)	No access	
2 (South)		No exit
3	No exit	
11A	No access	No exit

M23	Southbound	Northbound
7	No access from A23 northbound	No exit to A23 southbound

M25	Clockwise	Anticlockwise
5	No exit to A21 from M26 and no access to M26 from M25	No access to M26 from A21
9 (Central)		No access; no exit
9 (North)	No access; no exit	
19	No access	No exit
21	No exit to M1 southbound; no access from M1 northbound	No exit to M1 southbound; no access from M1 northbound

M27	Eastbound	Westbound
4 (West)	No access	No exit
4 (East)	No exit	No access
10	No exit	No access
12	No access	No exit

M40	Eastbound	Westbound
16	No access	No exit
14	No access	No exit
13	No exit	No access
8	No access	No exit
L	No exit	No access
7	No exit	No access
3	No exit	No access

M42	Southbound	Northbound
1	No access	No exit
7	Access from M6 only; no exit	Exit to M6 West only; exit to and access from unclassified road only
7A	Exit to and access from unclassified road only	Exit to M6 East only; exit to and access from unclassified road only
8	Exit to M6 only; no access	Access to M6 only; no exit

M45	Eastbound	Westbound
L	No access	No exit

M48	Eastbound	Westbound
29A	No access from A48 westbound	No exit to A48 eastbound

M53	Southbound	Northbound
11	No access	No exit

M56	Eastbound	Westbound
15	No exit	No access
9		No access to M6 southbound
8	No access; no exit	No exit
7		No access
4	No exit	No access
2	No exit	No access

M57	Southbound	Northbound
3	No access	No exit
5	No access	No exit

M58	Eastbound	Westbound
1	No exit	No access

M61	Southbound	Northbound
9	No exit	No access
3		No access
2		No access from A580 eastbound

M62	Eastbound	Westbound
14	No exit to A580; no access from A580 westbound	No exit to A580 eastbound; no access from A580
15	No exit	No access
23	No access	No exit

M63	Southbound	Northbound
7	No exit	
9	No exit to A5103 northbound; no access from A5103 northbound	
10	No exit to M56 or to A34 northbound	No exit to A34 northbound; no access from M56
11	No access	No exit
13	No exit	No access
14	No exit	No exit; no access
15	No access	

M65	Eastbound	Westbound
9	No access	No exit
11	No exit	No access

M66	Southbound	Northbound
L	access from A56 southbound only	Exit to A56 northbound only
1	No exit	No access
12	No access	

M67	Eastbound	Westbound
1	No access	No exit
2	No exit	No access

M69	Southbound	Northbound
2	No access	No exit

M180	Eastbound	Westbound
1	No access	No exit

M606	Northbound
L	No access

M621	Eastbound	Westbound
L	No exit	No access

A1(M)	Southbound	Northbound
57	No exit to A66(M)	No access from A66(M)
L	No access	No exit
5	No exit; no access	No exit
3	No access	
2	No exit	

A3(M)	Southbound	Northbound
L	Junction with unclassified road, no exit	Junction with unclassified road, no access

A38(M)	Southbound	Northbound
L	No access	No exit

A40(M)	Southbound	Northbound
L	No access	No exit

A48(M)	Eastbound	Westbound
29A	No exit	No access

A102(M)	Northbound	Southbound
L	No exit	No access

M8	Eastbound	Westbound
28A	No exit	No access
28	No exit	No access
25	No access from A739 northbound	No access from A739 northbound
23	No exit	No access
22	No exit	No access
21	No access	No exit
20	No exit	No access
18		No access
16	No exit	No access
14	No access	No exit
9	No access	No exit
8		No access from A8 eastbound, A89 eastbound or M73 southbound

M9	Eastbound	Westbound
8	No exit	No access from M876 northbound
6	No access	No exit
3	No exit	No access
2	No access	No exit
1A	No exit	No access

M73	Southbound	Northbound
3	No access from A80 northbound	No exit to A80 southbound
2	No access from A89; no exit to M8 (Junction 8) or A89	No exit to A89; no access from M8 (Junction 8) or A89

M74	Southbound	Northbound
2	No access	
3	No exit	No access
7	No access	No exit
9	No access	No exit; no access
10	No exit	
11	No access from B7078	No exit to B7078
12	No exit	No access from A70

M77	Southbound	Northbound
4	No access	No exit
L	No exit to A77 northbound	No access from A77 southbound

M80	Southbound	Northbound
L	No exit	No access
5	No exit	No access

M90	Southbound	Northbound
10	No exit to A912	No access from A912
8	No exit	No access
7	No access	No exit

M876	Eastbound	Westbound
2	No access	No exit

A1(M)	Southbound	Northbound
65	No exit to A1	No access from A1
57	No exit to A66(M)	No access from A66(M)

A74(M)	Southbound	Northbound
14 (North)	No access	No access; no exit
14 (South)	No access; no exit	
16	No exit	No access
18	No exit	No access
L	No access	No exit
L		No access
L	No exit	No access

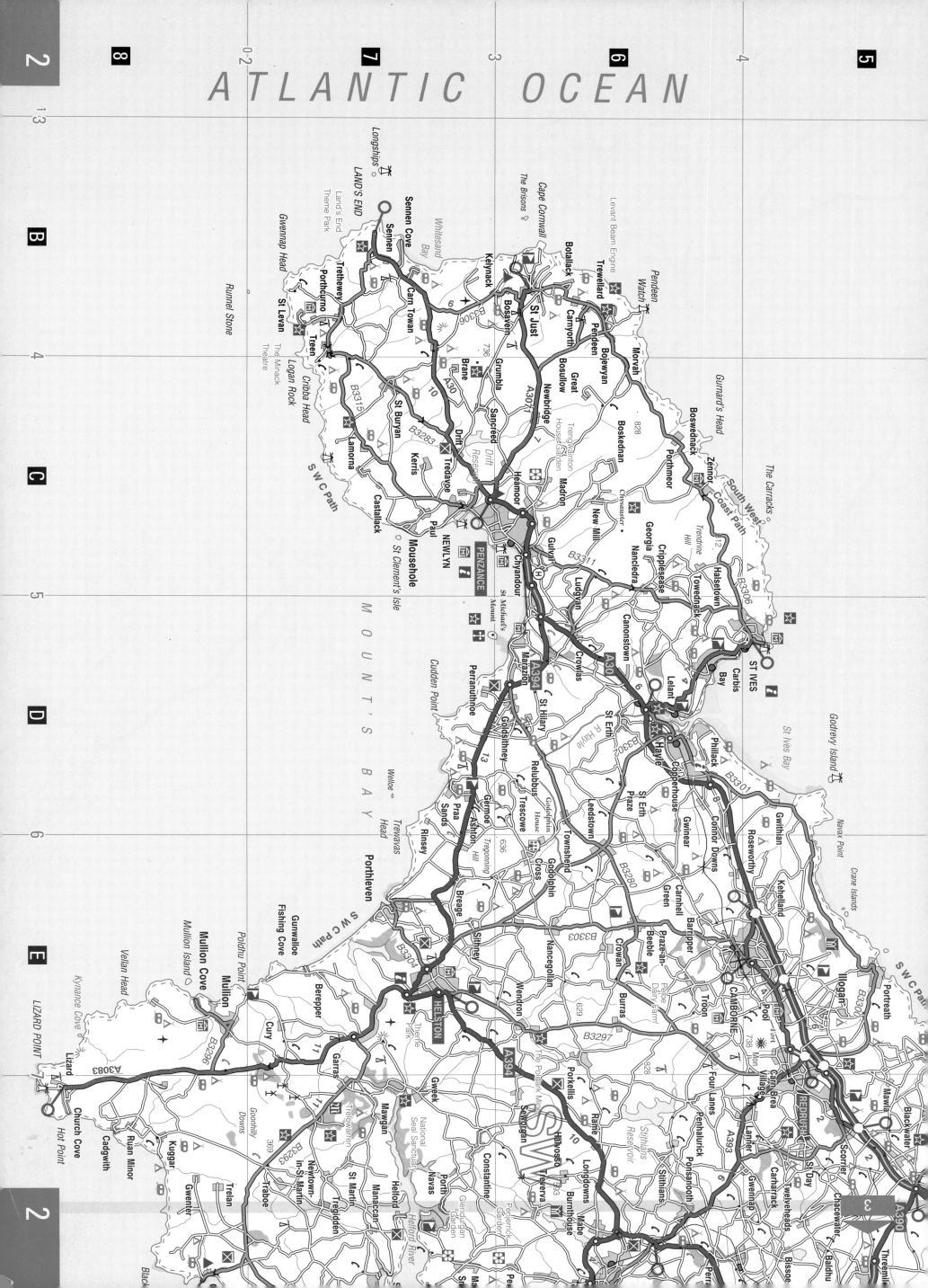

ENGLISH CHANNEL

Eddystone Rocks

Head

Great New
Stone
Bay

South West
Coast Path

364

NOSS MAYO

PLYMOUTH to
Roscoff   6-8 hrs
Santander   24 hrs
(summer only)

4 B C D E F 4

5 4 6 3 7 0·2 8

21

2 3 4 5

3

5

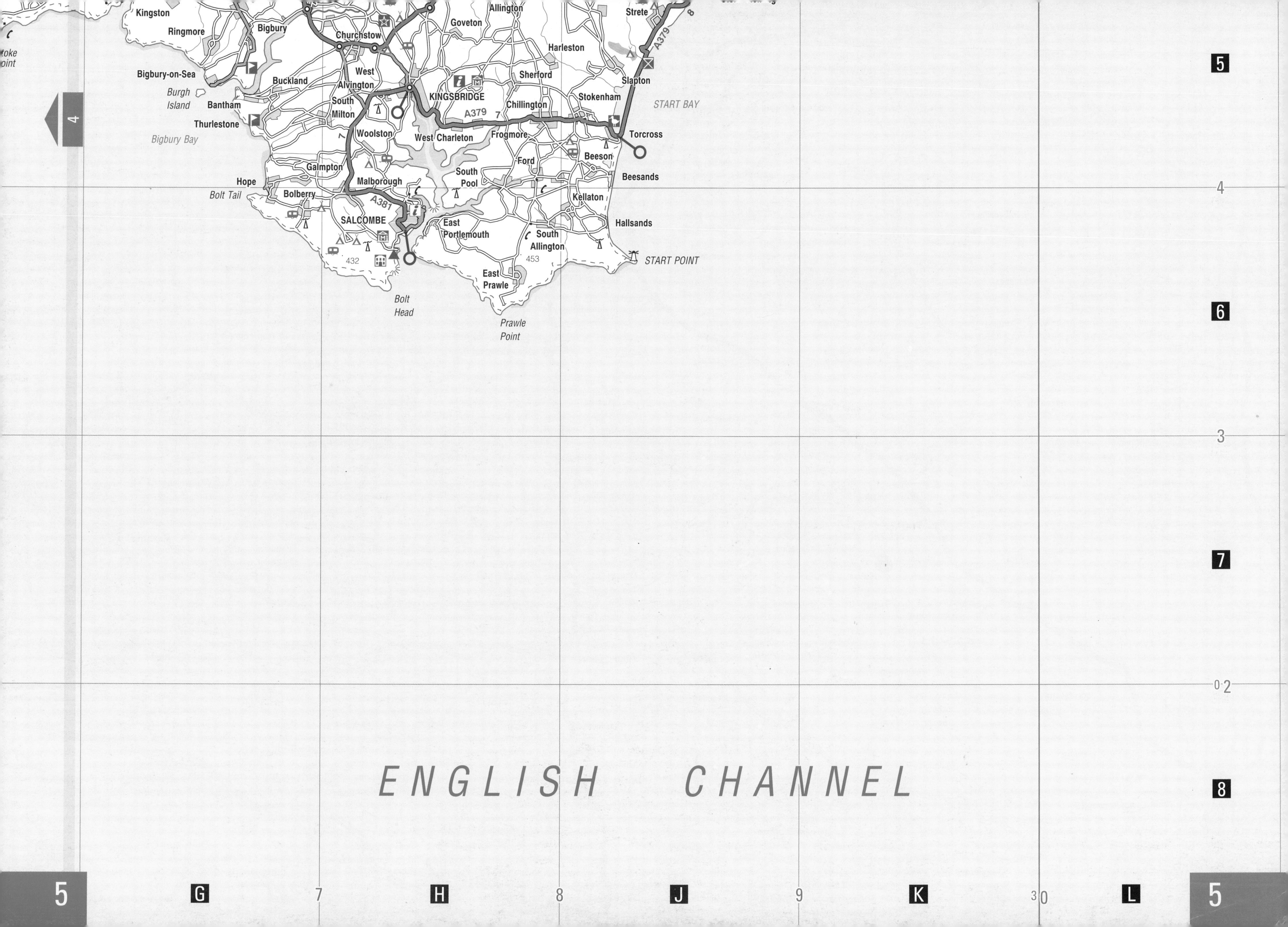

4

Kingston

Bigbury-on-Sea
Ringmore
Bigbury Bay
Burgh Island
Bantham
Thurlestone
Bigbury

Bolt Tail
Hope
Bolberry
Galmpton
Buckland
South Milton
West Alvington
Churchstow

432
SALCOMBE
A381
Malborough
Woolston
West

Bolt Head

KINGSBRIDGE
A379

East Portlemouth
West Charleton
South Pool
Prawle Point
East Prawle
Frogmore
Chillington
Sherford
Goveton
Allington

South Allington
453
Ford
Kellaton
Beeson
Stokenham
Harleston

Hallsands
Beesands
Slapton
START BAY
Strete
A379

START POINT
Torcross

E N G L I S H   C H A N N E L

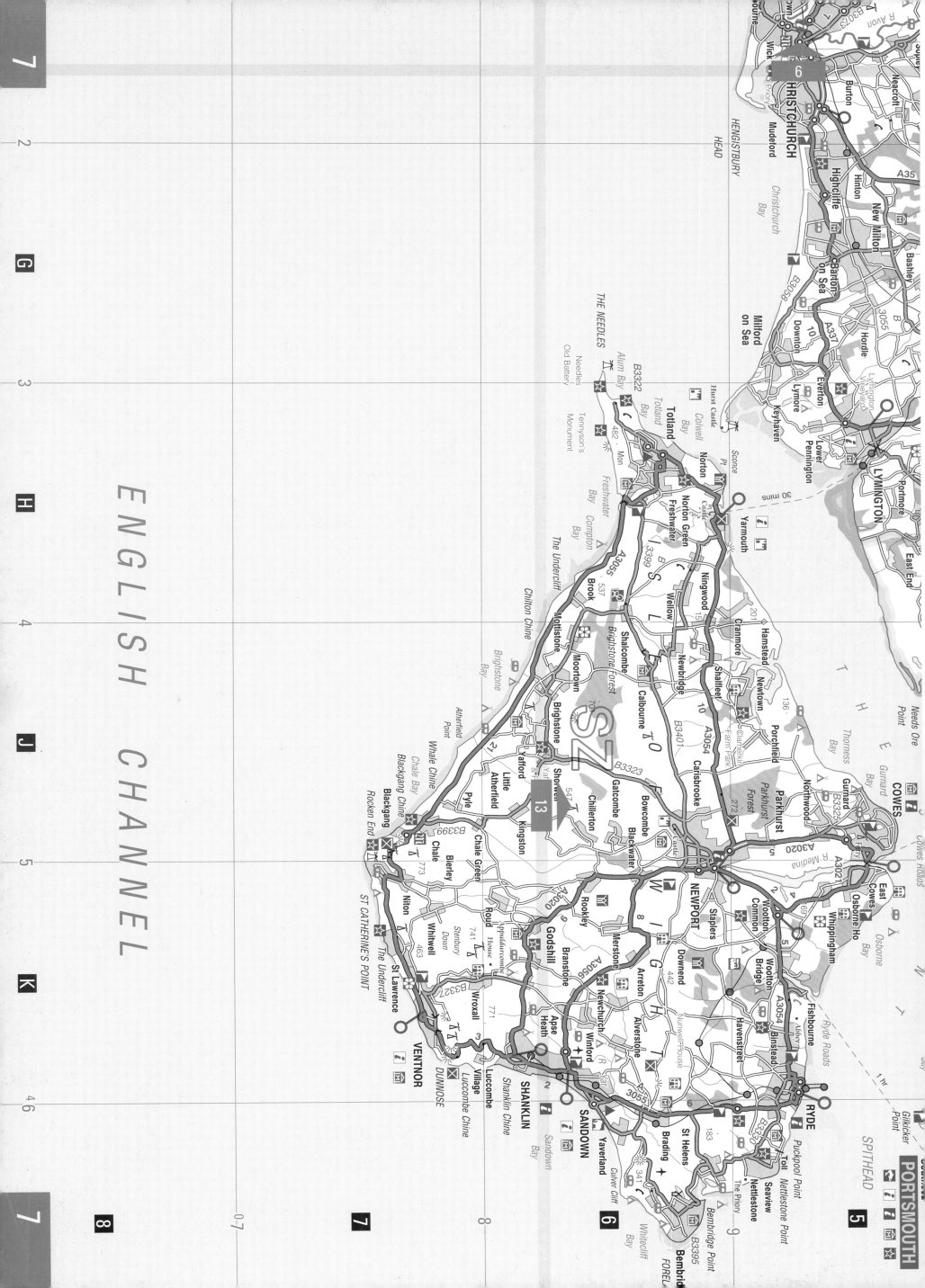

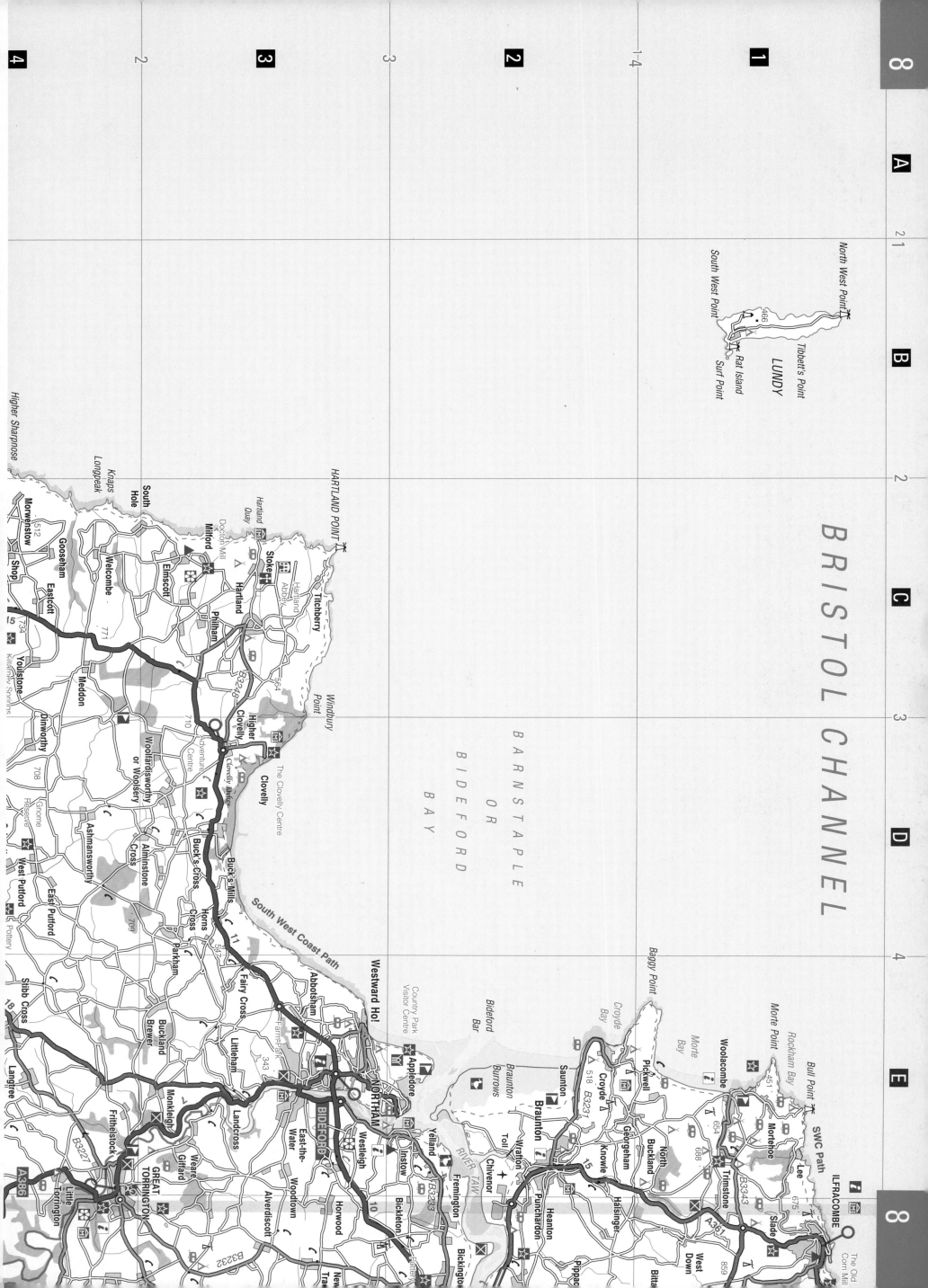

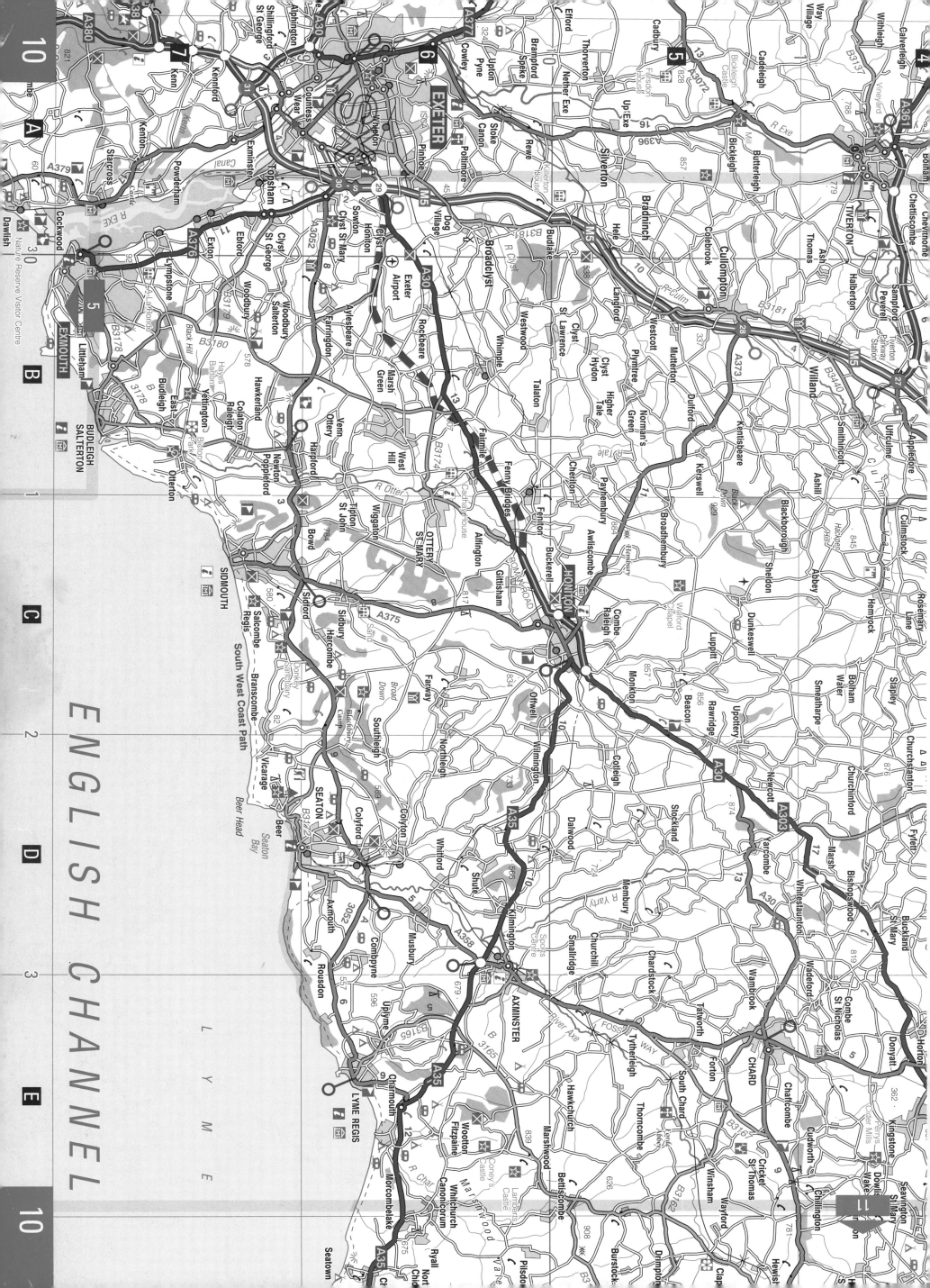

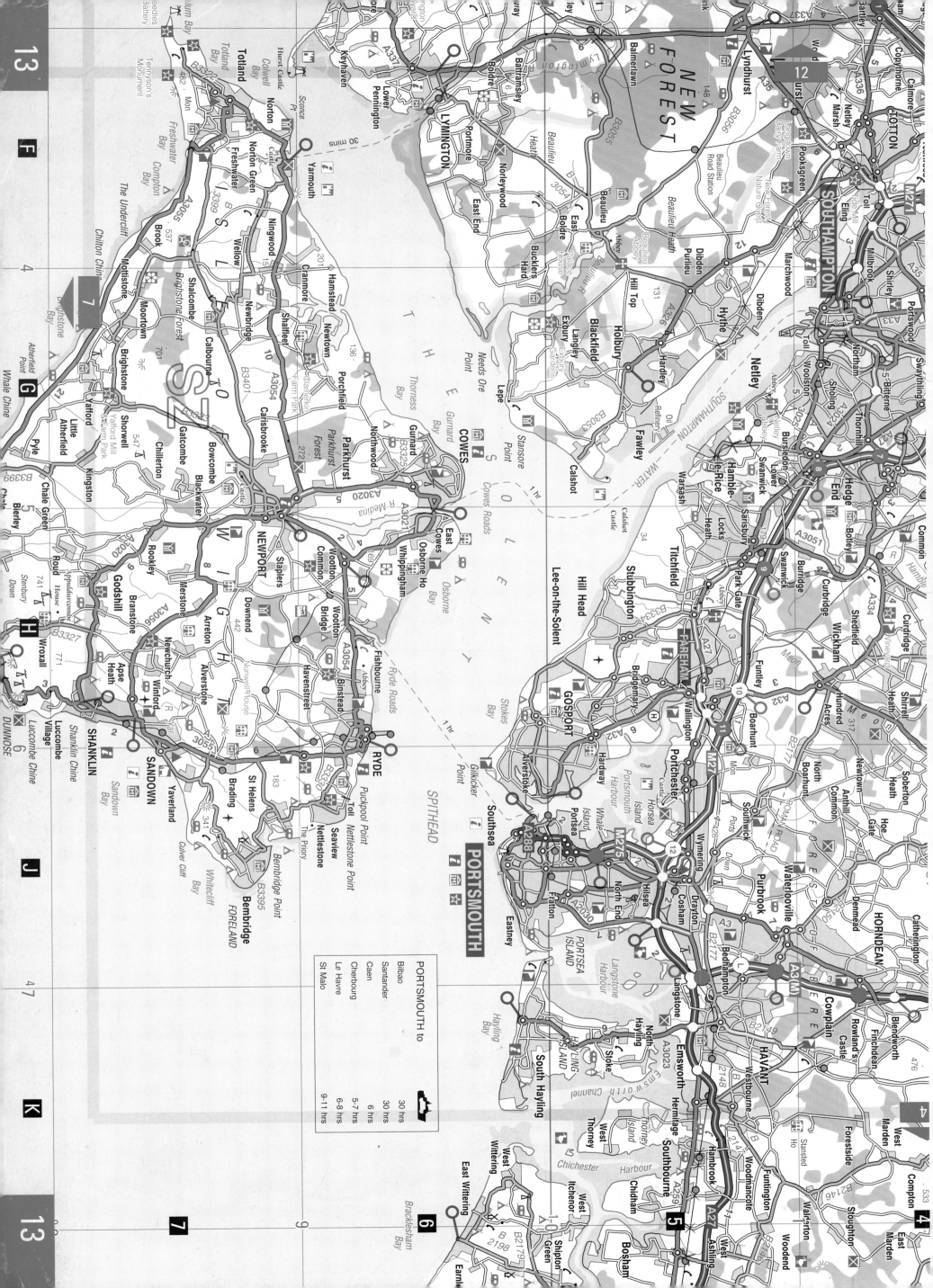

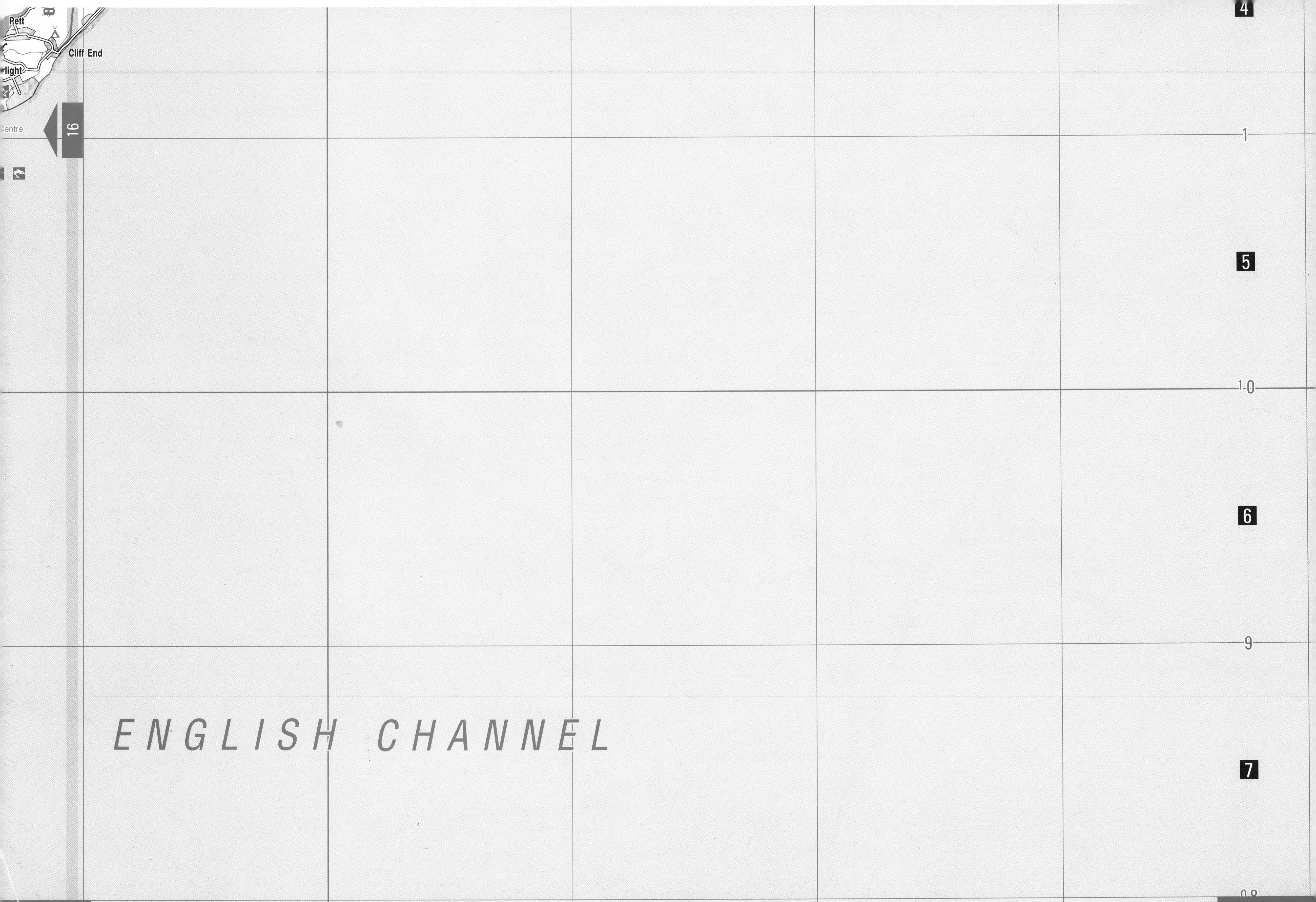
Pett
Cliff End
16
ENGLISH CHANNEL
G
H
J
K
L
4
5
6
7

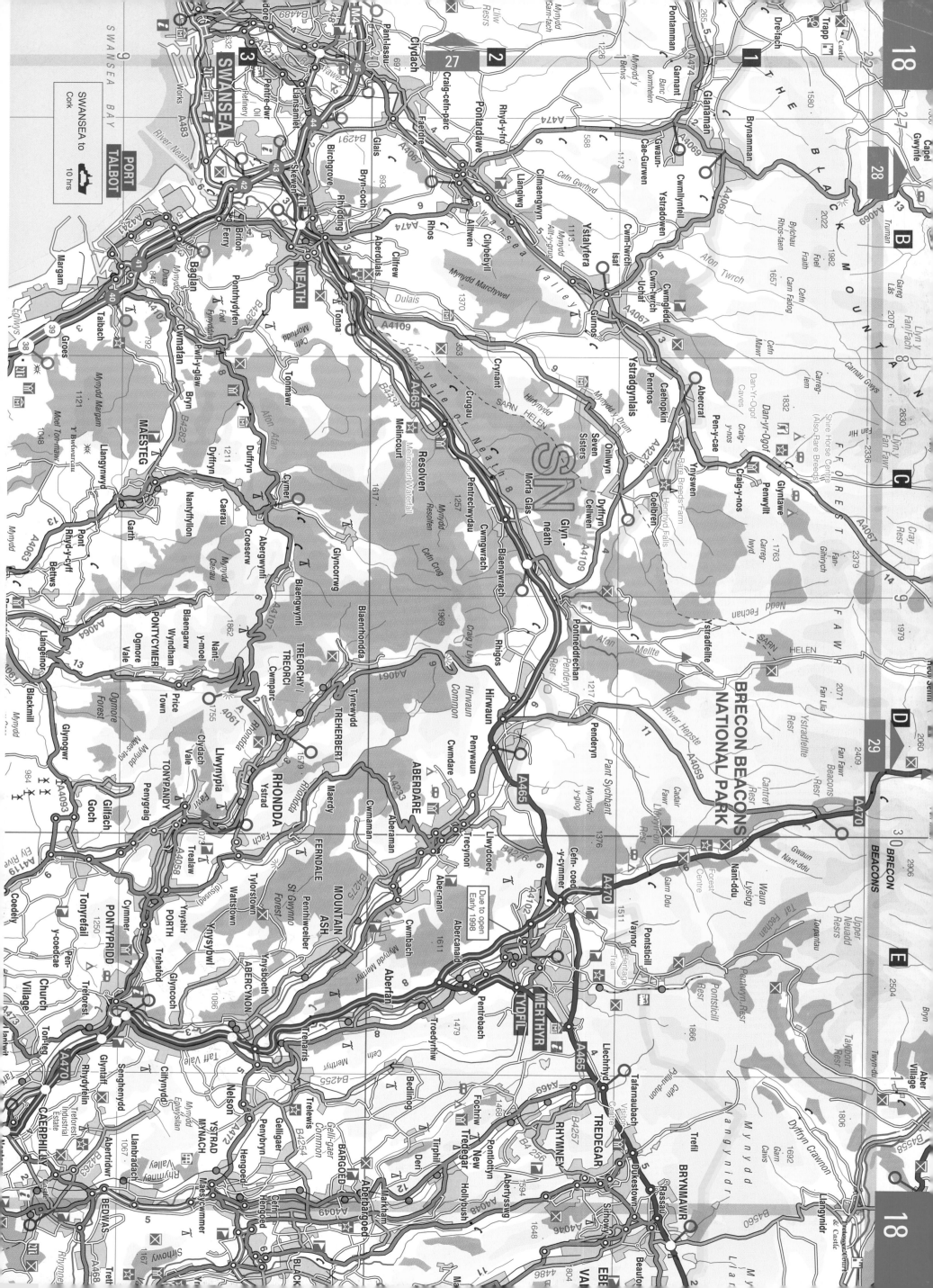

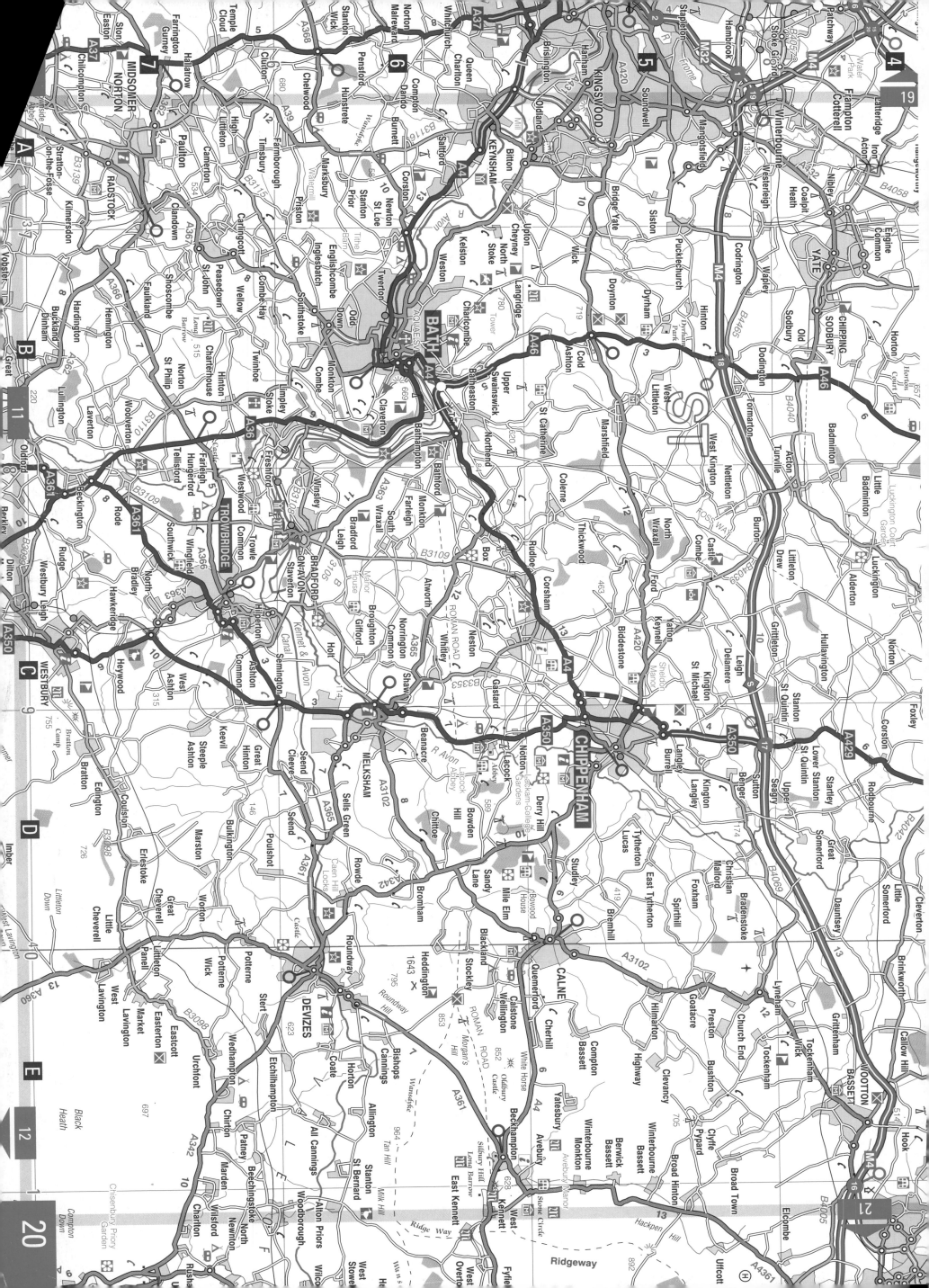

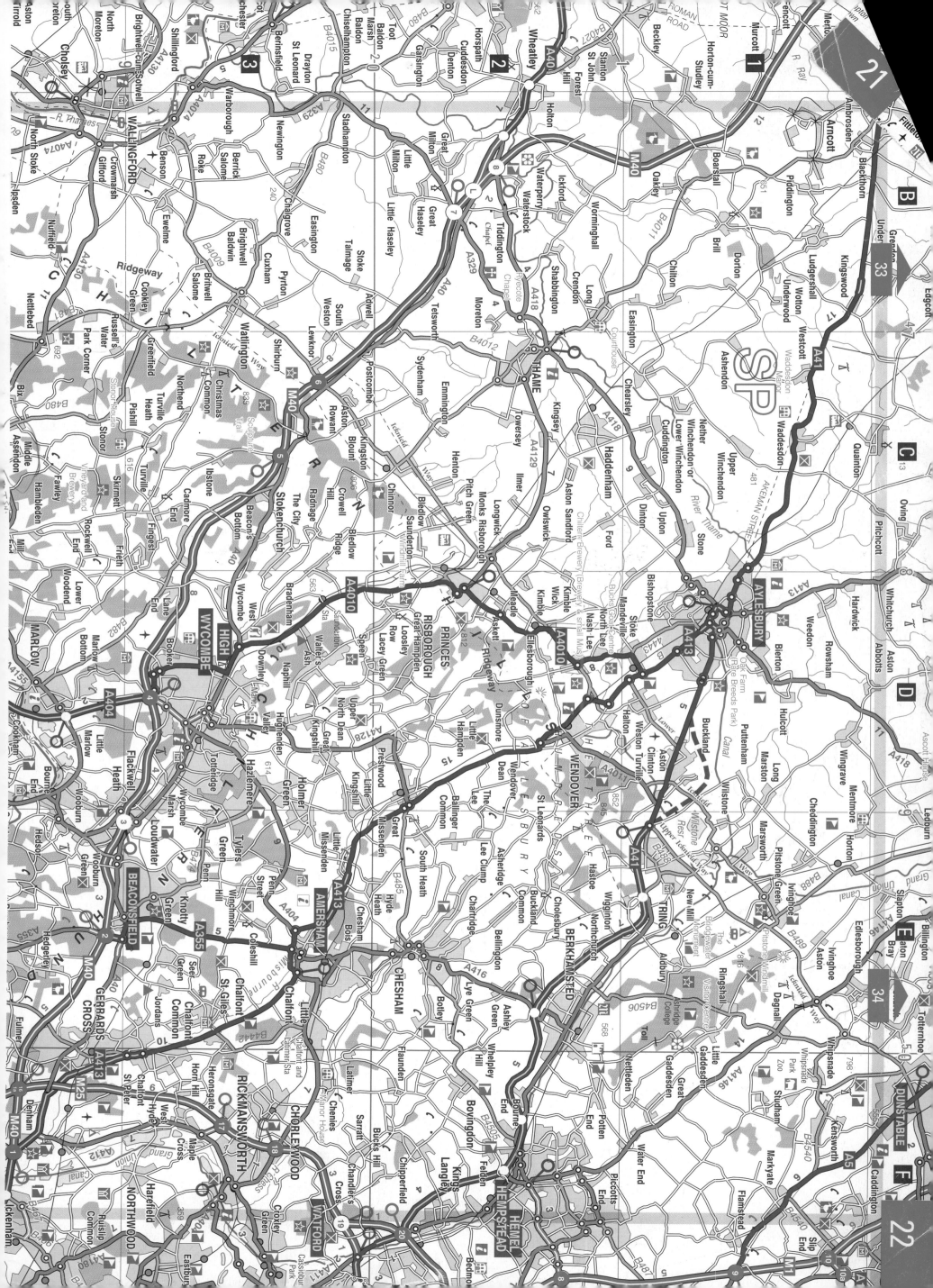

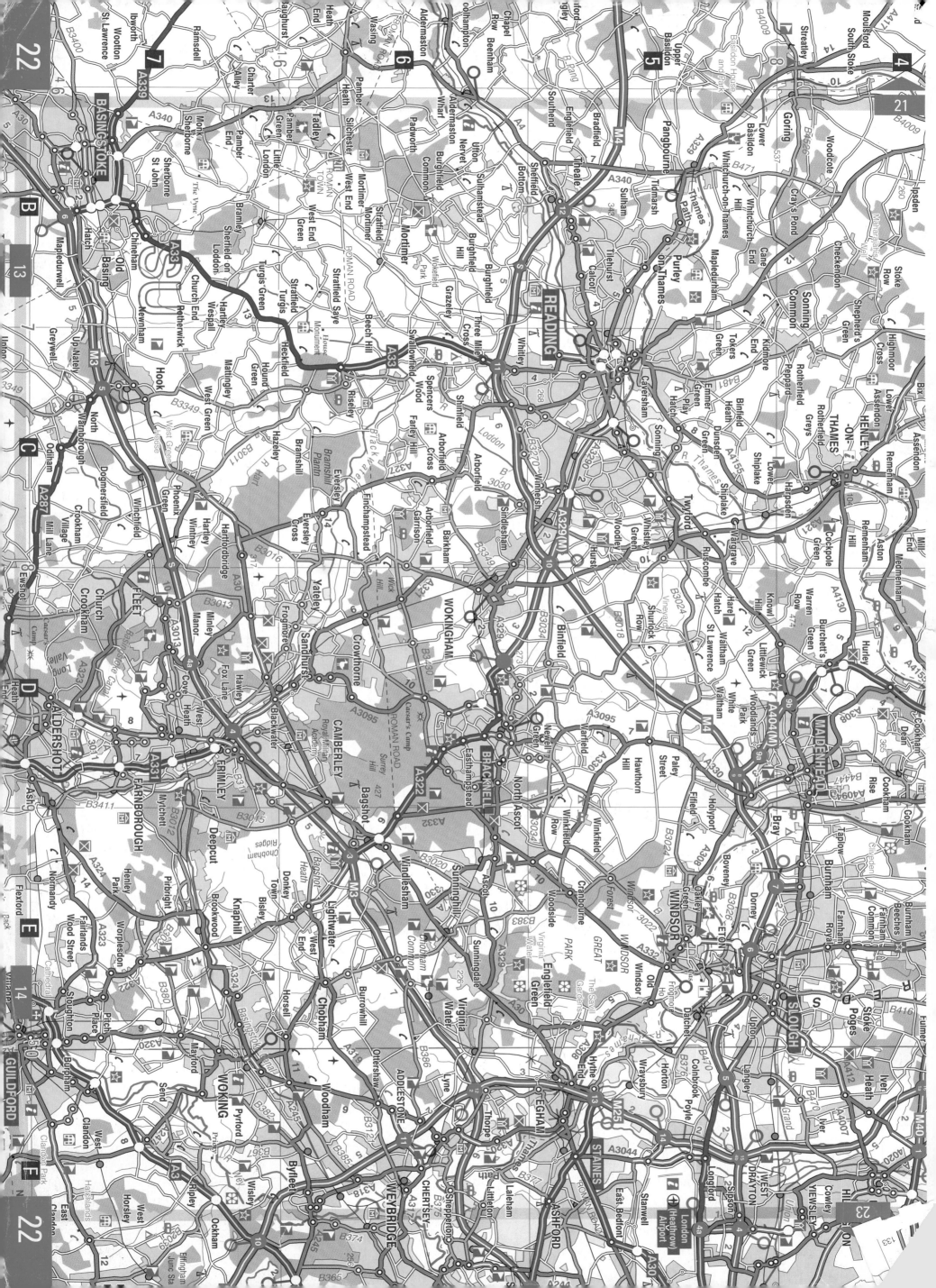

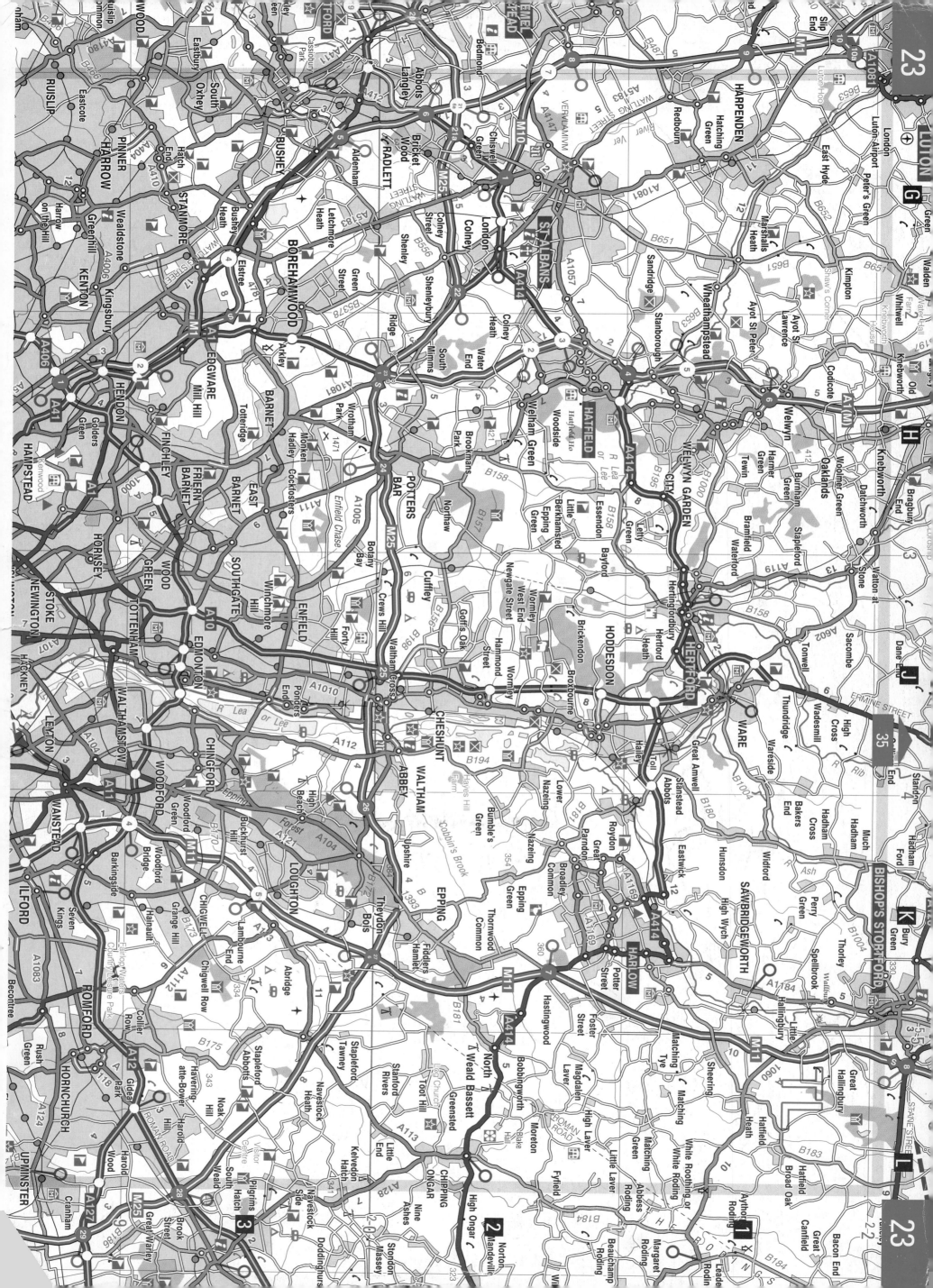

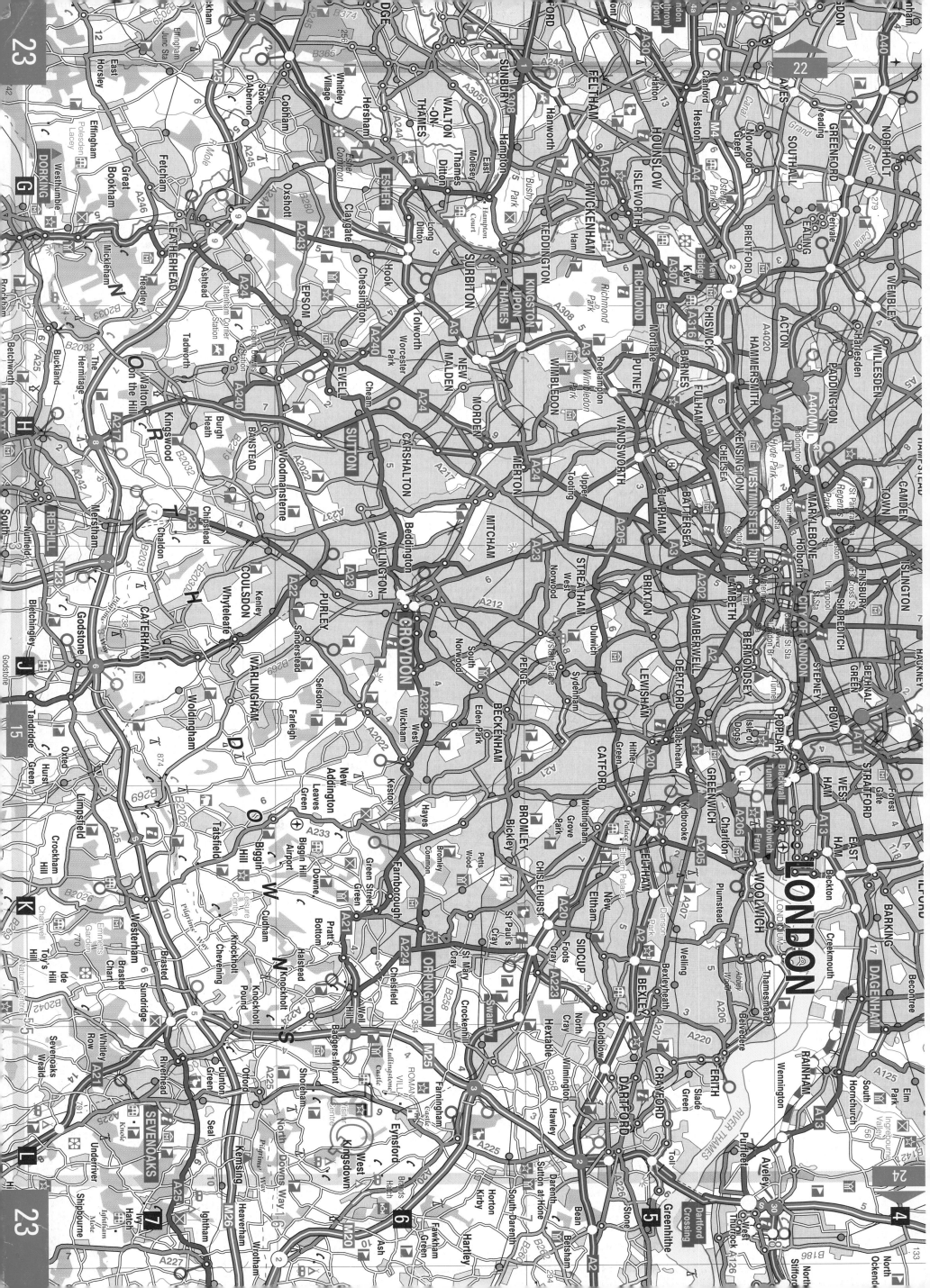

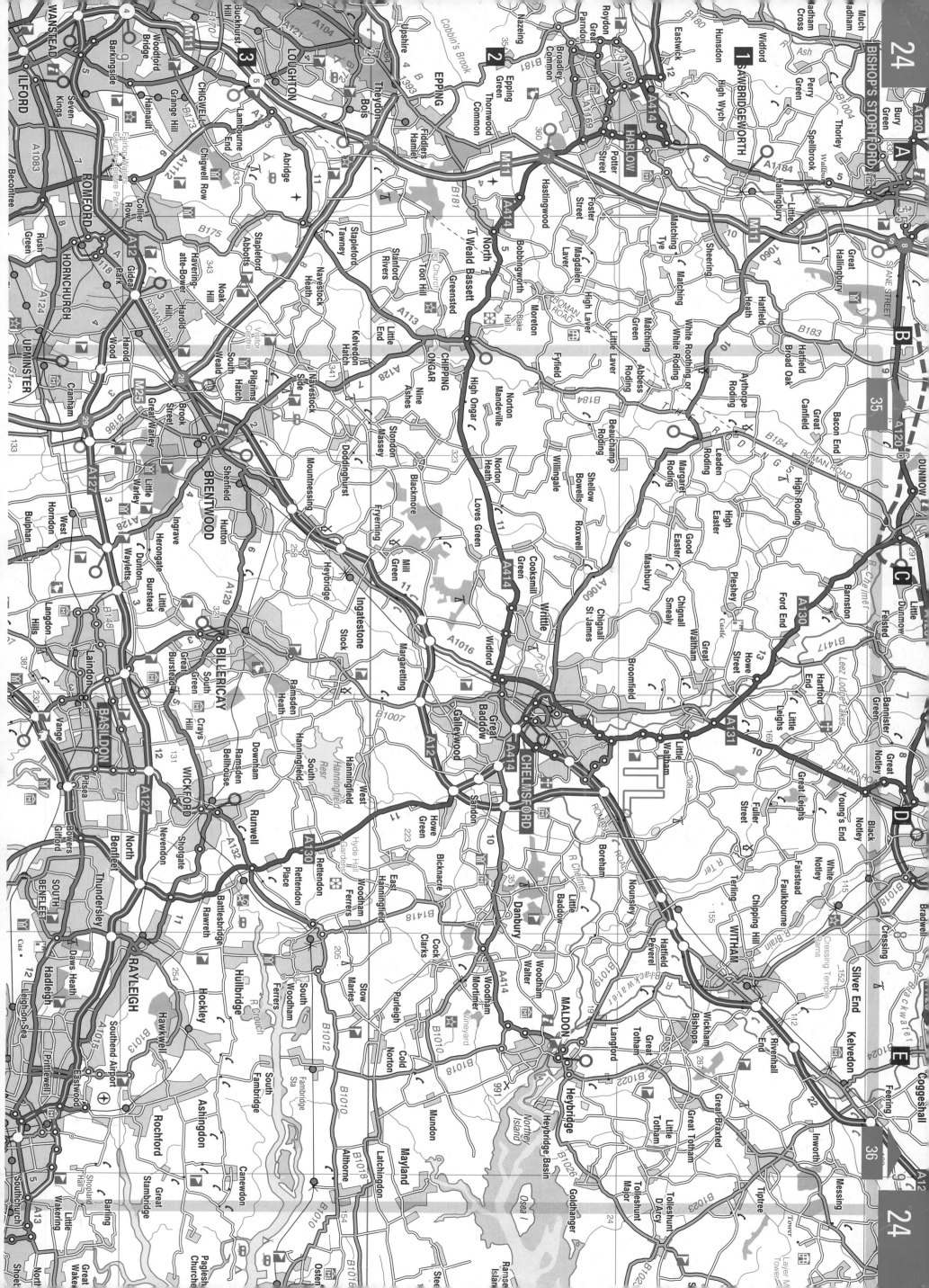

NORTH SEA

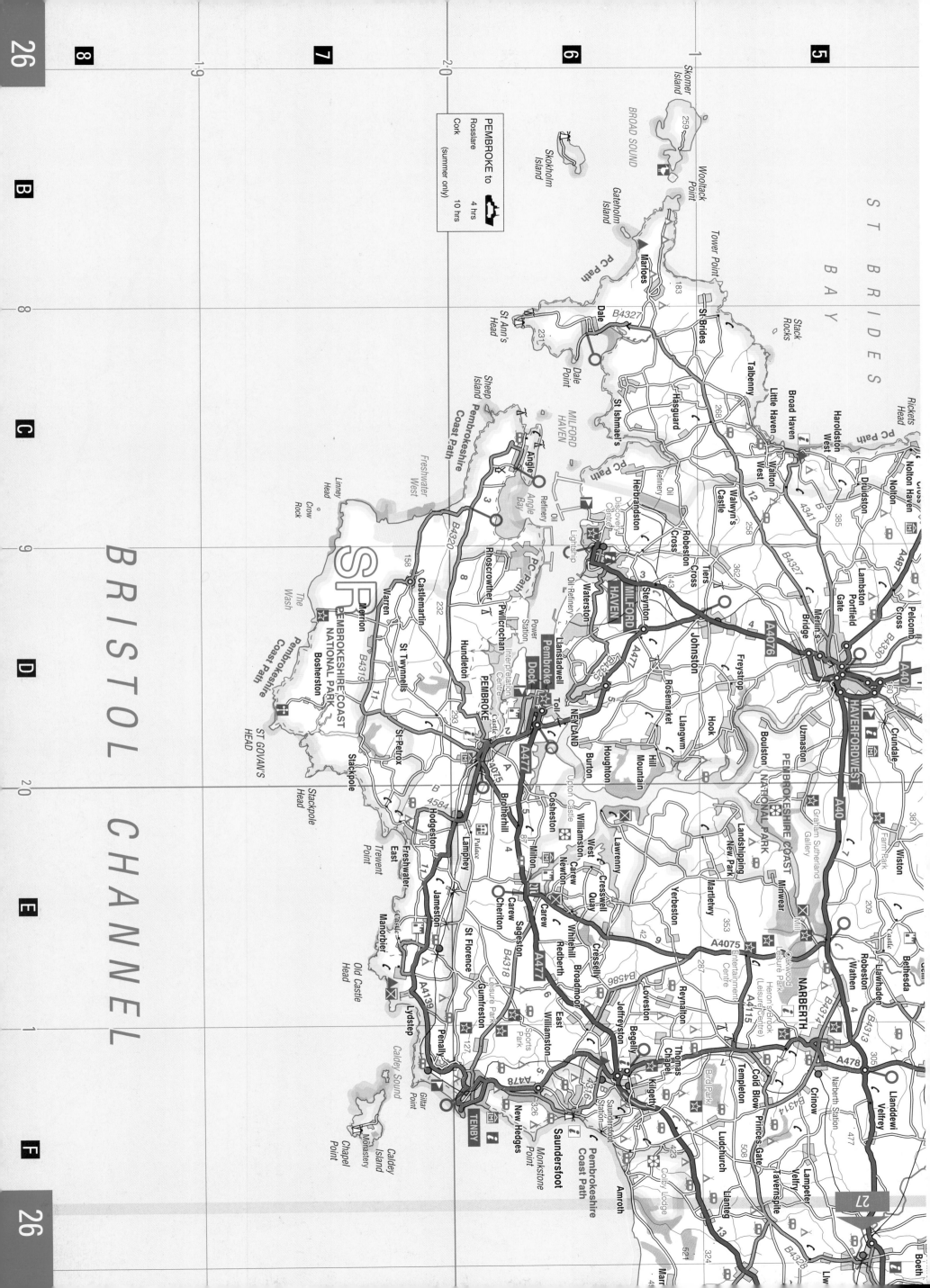

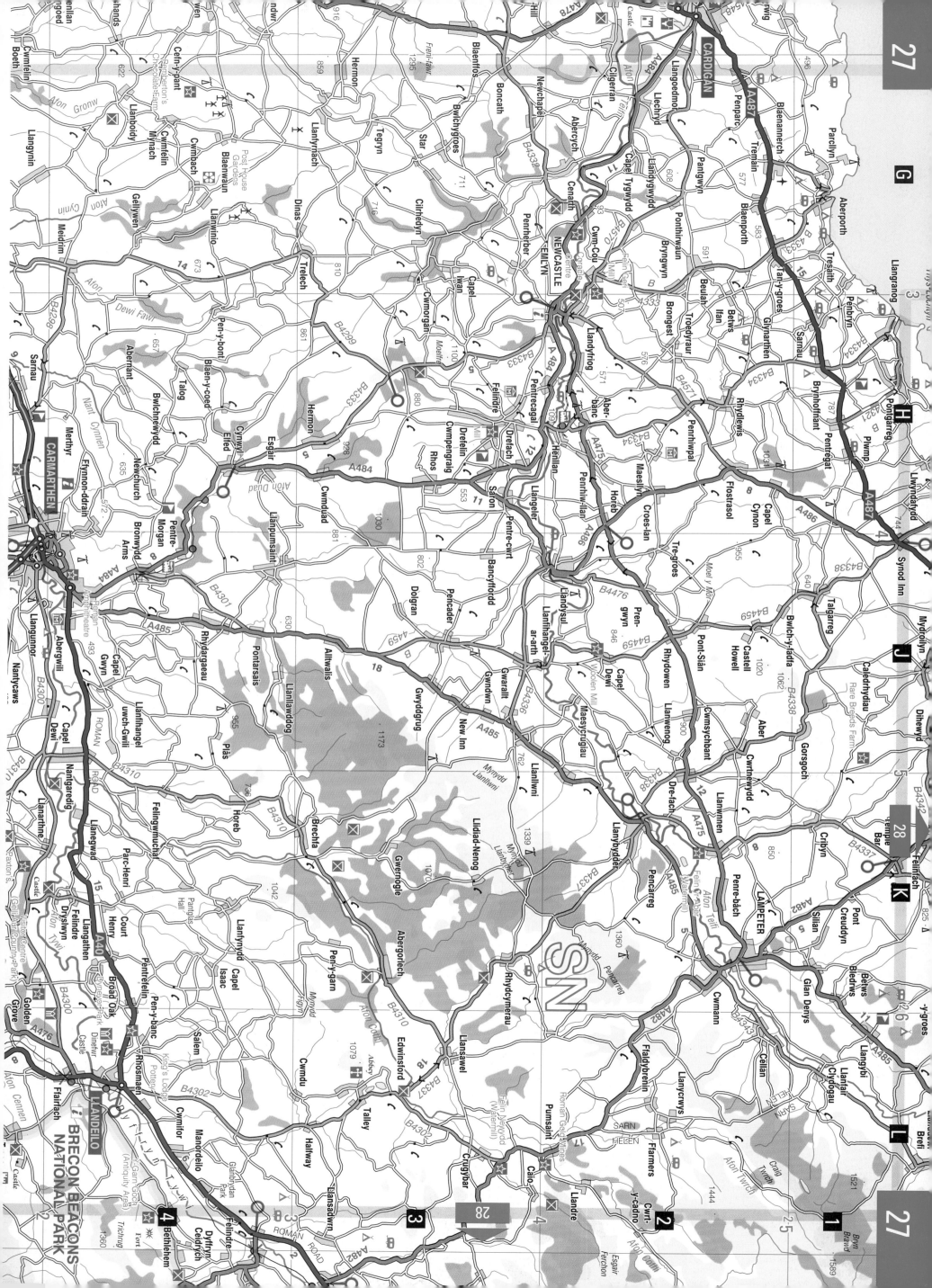

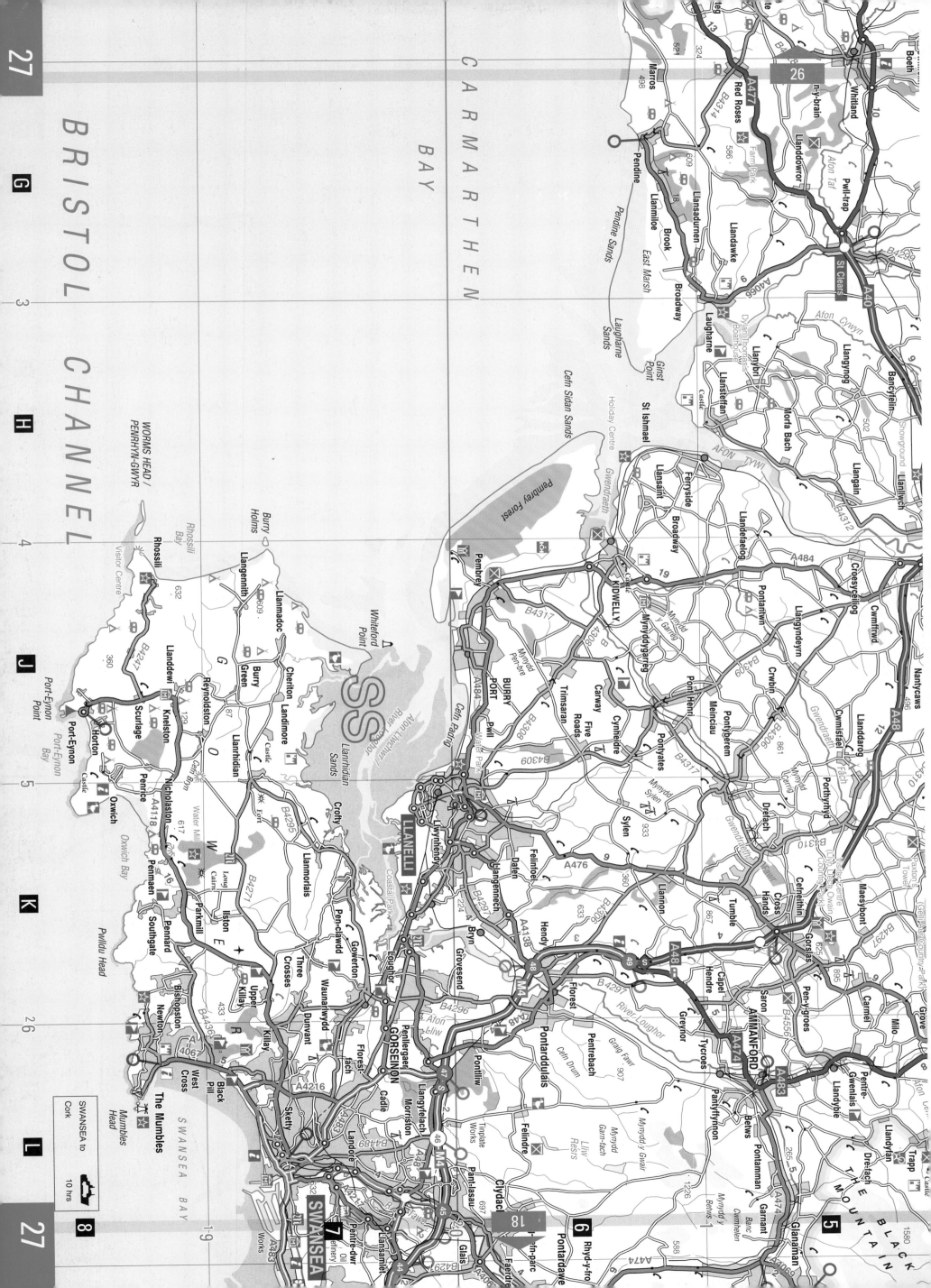

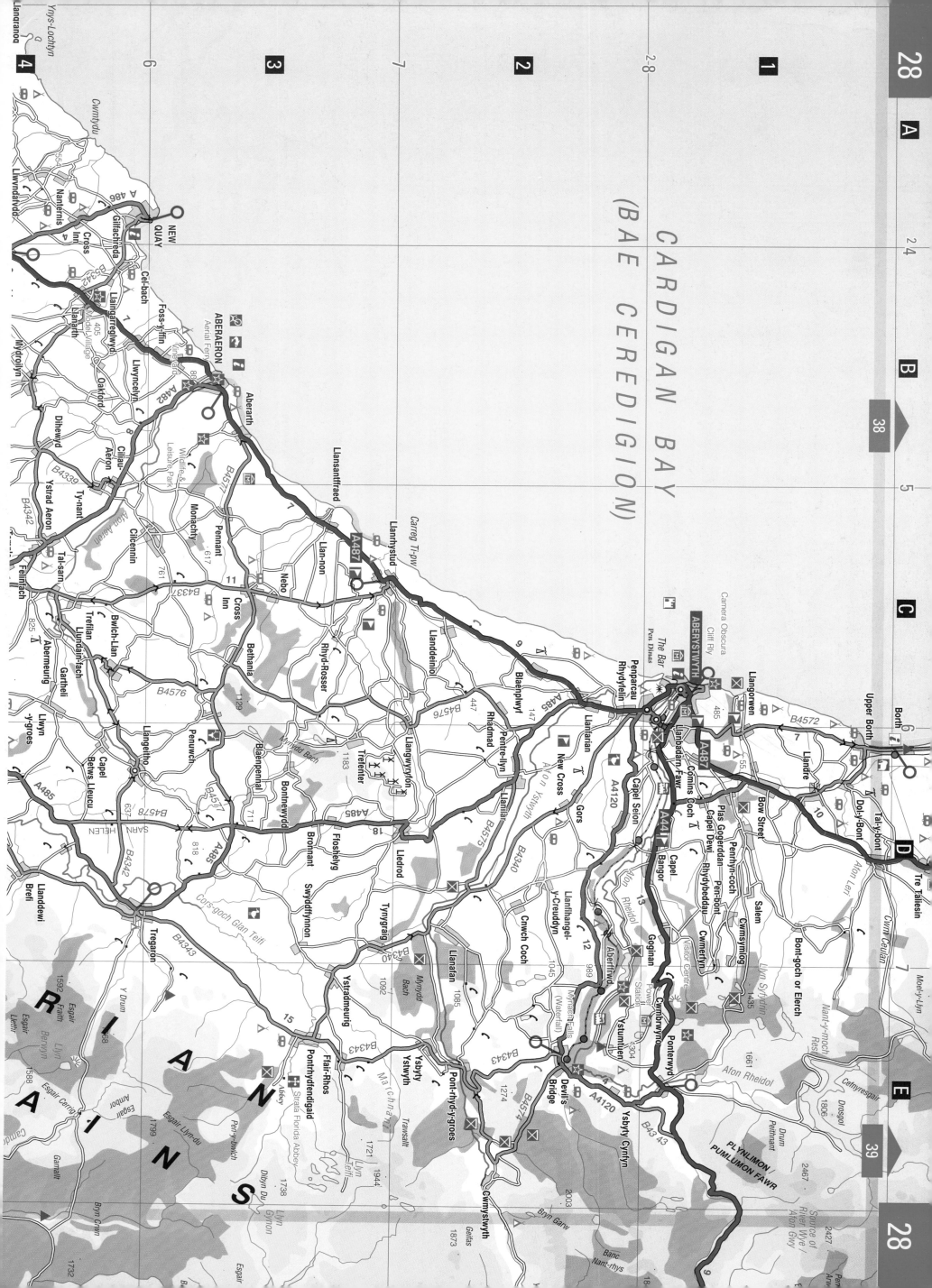

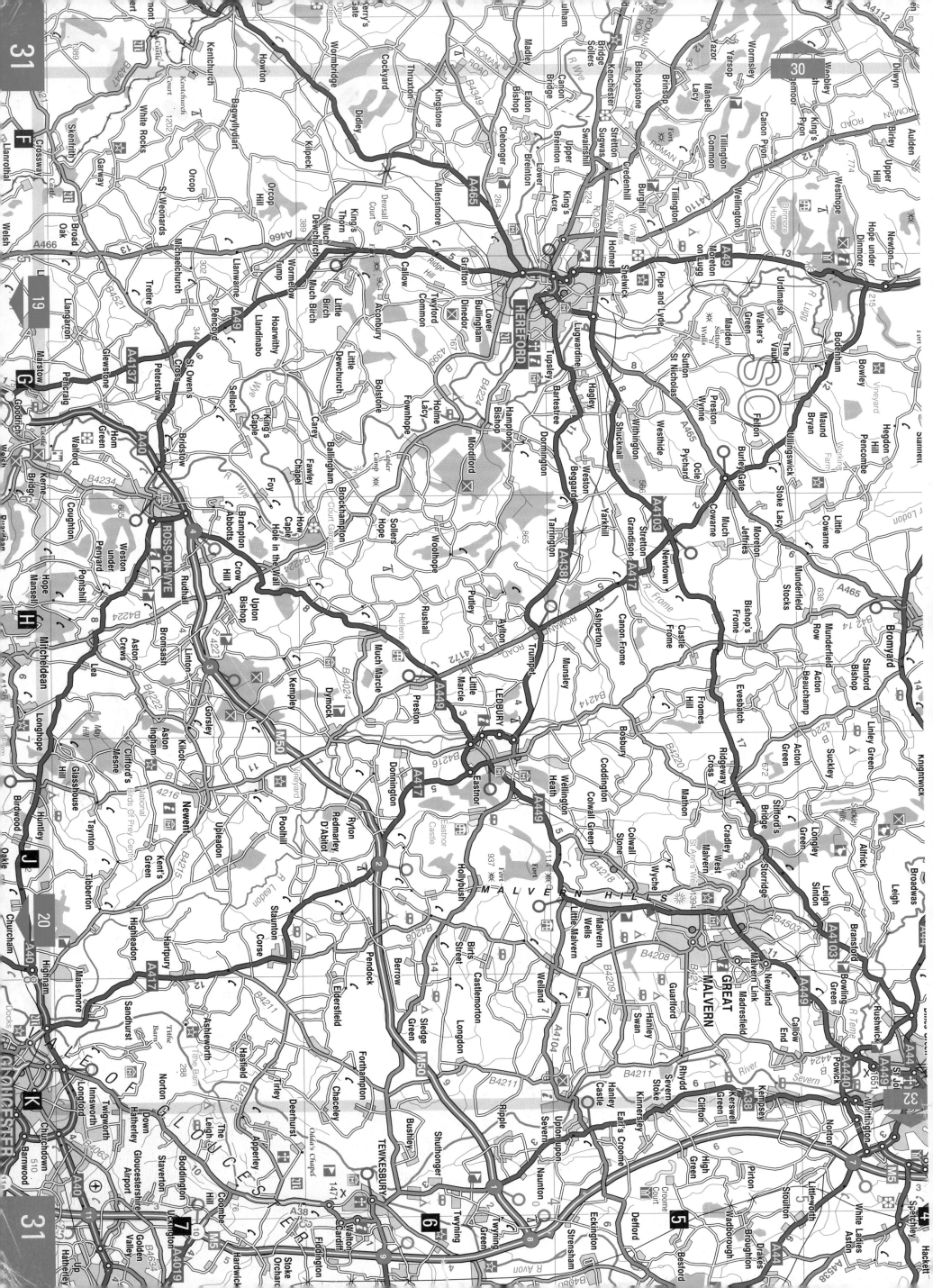

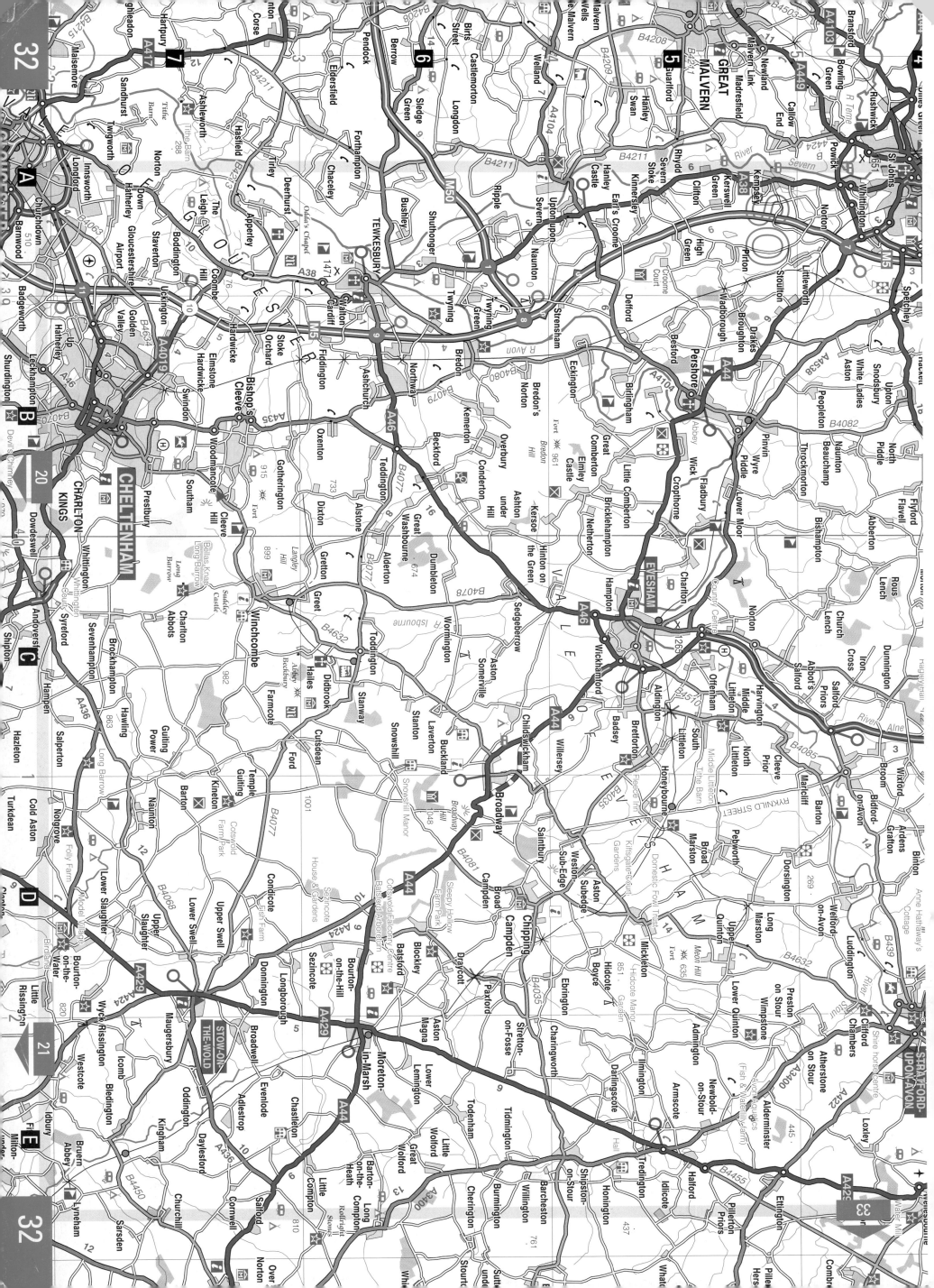

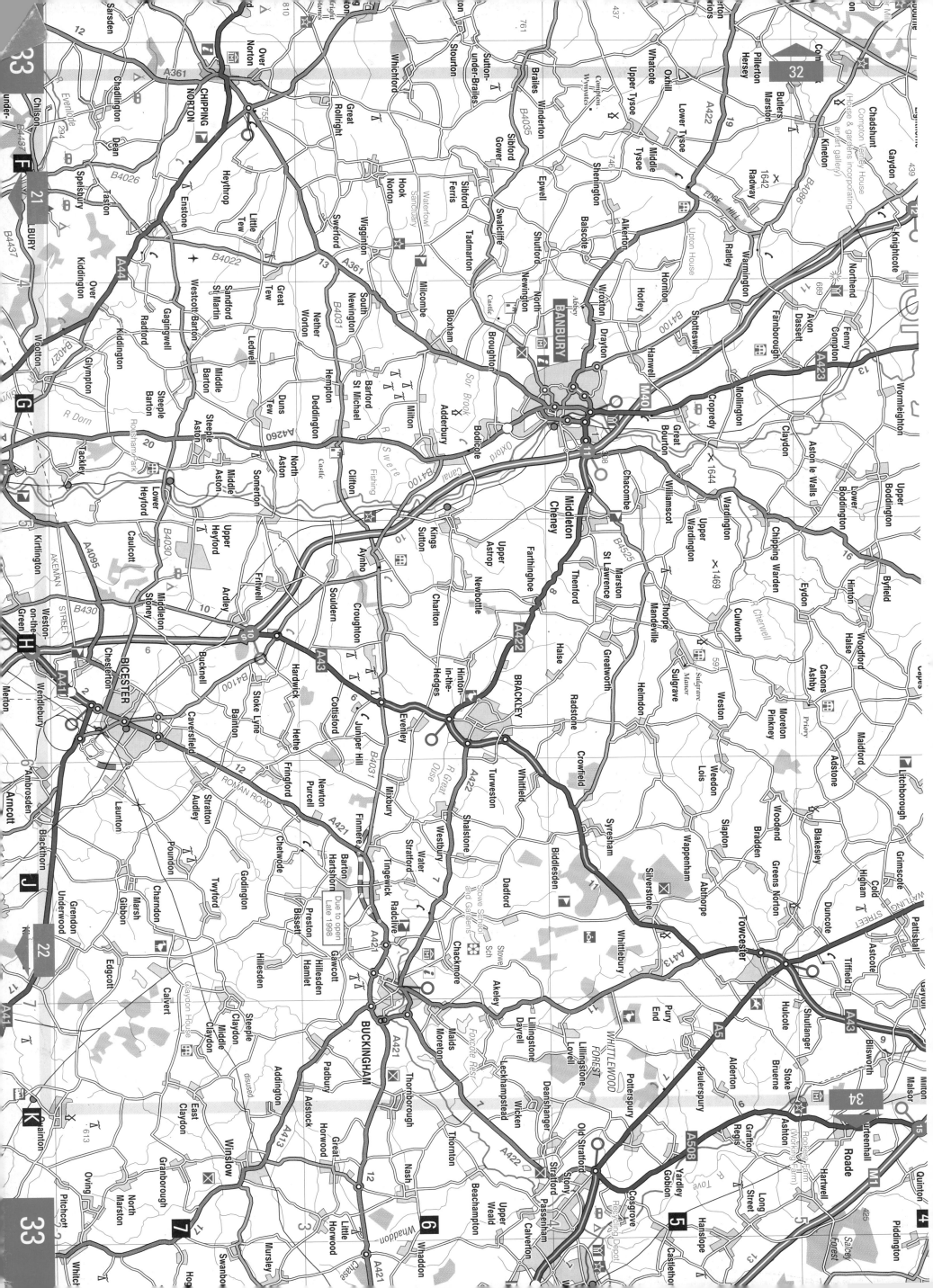

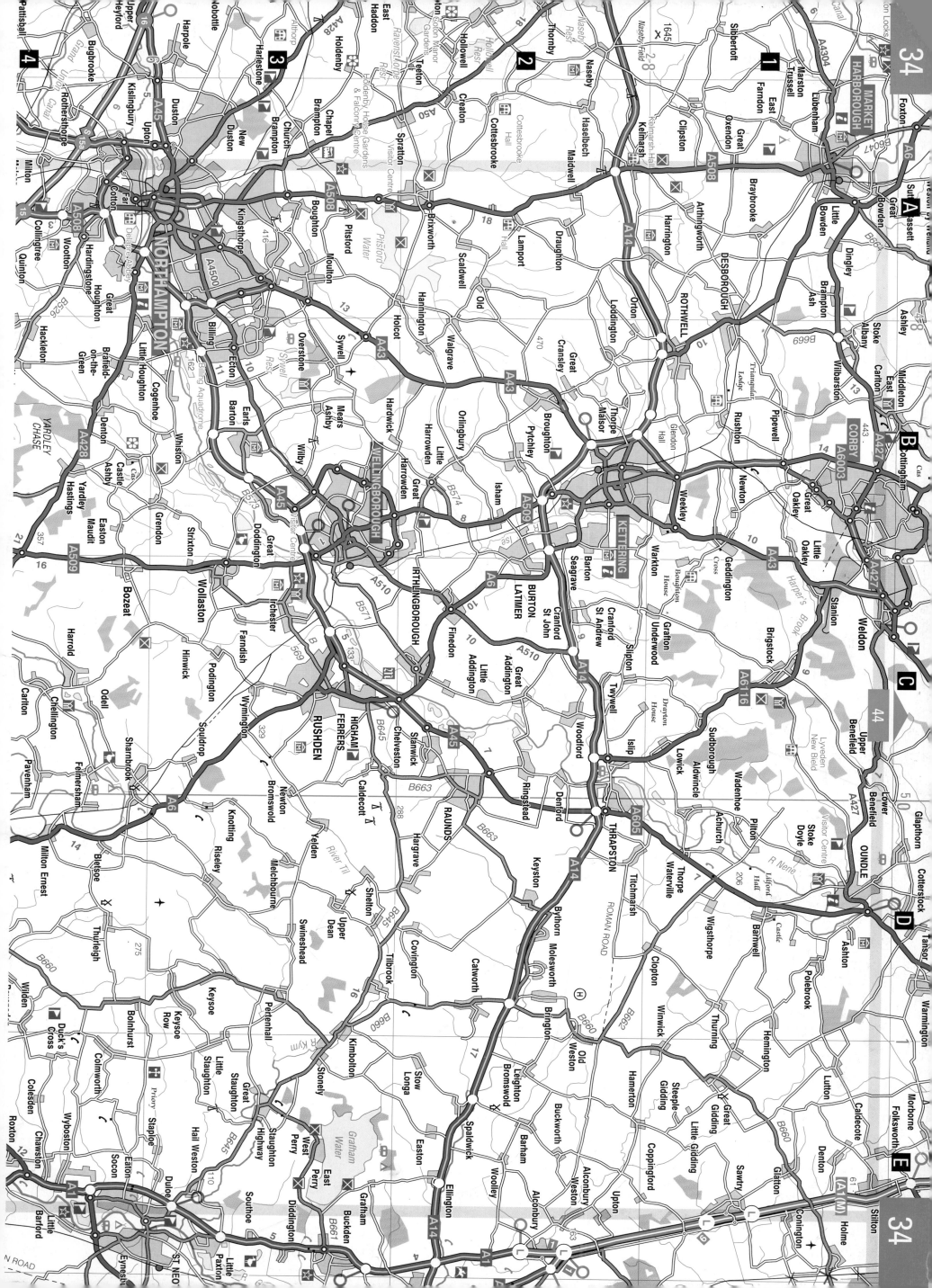

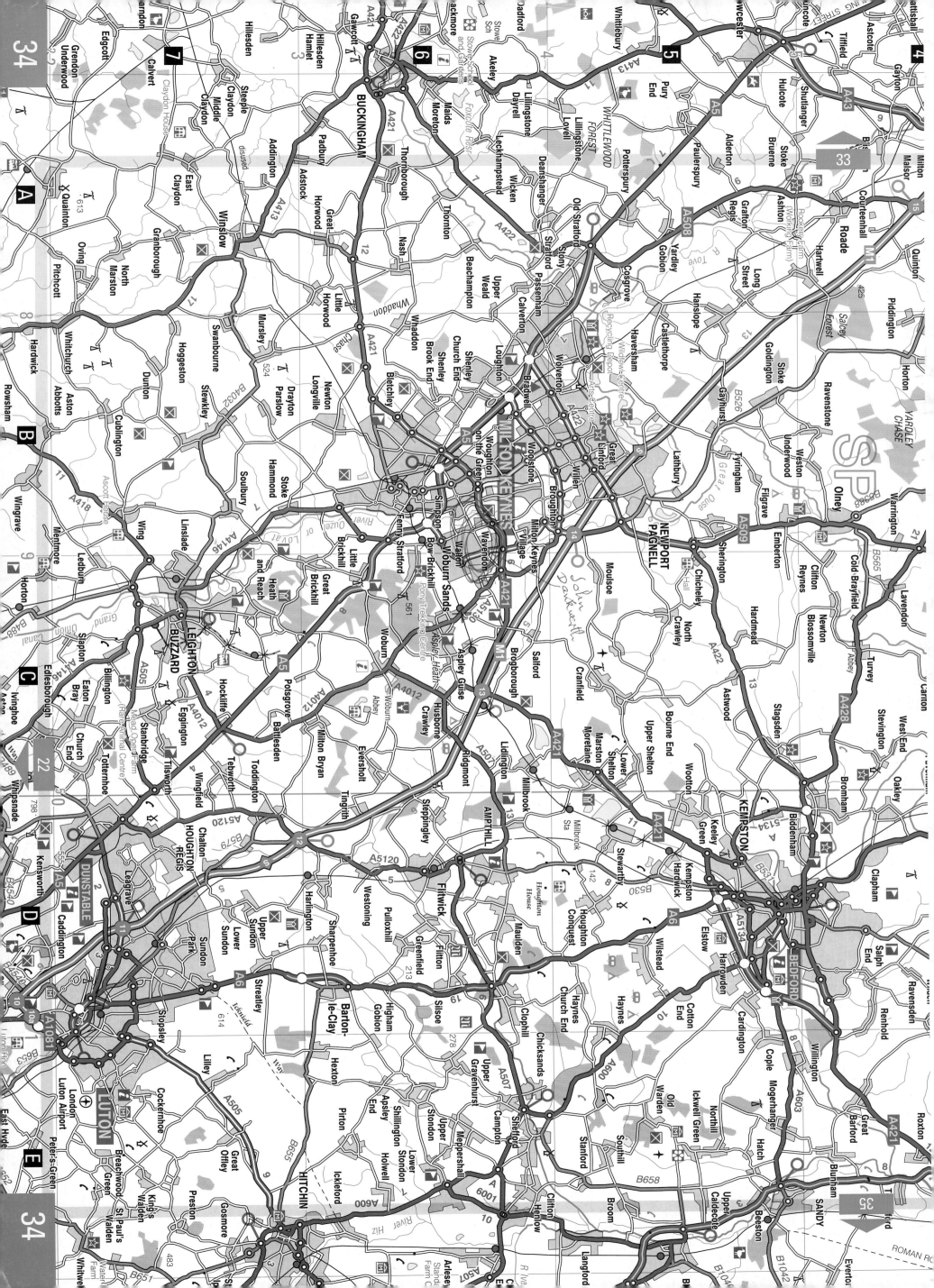

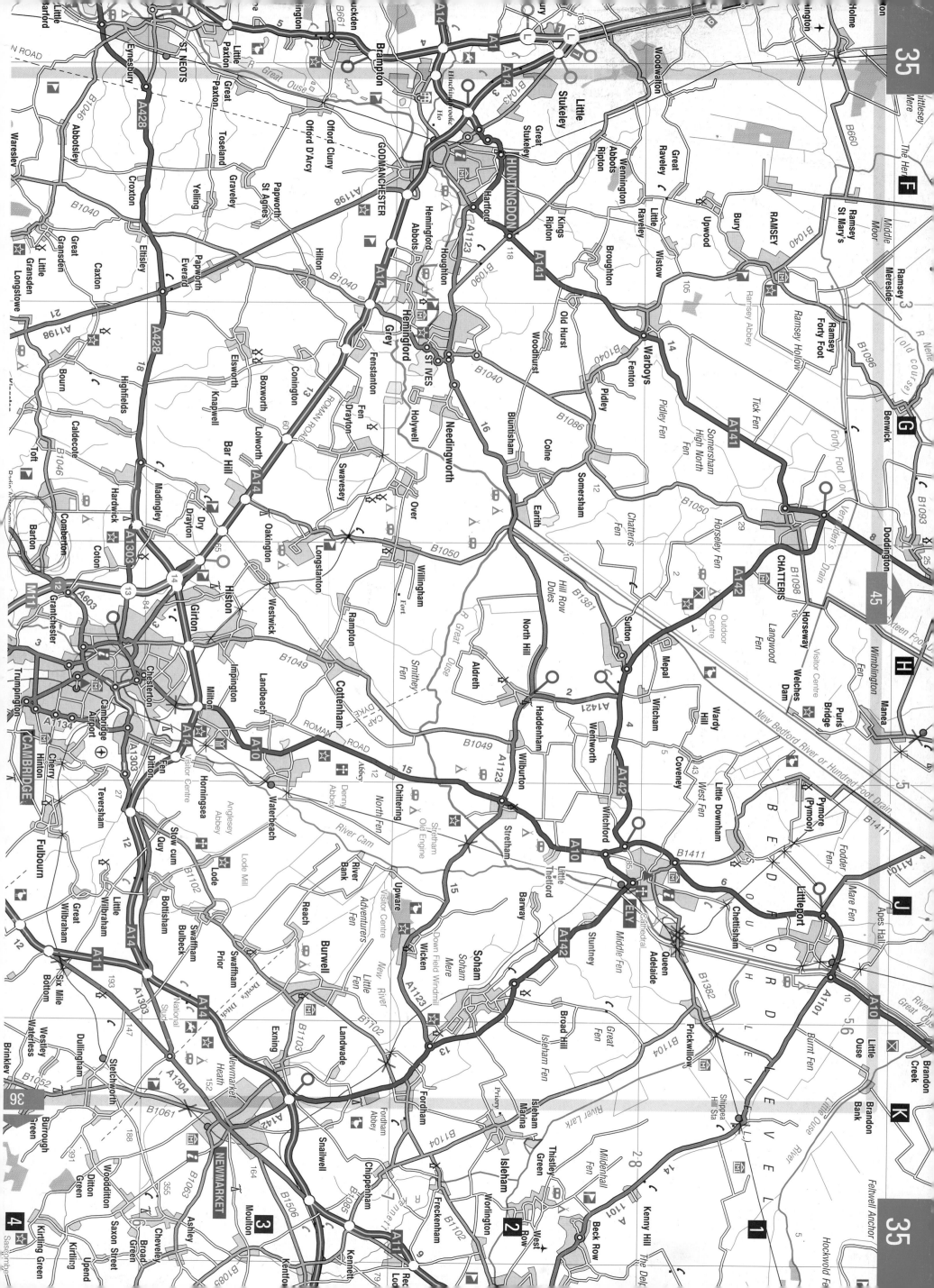

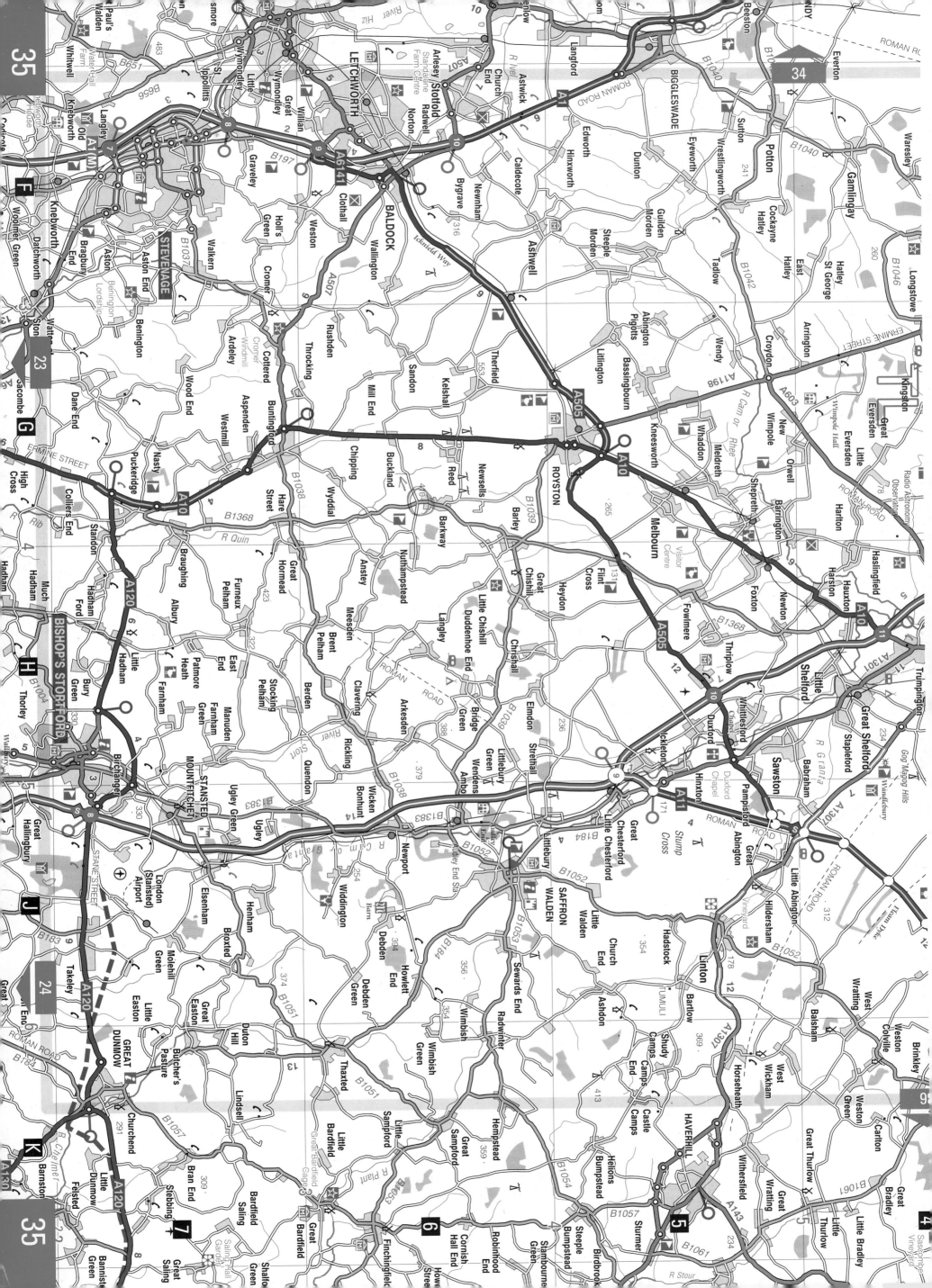

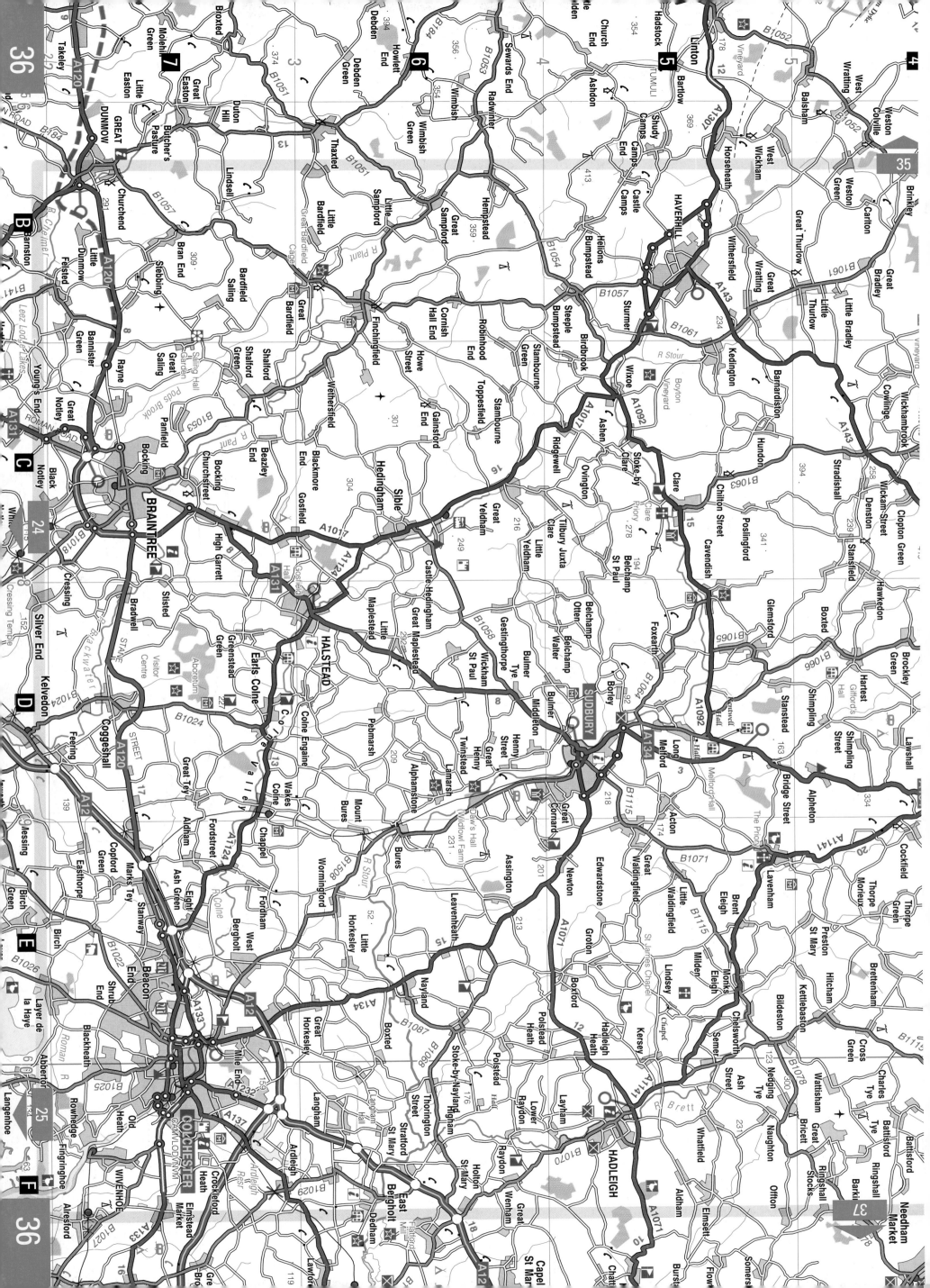

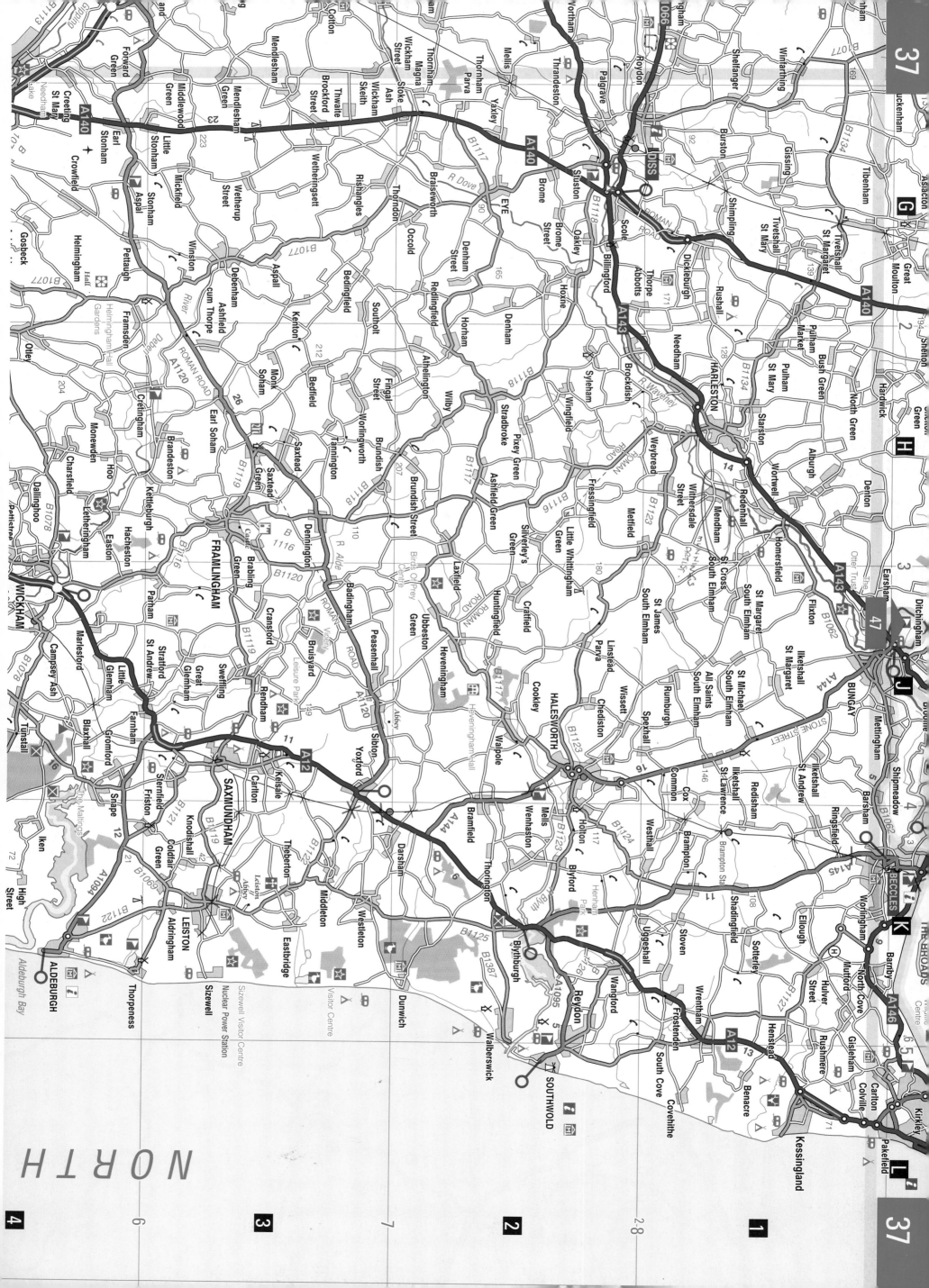

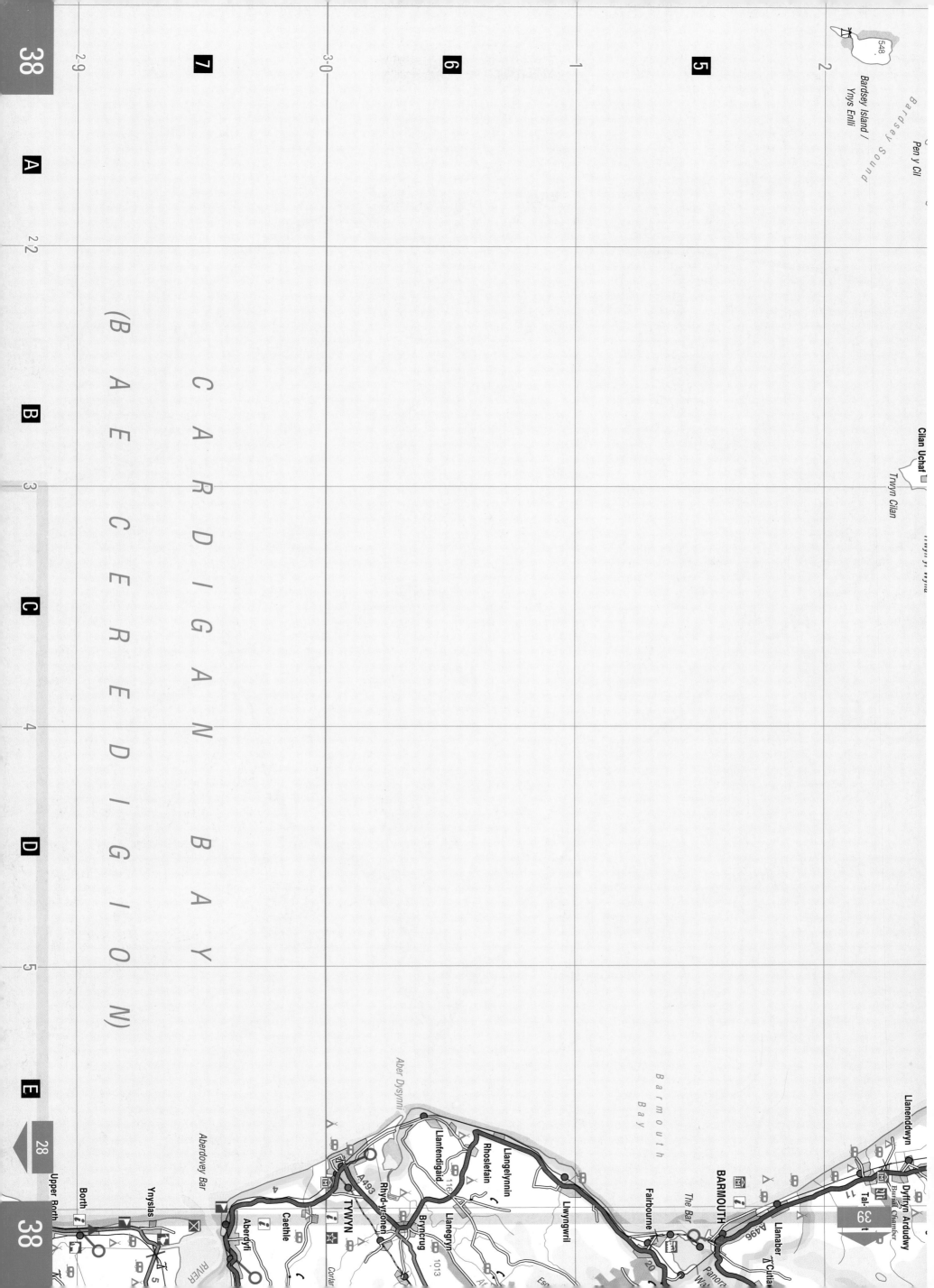

548

Bardsey Island /
Ynys Enlli

Pen y Cil

Bardsey Sound

Cilan Uchaf
Trwyn Cilan

Trwyn yr Wylfa

29   2   A   22   B   3   C   4   D   5   E   28   38

5

1

6

30

7

(BAE CEREDIGION)

CARDIGAN BAY

*Barmouth
Bay*

Llaneiddwyn
Dyffryn Ardudwy

BARMOUTH
The Bar

Fairbourne

Llwyngwril

Llangelynnin
Rhoslefain

Llanegryn
Bryncrug

Llanfendigaid
Rhyd-y-ronen

TYWYN
Caethle
Aberdyfi

Aber Dysynni

Aberdovey Bar

Ynyslas

Borth

Upper Borth

A493

1013

1167

Llanaber
Llanaber
A496
Cutiar
Tal-

Panora.

39

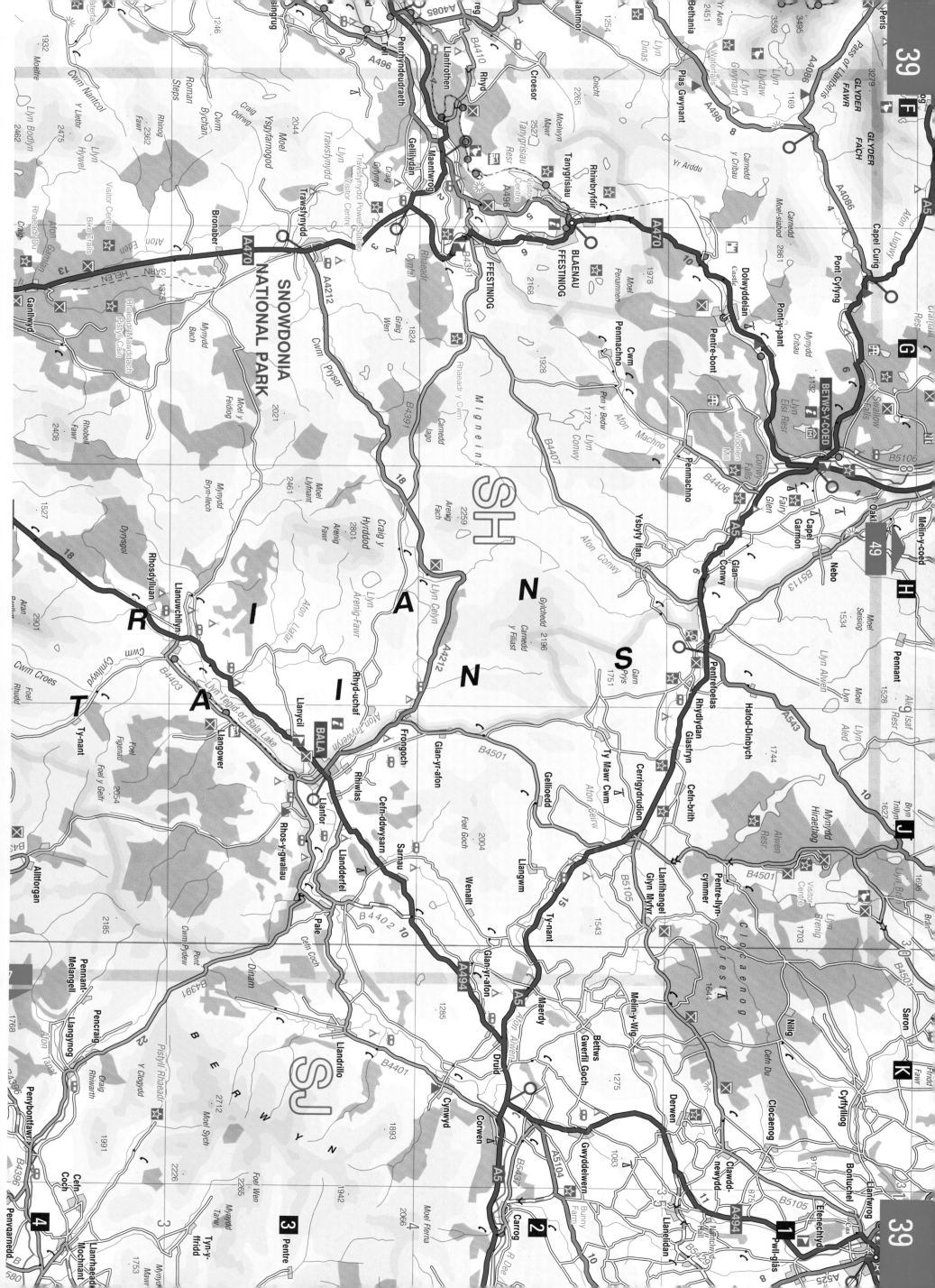

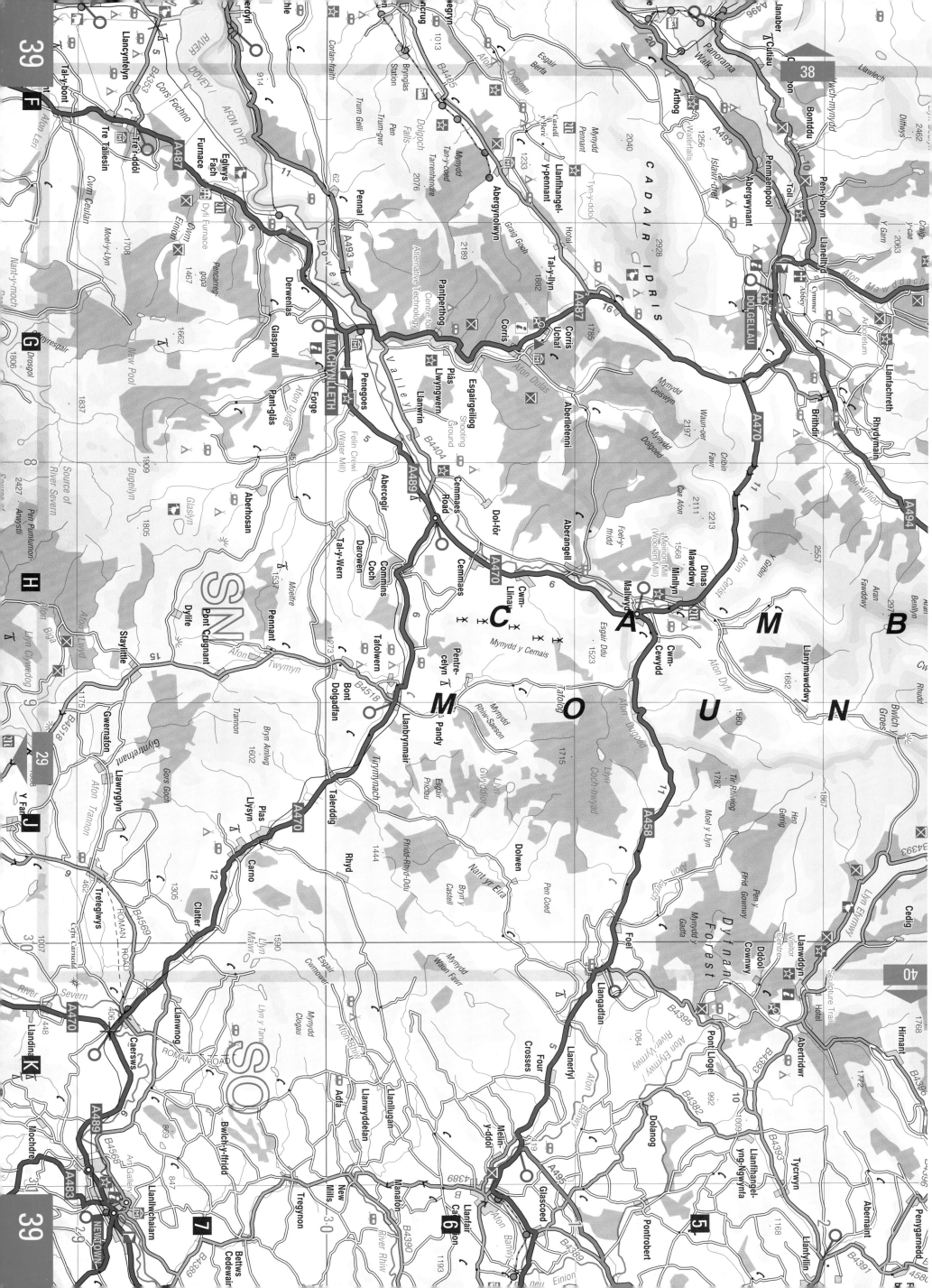

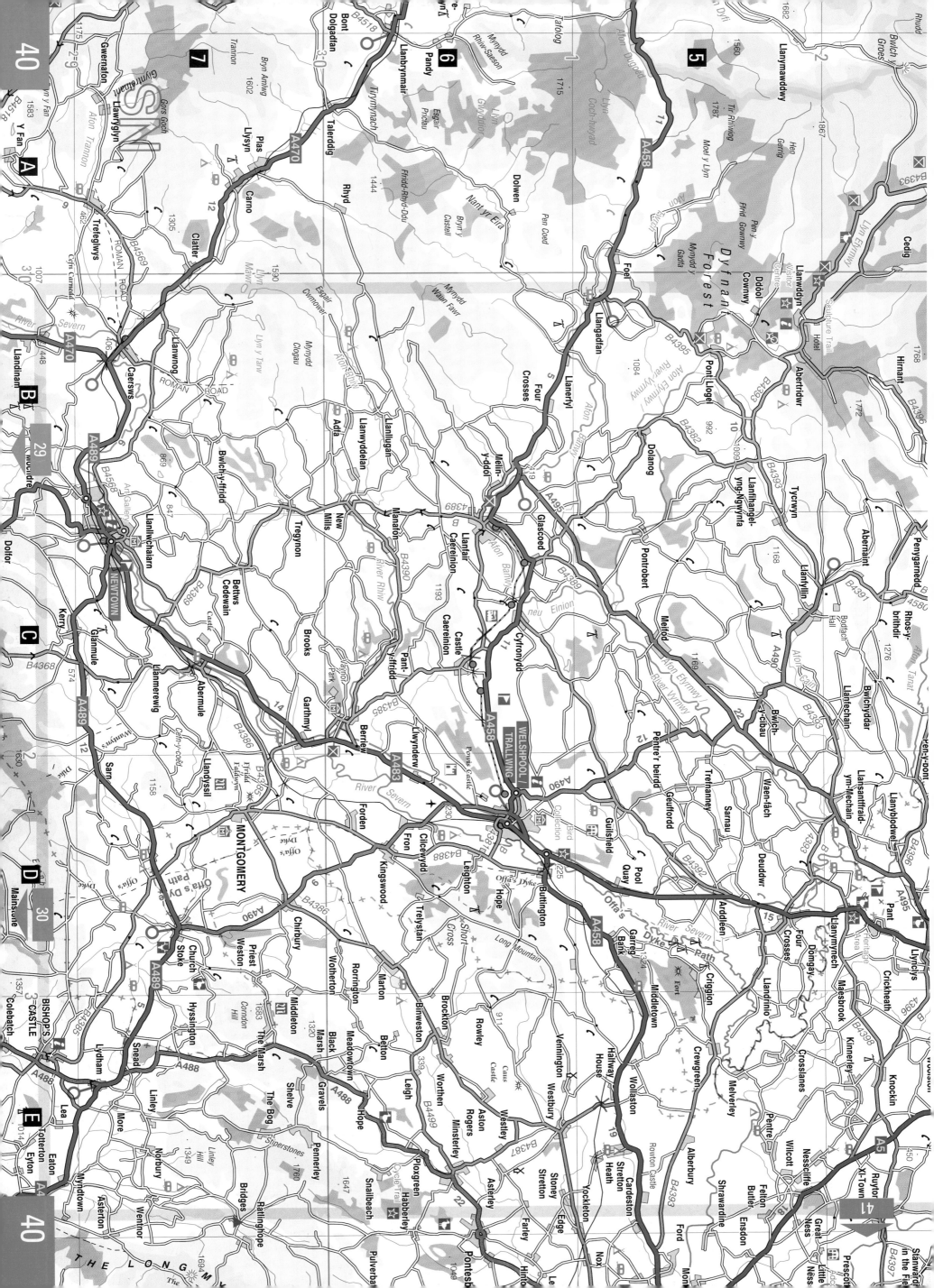

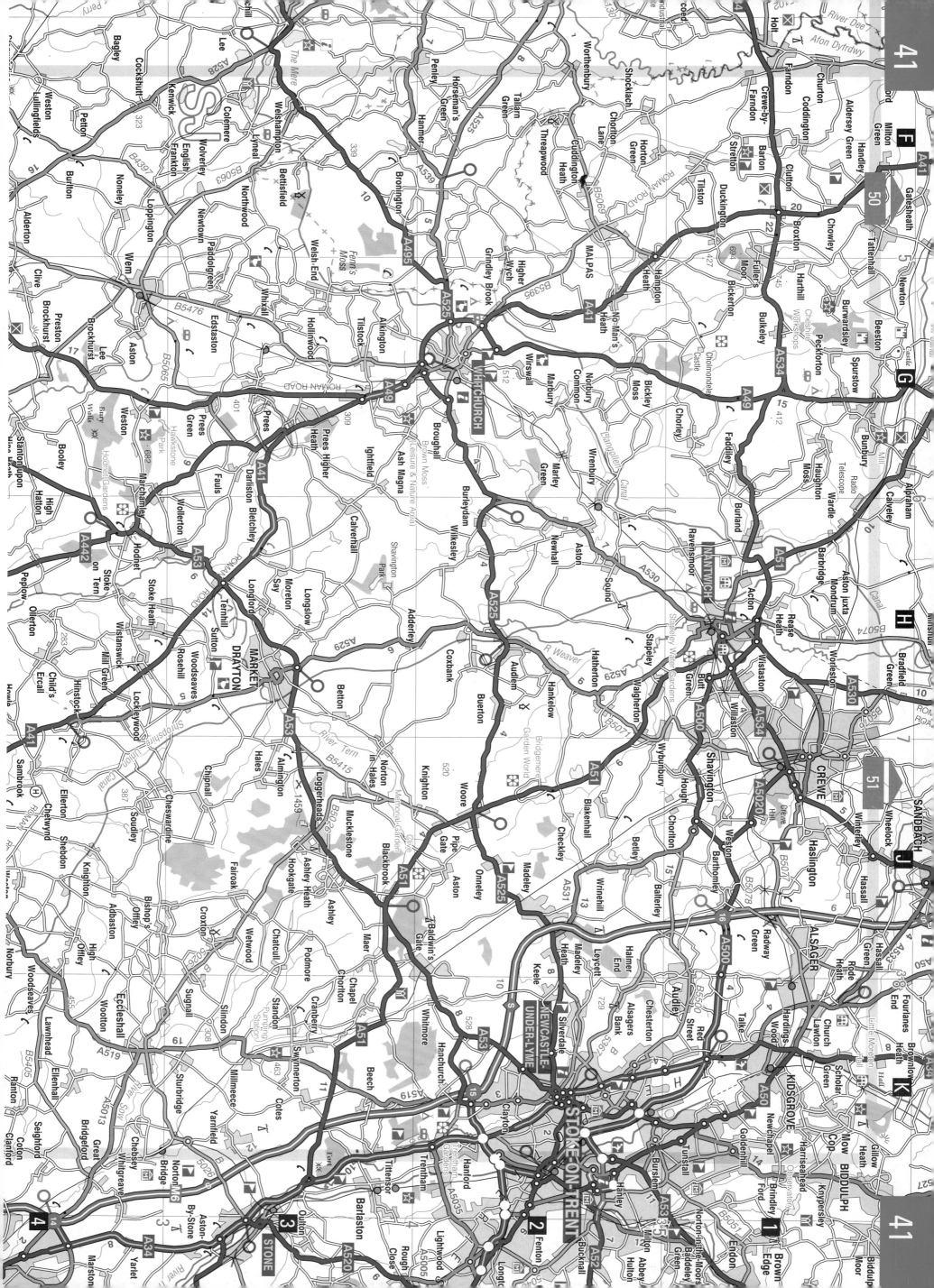

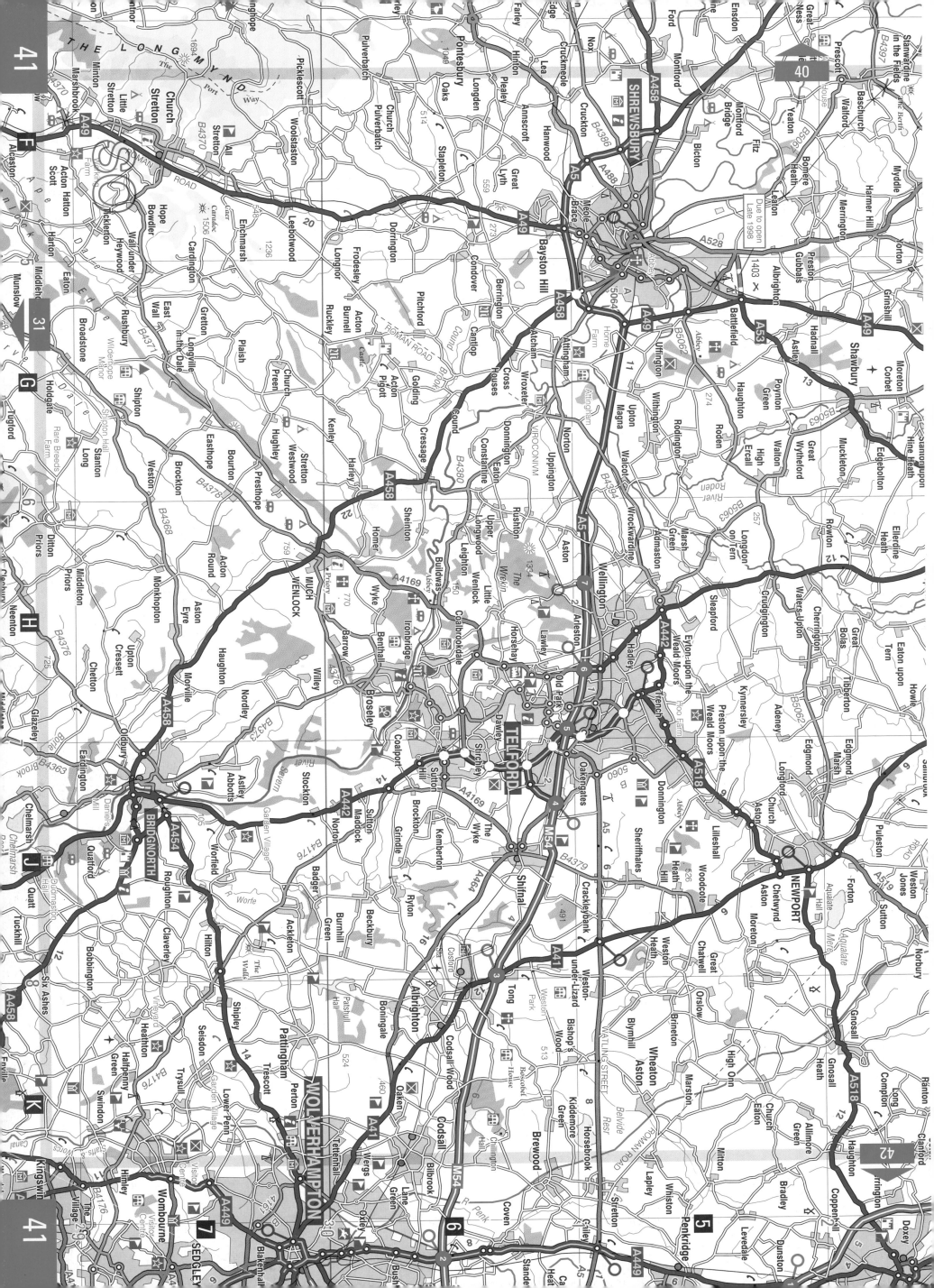

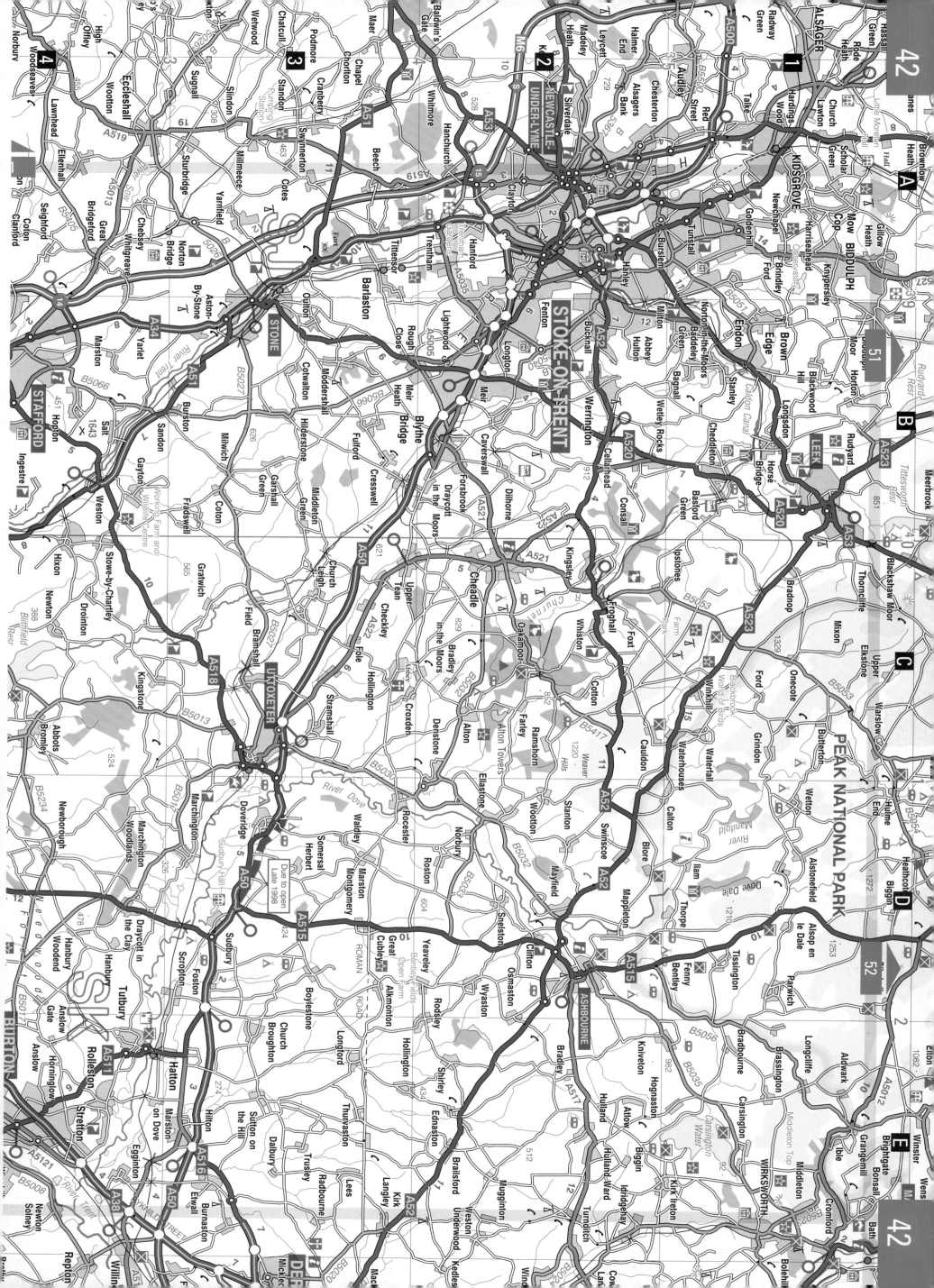

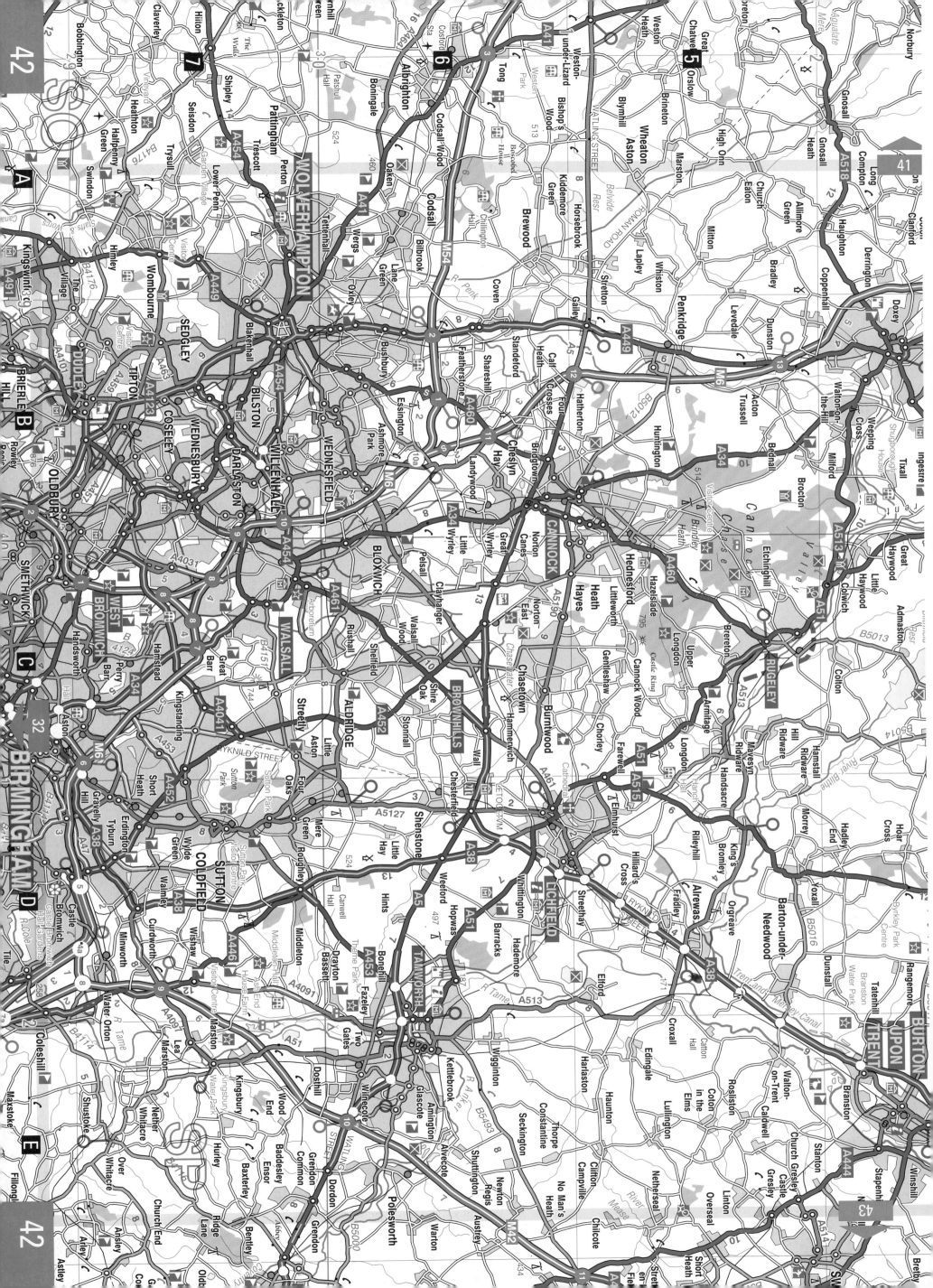

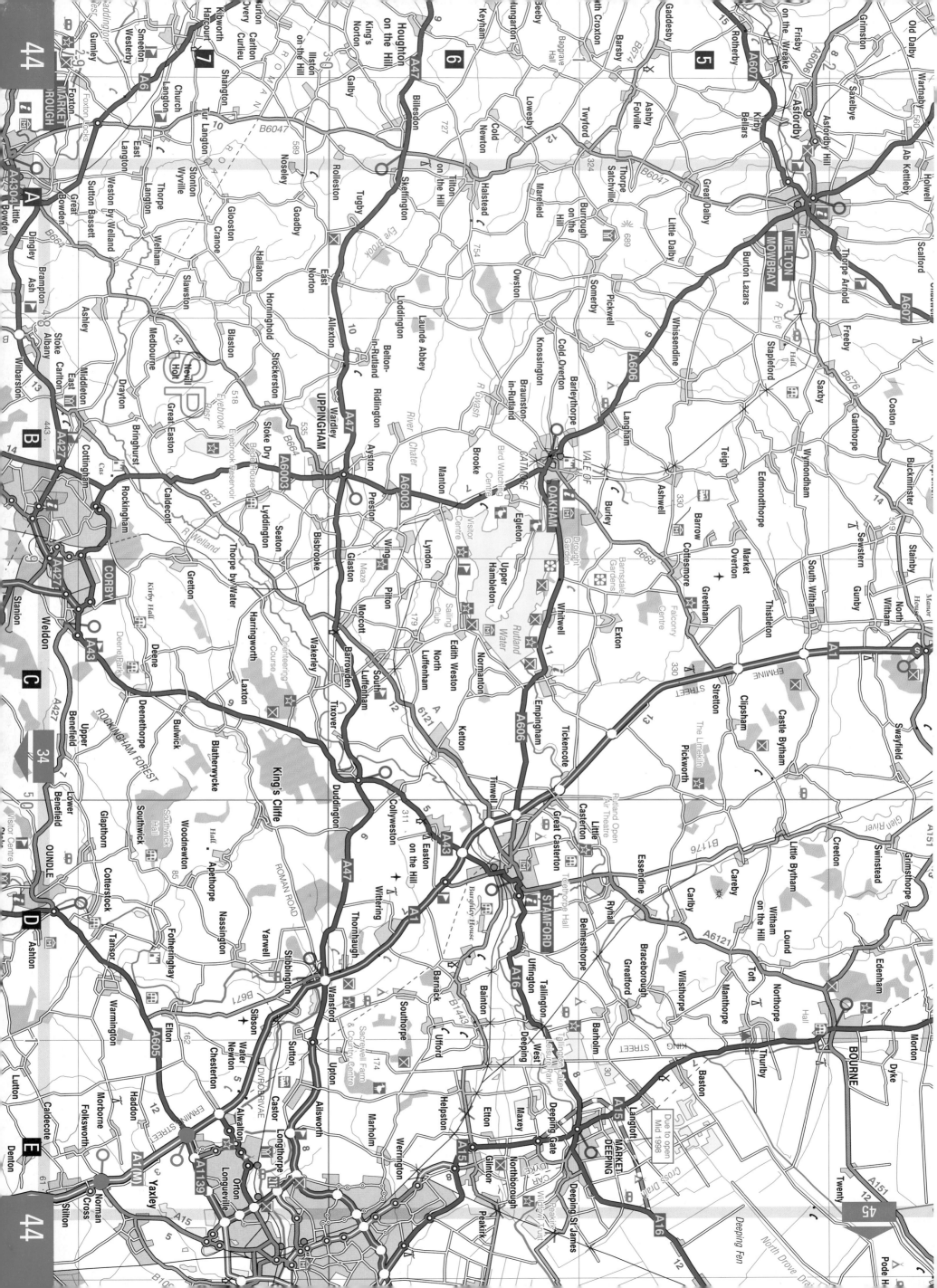

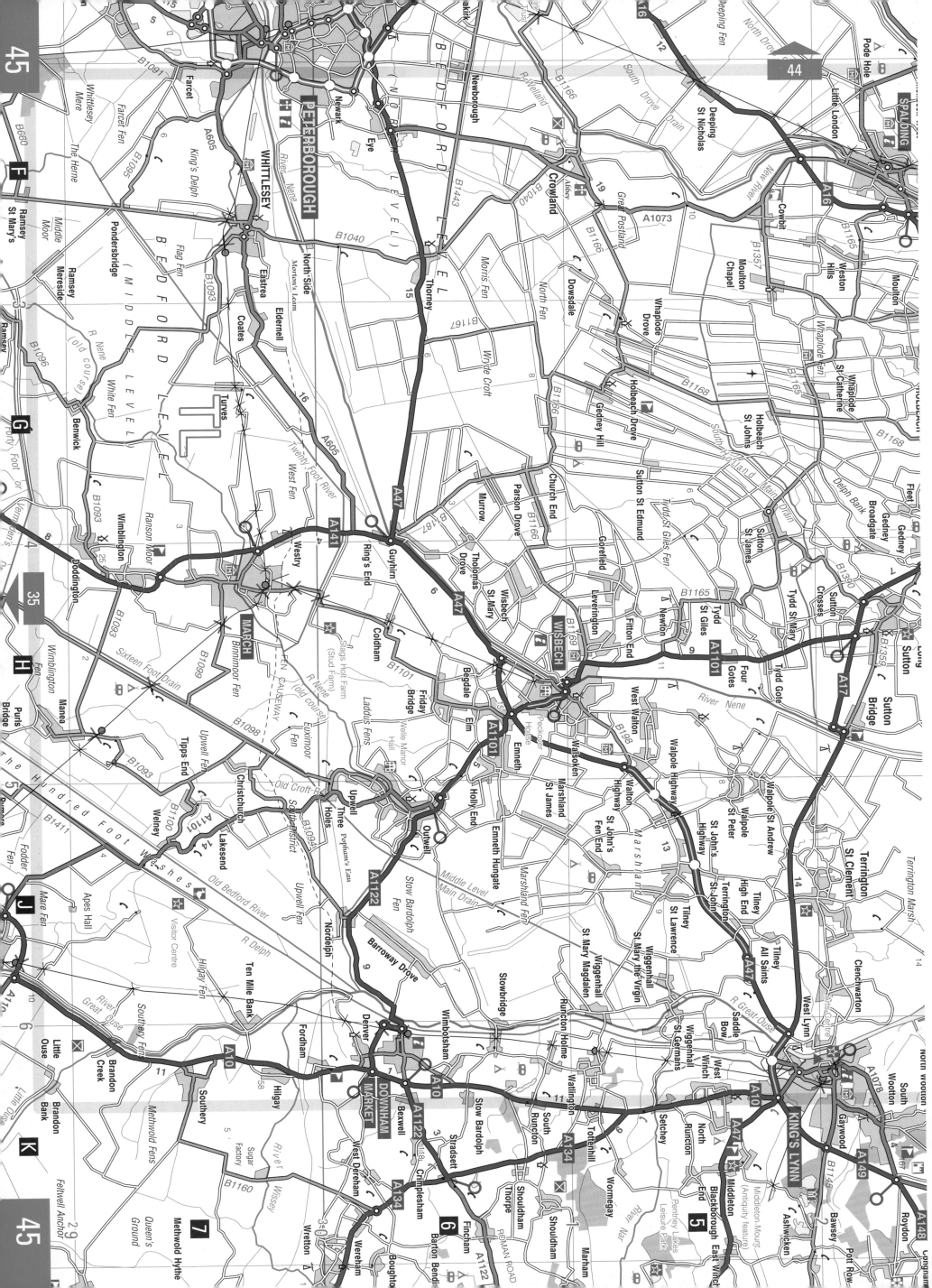

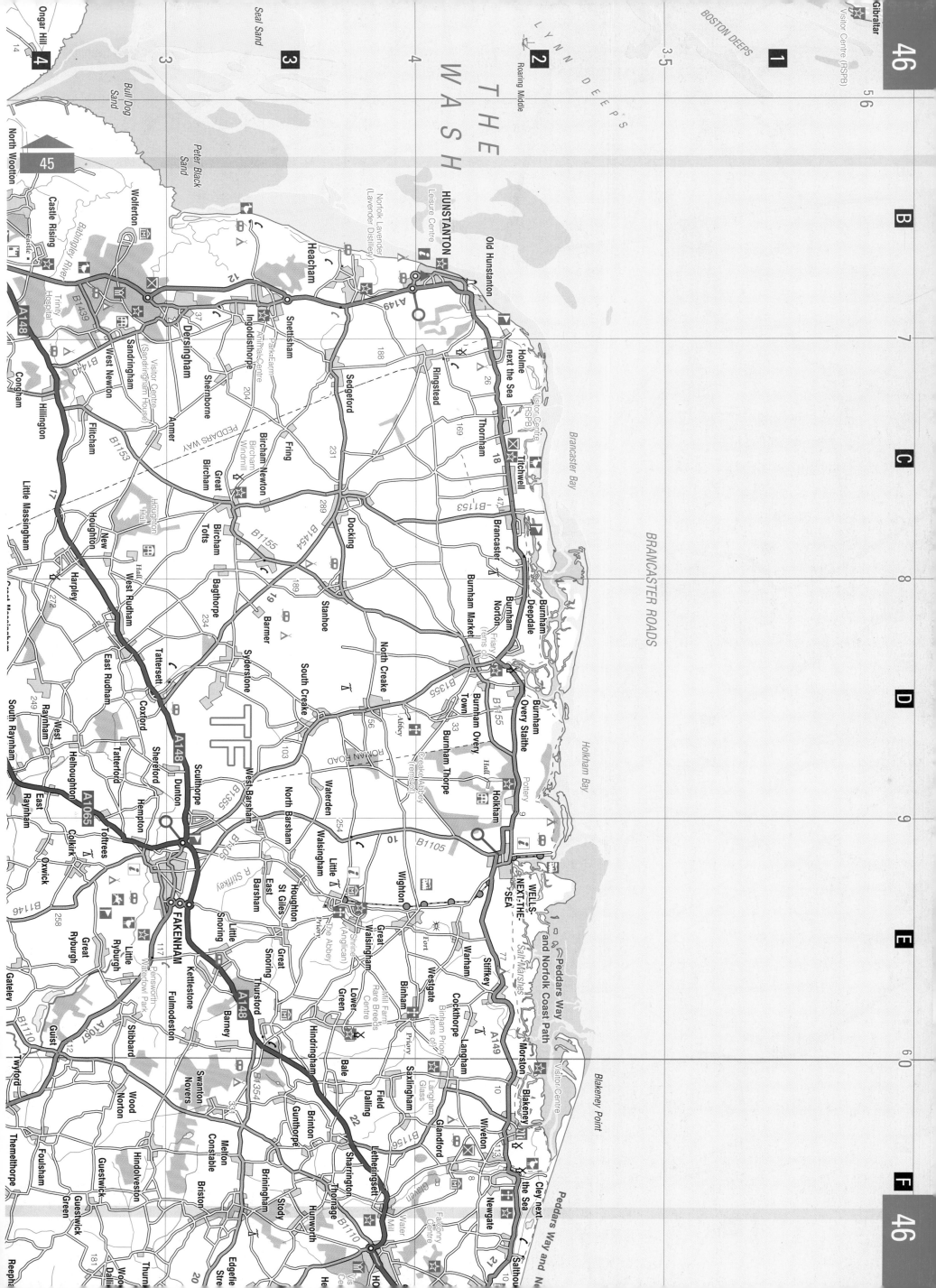

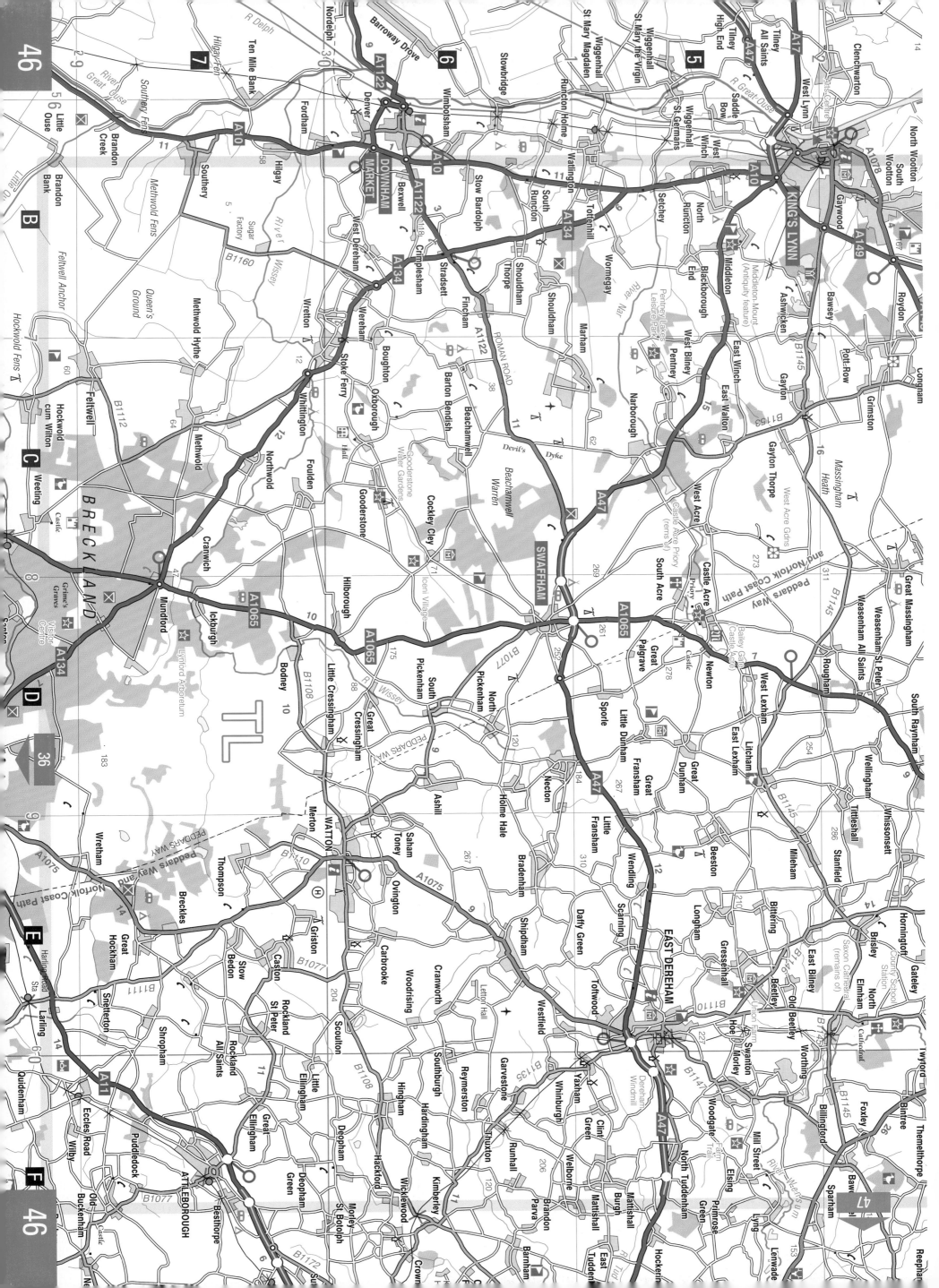

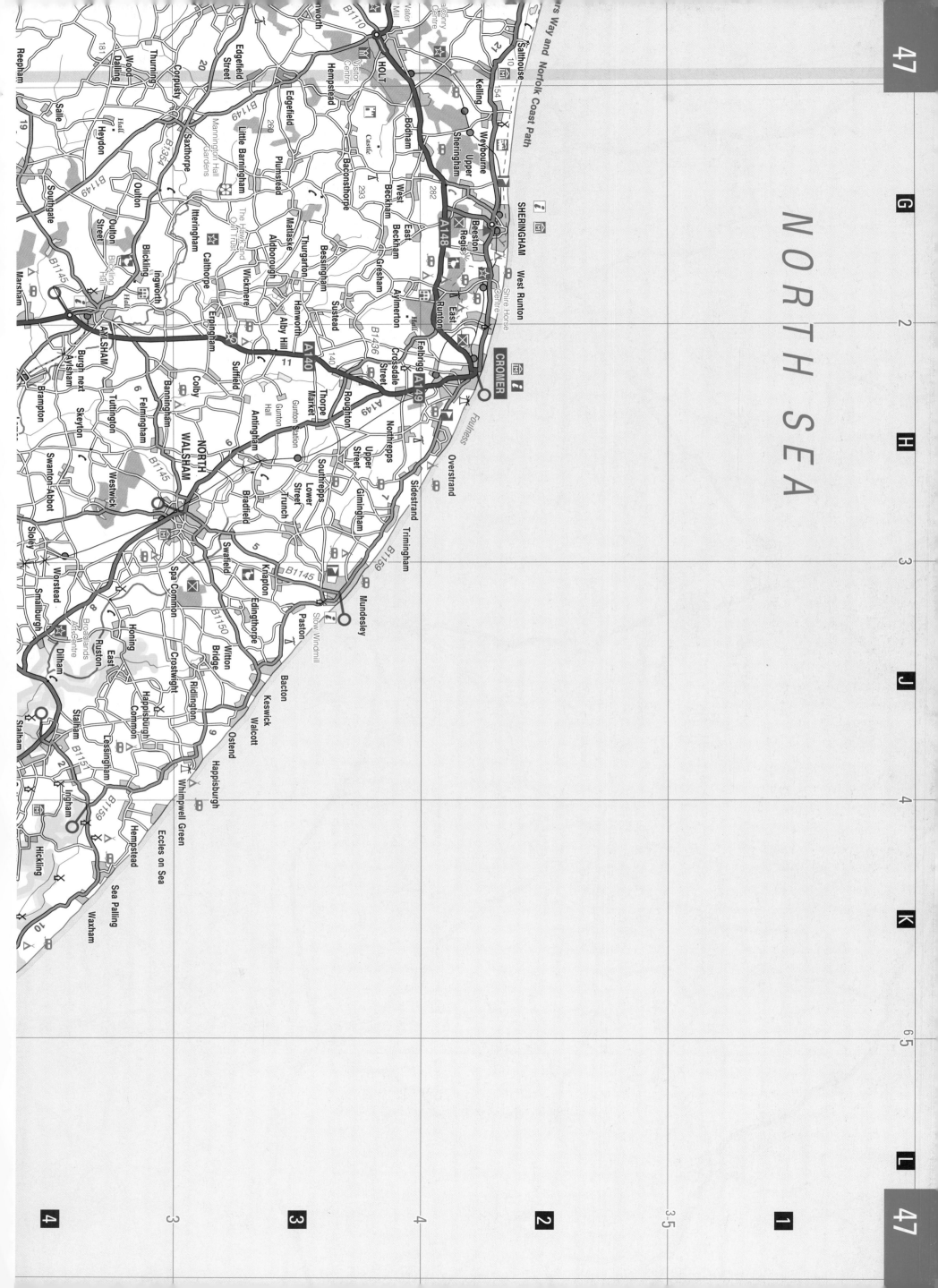

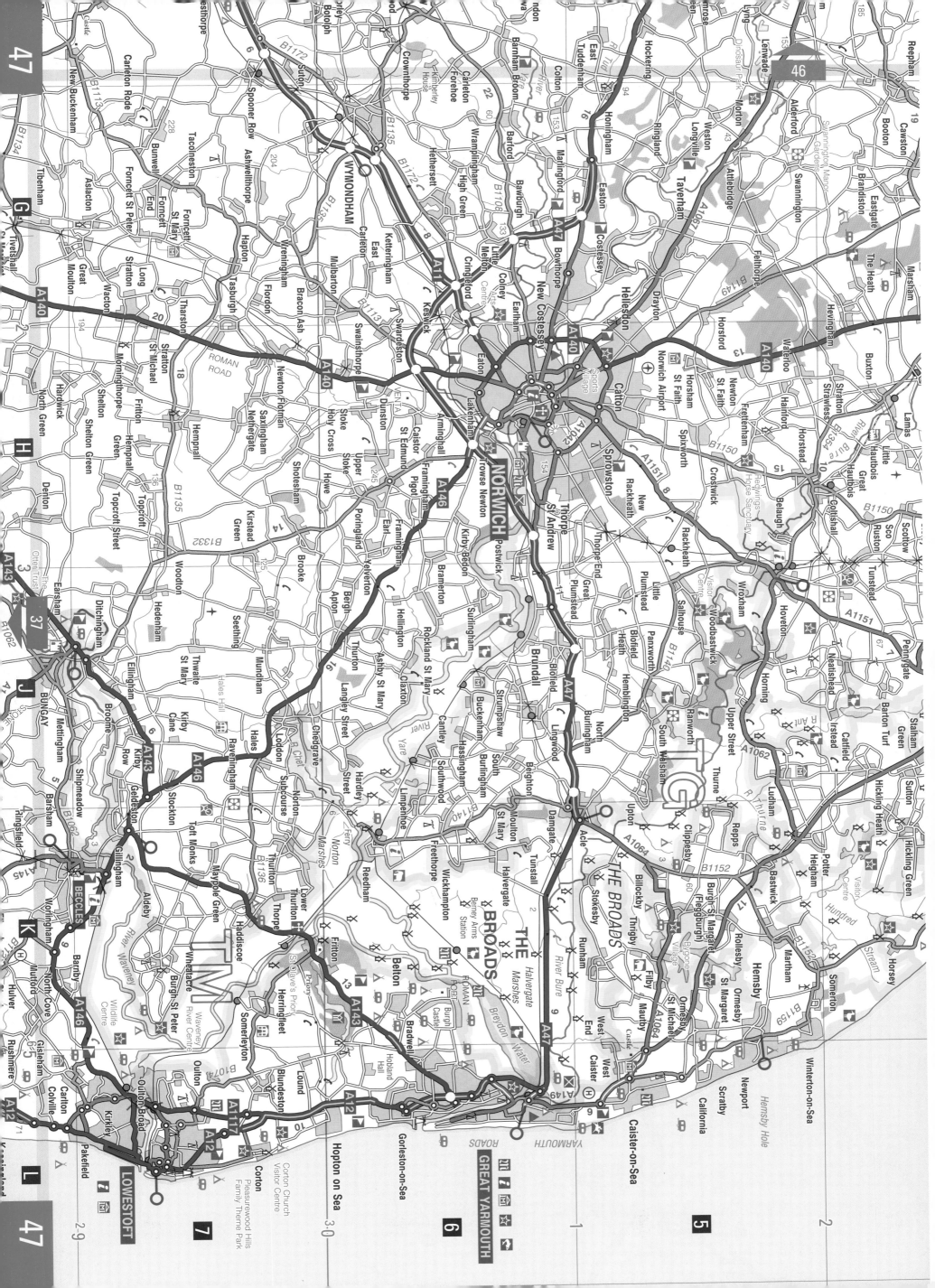

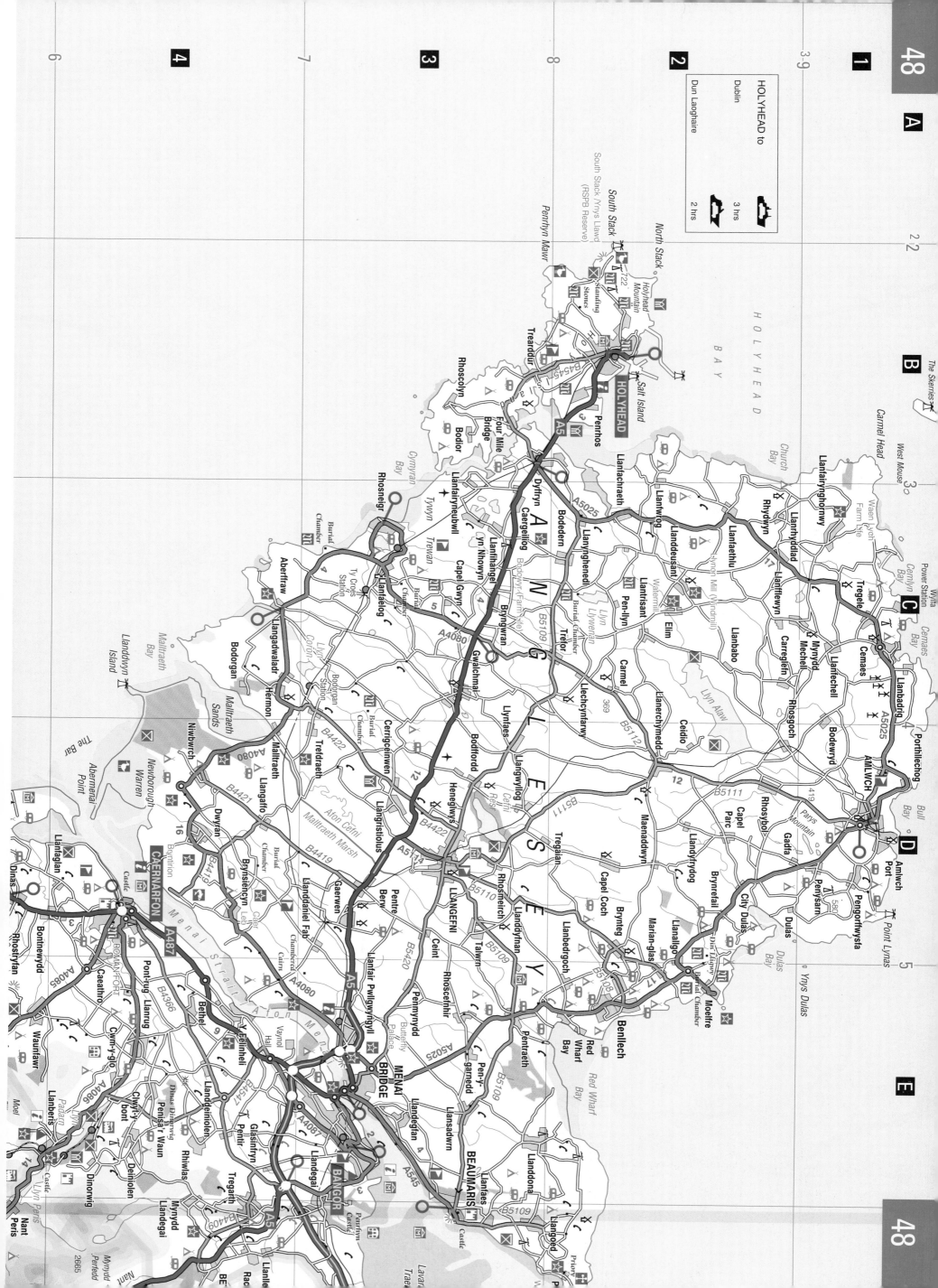

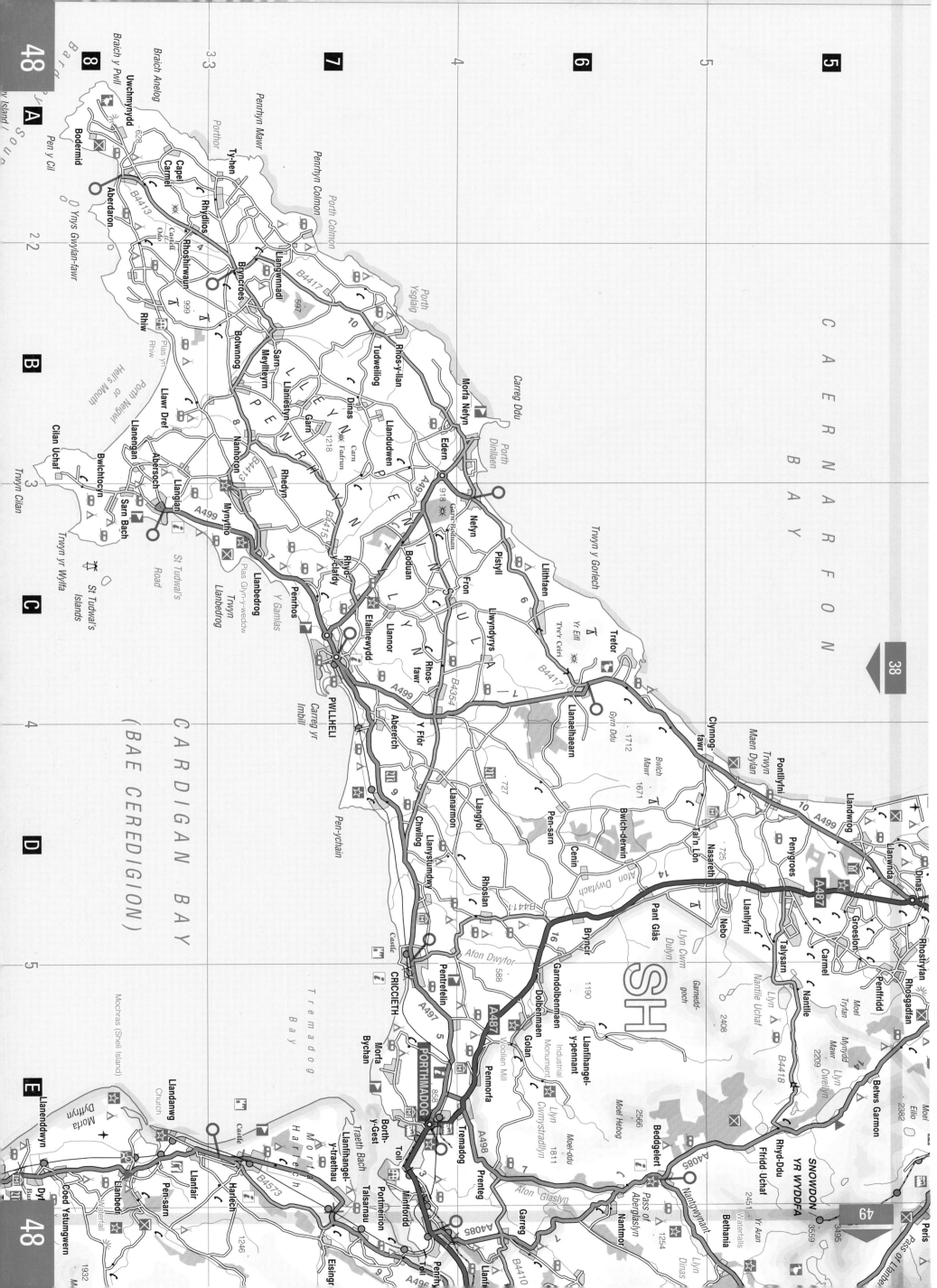

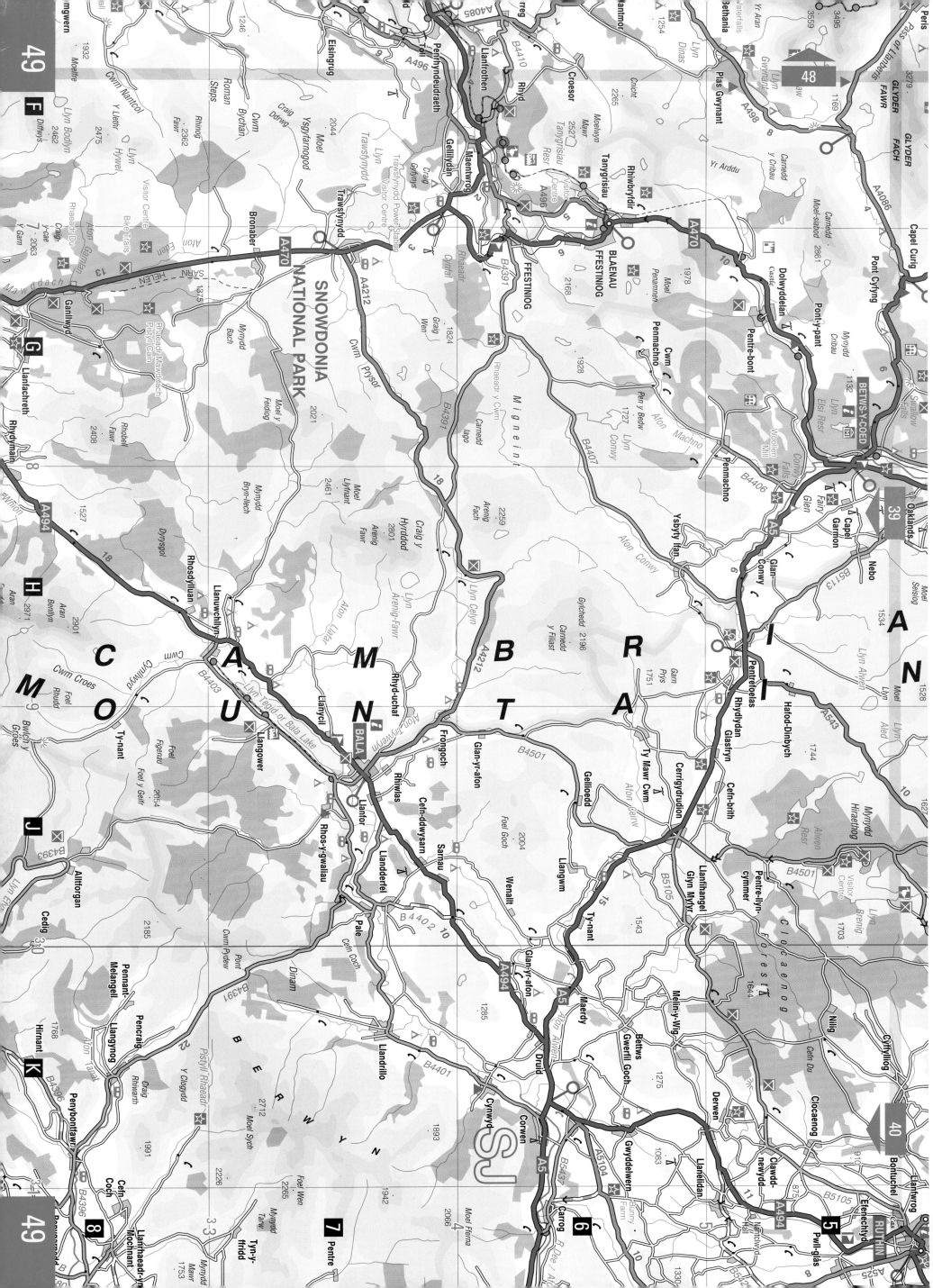

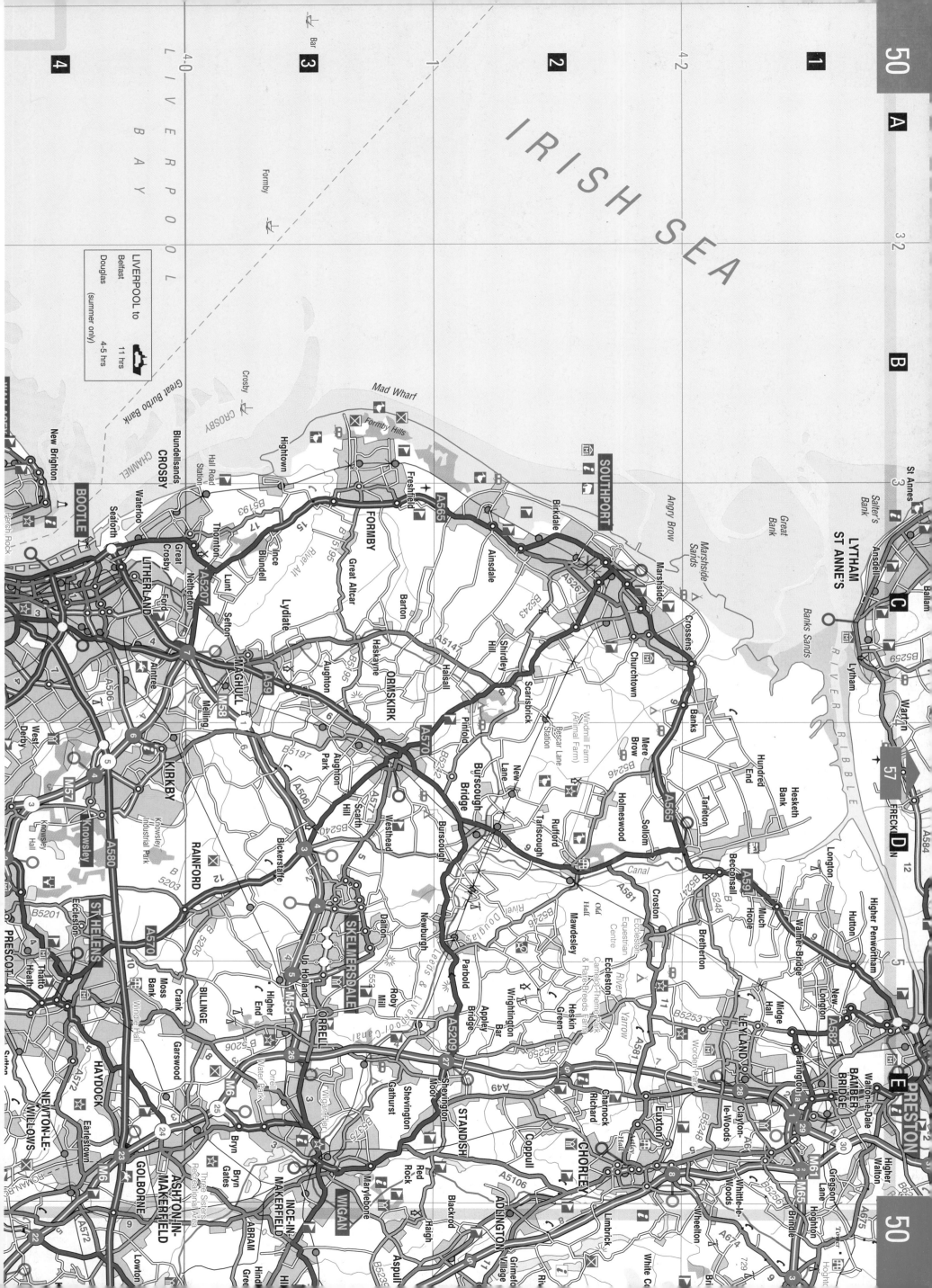

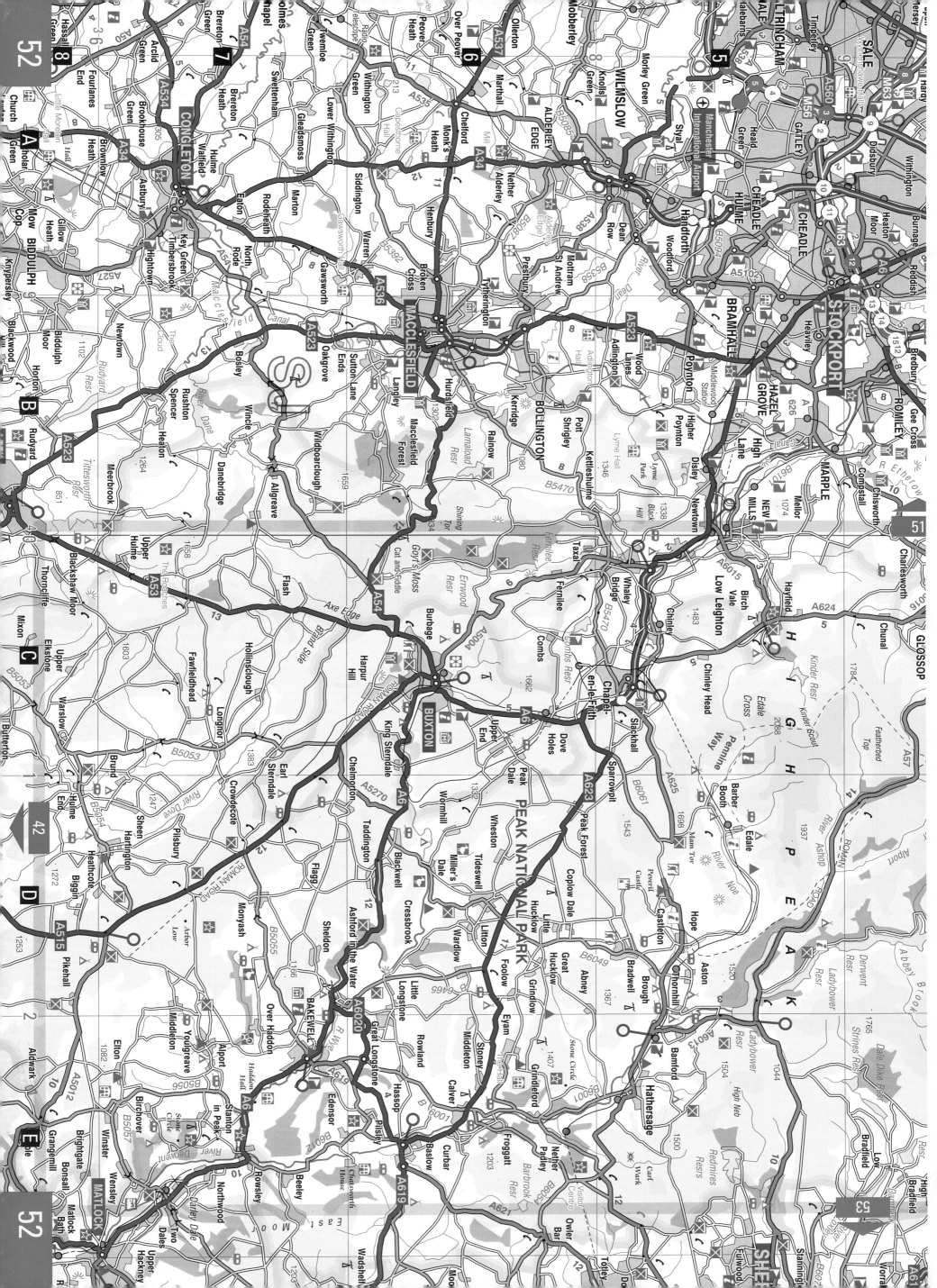

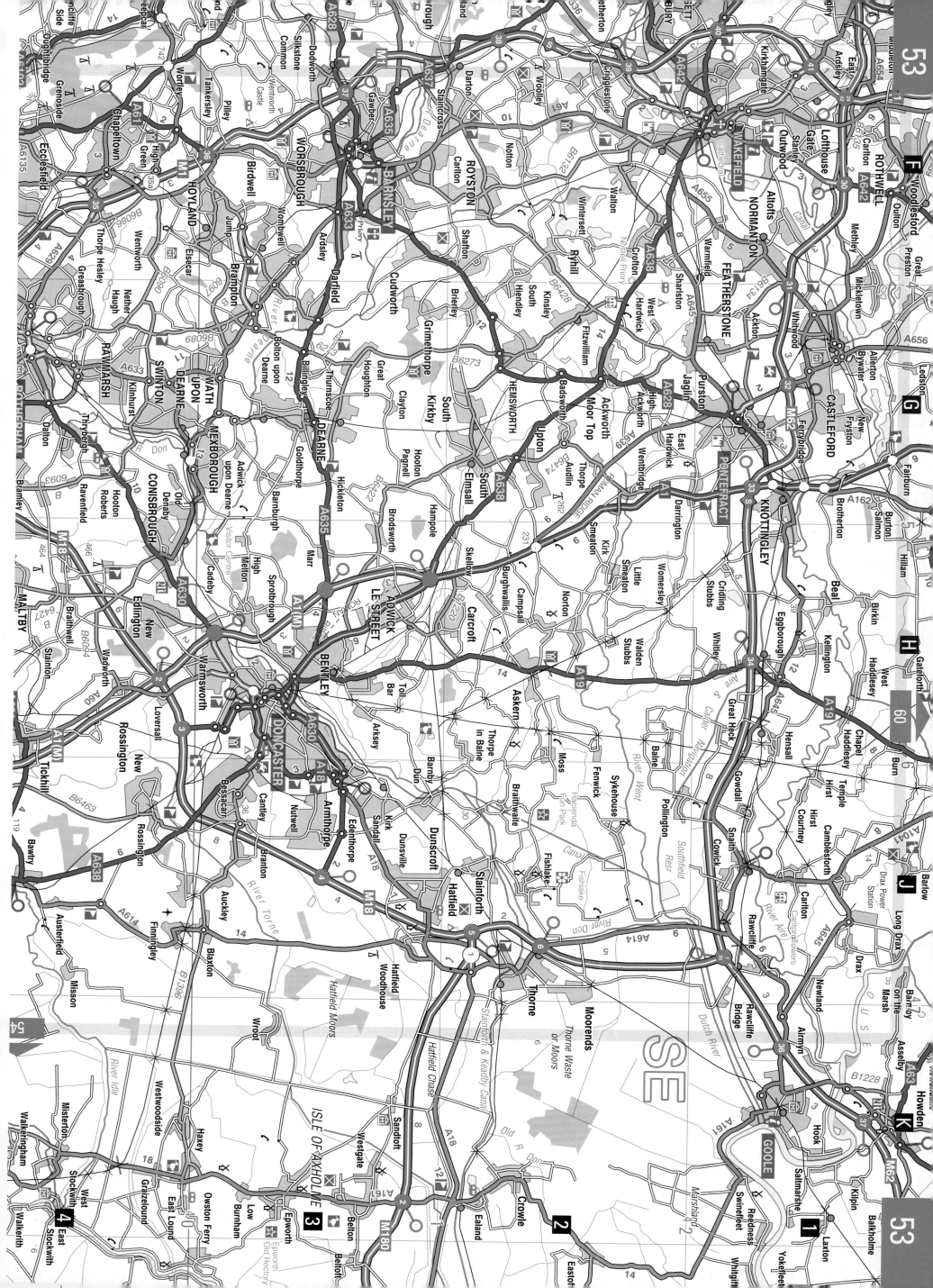

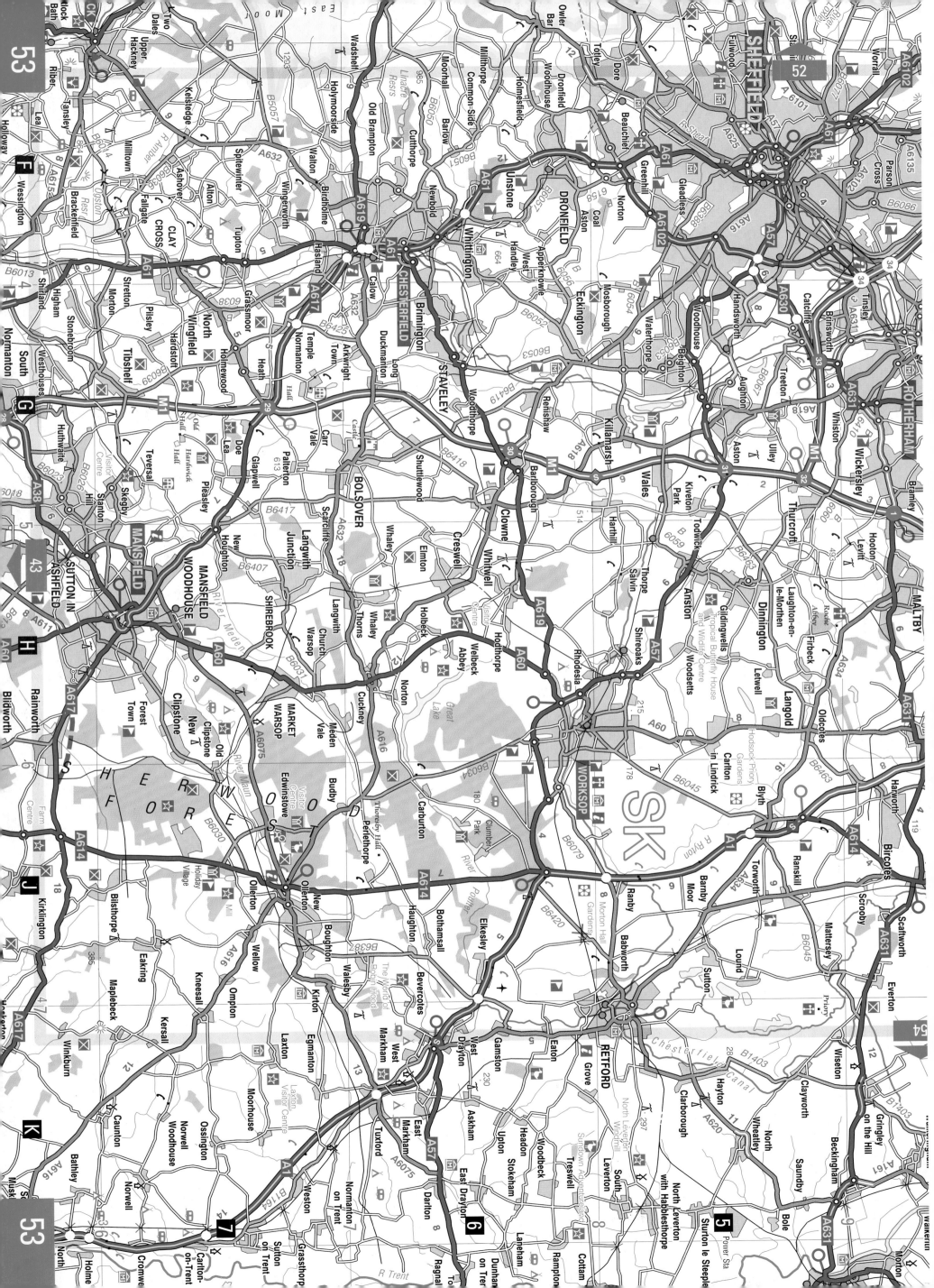

NORTH SEA

GRIMSBY

CLEETHORPES

WITHERNSEA

HEDON

Immingham

SPURN HEAD

MOUTH OF THE HUMBER

RIVER HUMBER

Discovery Centre
Butterfly Gardens
Pleasure Island Theme Park
Haile Sand Fort

Due to open Mid 1998

KINGSTON UPON HULL to
Rotterdam (Europort)   14 hrs
Zeebrugge   14 hrs
South East Chequer

Donna Nook

Saltfleet

North Somercotes

South Somercotes

Conisholme

Grainthorpe

Marshchapel

North Cotes

North Coates

Tetney Lock

Tetney

Humberston

Covenham
St Mary

Covenham
St Bartholomew

Yarburgh

Fulstow

North
Thoresby

Grainsby

Holton le
Clay

New Waltham

Waltham

Scartho

Ashby
cum Fenby

Brigsley

Barnoldby
le Beck

Bradley

Great
Coates

Aylesby

Laceby

Healing

Stallingborough

Riby

Keelby

Brocklesby

Habrough

South
Killingholme

North
Killingholme

Thornton
Abbey

East
Halton

East Halton
Skitter

Oil Terminal

Power Station

Oil Refineries

Immingham
Docks

Paull

Thorngumbald

Burstwick

Keyingham

Halsham

Ottringham

Patrington

Winestead

Welwick

Weeton

Skeffling

Easington

Kilnsea

Out
Newton

Holmpton

Hollym

Rimswell

Waxholme

Sunk Island

Salthaugh
Grange

The Old Hall

Pauli Holme
Sands

Fouholme
Sands

Cherry Cobb
Sands

Sunk Island Sands

Bull Sand Fort

Dolphin

Spurn

Visitor Centre

Beelsby

Hatcliffe

Irby Upon
Humber

Windmill

Binbrook

Swinhope

Thorganby

Croxby

Rothwell

Cabourne

Swallow

Cuxwold

Thoresway

Stainton
le Vale

Ludborough

North
Thoresby

Wold
Newton

East
Ravendale

Consortium

T A

A18

A46

A1173

A1173

A46

A180

A160

A16

A18

B1225

B1203

B1201

B1211

B1210

B1219

B1362

B1242

B1445

B1033

A1033

A1031

A1098

A1033

G

H

J

K

55

61

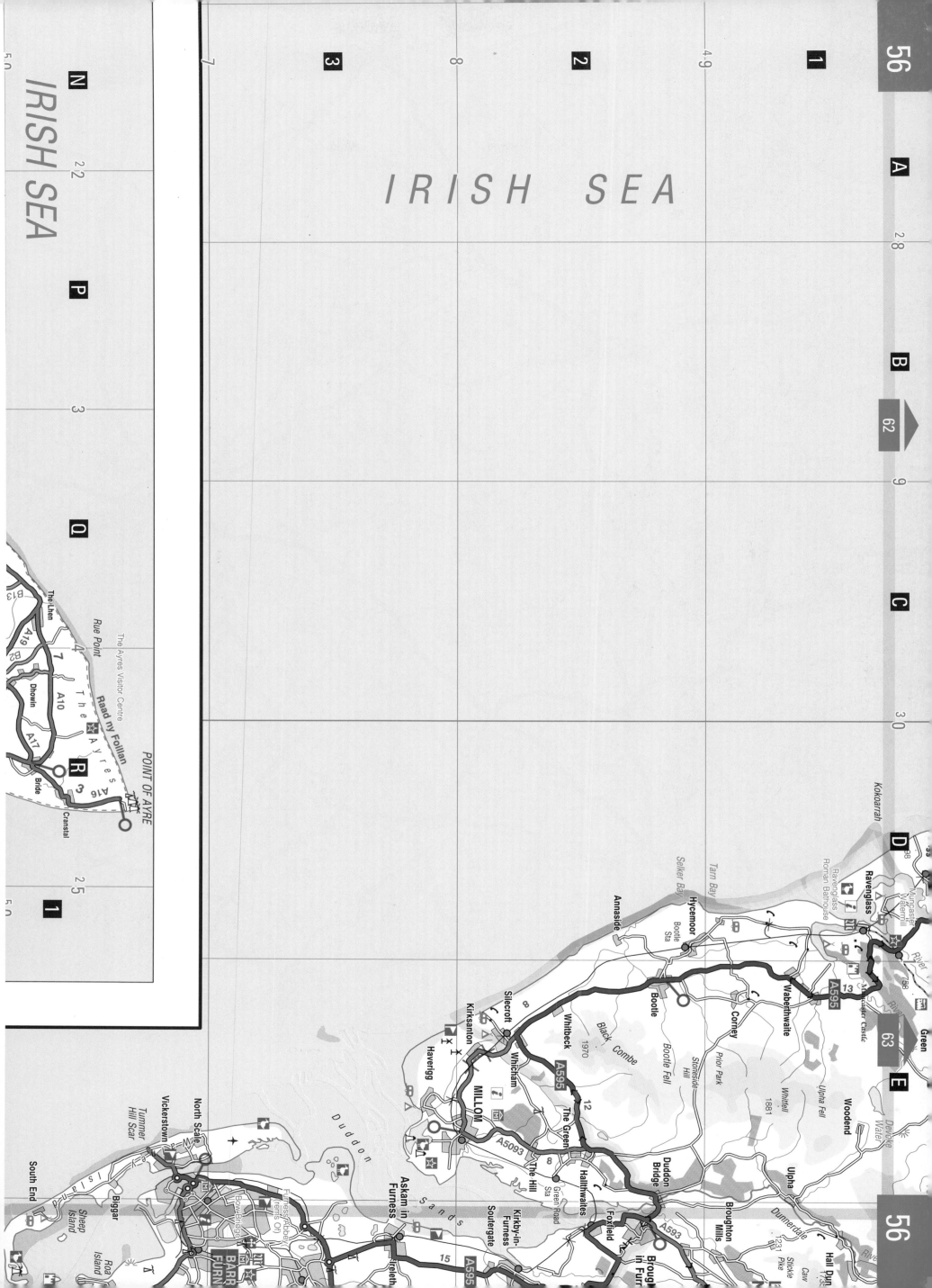

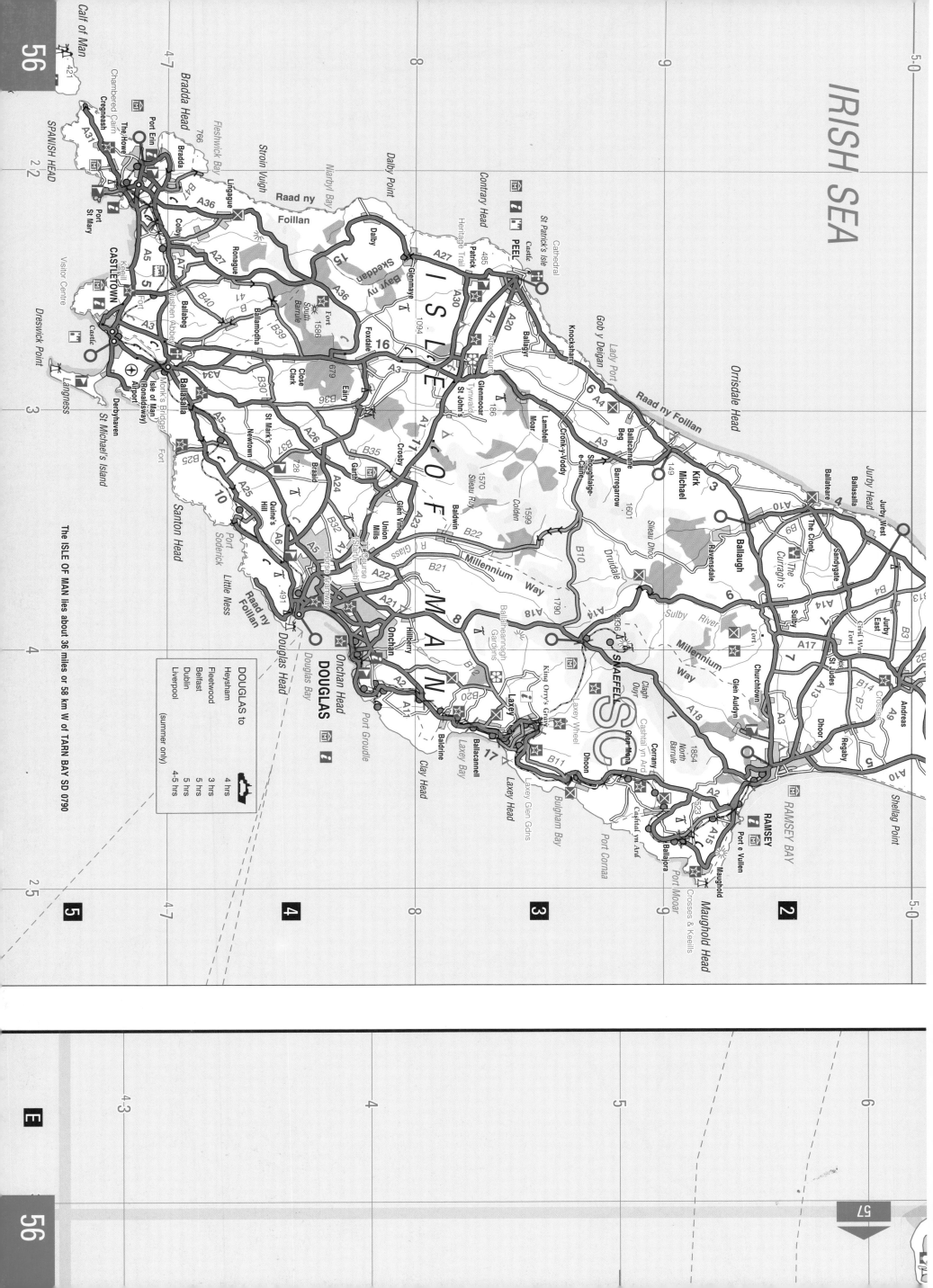

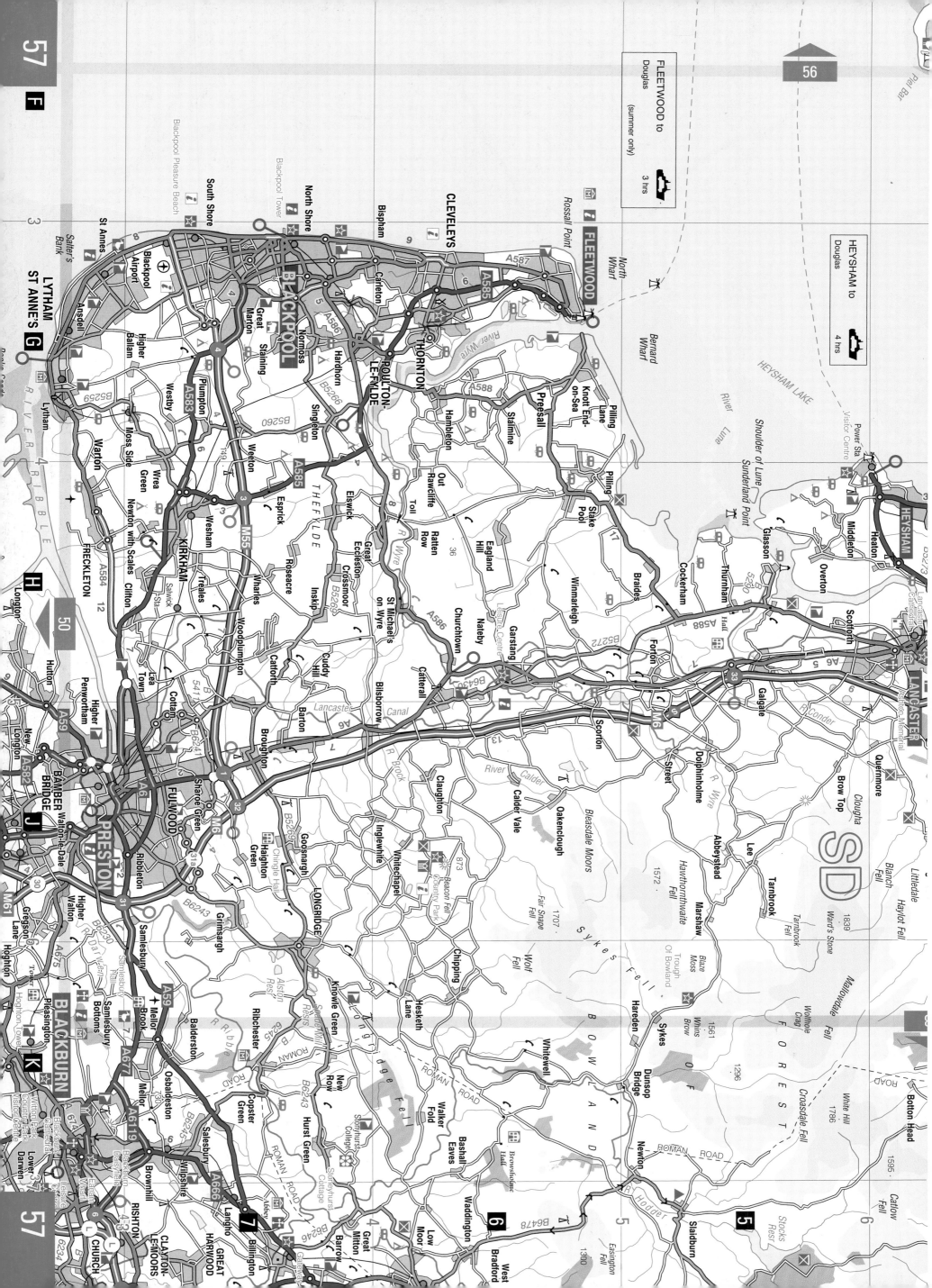

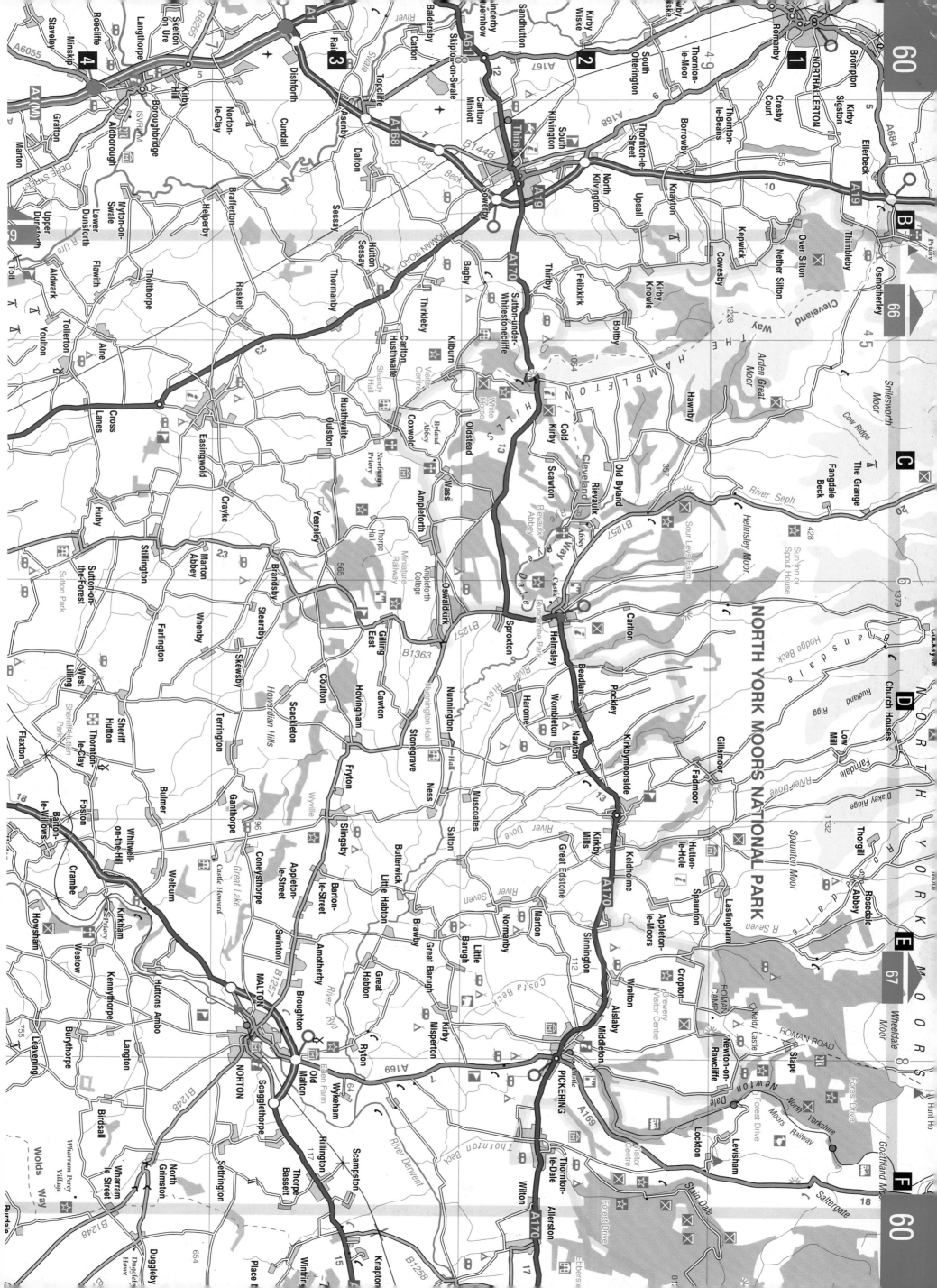

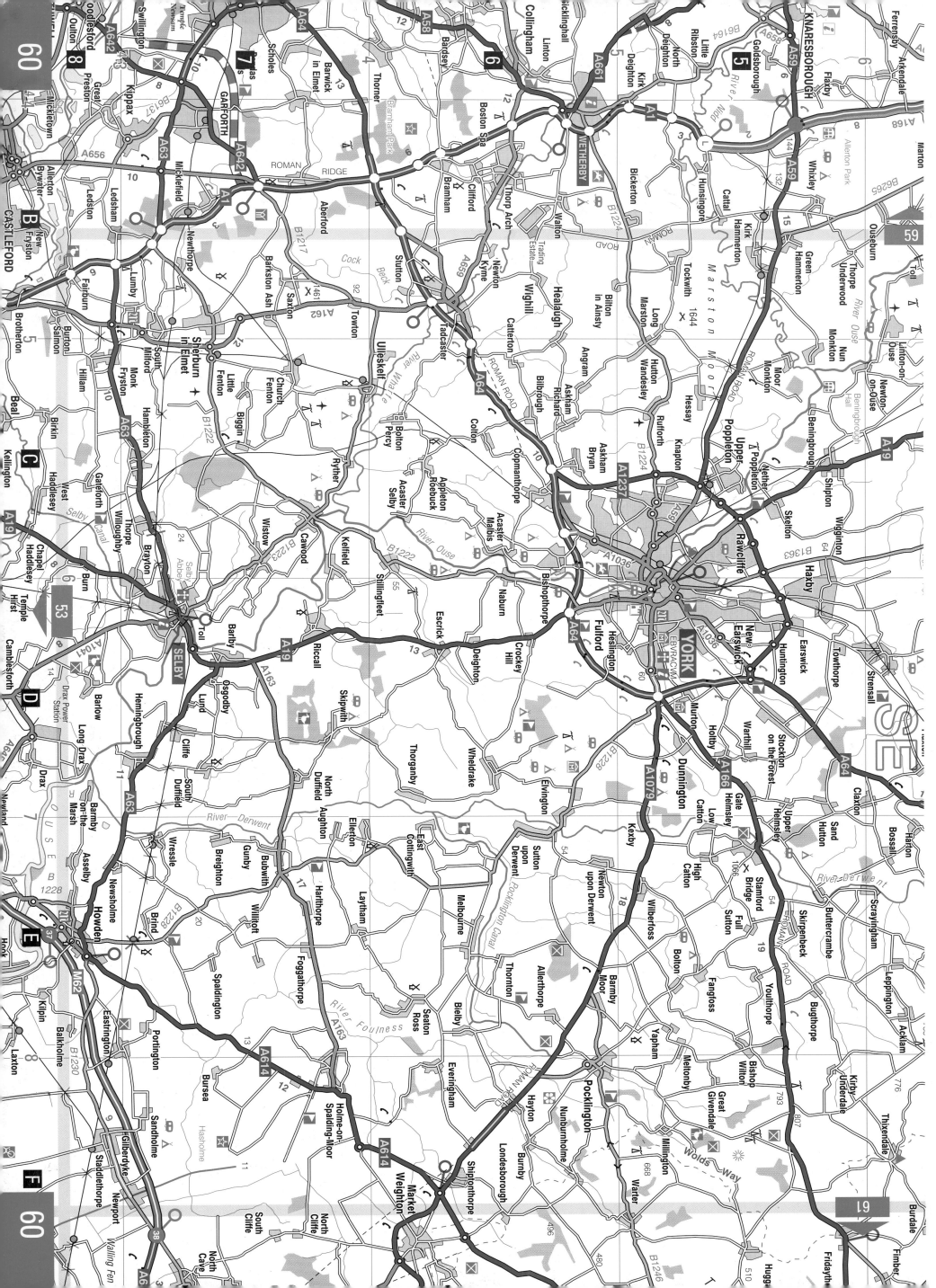

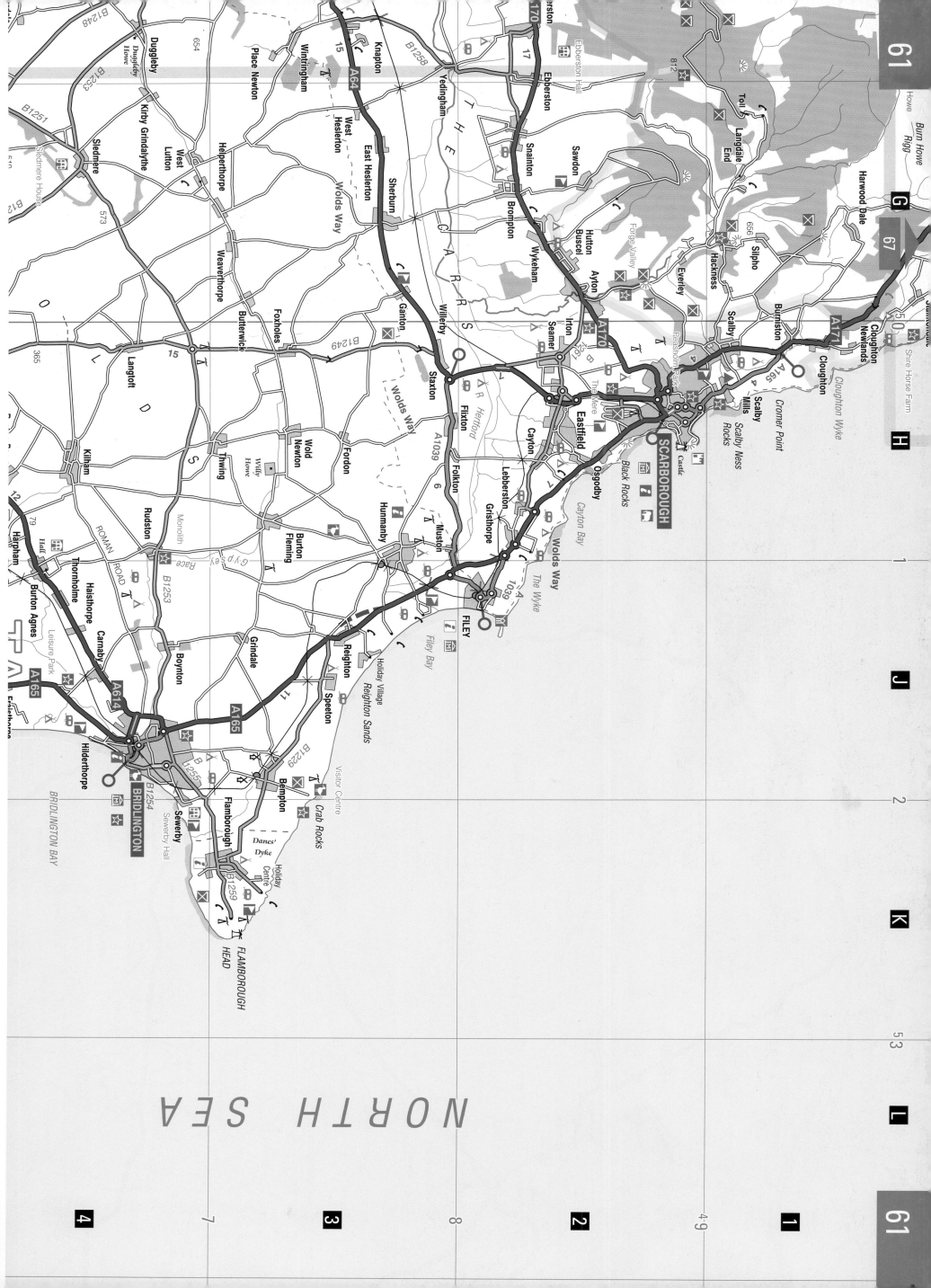

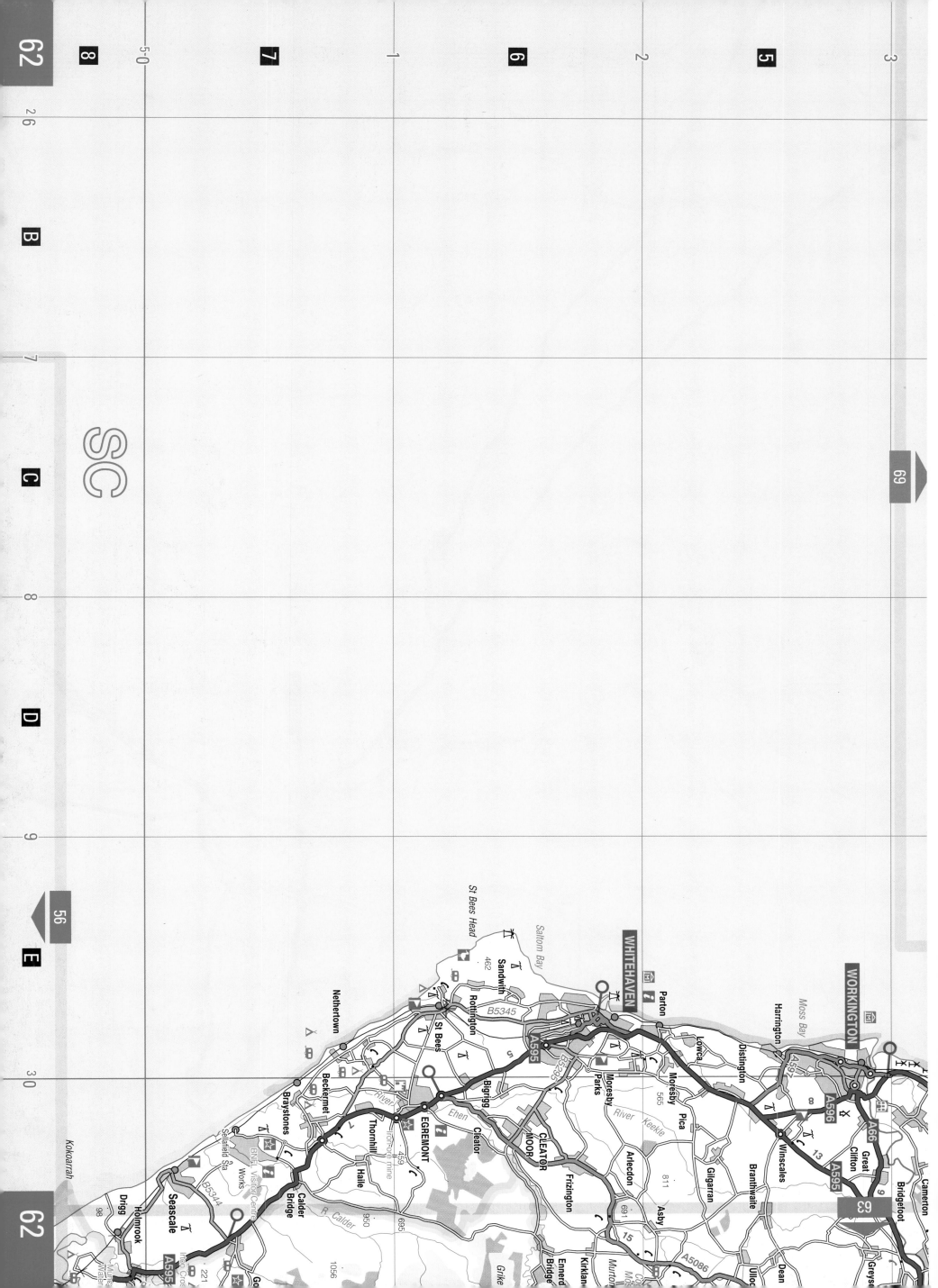

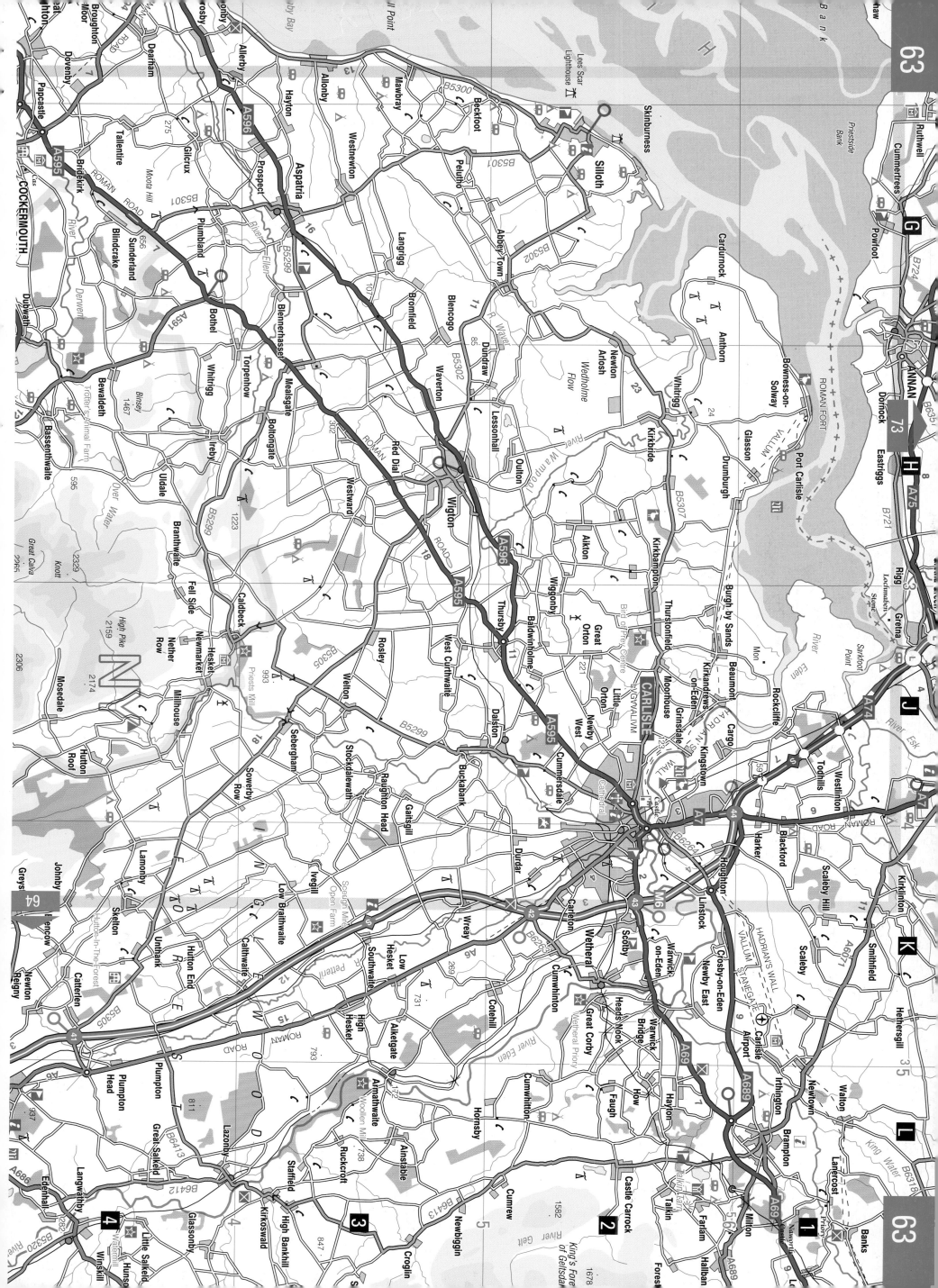

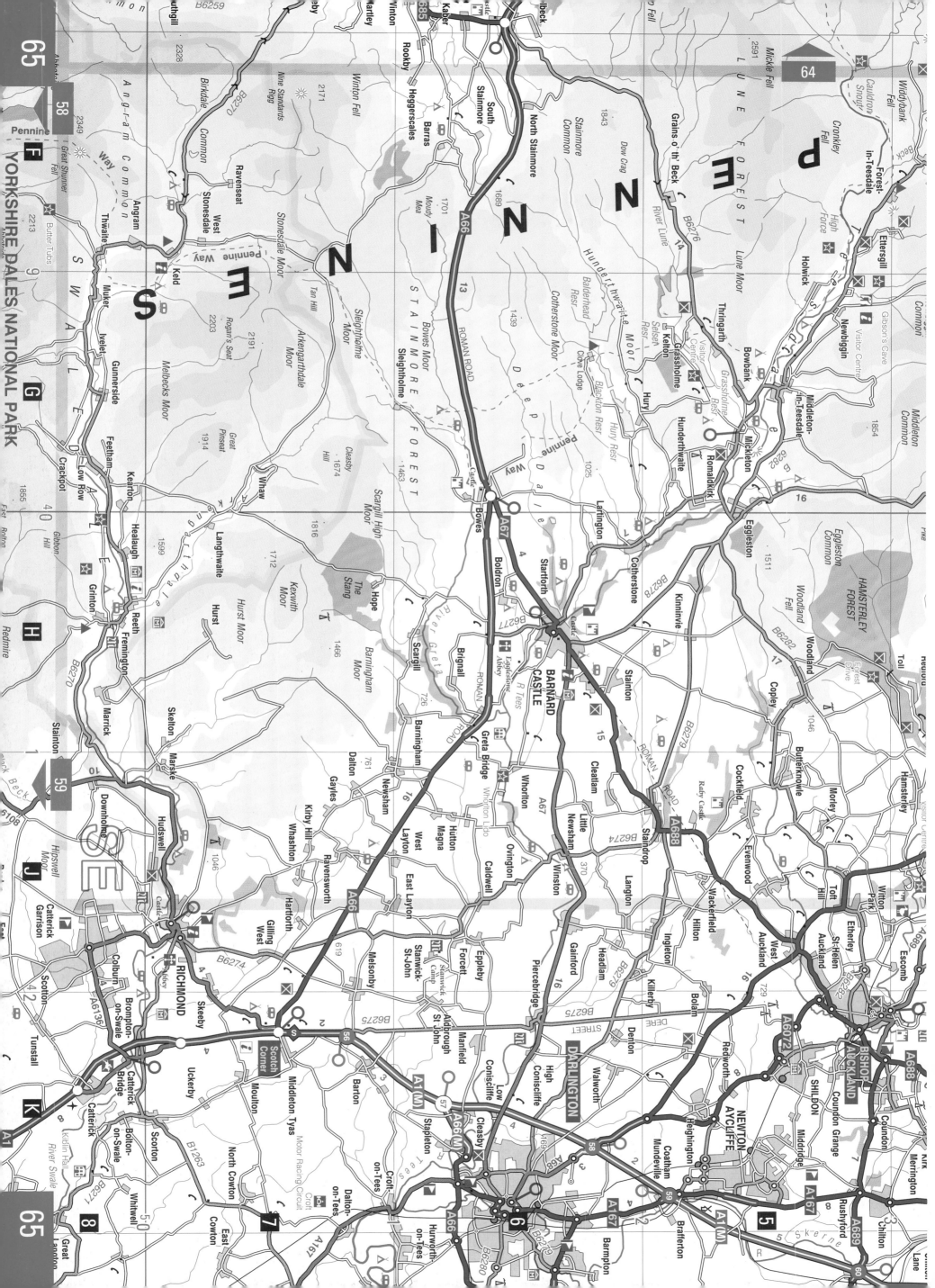

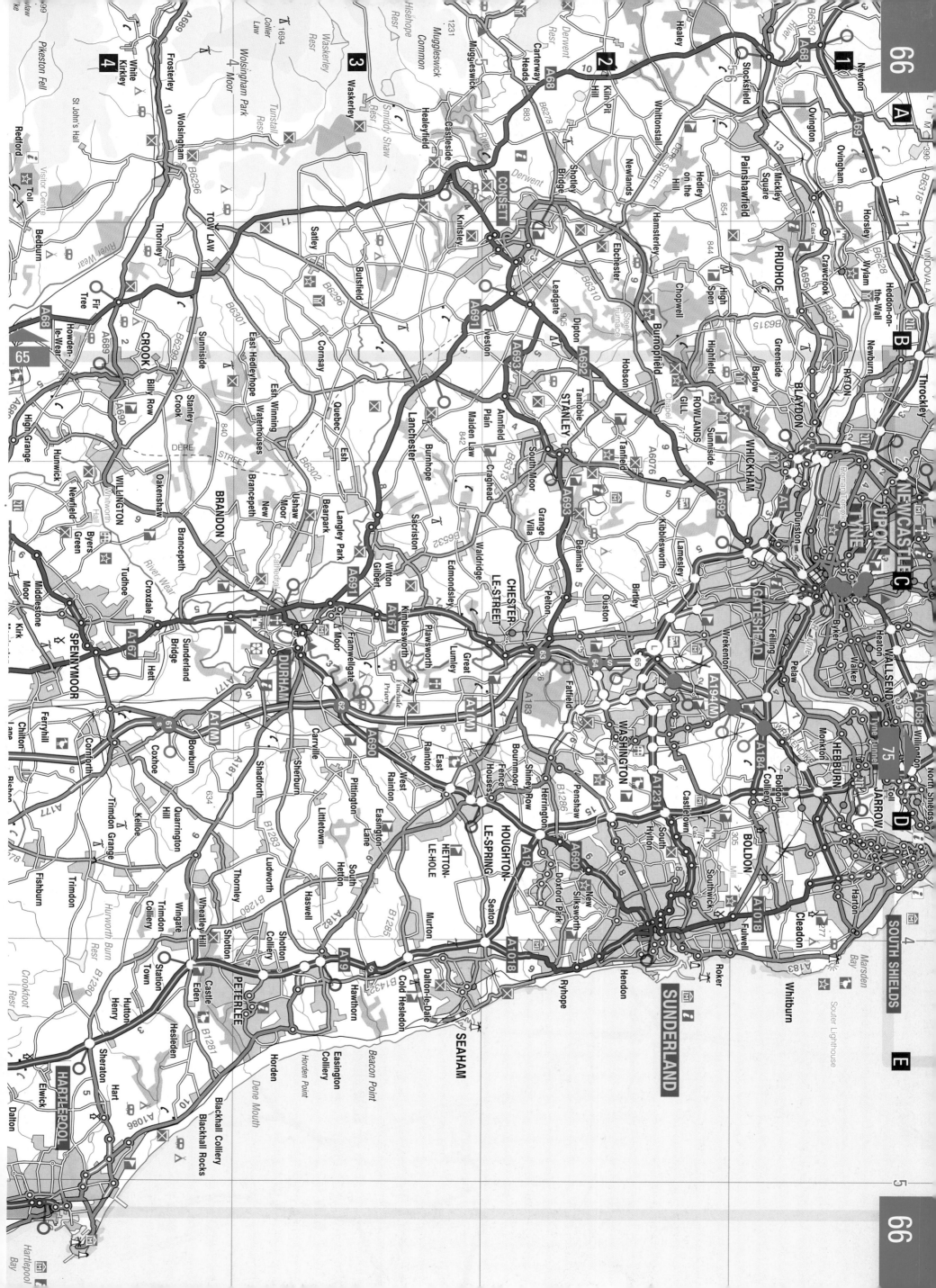

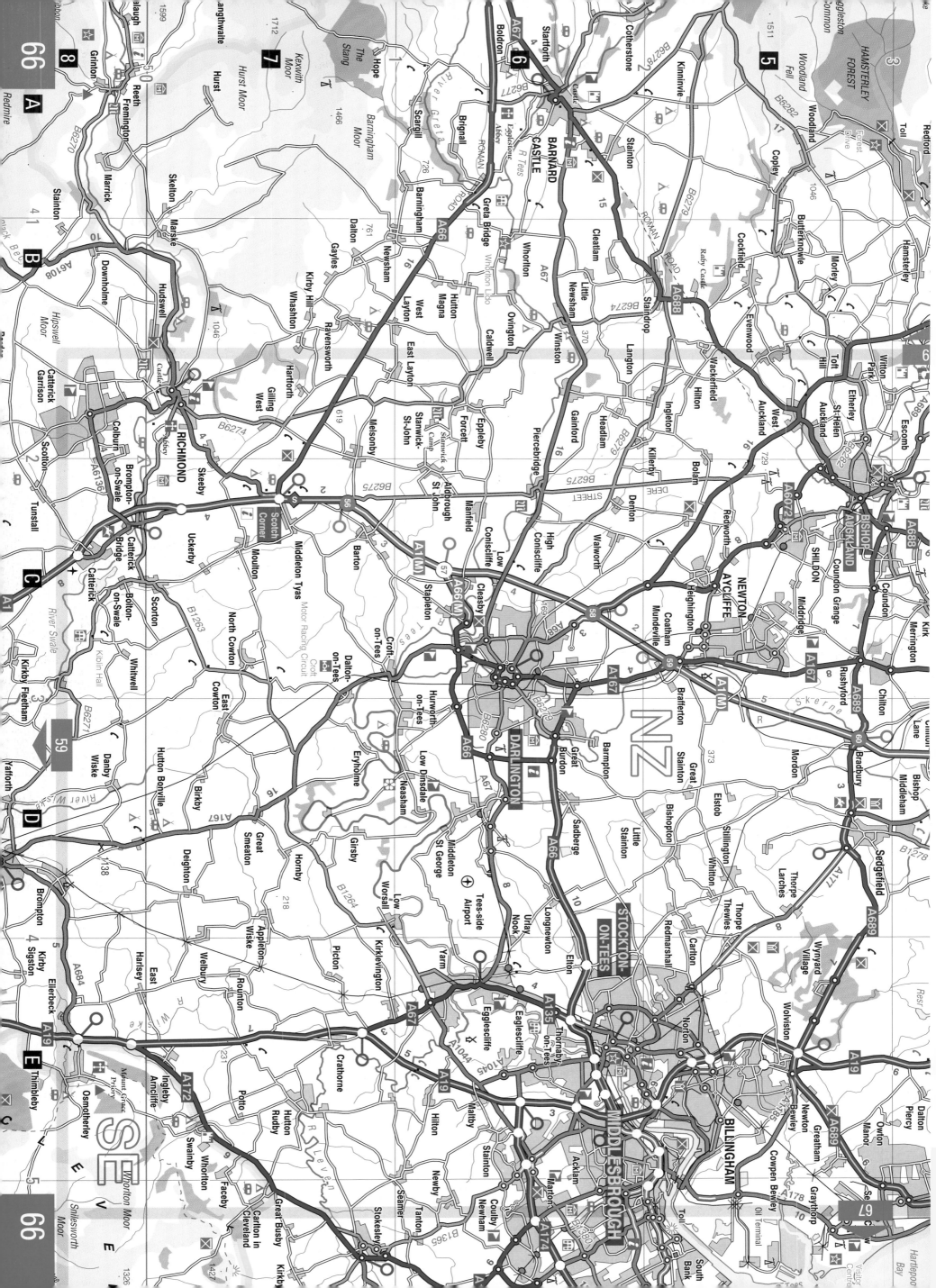

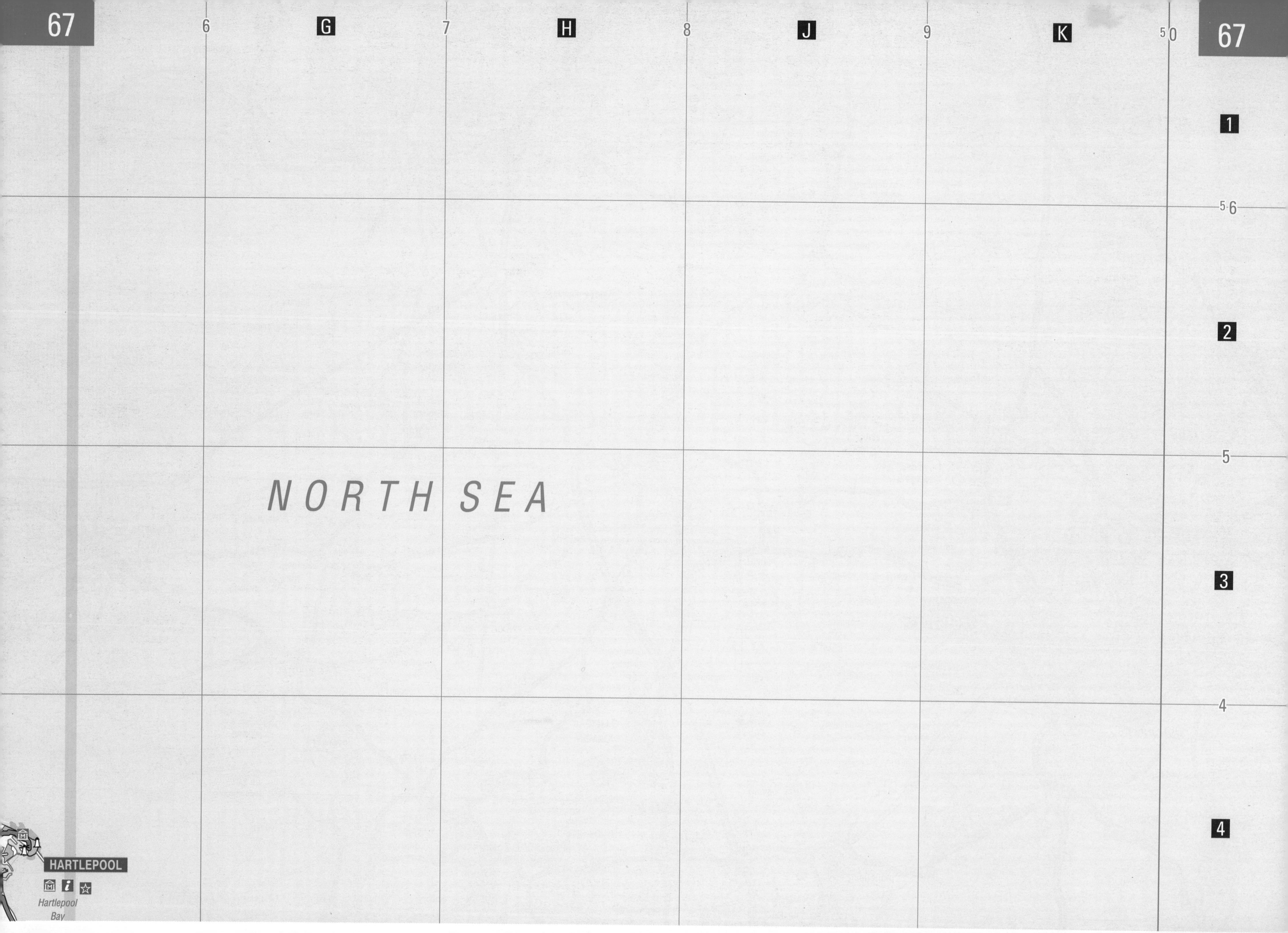
67
6
G
7
H
8
J
9
K
50
67
1
56
2
5
NORTH SEA
3
4
4
HARTLEPOOL
Hartlepool Bay

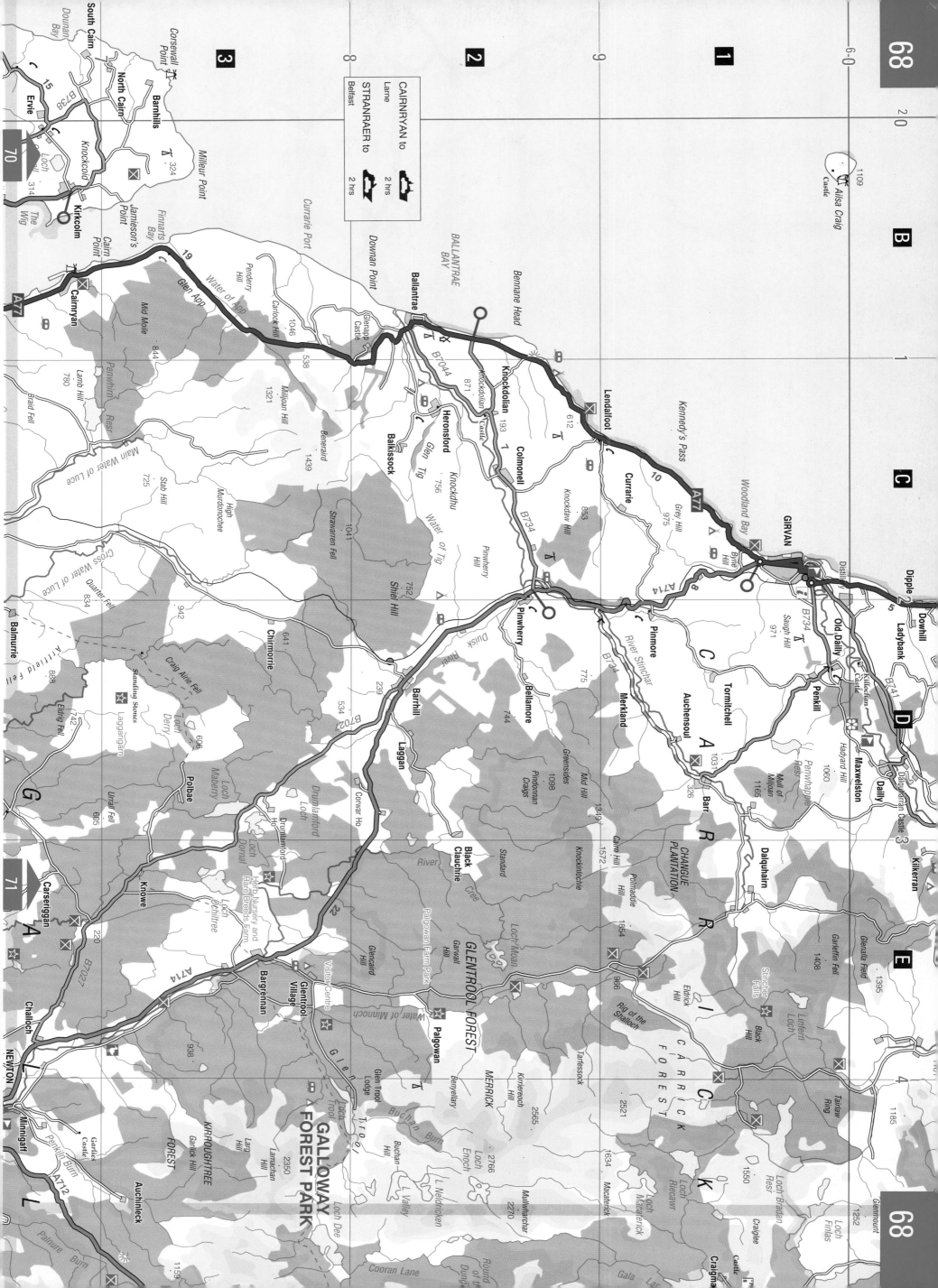

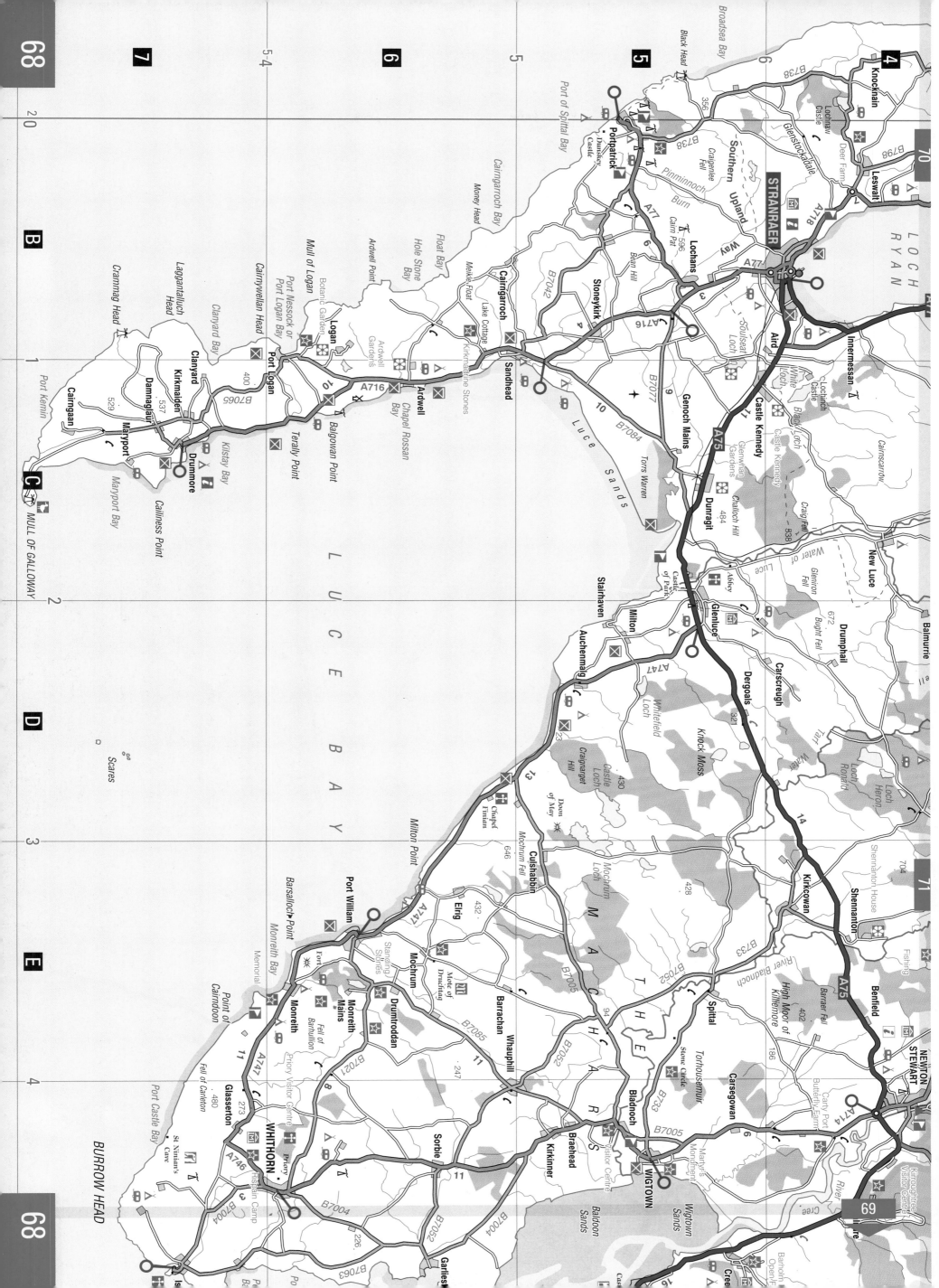

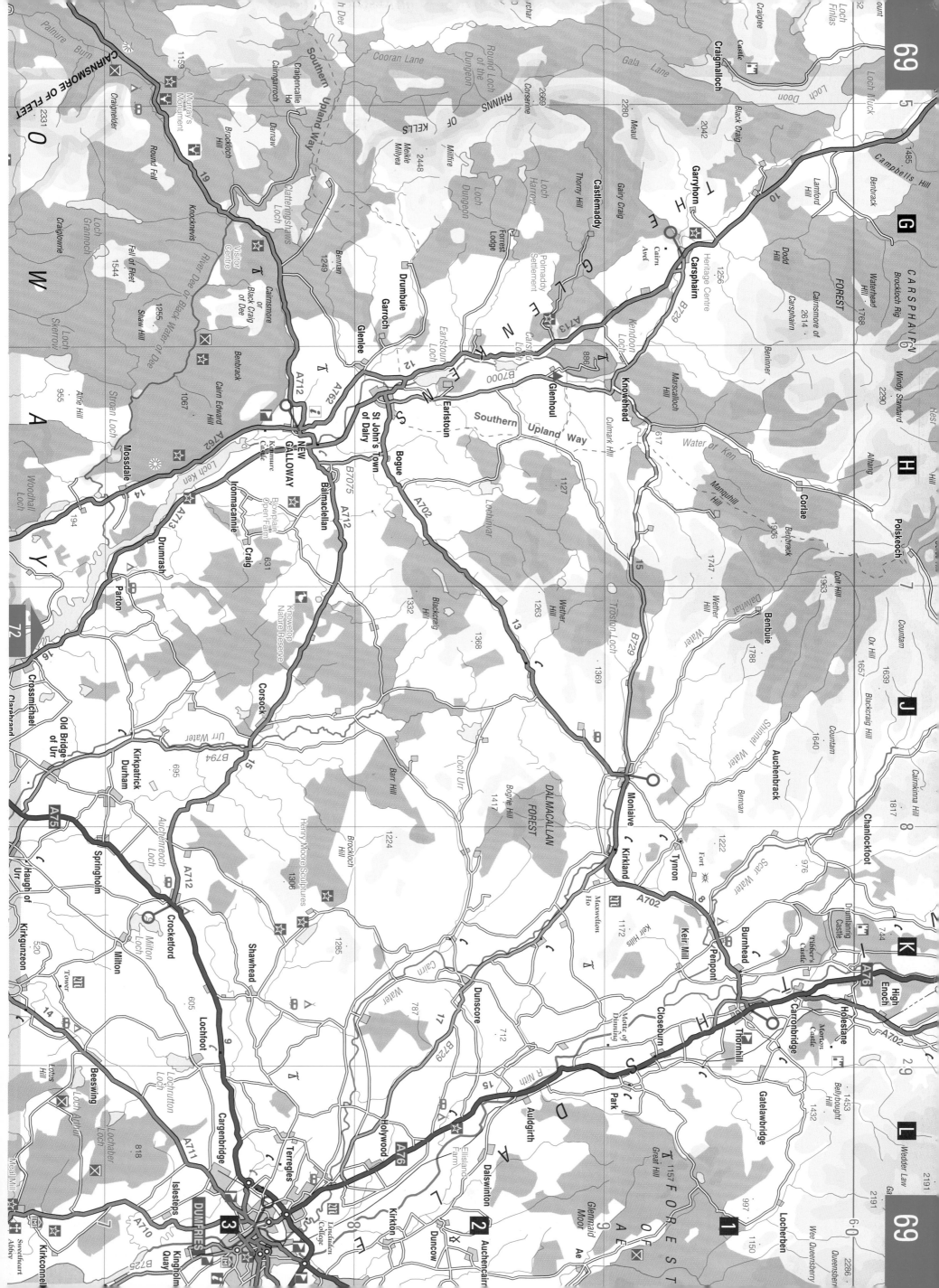

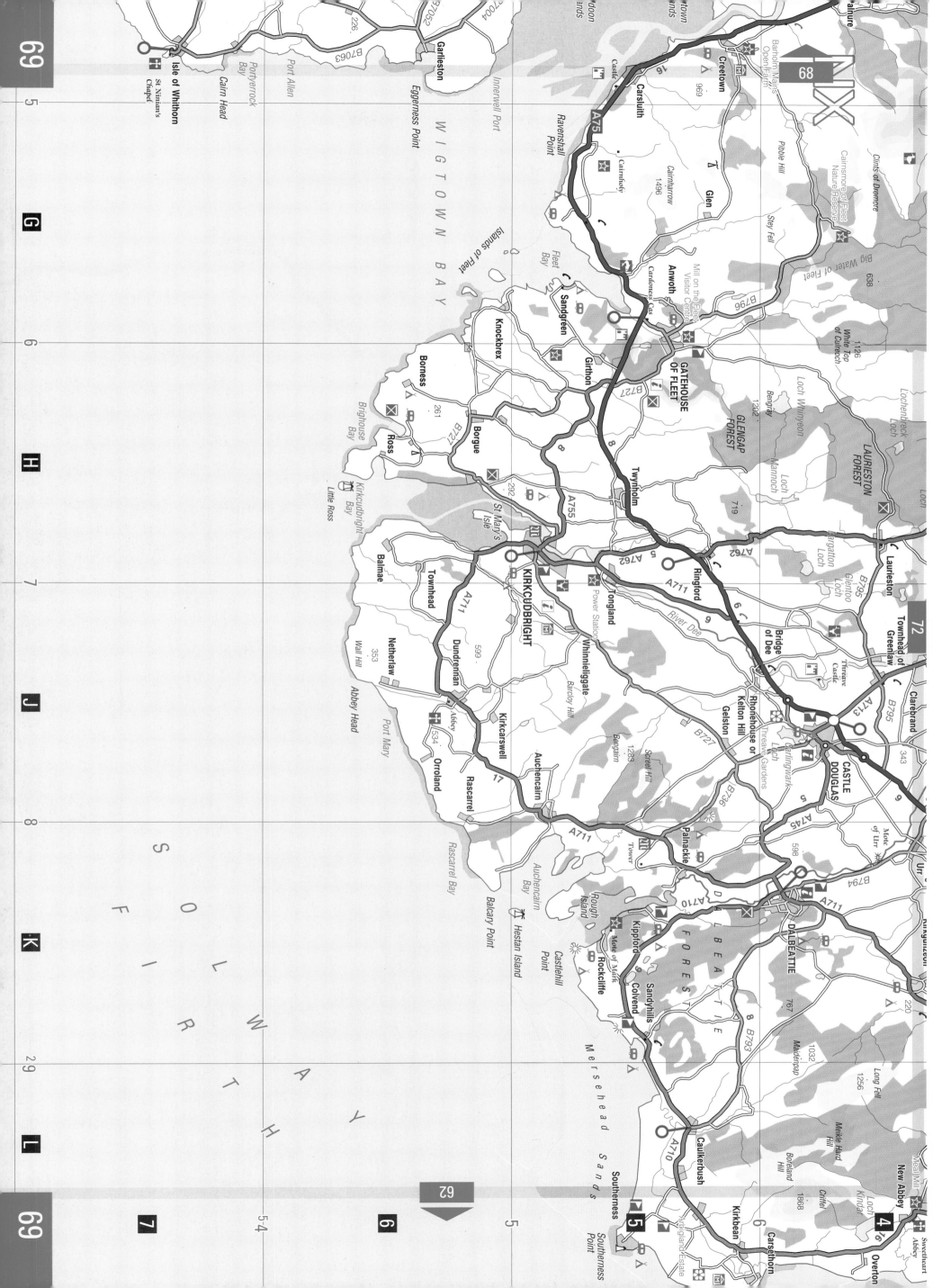

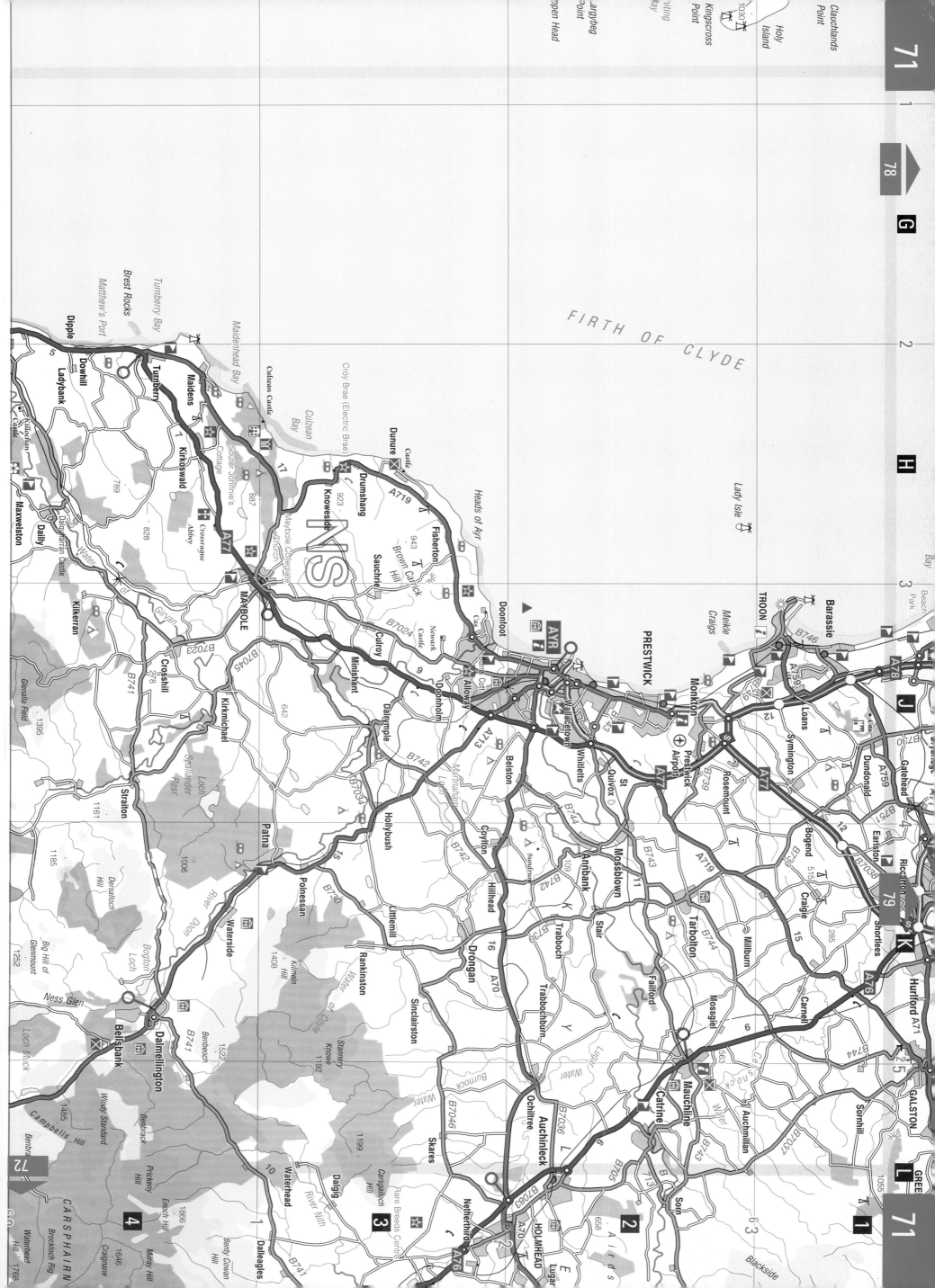

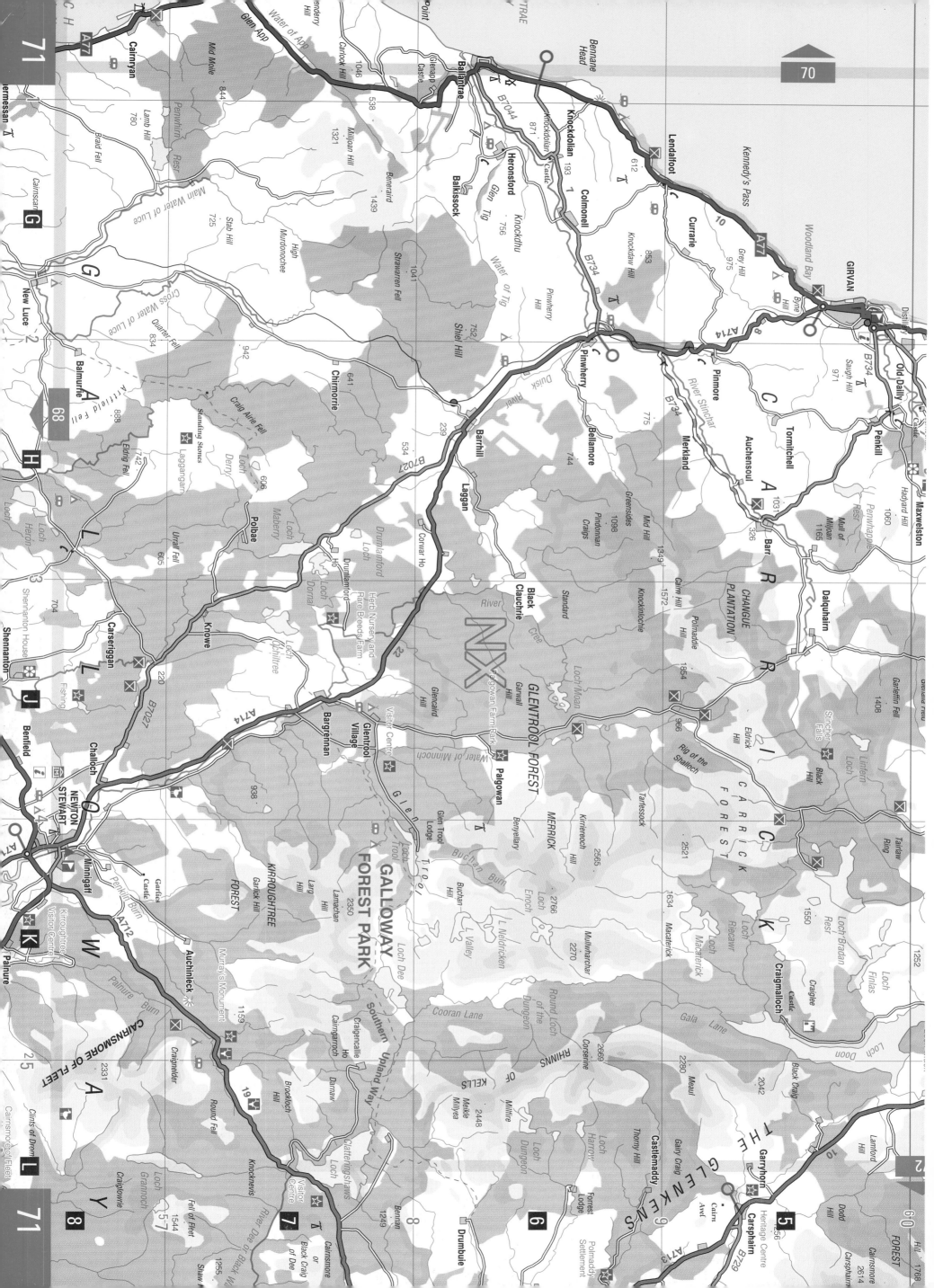

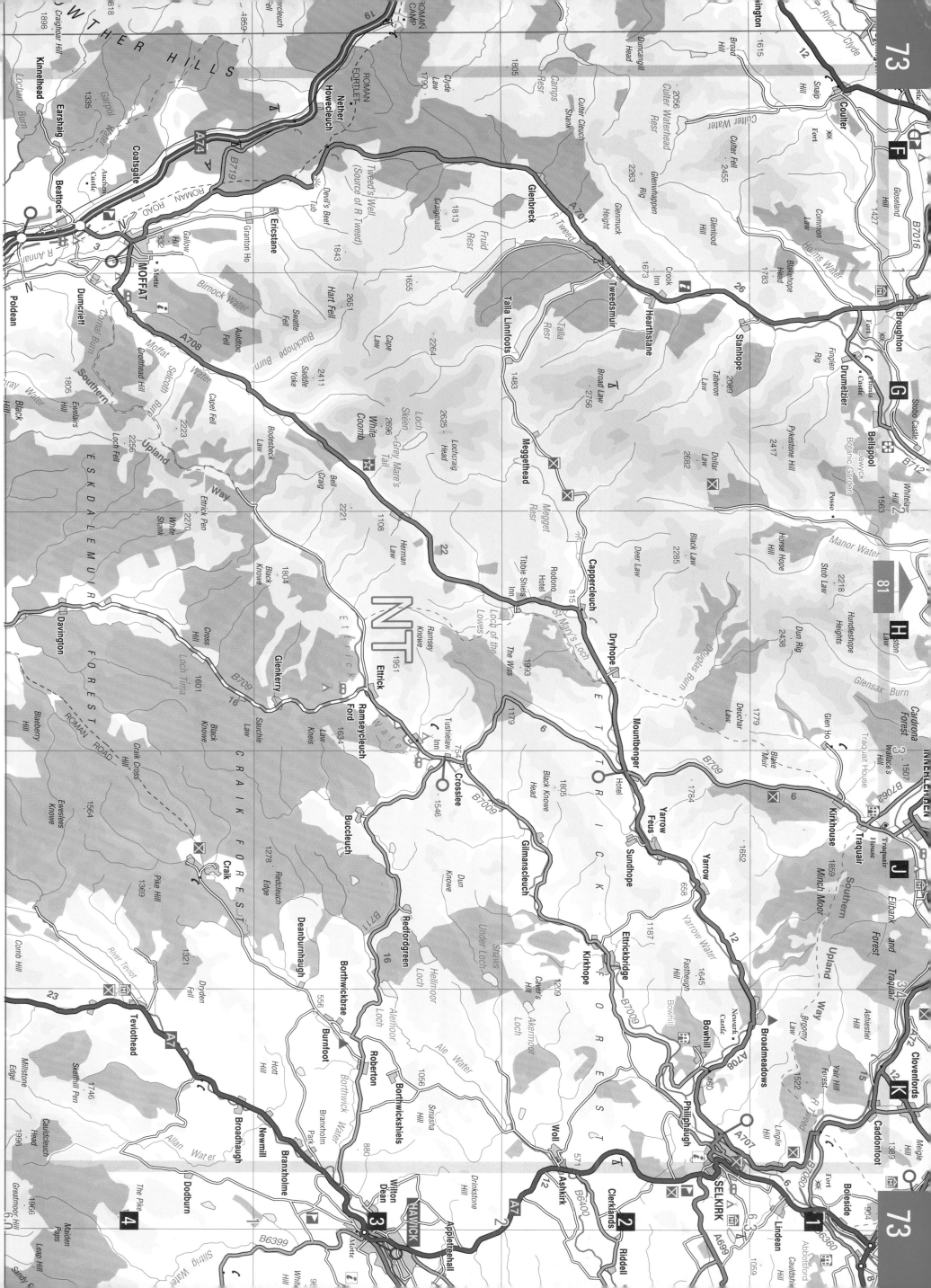

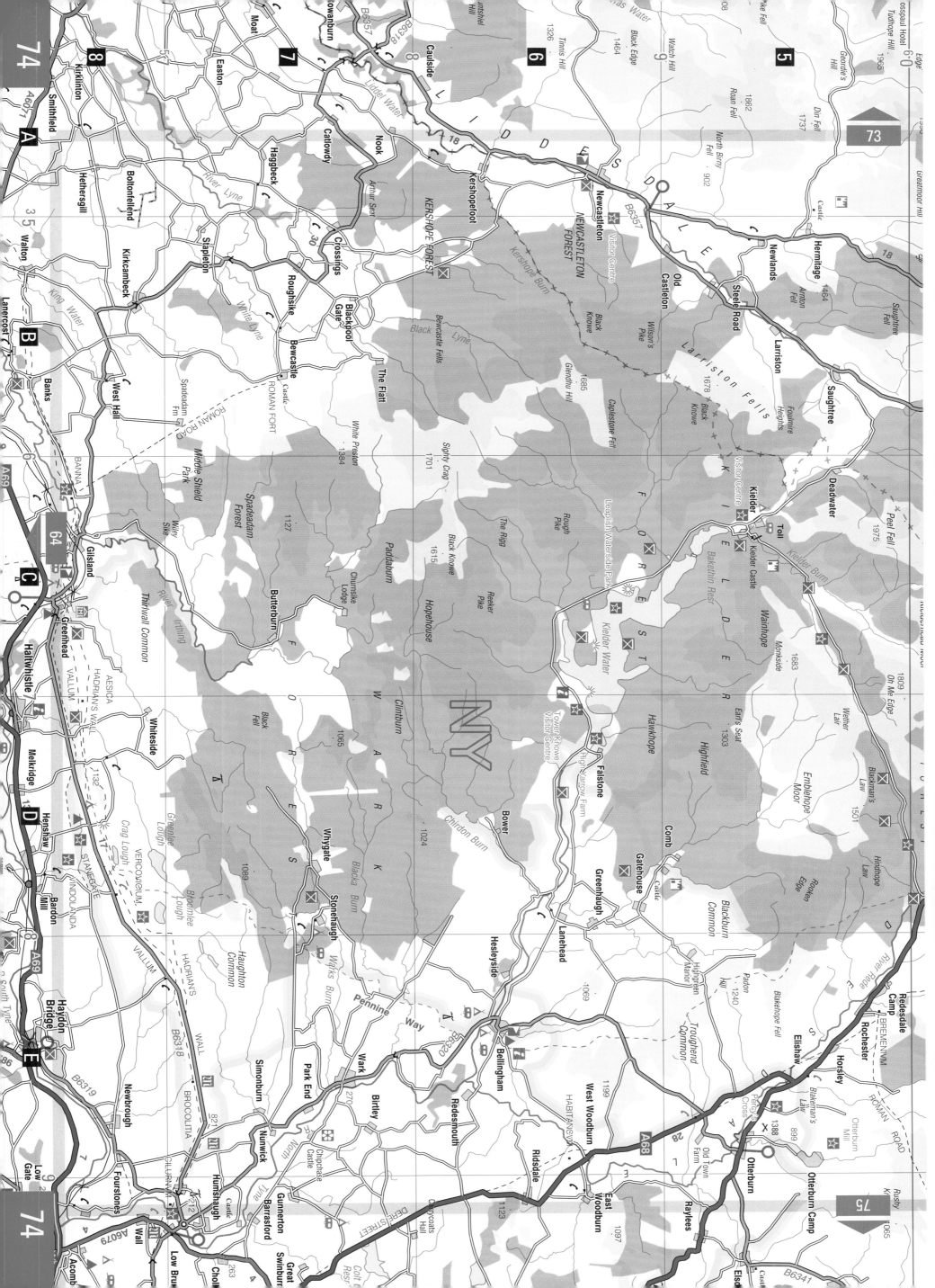

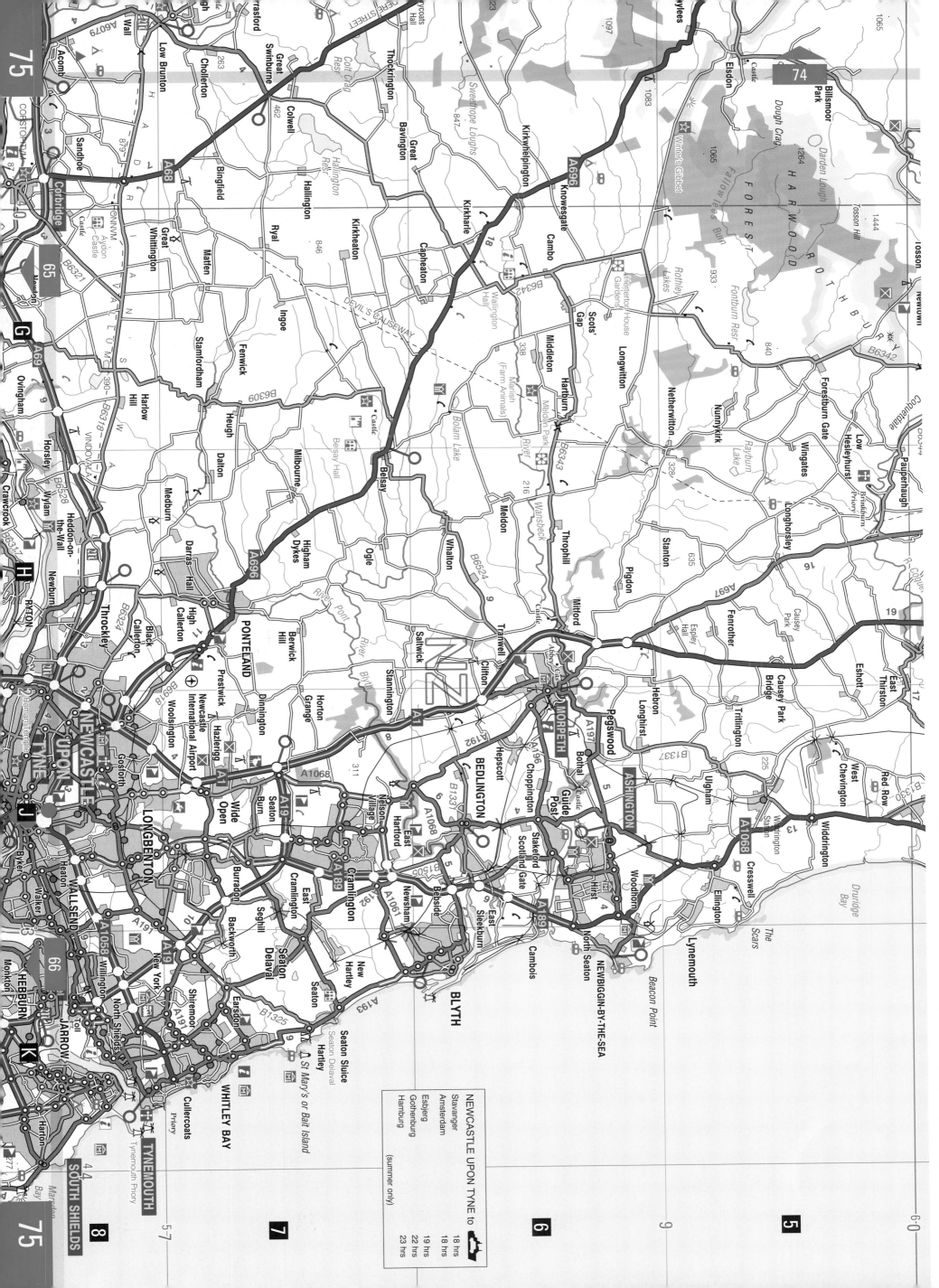

A

B

C

D

E

1

2

3

4

7·0

12

3

4

5

9

8

7

INNER HEBRIDES

Dubh Artach

An Clachan

Sanaigmore

Tòn Mhòr

Carraig Bhàn

Kilnave

Ardnave

Eilean Beag

Nave Island

Ardnave Point

Gortantaoid Point

57

Killinallan

Loch Gruinart

Gortantaoid

Beinn Bhreac

940

Sgairail

Giùr-bheinn

1037

965

Sgarbh Dubh

Loch Smigeadail

1195

Bunnahabhain

Sgarbh Breac

Bachlaig

Rubha Bholsa

Post Rocks

RUBH' A' MHAIL

Caol Ila

Port Askaig

Feolin Ferry

S O U N D

O F

Loch a' Chnuic Bhric

Inver Cottage

Gleann Astaile

Abhainn Gleann

Ubhamadair

J U R A

F O R E S T

Rubh' Aird na Sgitheich

Allt na Gile

Beinn an-Òir

2576

2477

Glen Batrick

Corran R

Glas Bheinn

1839

PAPS OF JURA

Leargybreck

Knockrome

Ardfernal

A846

24

Loch na Mìle

Lowlandman's Bay

An Dùnan

Port Doir' a' Chrorain

Lagg

Gate House

Loch an Aircill

Beinn Bhreac

1439

1029

Liundale

Loch Lesgamaill

J U R A

Cruib

1036

Choc

927

Gleann Aoistail

Rubh' a' Chamais

Tarbert

Beinn Sgaillinish

622

Skervuile Lighthouse

Rubha nan Crann

Rubh' an t-Sàilein

Rubh' a' Chrois-aoinidh

Shian Bay

Loch Righ Mòr

575

Shian River

Rainberg Mòr

Allt an Tairbh

1487

Loch Tarbert

an lìne

Corpach Bay

Maol nan Damh

887

Cruach an Uillt Fheàrna

1106

Beinn Bhreac

1532

1564

Rubha na h-Uamha-sàile

Glendebadel Bay

Glasa

COLONSAY

Kiloran Bay

An Rubha

Eilean a' Chladaich

Kilchattan

B8086

Beinn Bhreac

456

468

Uragaig

Cailleach Uragaig

Carnan Eoin

Port Ceann a' Ghàrraidh

Balnahard

Rubh' a' Geodha

Port na Cuilce

Eilean nan Ròn

Dubh Eilean

304

Priory

Oronsay Fm

ORONSAY

Caolas Mòr

Ceann Riobha

Eilean Ghaoideamal

Eilean Treadhrach

Garvard

B8085

Scalasaig

Fada

B

446

Colonsay House

Kiloran

B8087

Port a' Bhata

Uragaig

Meall an Arbhair

Rubha Dubh

Loch Staosnaig

Port-an-Obain

COLONSAY to Oban

2 hrs

1 hr (summer only)

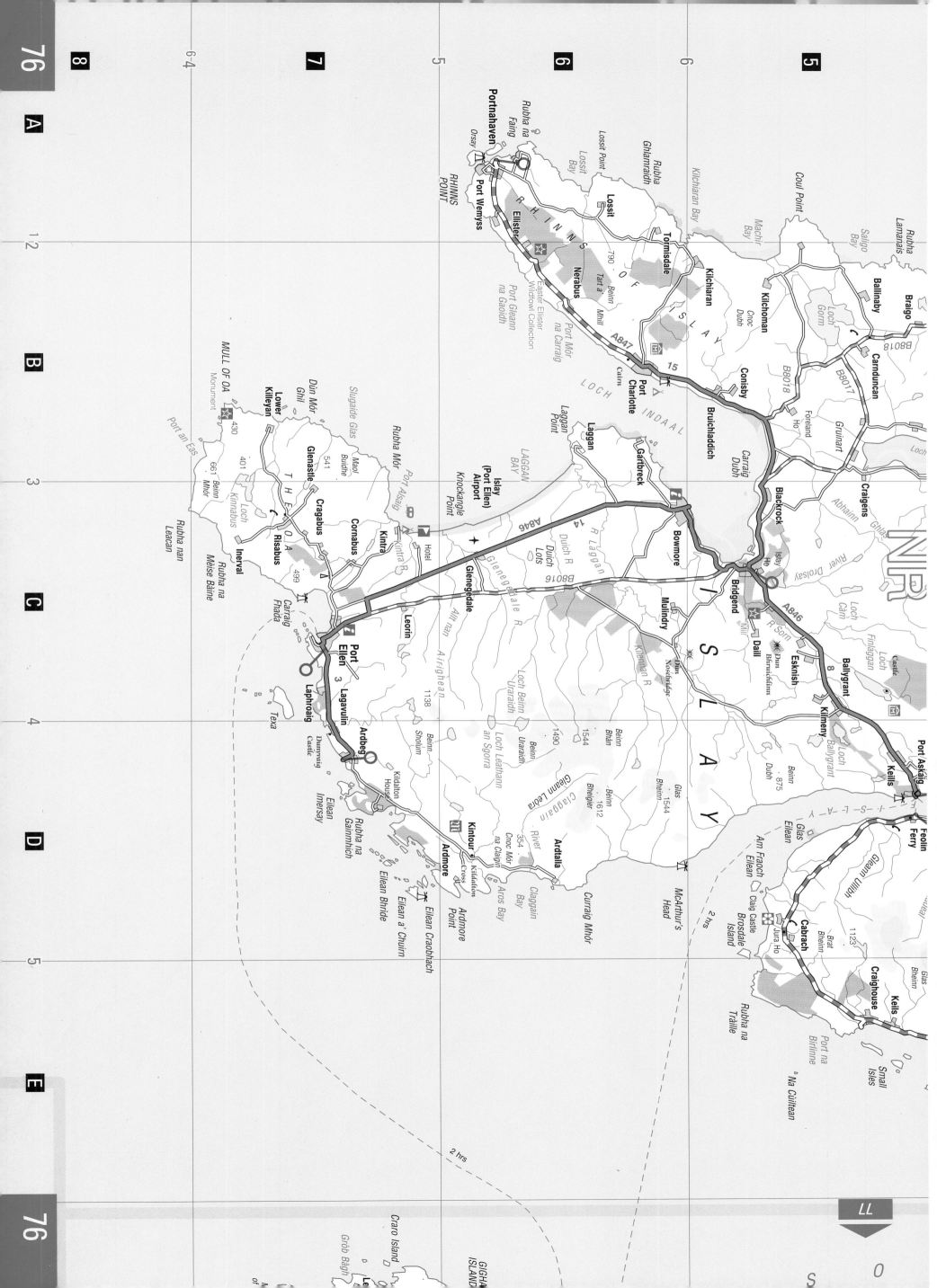

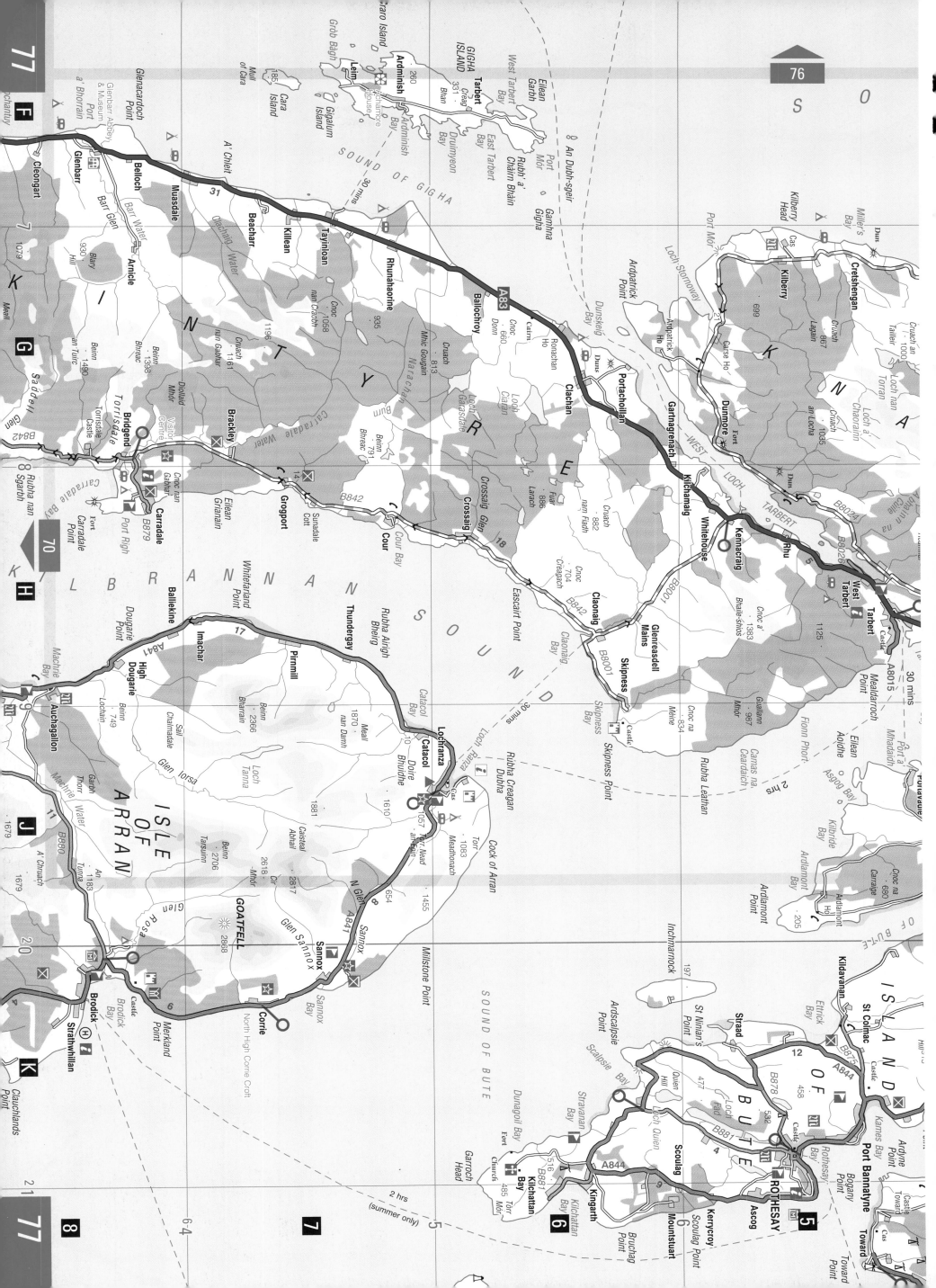

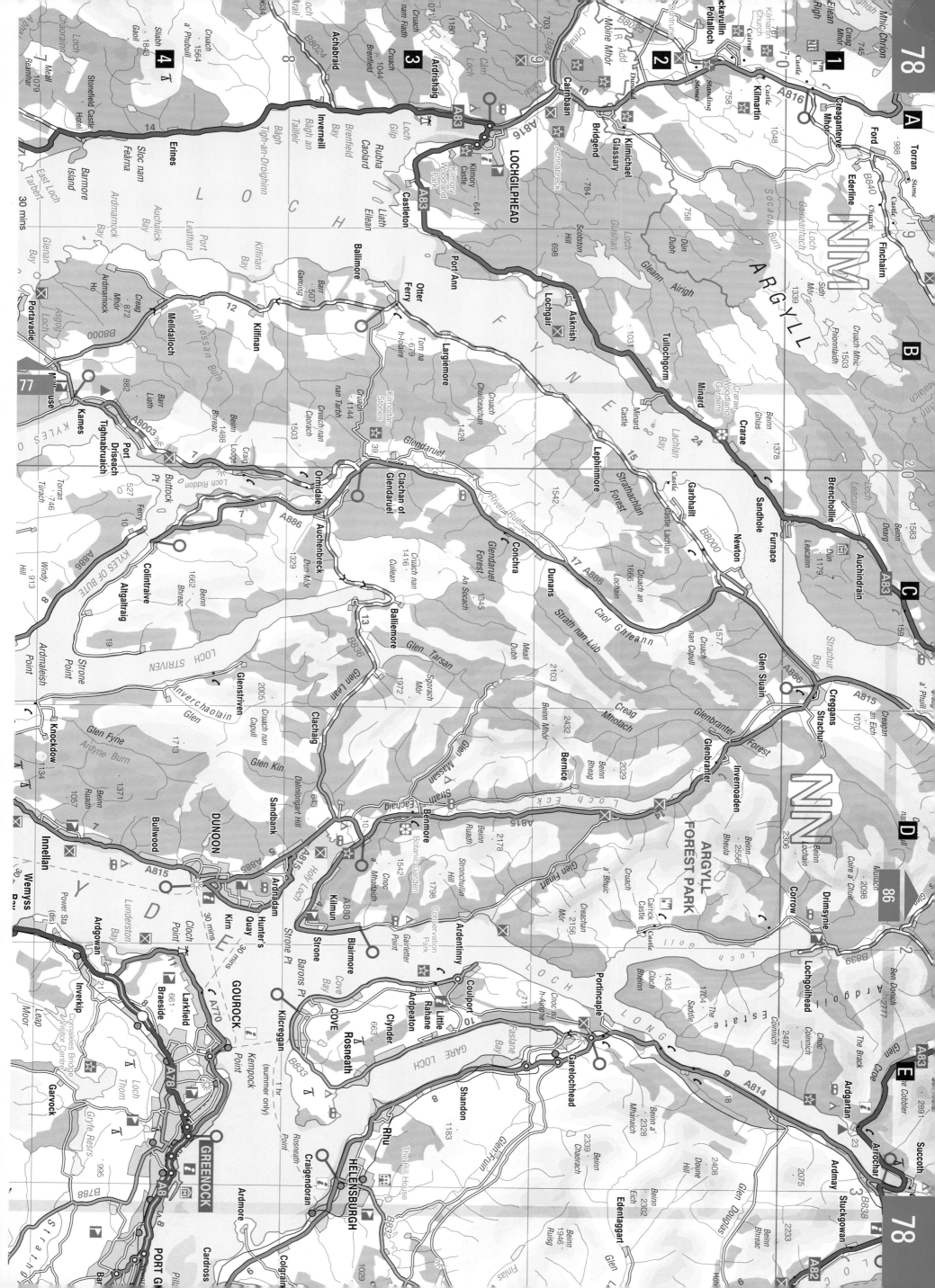

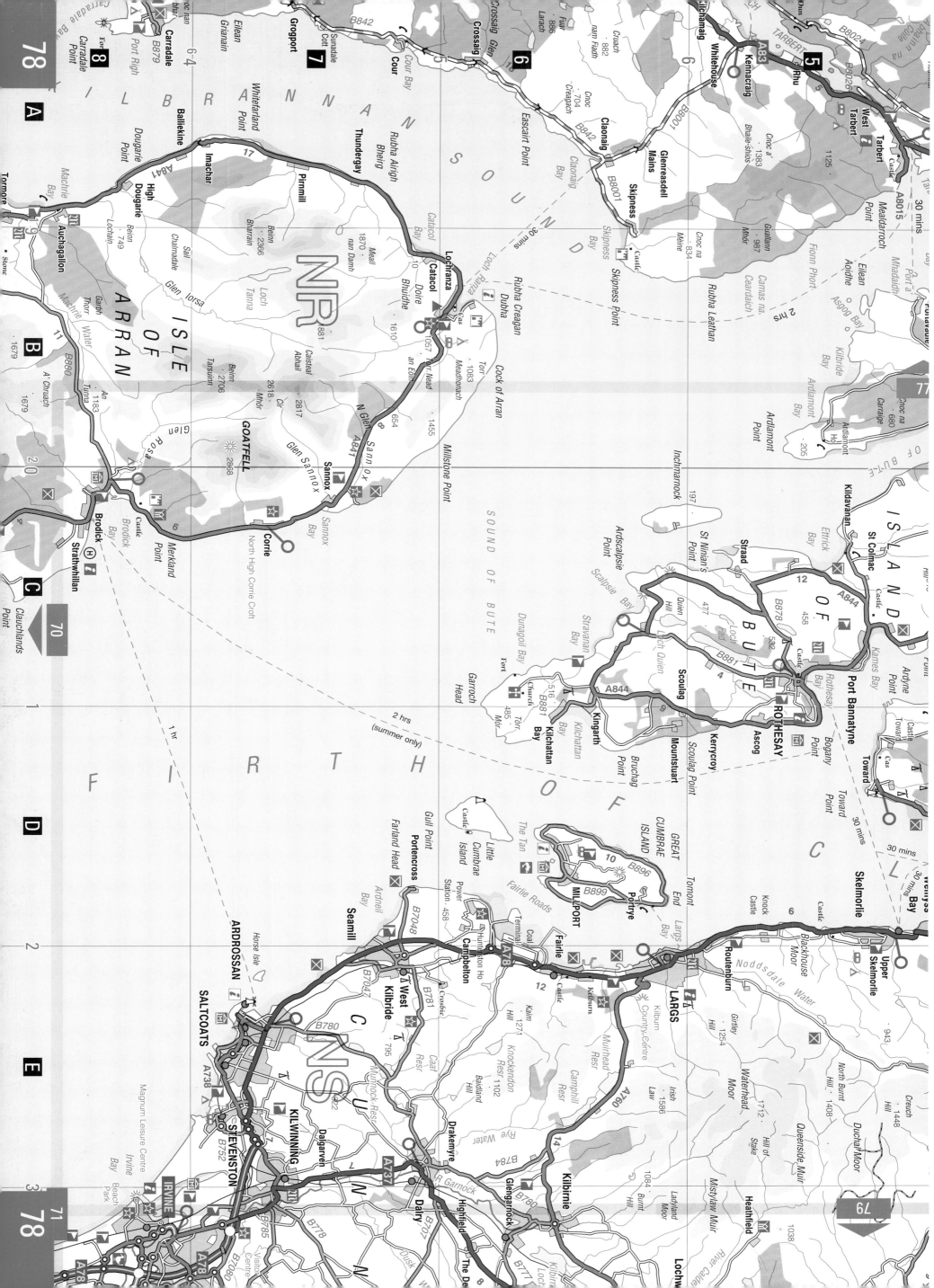

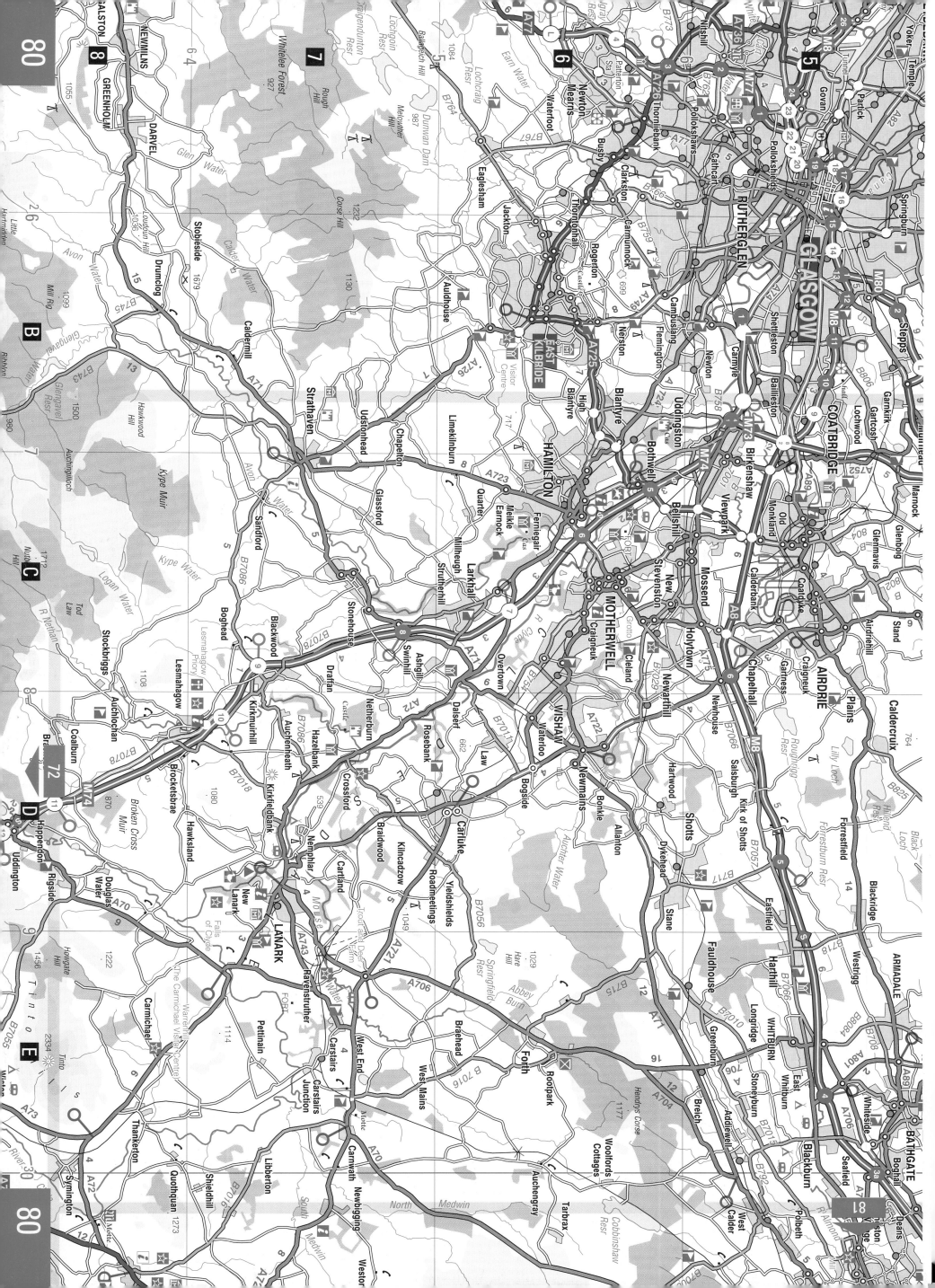

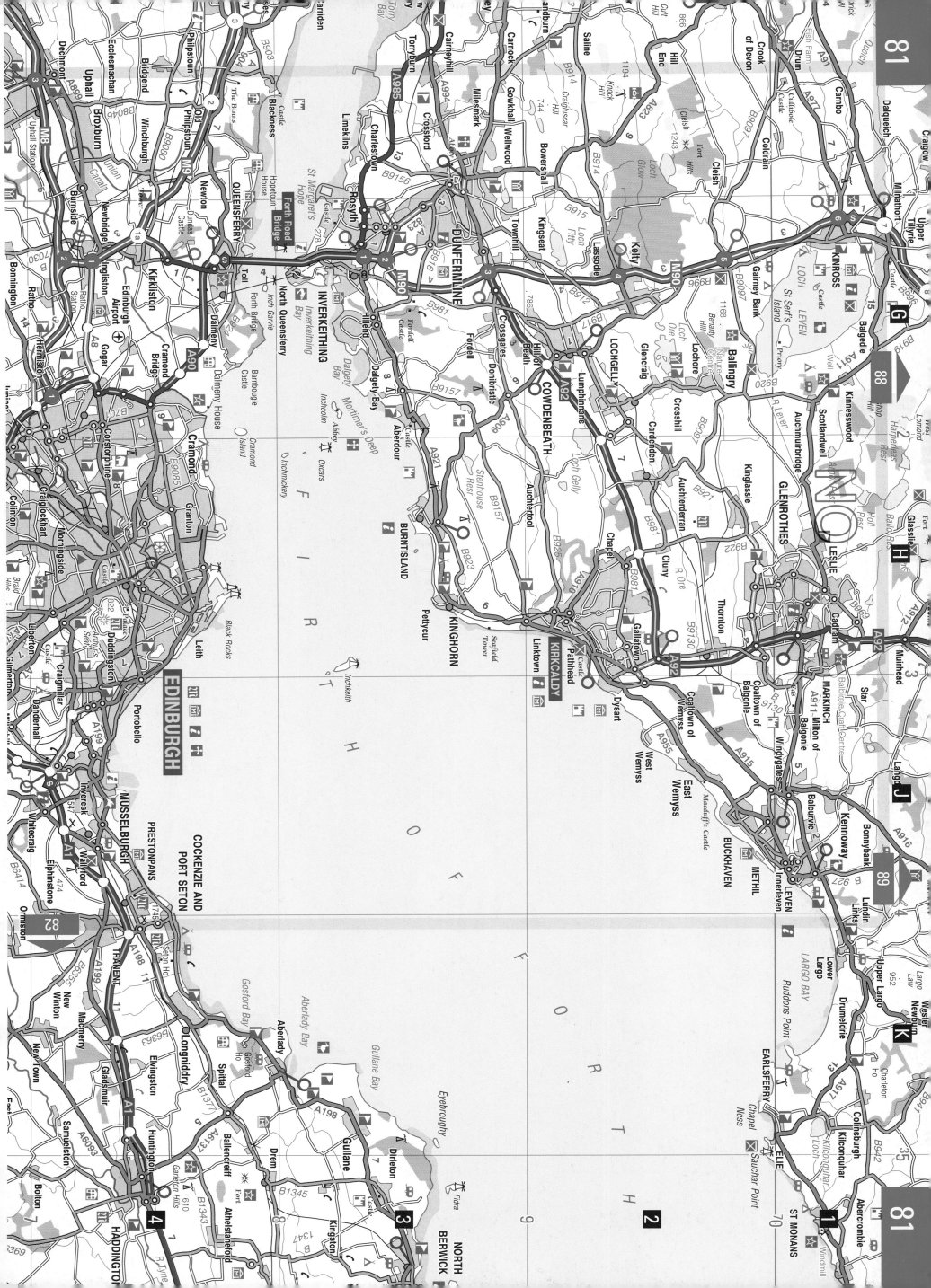

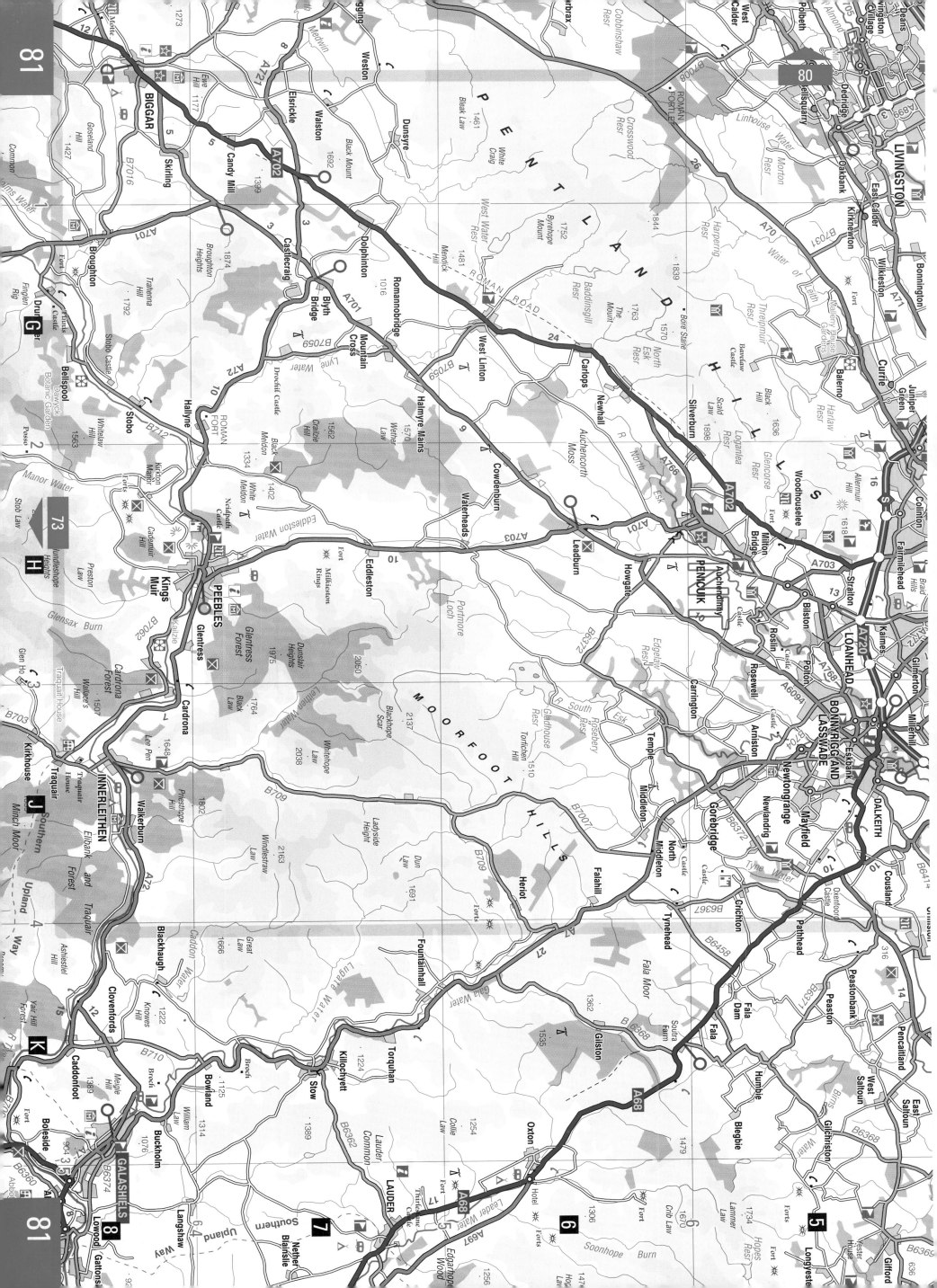

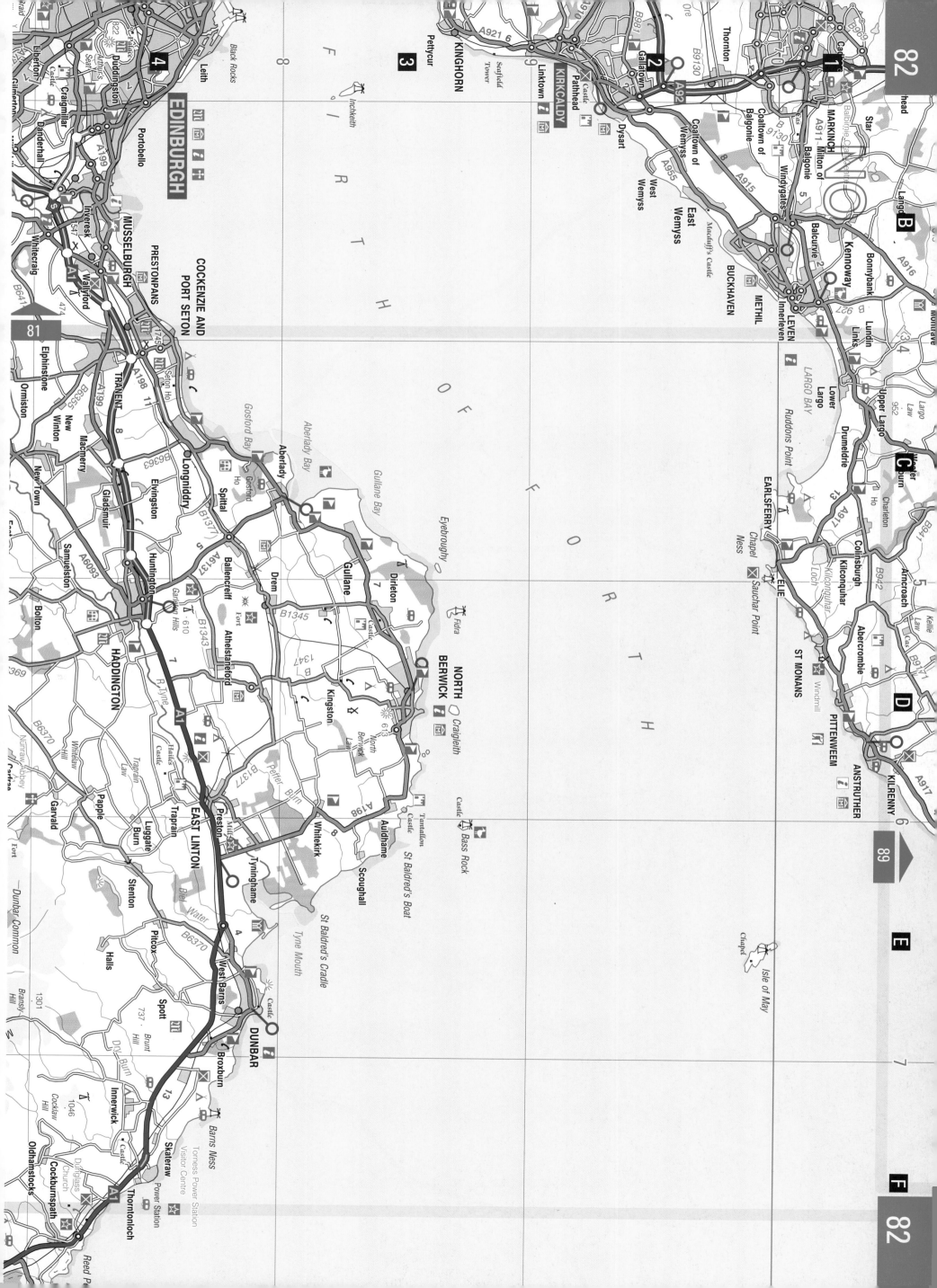

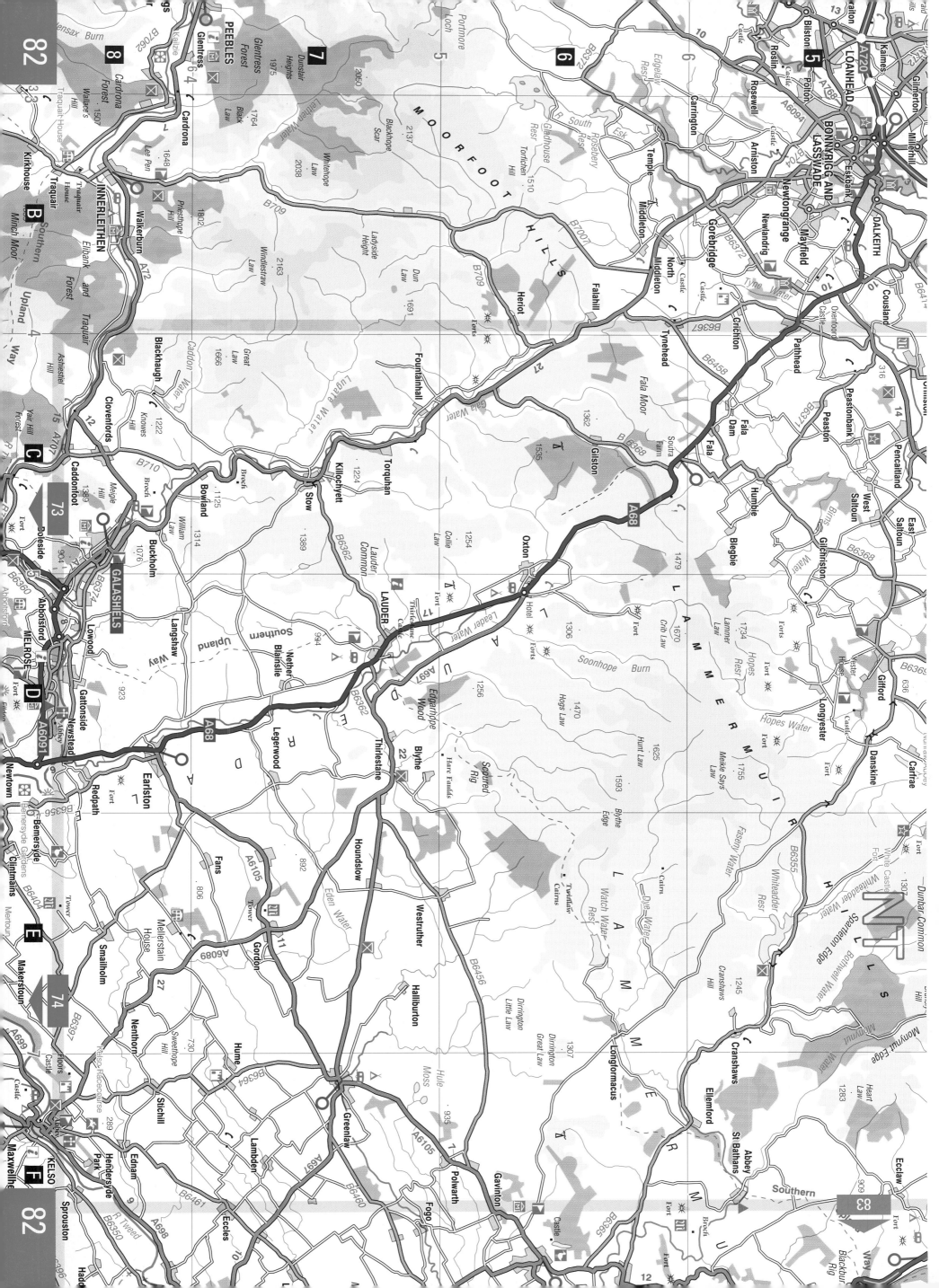

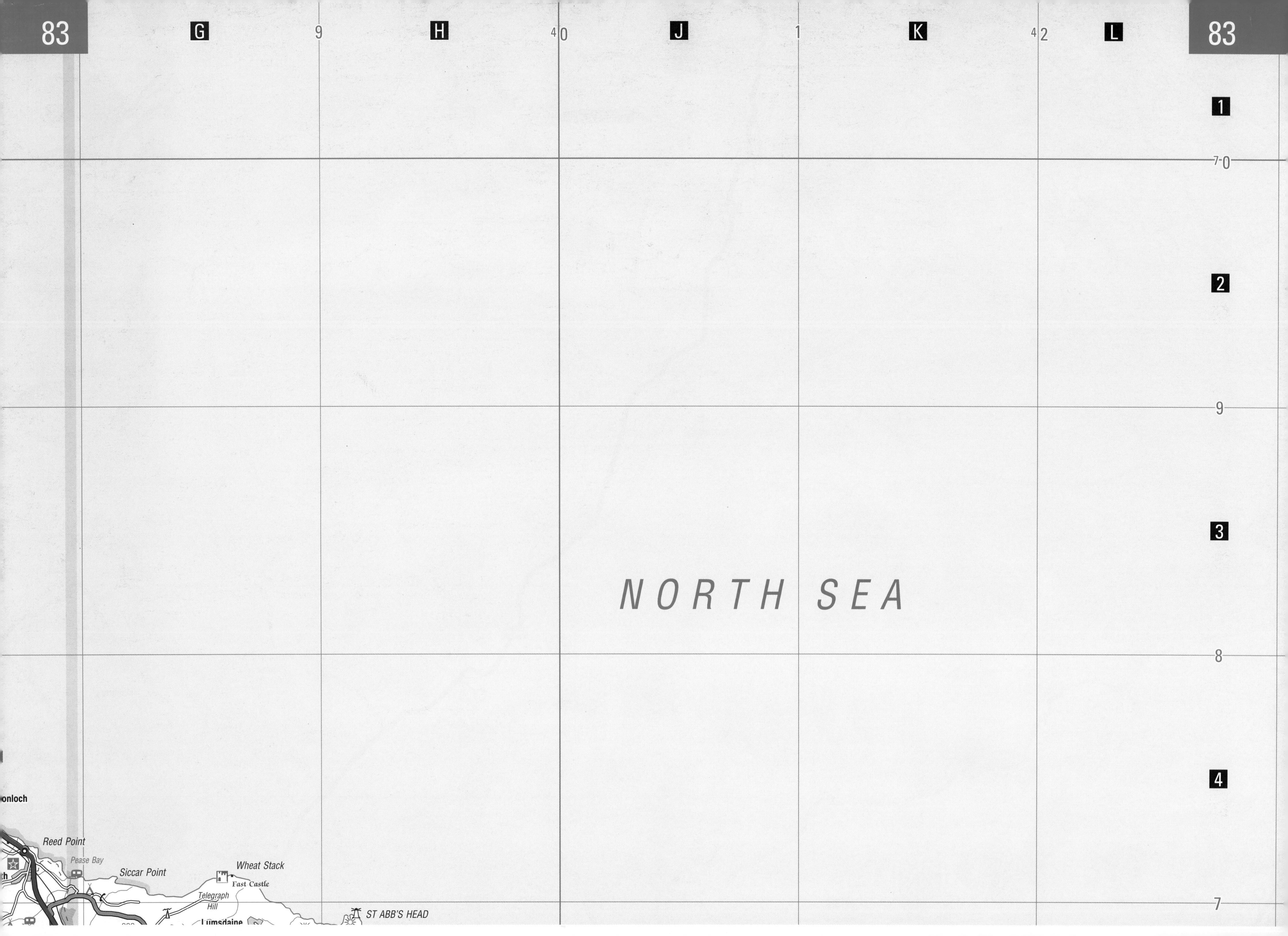
G
9
H
40
J
1
K
42
L
1
70
2
9
3
NORTH SEA
8
4
7
onloch
Reed Point
Pease Bay
Siccar Point
Wheat Stack
Fast Castle
Telegraph Hill
Lumsdaine
ST ABB'S HEAD

83

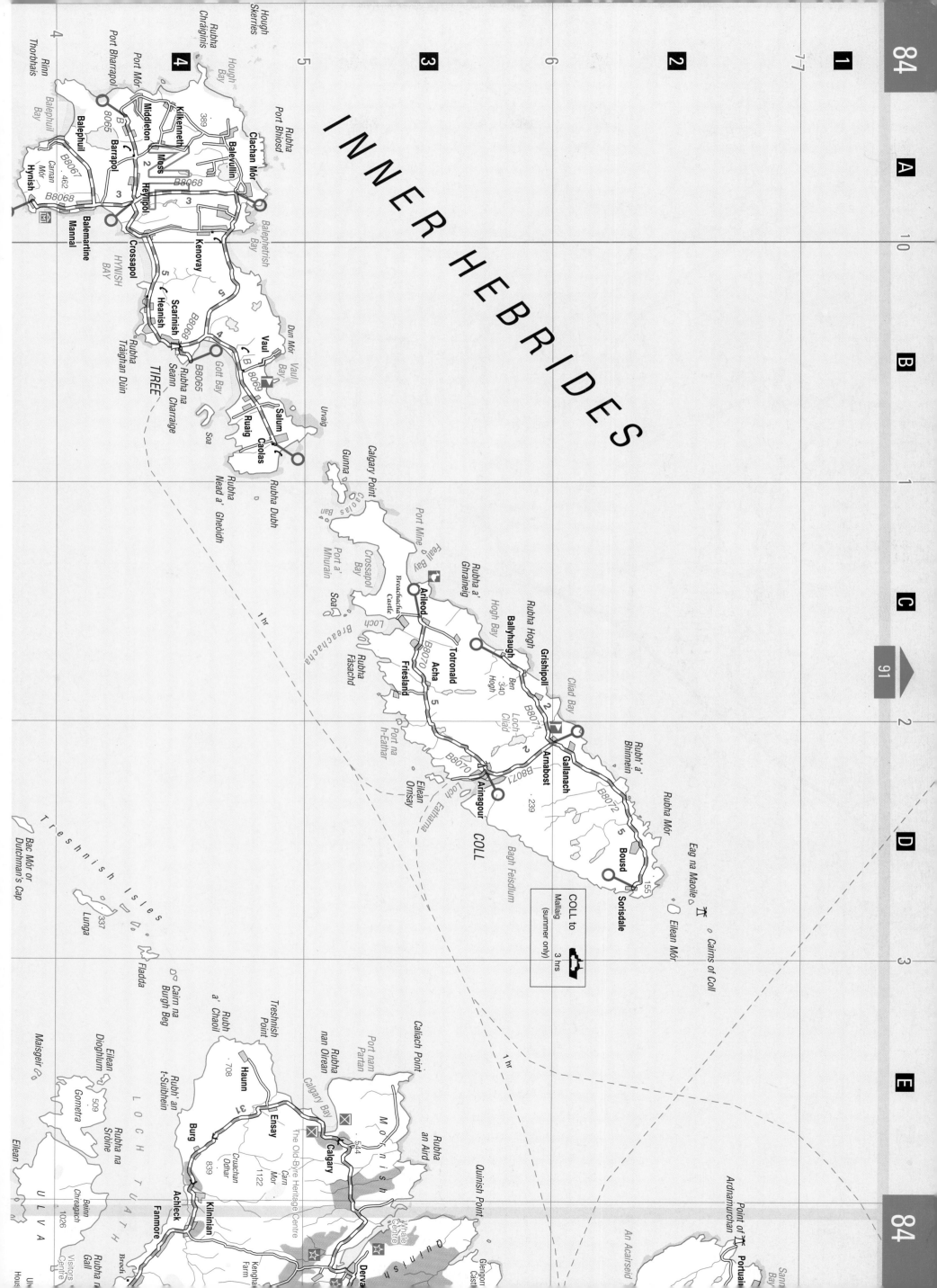

INNER HEBRIDES

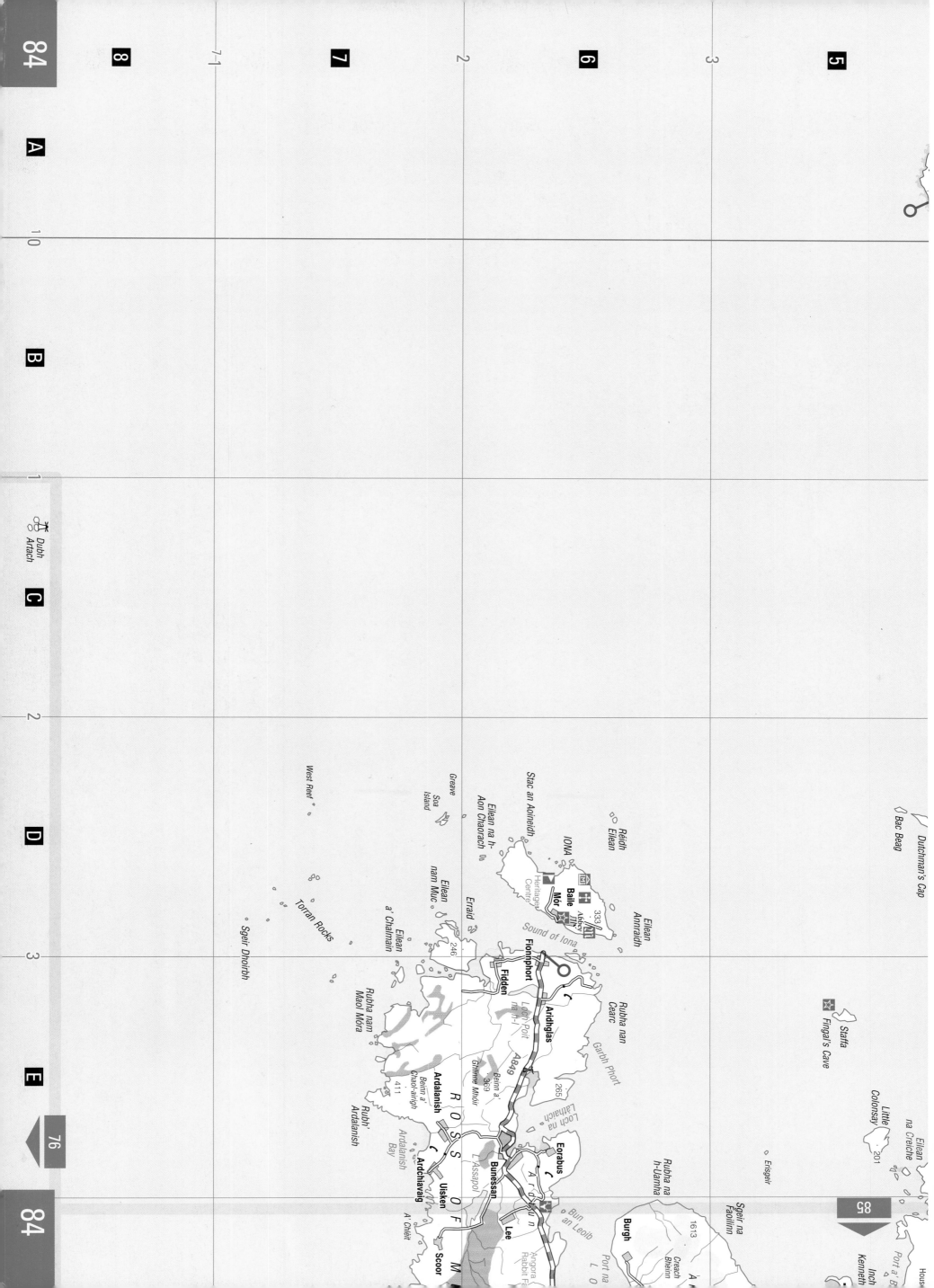

76

85

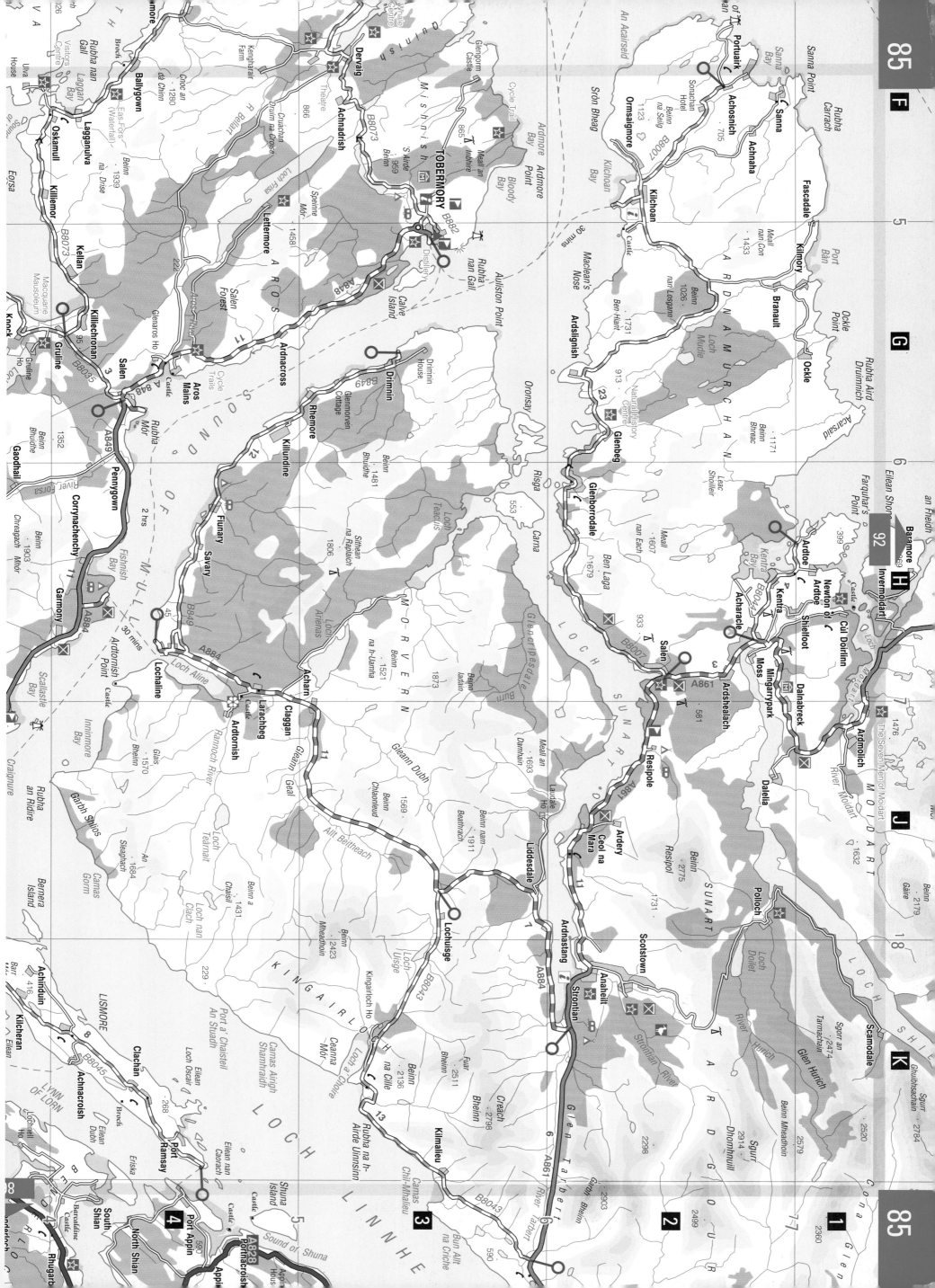

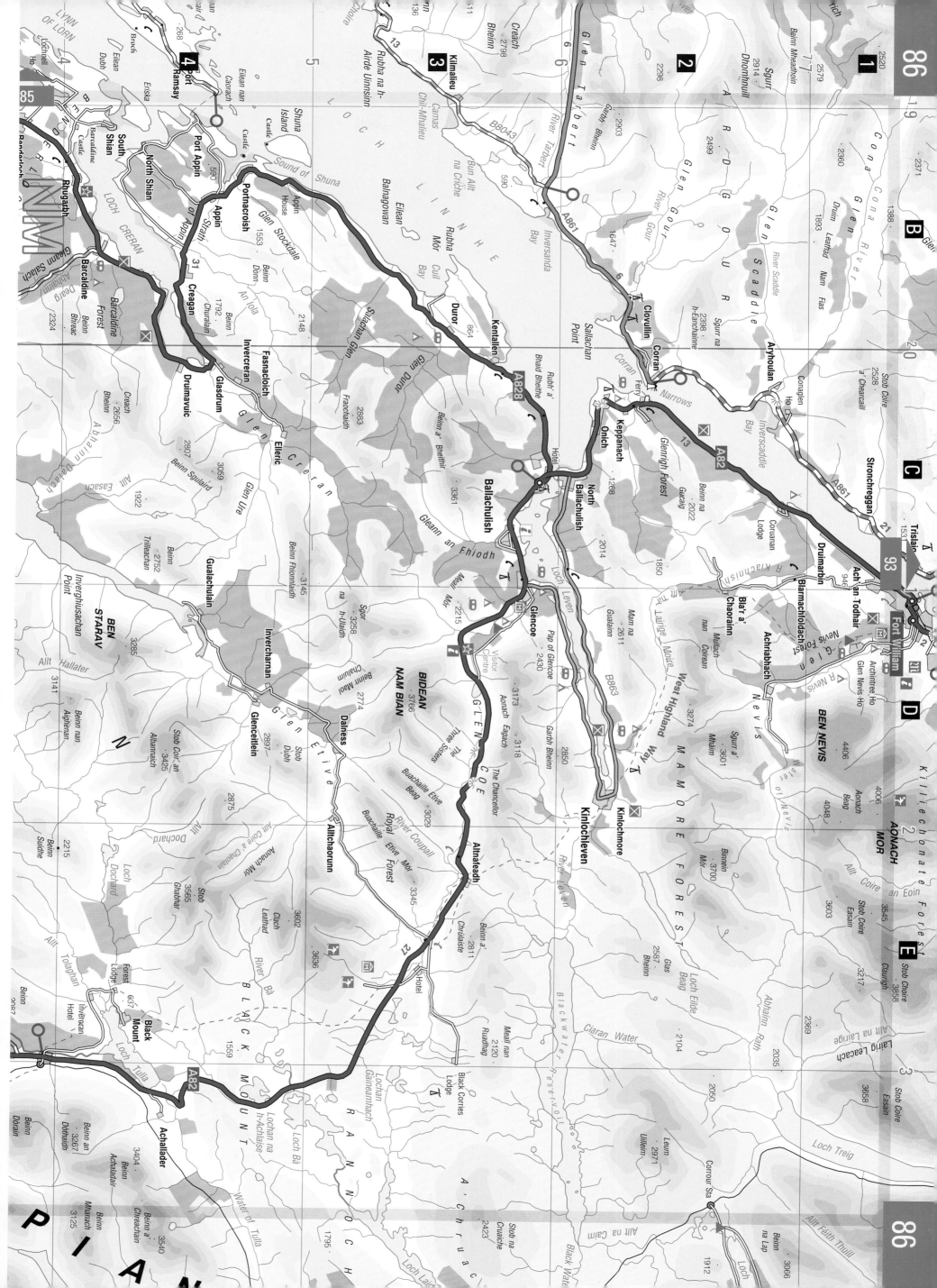

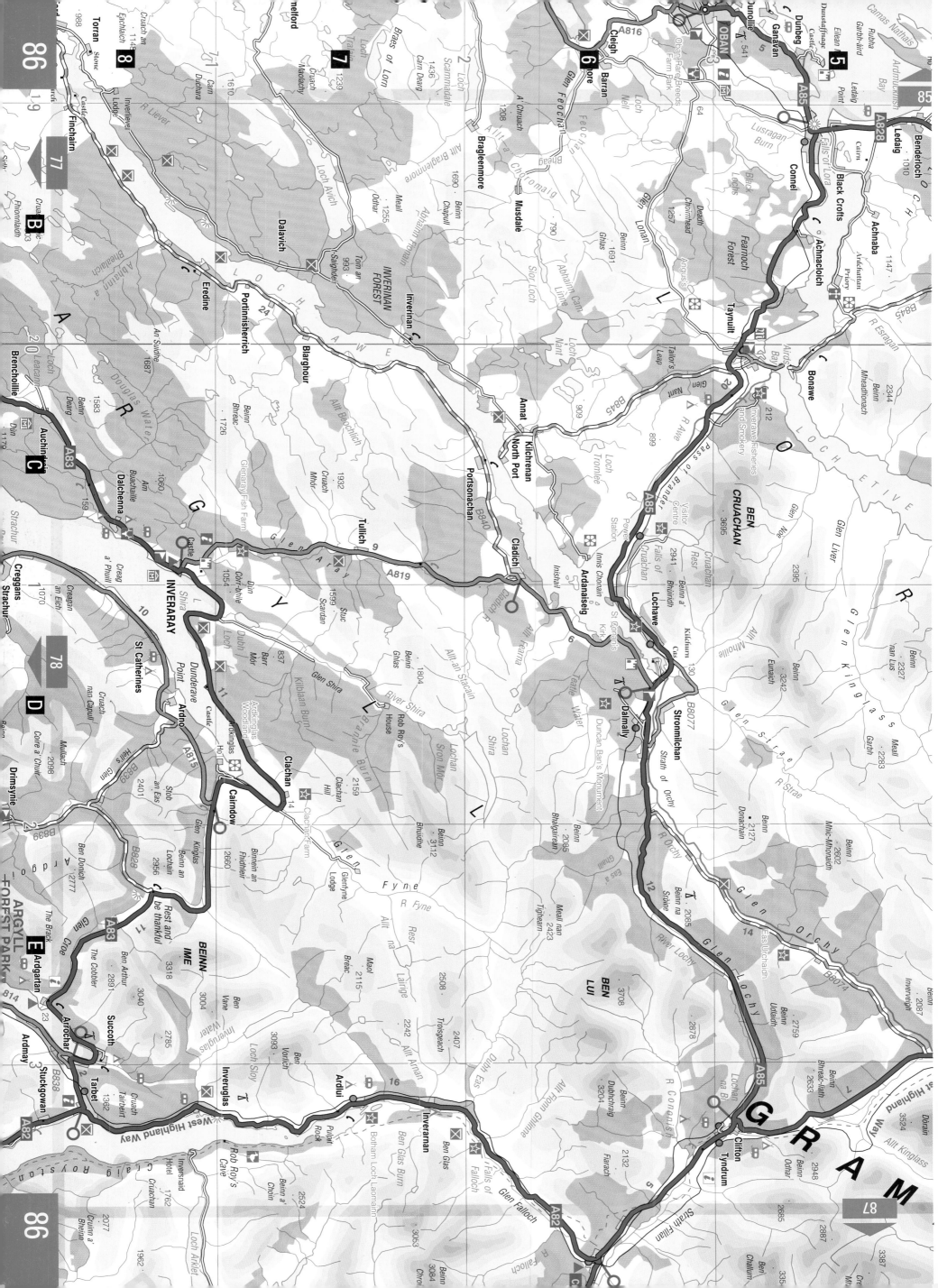

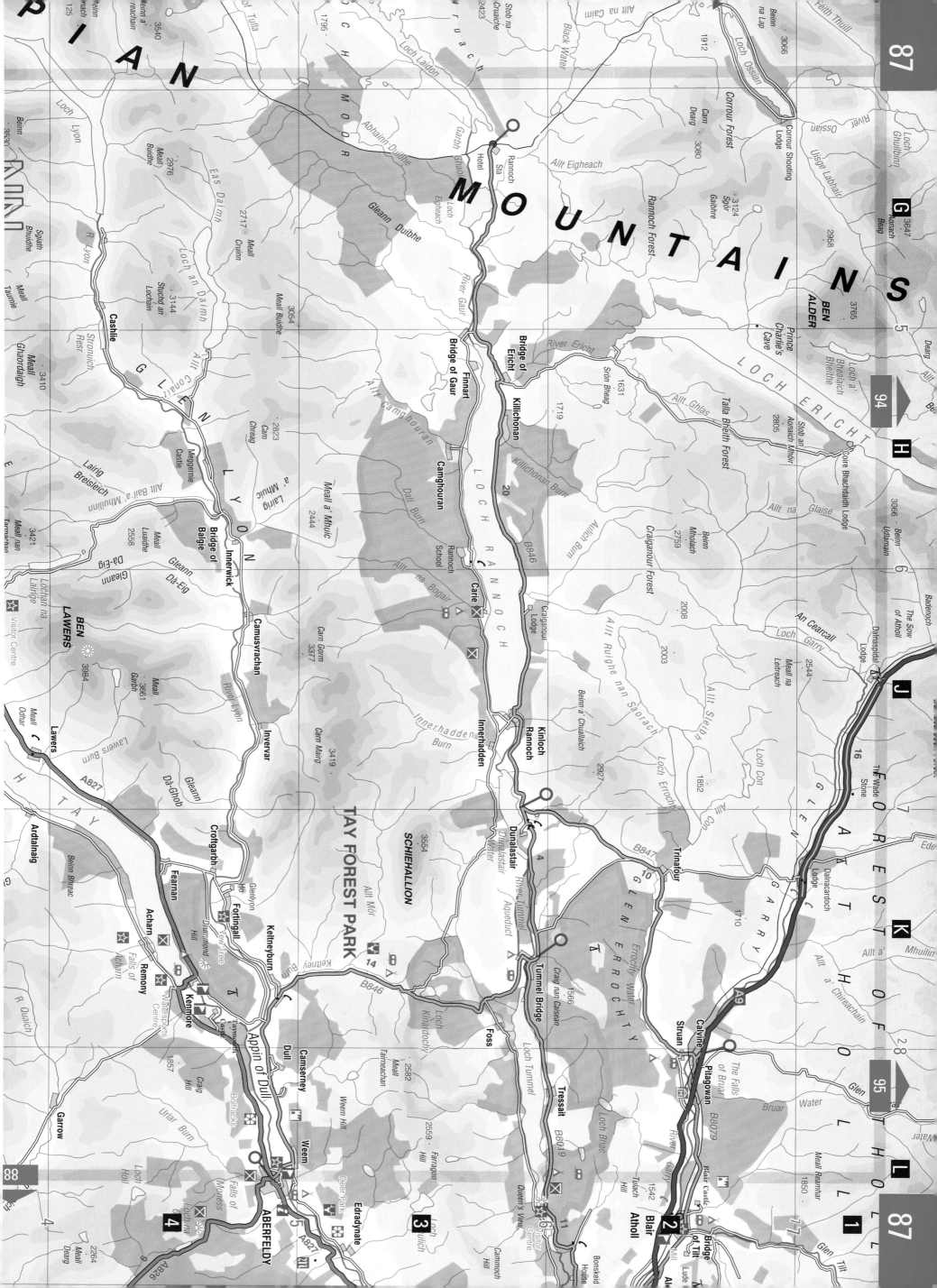

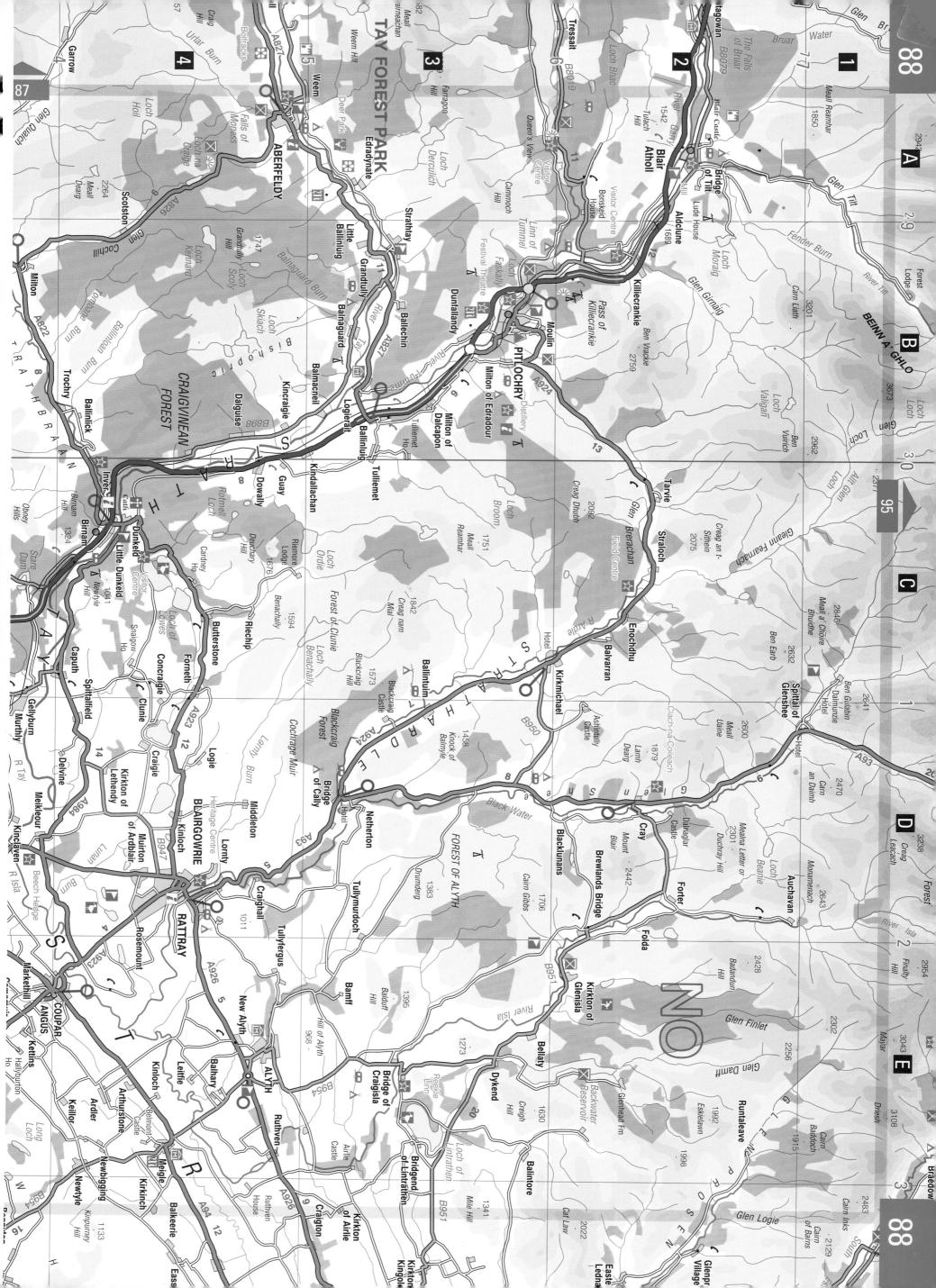

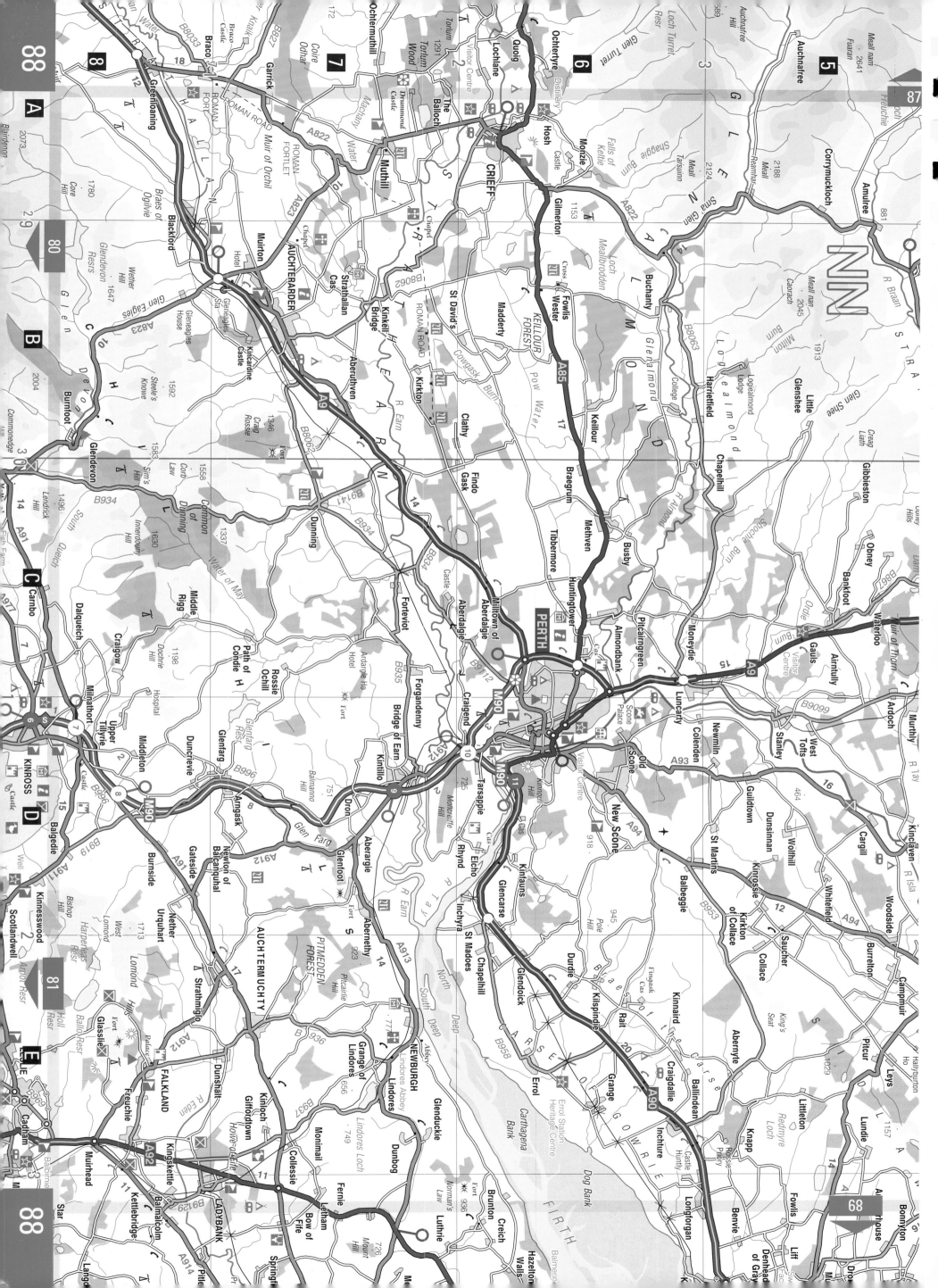

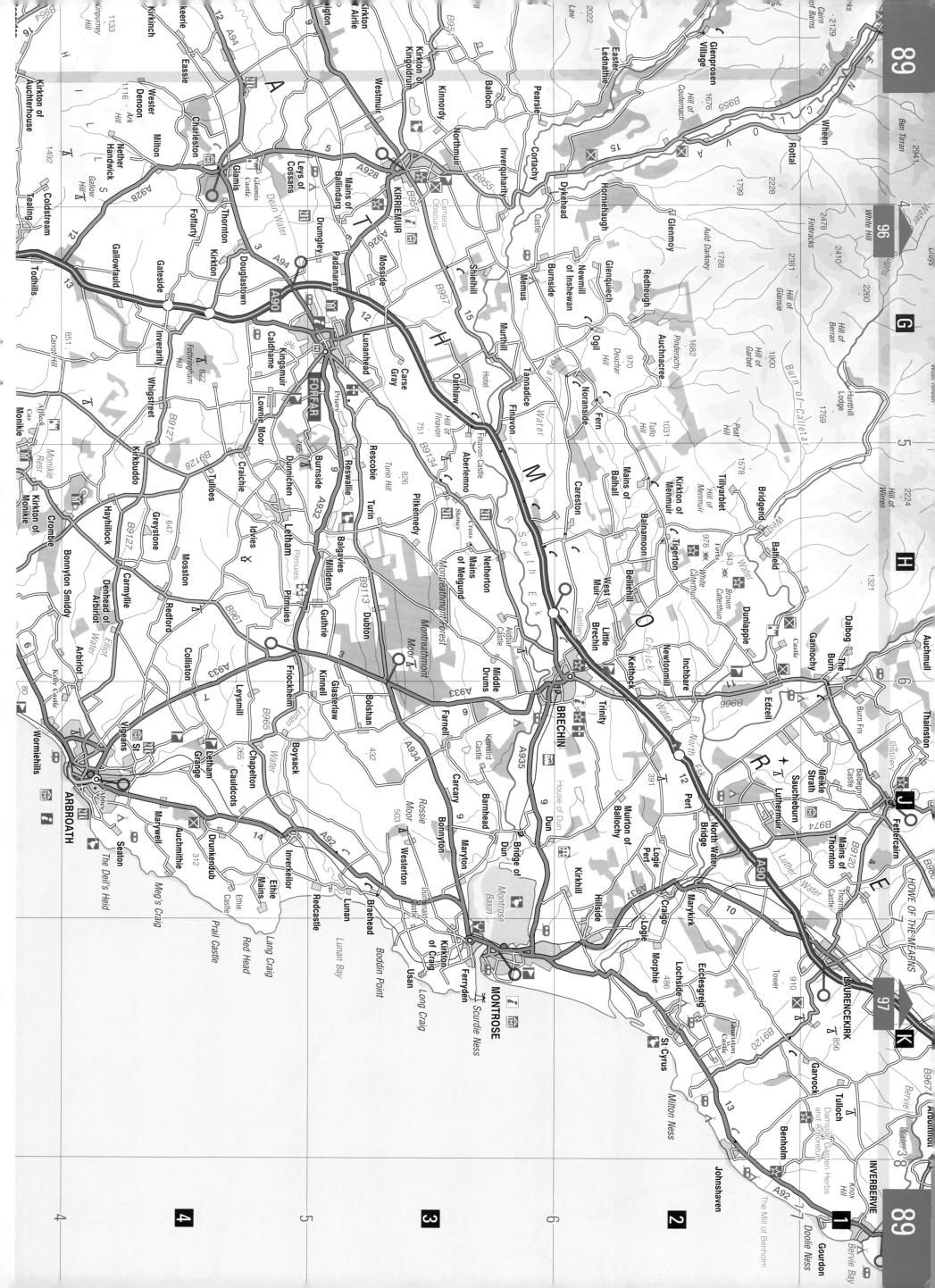

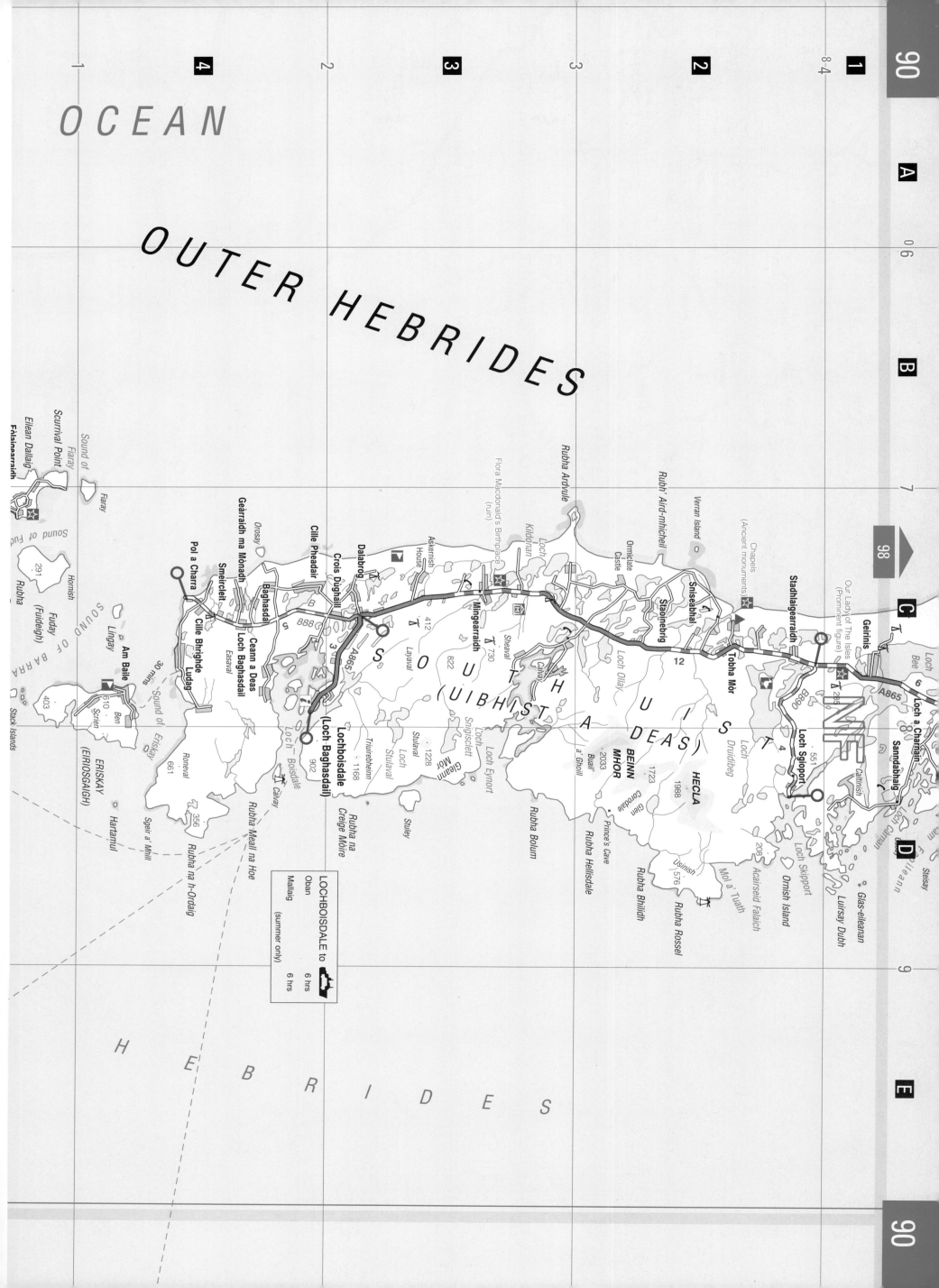

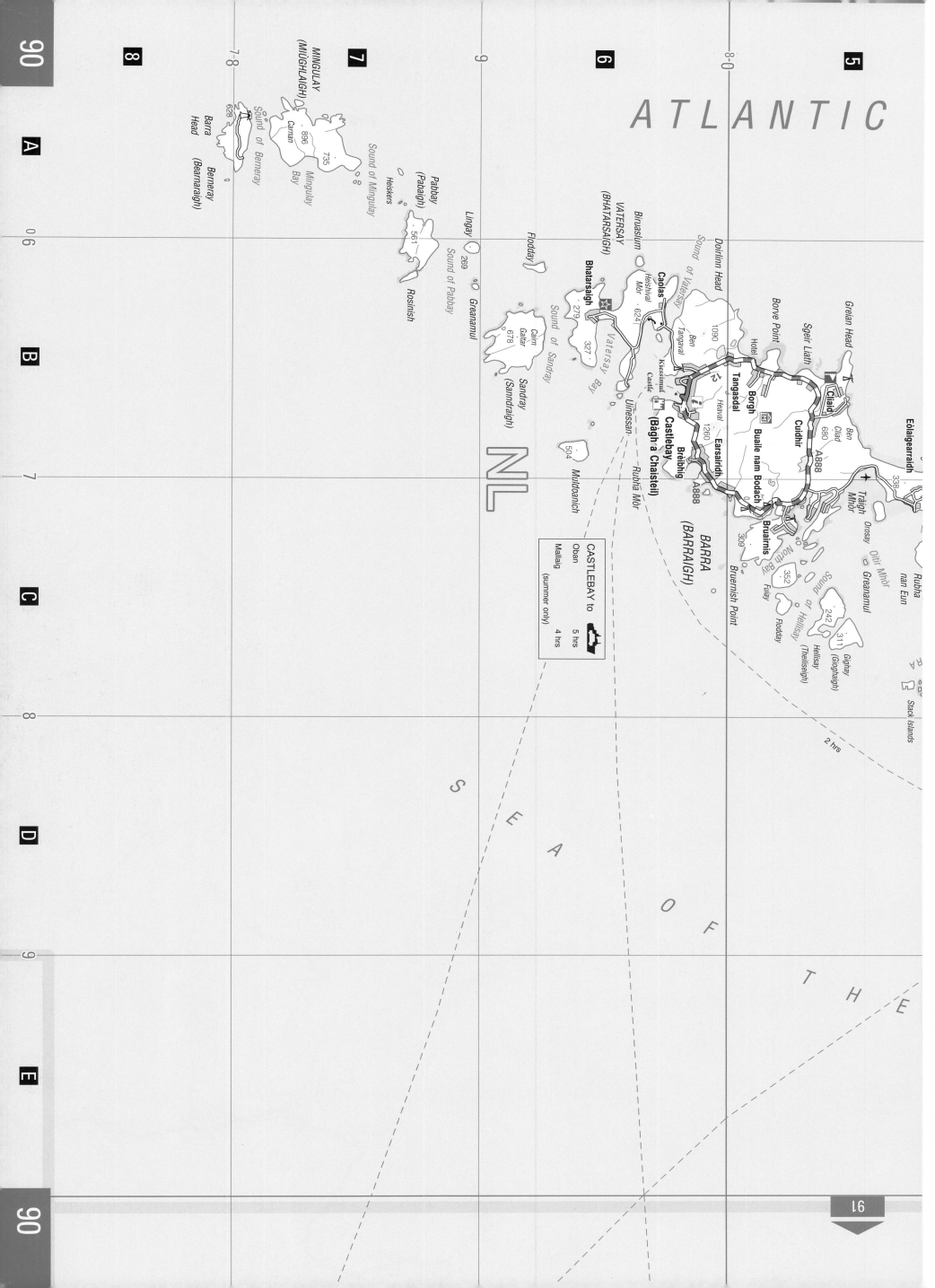

ATLANTIC

SEA OF THE

NL

CASTLEBAY to
Oban   5 hrs
Mallaig   4 hrs
(summer only)

MINGULAY
(MIÙGHLAIGH)

Carnan
896

735

Mingulay
Bay

Sound of Berneray

Barra
Head

Berneray
(Bearnaraigh)

628

Sound of Mingulay

Heiskers

Pabbay
(Pabaigh)
561

Sound of Pabbay

Rosinish

Lingay
269

Greanamul

Flodday

Sound of Sandray

Càirn
Galtar
678

Sandray
(Sandraigh)

Biruaslum

Heishival
Mòr
624

Bhatarsaigh
279

Caolas

327

Uinessan

Muldoanich
504

VATERSAY
(BHATARSAIGH)

Dòirlinn Head

Sound of Vatersay

Ben
Tangaval
1090

Vatersay Bay

Rubha Mòr

Kisimul
Castle

Castlebay
(Bàgh a Chaisteil)

Breibhig

Borve Point

Hotel

Sgeir Liath

Greian Head

Borgh
Tangasdal

Heaval
1260

Earsairidh

Bualle nam Bodach

Breibhig

BARRA
(BARRAIGH)

A888

A888

Eòlaigearraidh

Ben
Cliad
680

Cuidhir

Cliaid

Traigh
Mhòr

338

Orosay

Oitir Mhòr

Oitir Greanamul

Rubha
nan Eun

Bruairnis
309

Bruairnish Point

North Bay

Sound of Fuiay

Fuiay

352

Flodday

Sound of Hellisay

Hellisay
(Theiliseigh)

242

Gighay
(Gioghaigh)
311

Stack Islands

90

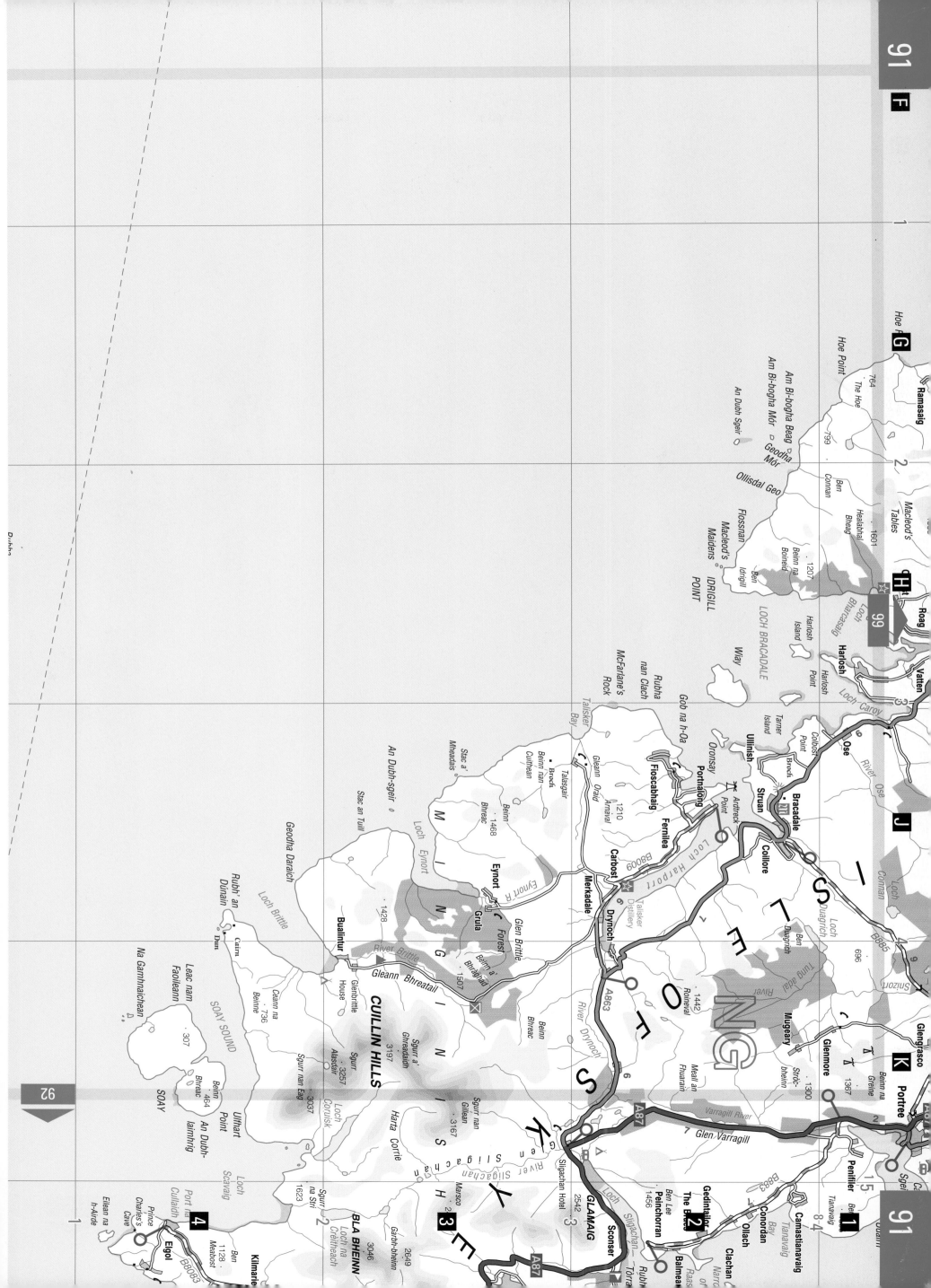

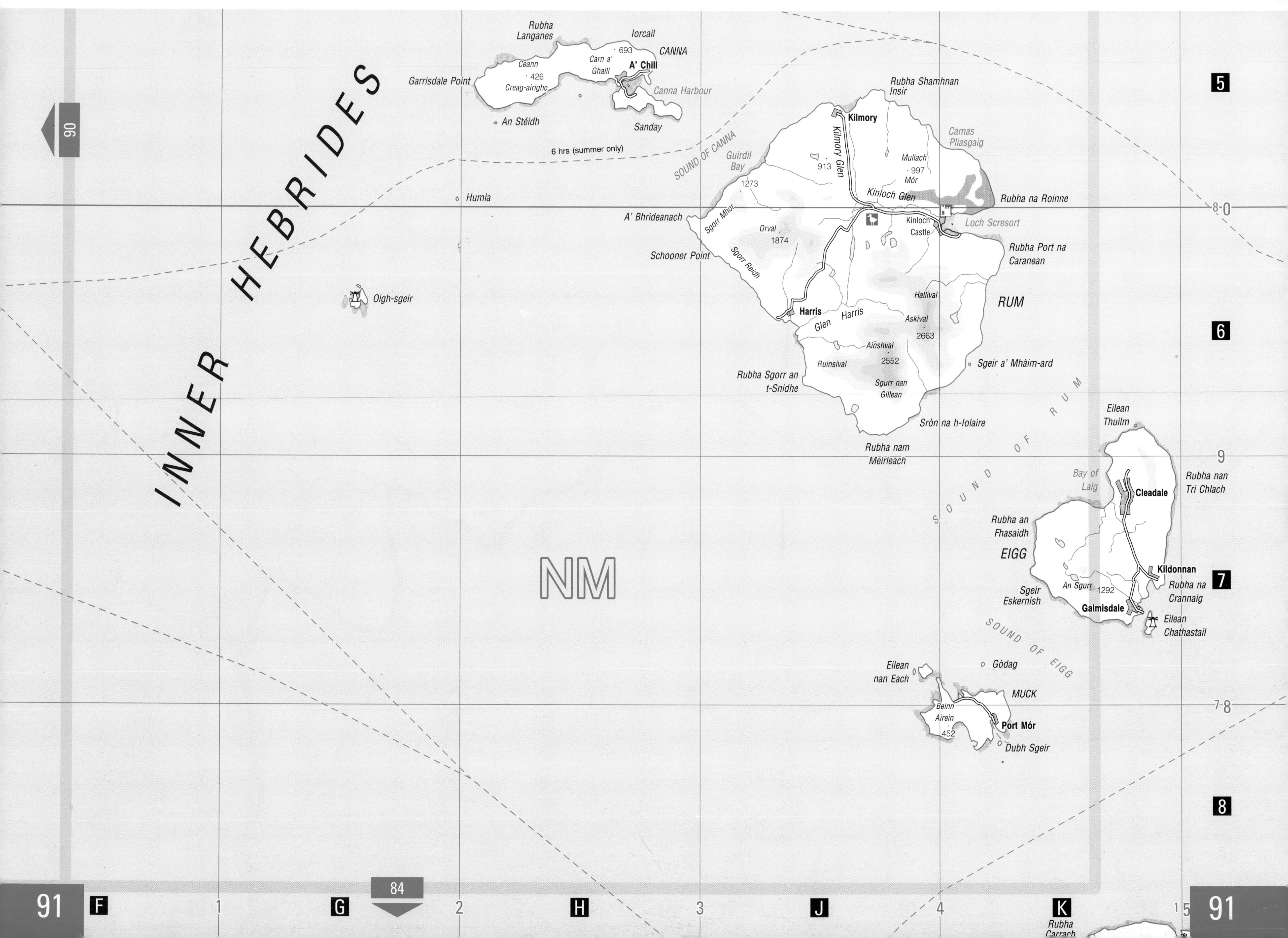

F

G

84

H

J

K

1

2

3

4

15

8

7-8

6

9

8-0

5

INNER HEBRIDES

NM

Oigh-sgeir

Garrisdale Point

Humla

Rubha Langanes

An Stéidh

Ceann a'
Creag-airighe

Ceann
426

Carn a'
Ghaill
693

Iorcail

CANNA

Sanday

A' Chill

Canna Harbour

6 hrs (summer only)

Guirdil
Bay

SOUND OF CANNA

A' Bhrideanach

Schooner Point

Sgorr Mhór

Sgorr reidh

1273

Orval
1874

913

Kilmory Glen

Rubha Sharnhan
Insir

Rubha Sgorr an
t-Snidhe

Harris

Ruinsival

Glen   Harris

Ainshval
2552

Askival
2663

Mullach
Mór
997

Kilmory

Camas
Pliaspaig

Sgurr nan
Gillean

Halival

Kinloch
Castle

Kinloch
Glen

Rubha nam
Méirleach

Sròn na h-Iolaire

Sgeir a' Mhaim-ard

RUM

Kinloch

Loch Scresort

Rubha Port na
Caranean

Rubha na Roinne

SOUND
OF
RUM

Eilean
nan Each

Benn
Airein
452

Gòdag

Duibh Sgeir

MUCK

Port Mór

Rubha an
Fhasaidh

Sgeir
Eskernish

EIGG

An Sgurr
1292

Galmisdale

SOUND OF EIGG

Bay of
Laig

Eilean
Thuilm

Eilean nan
Tri Chlach

Cleadale

Kildonnan

Rubha na
Crannaig

Eilean
Chathastail

Rubha
Carrach

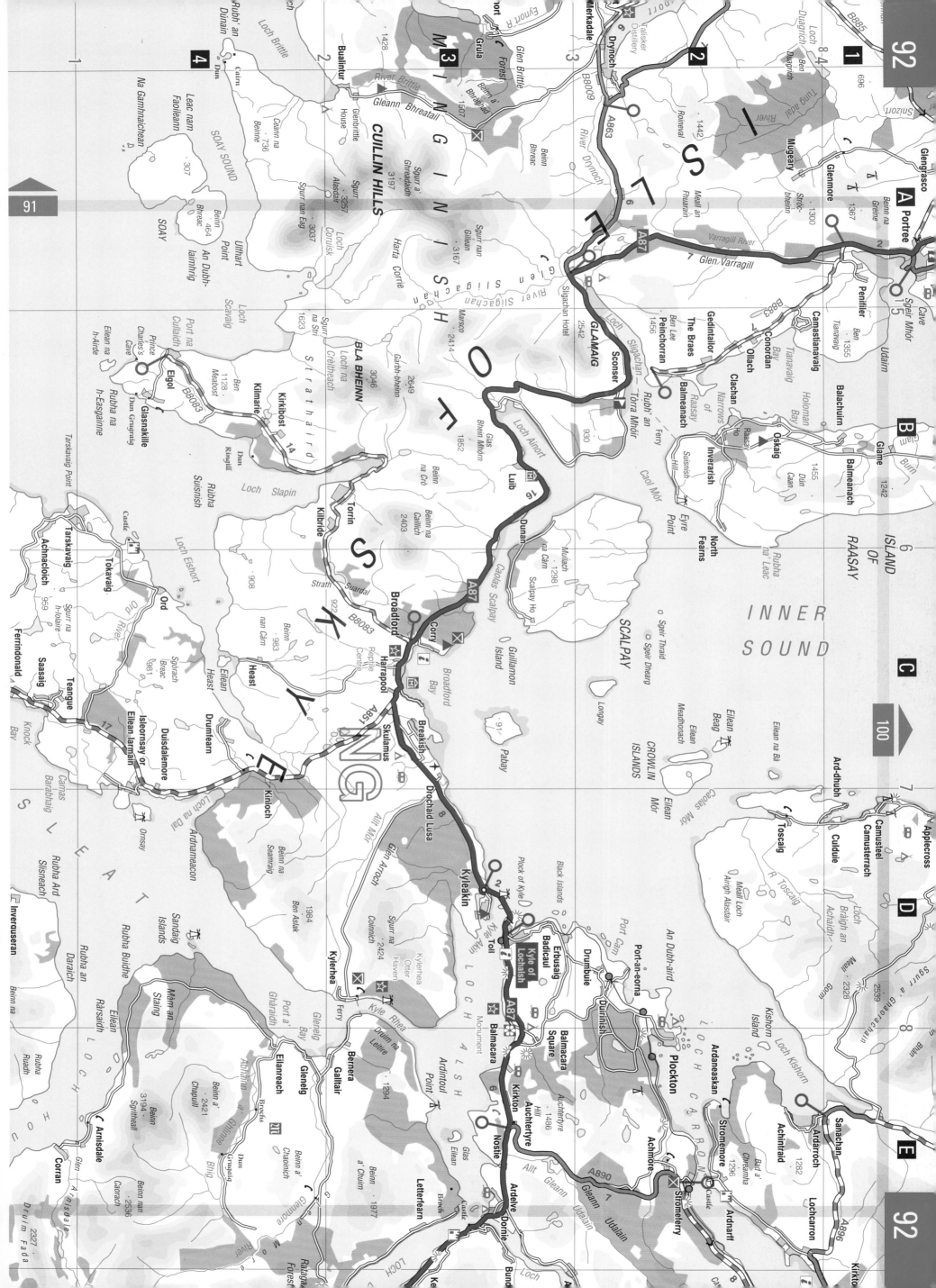

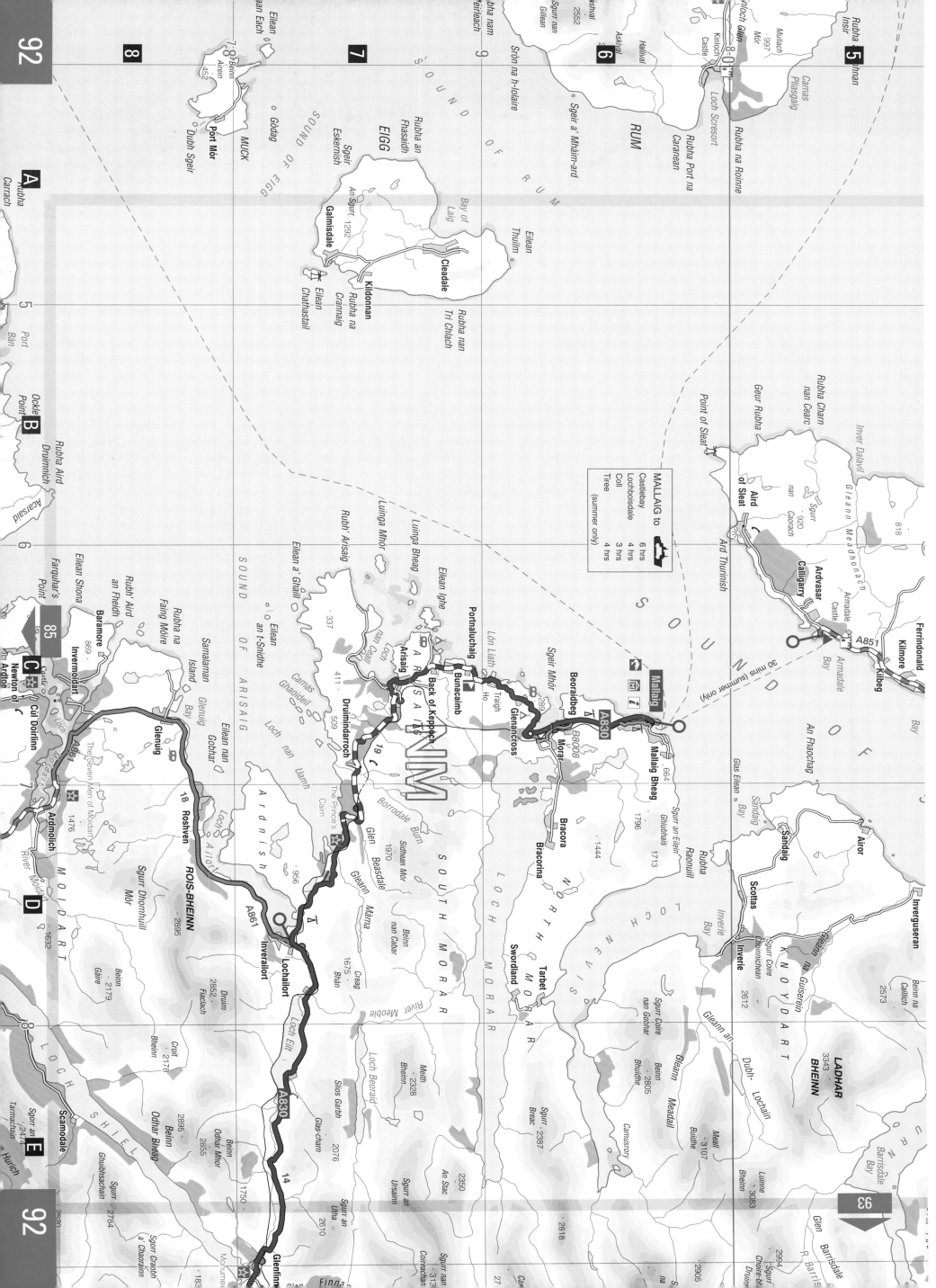

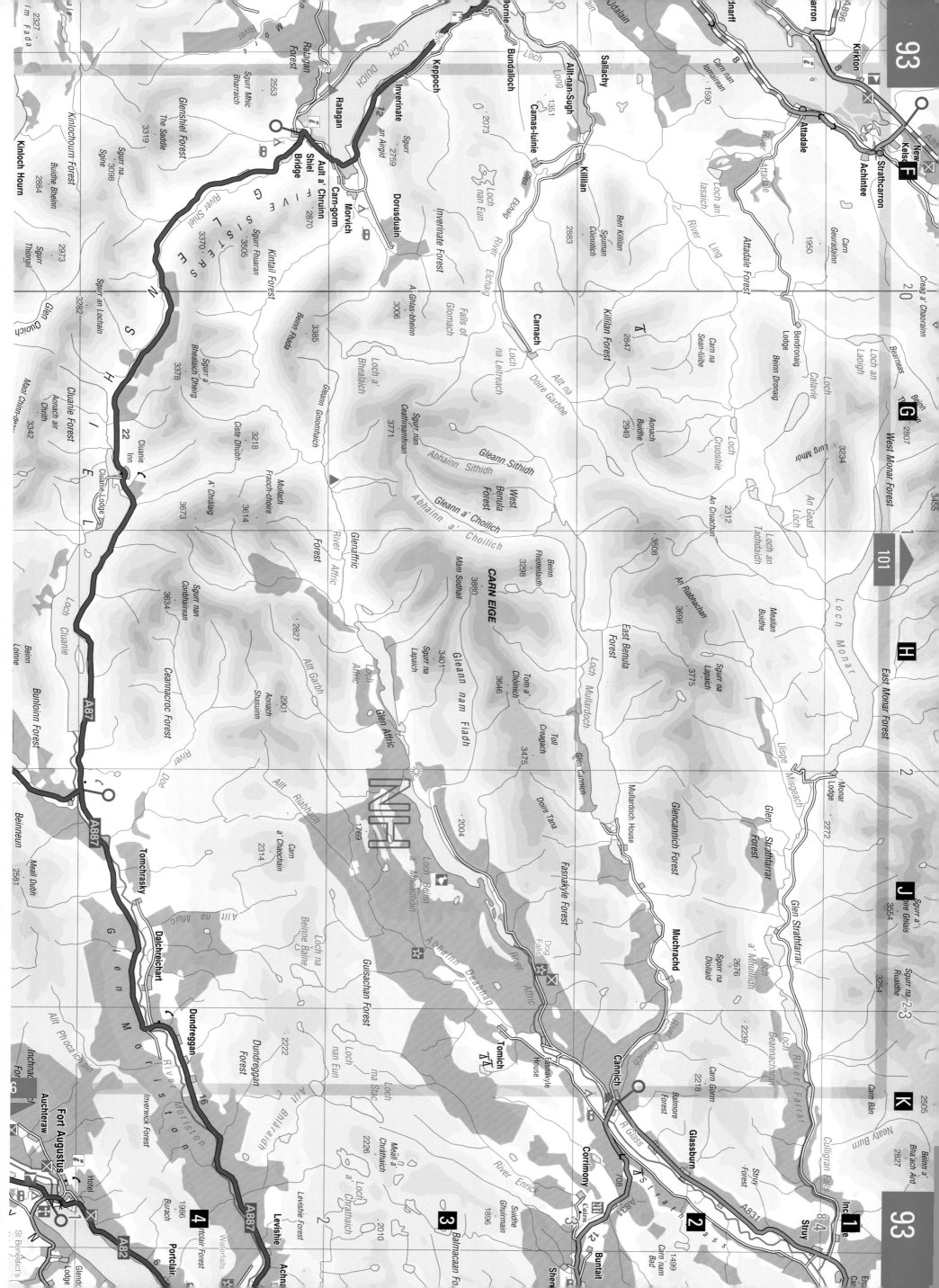

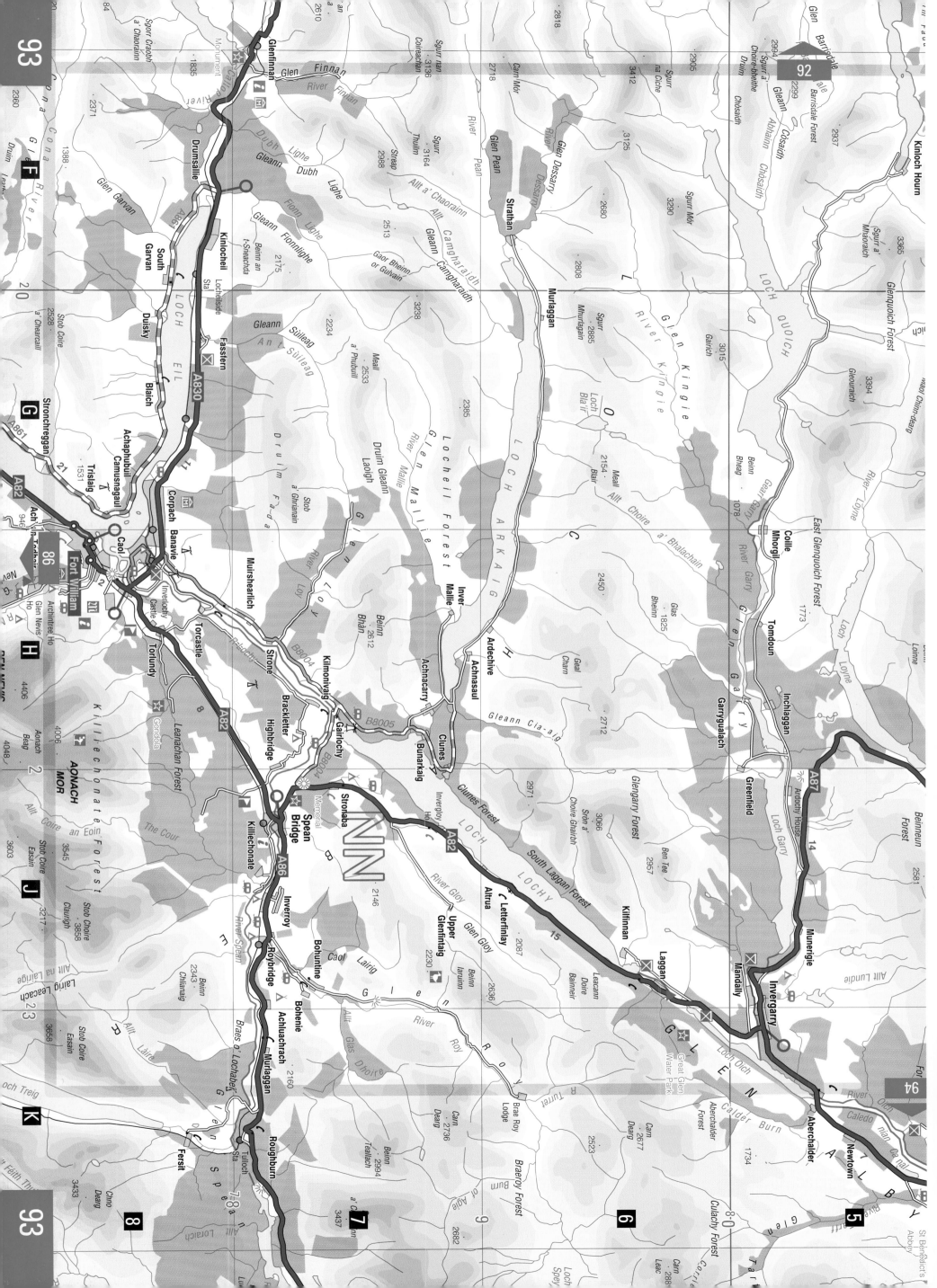

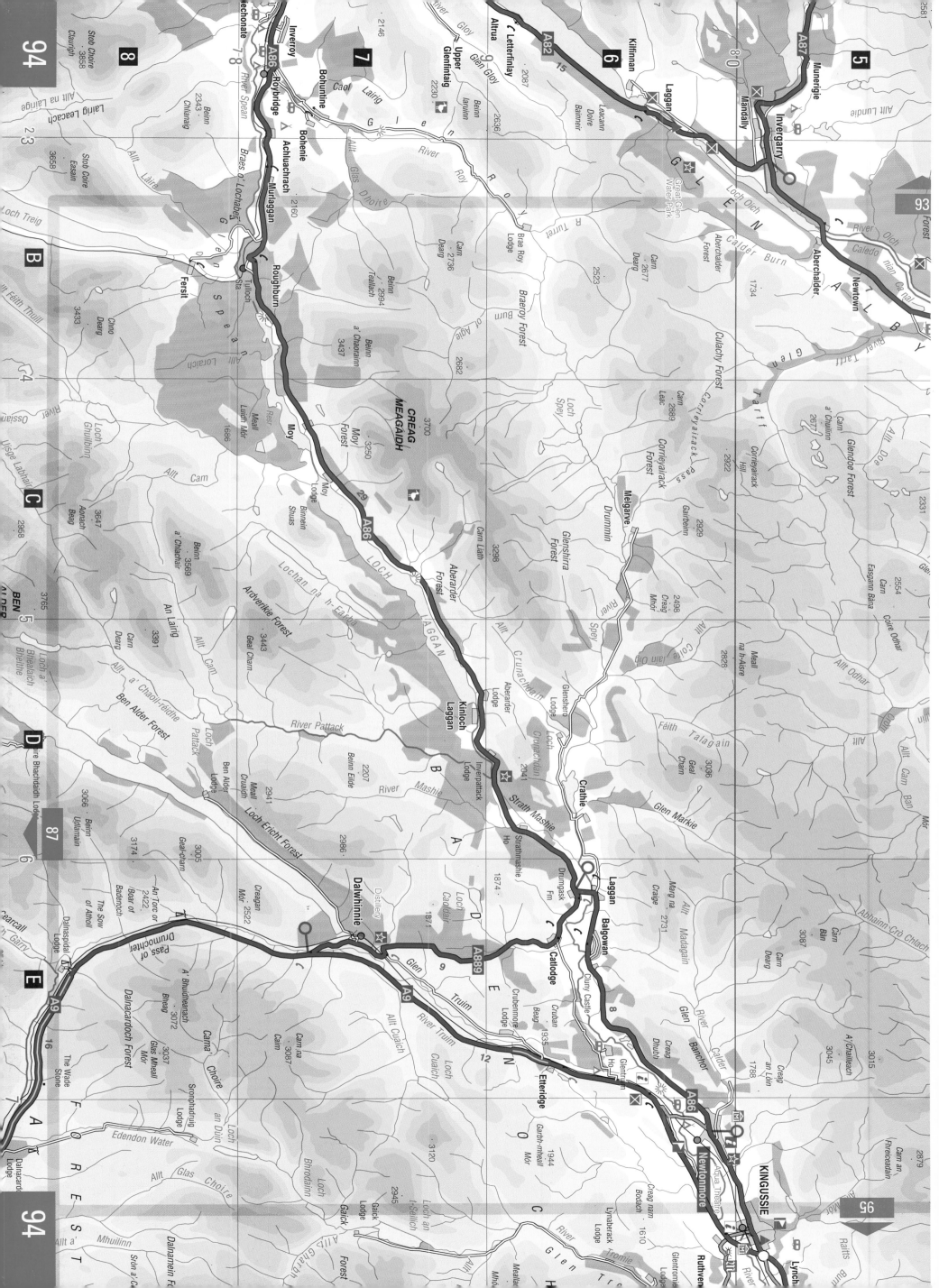

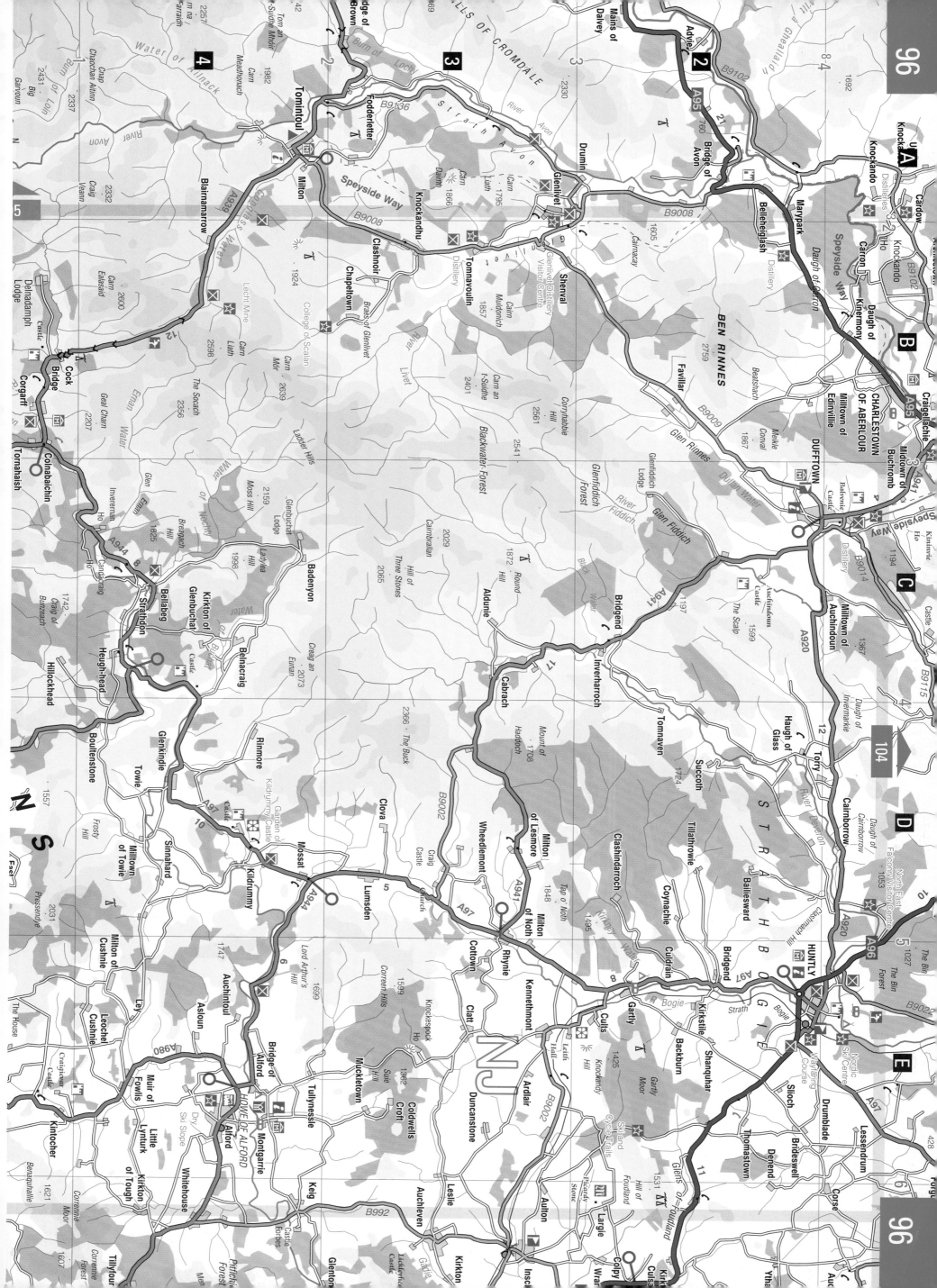

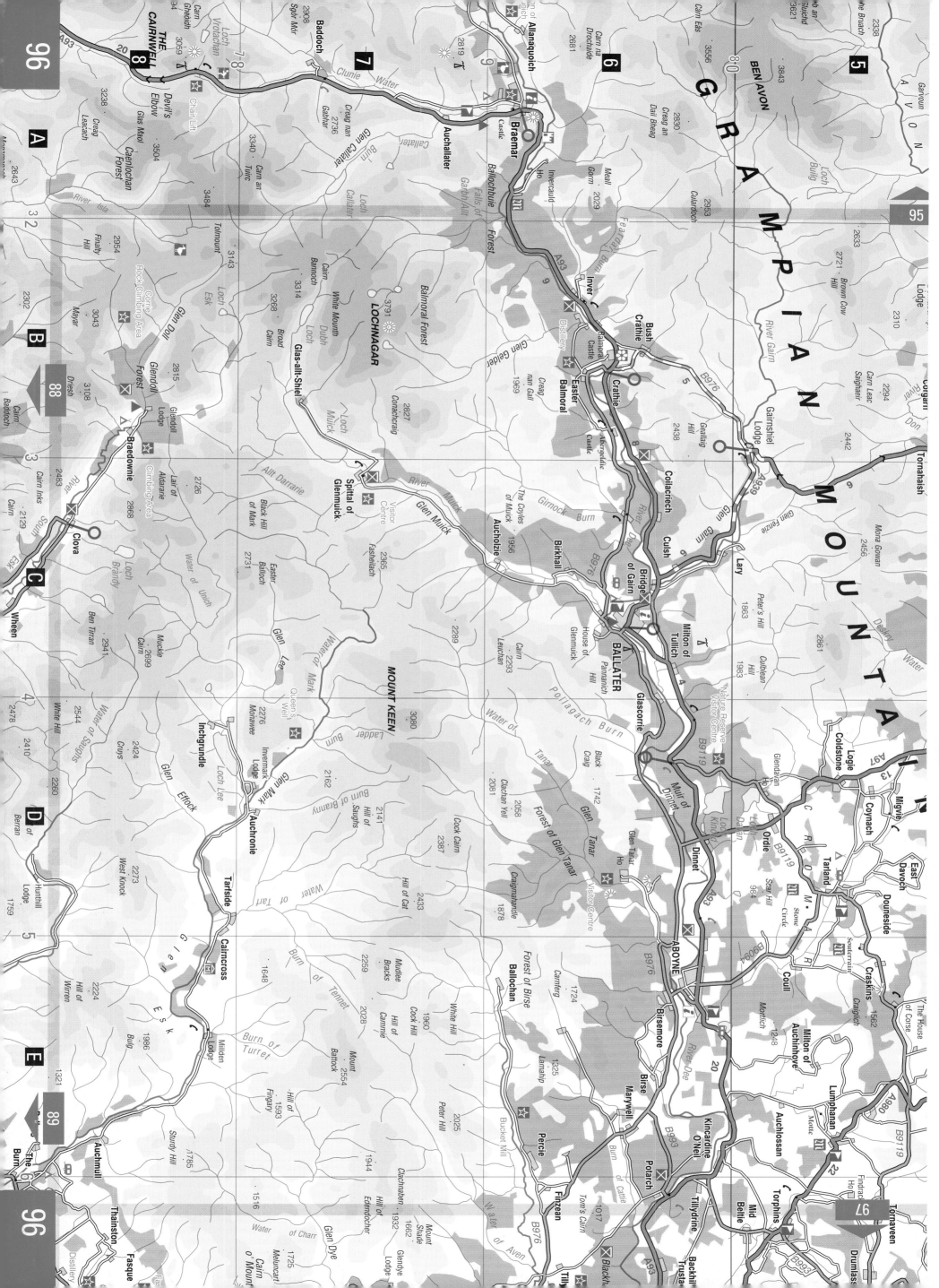

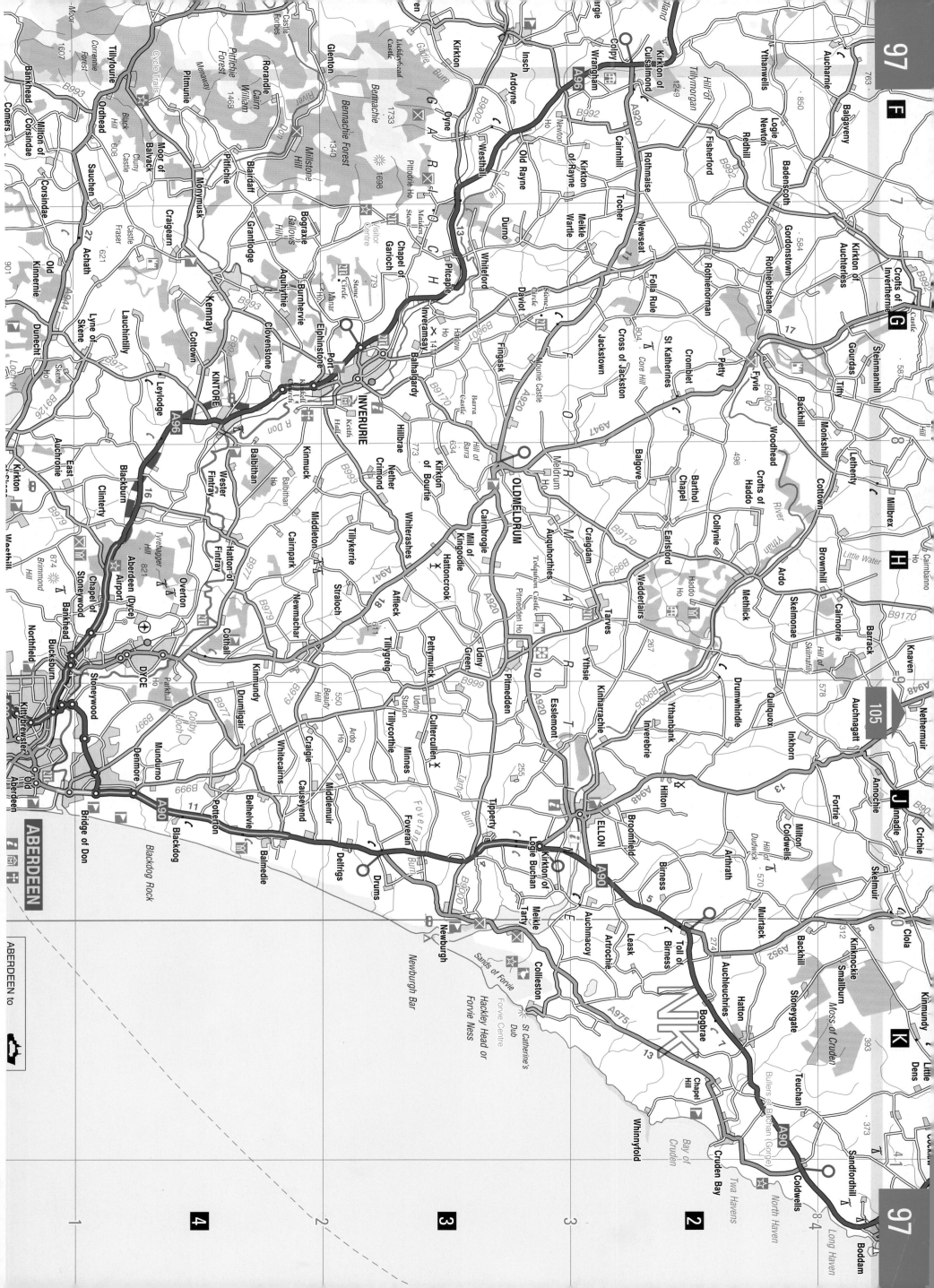

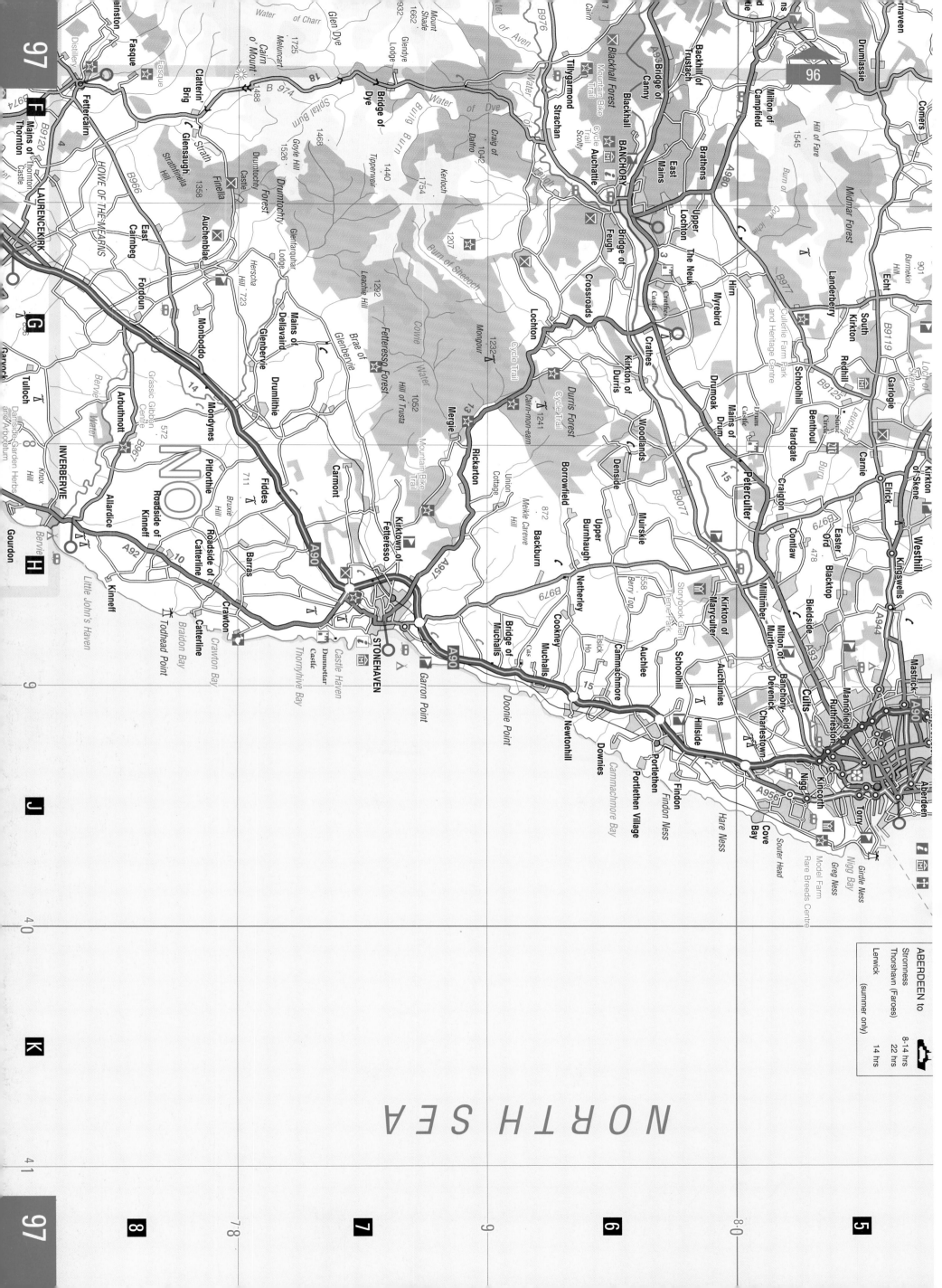

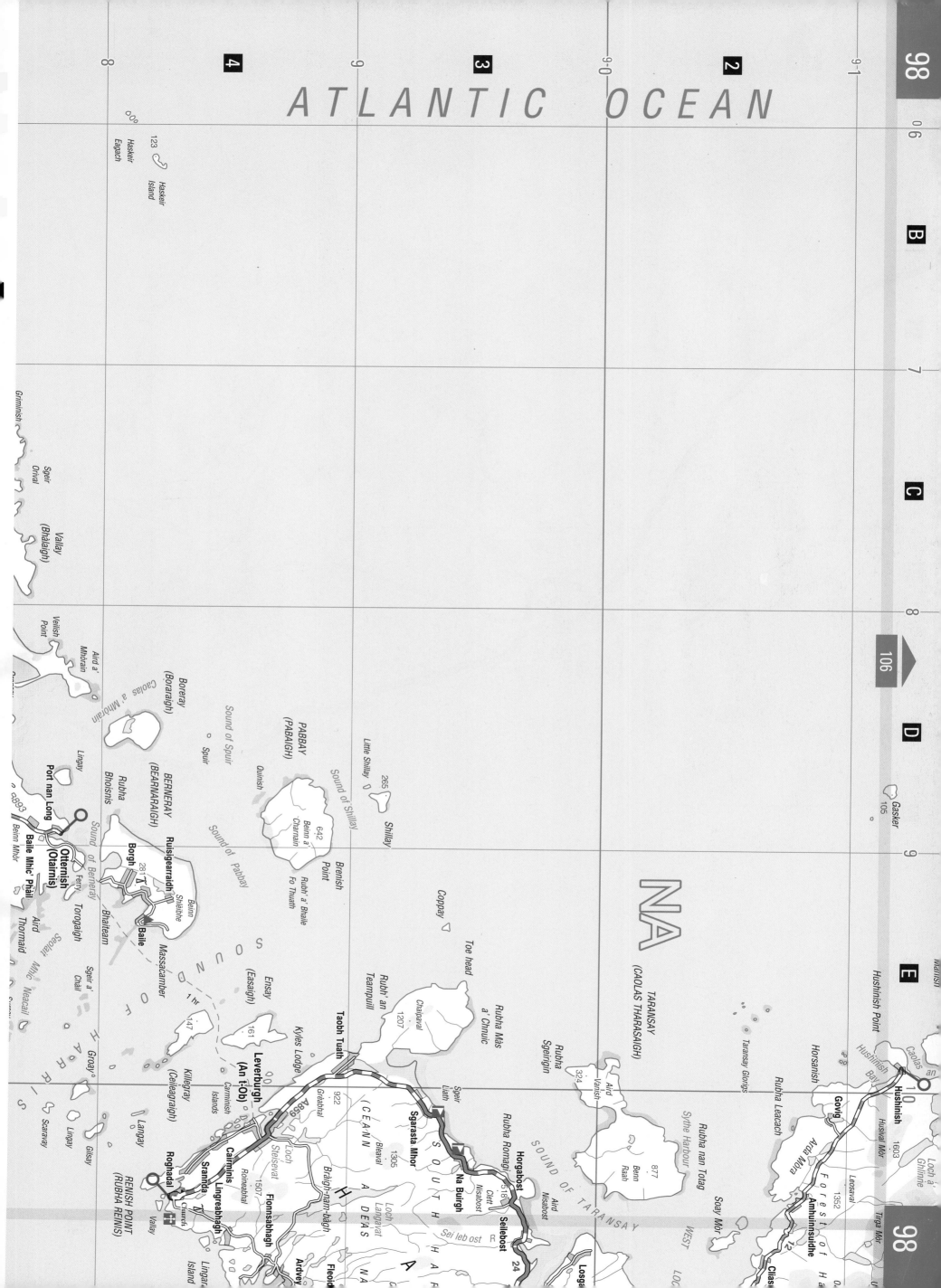

ATLANTIC OCEAN

Haskeir
Island
123
Haskeir
Eagach

Grmmnish

Sgeir
Orival

Valay
(Bhàlaigh)

Veilish
Point

Aird a'
Mhórain

Boreray
(Boraraigh)

Caolas a'Mhórain

Lingay

Sound of Spuir

Spuir

Quinish

Little Shillay

265

Shillay

642

Benin a'
Charnain

Rubh a' Bhaile
Fo Thuath

Brenish
Point

Sound of Shillay

PABBAY
(PABAIGH)

BERNERAY
(BEARNARAIGH)

Rubha
Bhoisnis

Ruisigearraidh

Borgh

281

Benn
Shlèibhe

Baile

Sound of Berneray

Sound of Pabbay

Coppay

Toe head

Rubh' an
Teampuill

Rubha Màs
a' Chnuic

Rubha
Sgeirigin

NA

TARANSAY
(CAOLAS THARASAIGH)

Gasker

105

Hushinish Point

Horsanish

Taransay Glorps

Rubha nan Totag

Soay Mòr

Sythe Harbour

Rubha Leacach

Govig

Hushinish

Caolas an

Loch a'
Ghlinne

Amhuinnsuidhe

Clisi

Forest of H

Arda Mòra

Husival Mòr

1603

Leosaval
1352

Tirga Mòr

WEST

Port nan Long

Baile Mhic' Phàil

Otternish
(Otairnis)

Ferry

Torogaigh

Aird
Thormaid

Sgeir a'
Chàil

Seòlaid Mhic Neacail

Massacamber

1 hr

147

Ensay
(Easaigh)

161

Kyles Lodge

Groay

Killegray
(Ceileagraigh)

SOUND OF HARRIS

Langay

Scaravay

Lingay

Gilsay

Lingay

Carminis
Islands

Leverburgh
(An t-Ob)

Taobh Tuath

Gréabhal

922

Sgeir
Liath

Chaipaval
1207

Aird
Vanish

324

Benn
Raah

877

Aird
Nisabost

Roghadal

RENISH POINT
(RUBHA REINIS)

Valay

Cairinis

Lingreabhagh

Srannda

Fionsabhagh

Ardvey

Fleoid

Church

A859

CEANN A DEAS NA

Loch
Steisevat

Roineabhal
1507

Bleaval
1305

Bràigh-nam-bàgh

Loch
Langavat

Sei leb ost

SOUTH HARRIS

Horgabost

Nisabost

Seilebost

Sgarasta Mhor

Na Buirgh

Rubha Romagi

SOUND OF TARANSAY

Losga

24

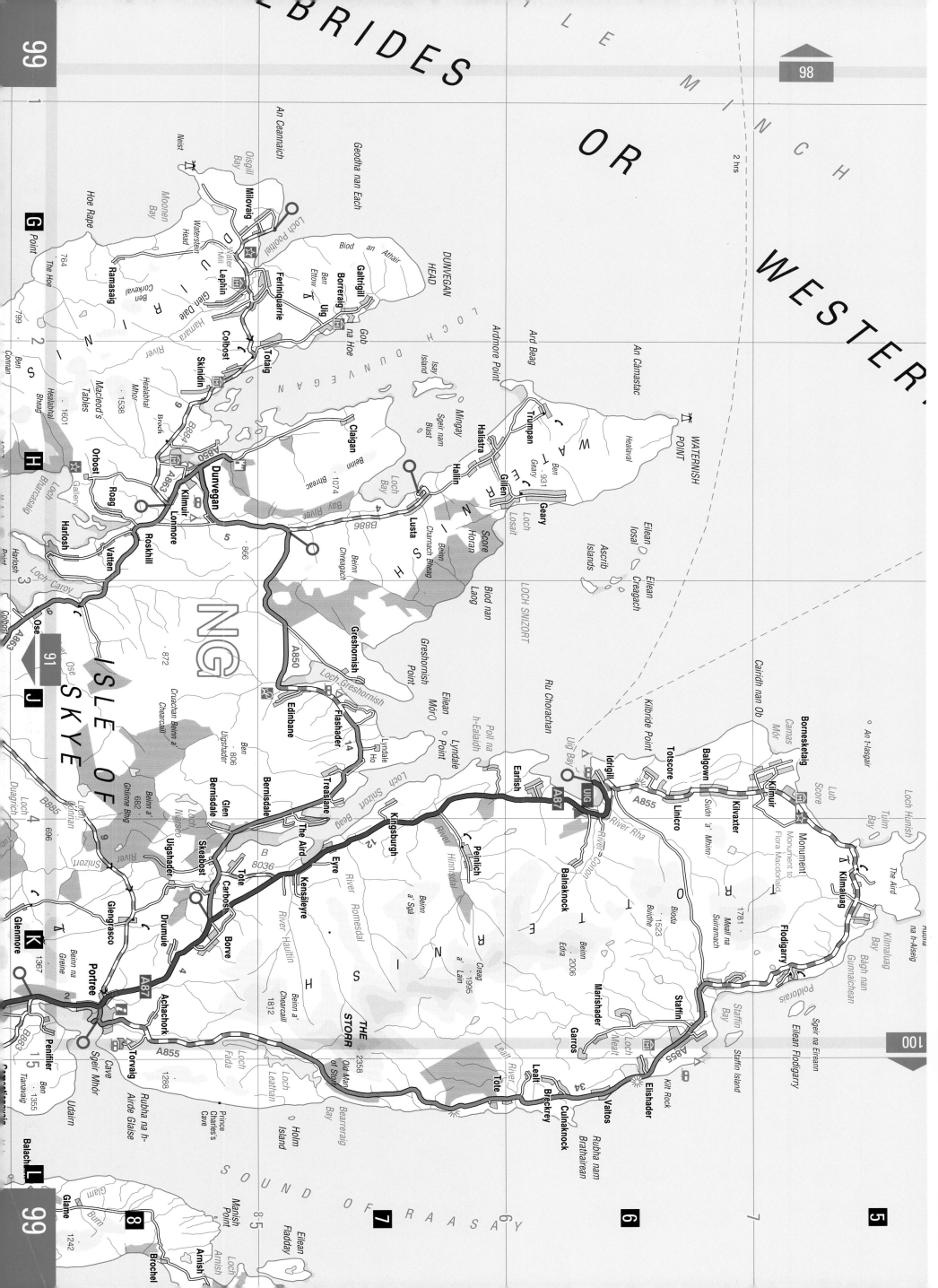

THE MINCH

Gob na Mìlaid

Sròanach

247

Shìant Islands

Garbh Eilean
528

Cadha na Gaoidhsich

Eilean an Tighe

Eilean Mhuire

Sgeir nam Maol

RUBHA HUNISH

Eilean Trodday

Rubha na h-Aiseig

Longa Island
230

Caolas Beag

Rubha Bàn

Big Sand

North Erradale

B8021

Lonemore

Strath

Gairloch

Rubha Reigh

Sròn na Clèite

Melvaig

Aultgrishan

Seana Chamas

Port Erradale

Peterburn

R. Sand

An Cuaidh
972

Cnoc Breac
962

Sròn a' Gheodha Dhuibh

Camas Mòr

Loch an Draing

Loch Squod

Eilean Furadh Mòr

271

340

Rubha nan Sasan

Greenstone Point

Rubha Mòr

Gob a' Chuaille

Slaggan Bay

Opinan

Rubha Beag

Inverasdale

Cove

B8057

LOCH EWE

Isle of Ewe

233

Naast

Midtown

Brae

Rubha' Ard na Bà

Loch Bad a' Chreamh

749

Poolewe

Londubh

Loch Tollaidh
1140

1123

R. Ewe

Loch Kernsary

Inverewe

Rubha' a' Bhàid

593

Tournaig

Drumchork

Tighnafiline

Aultbea

Buainaluib

Ormiscaig

Mellon Charles

Beinn Dearg Mhòr
513

Mellon Udrigle

Achgarve

478

Laide

Sand

A832

Loch na Beiste

820

Beinn Dearg Bad Chaille
897

Loch Fada

Meall na Mèine

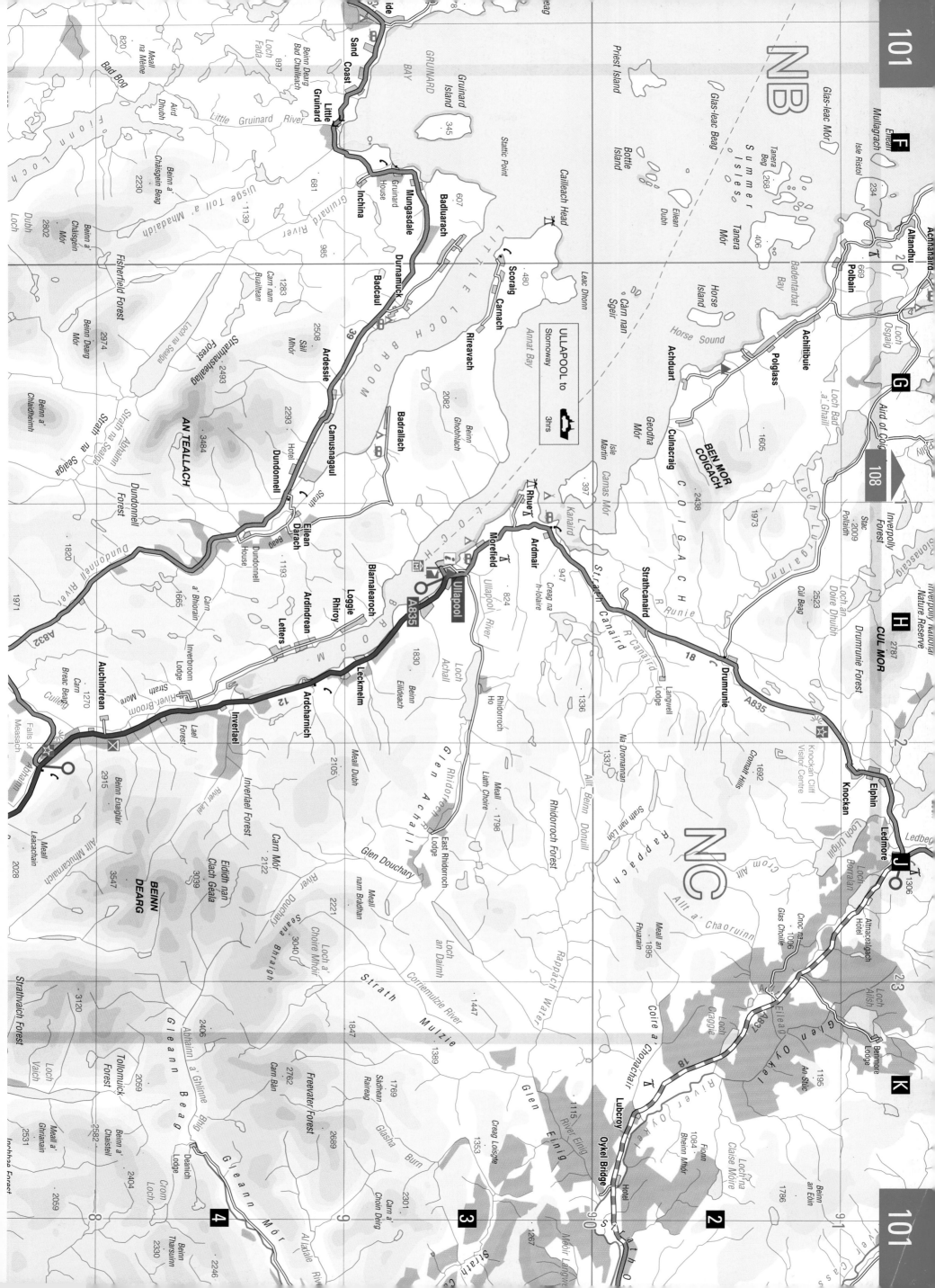

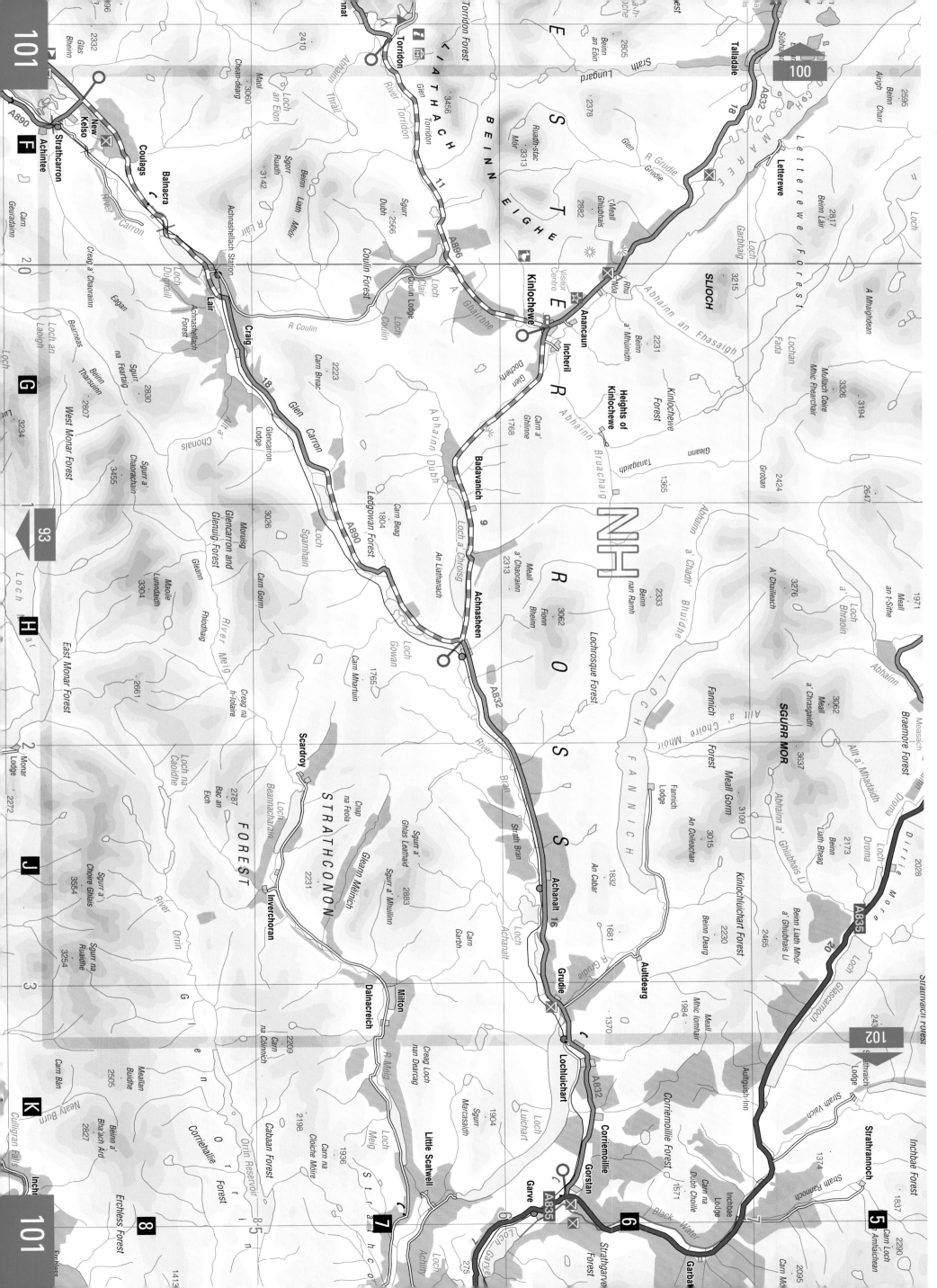

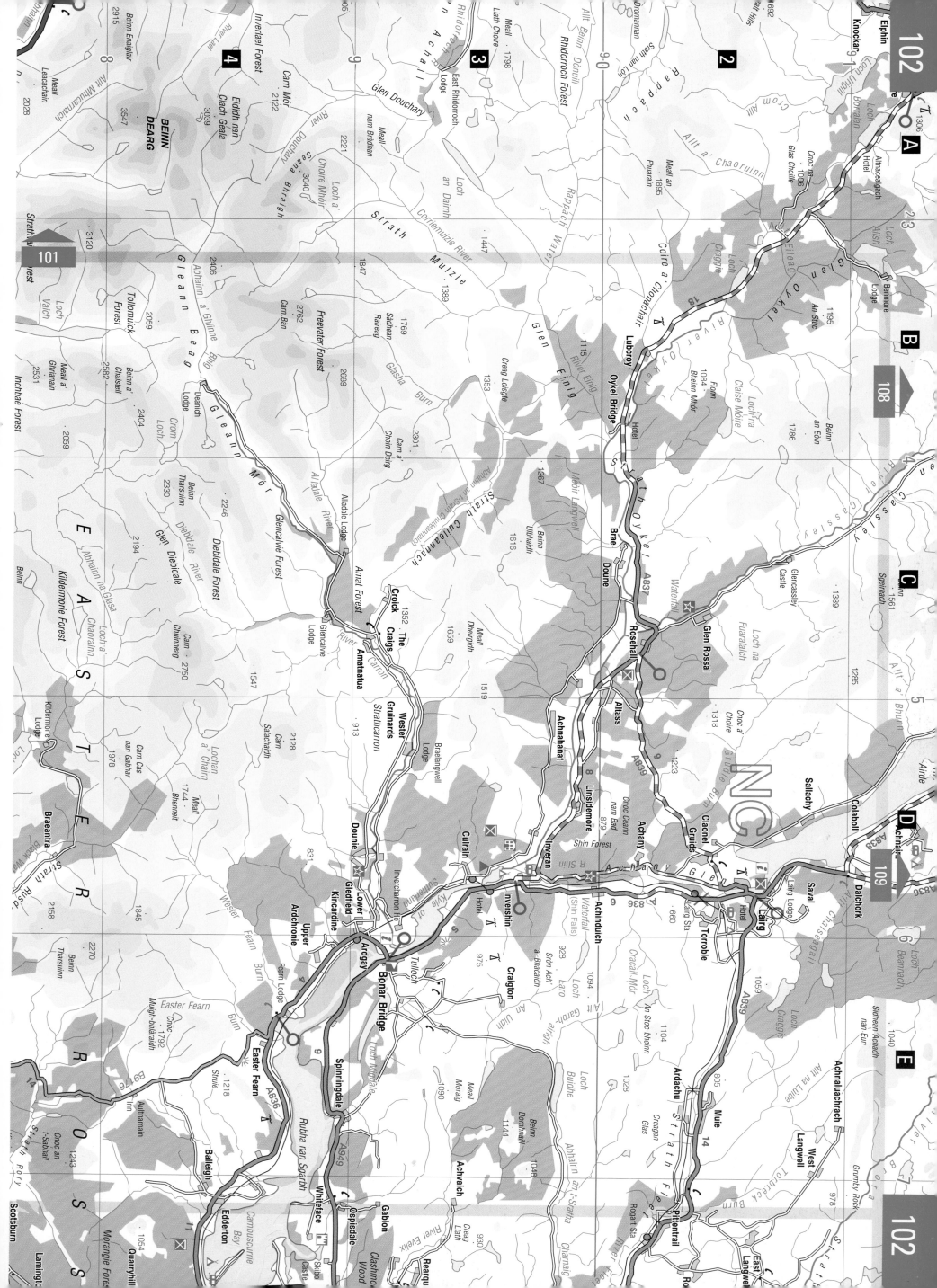

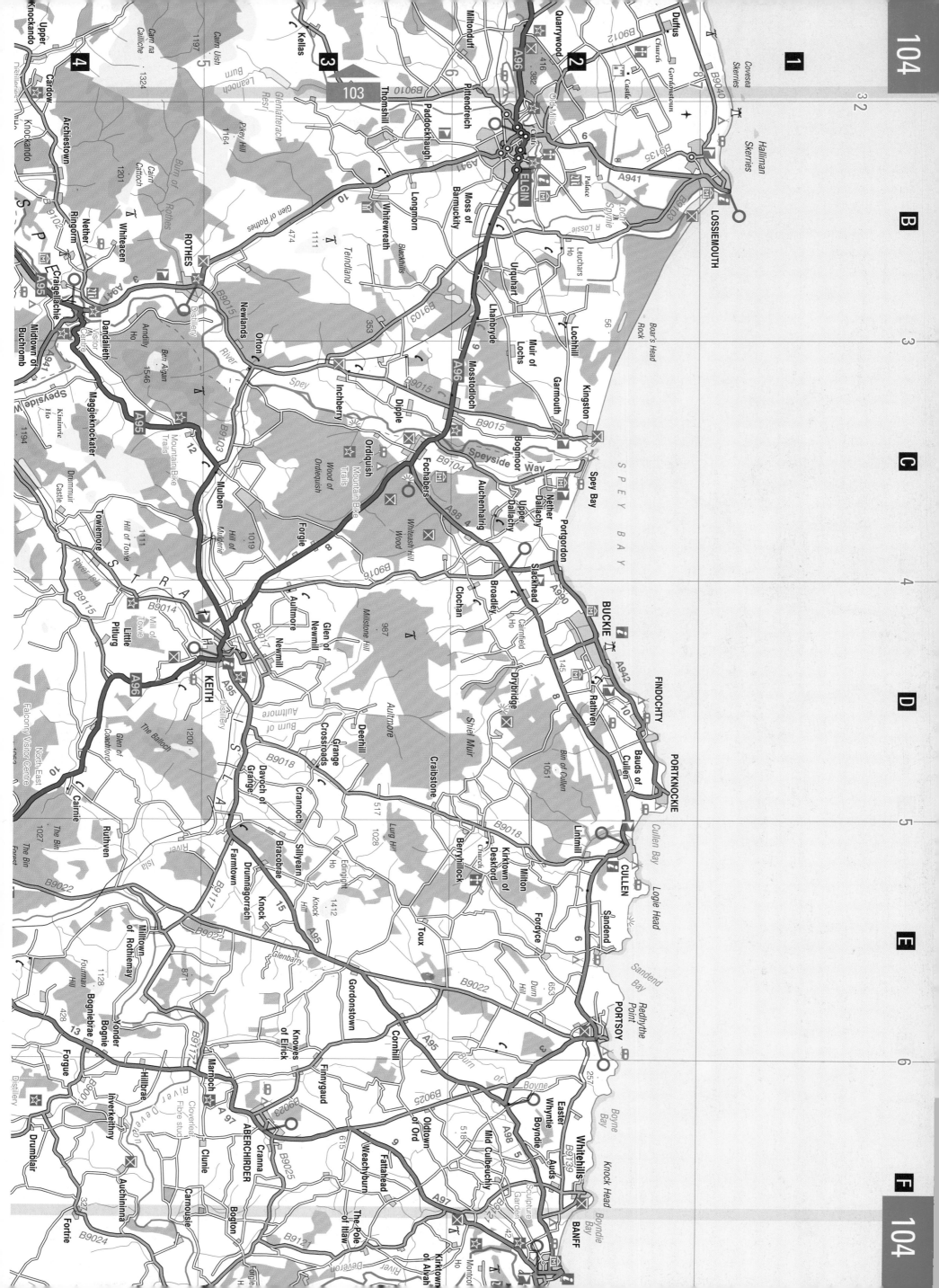

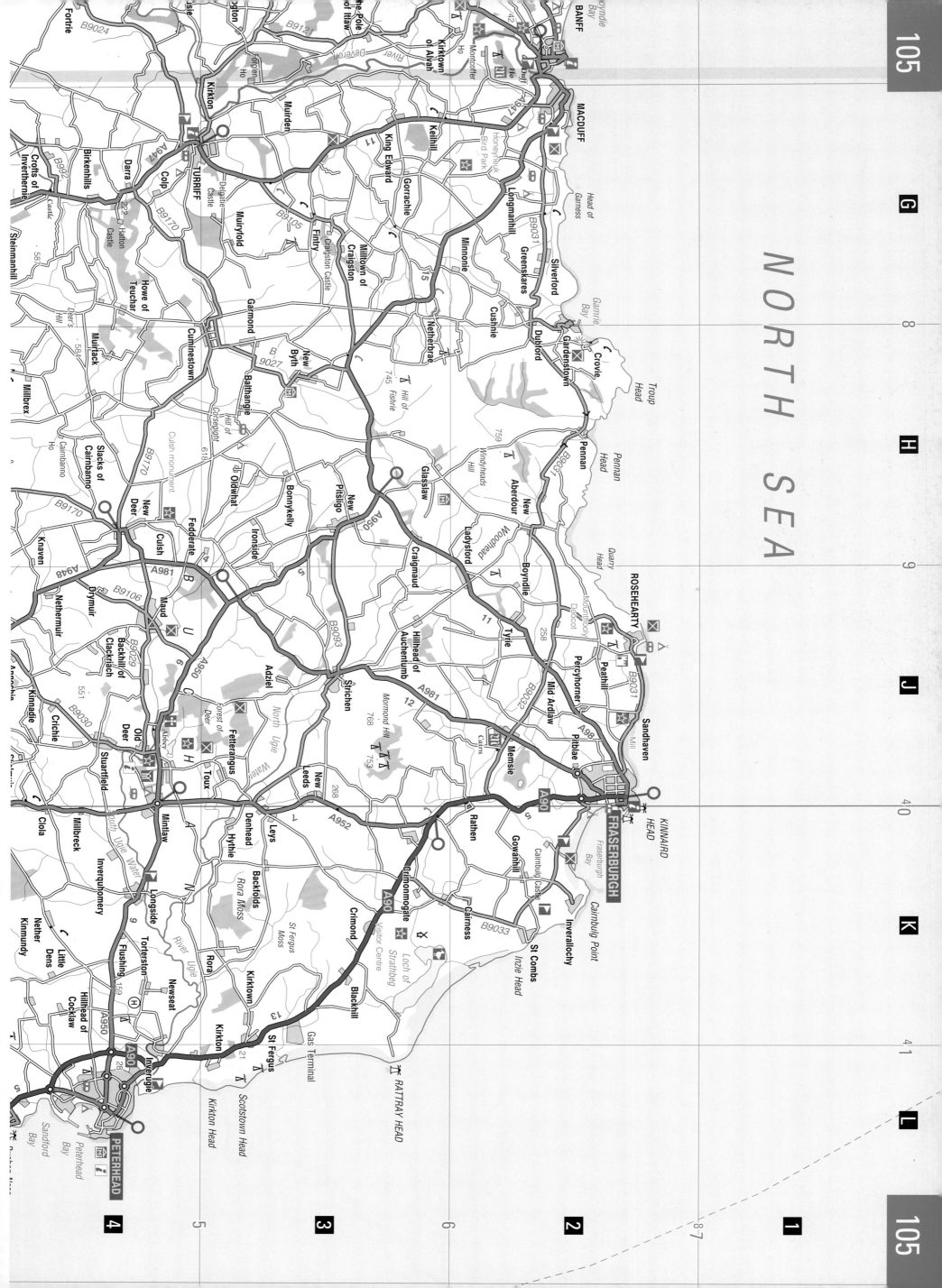

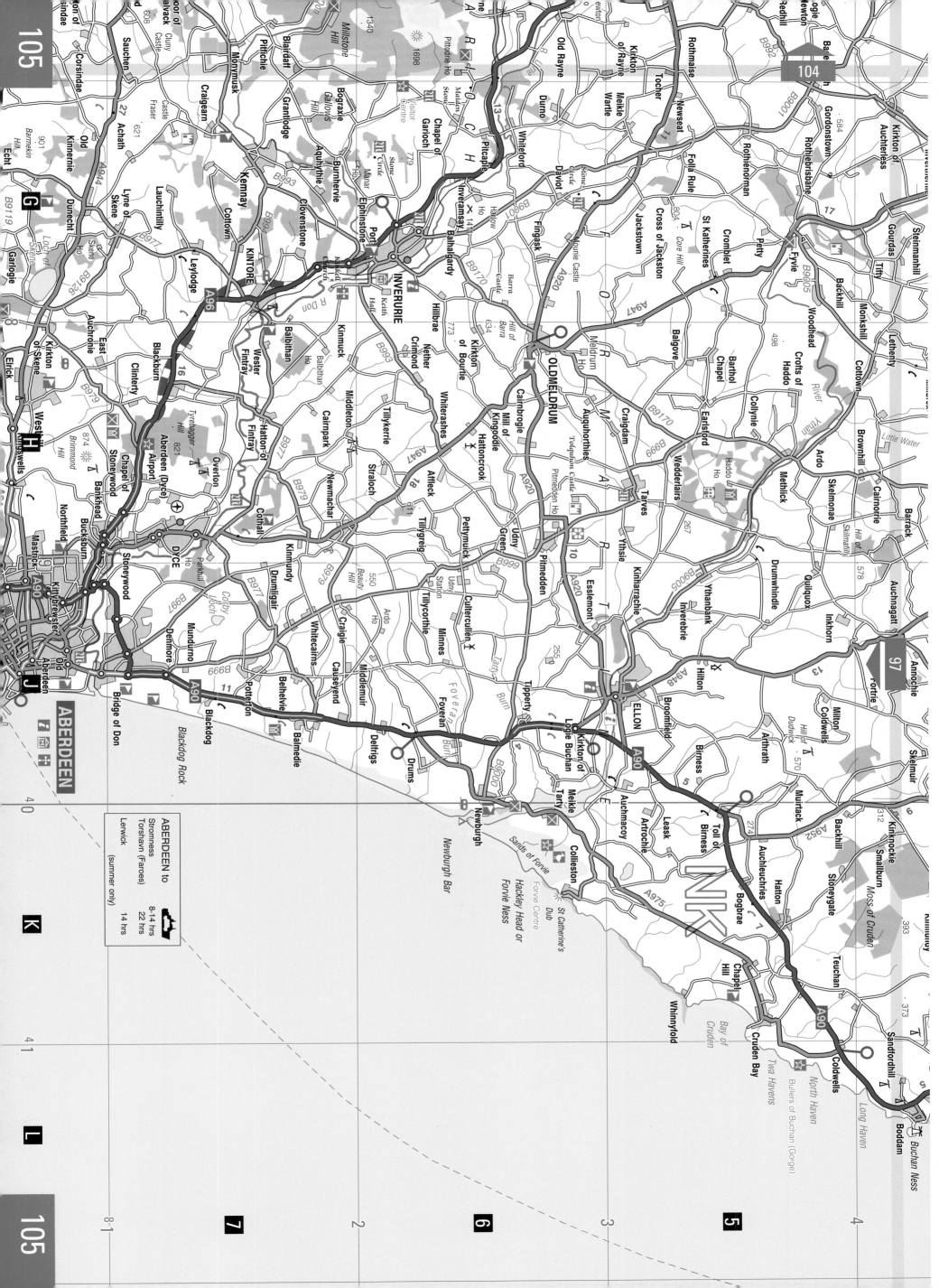

A

B

C

D

E

8·9

07

8

9

10

1

7

2

6

3

5

Flannan Isles

OCEAN

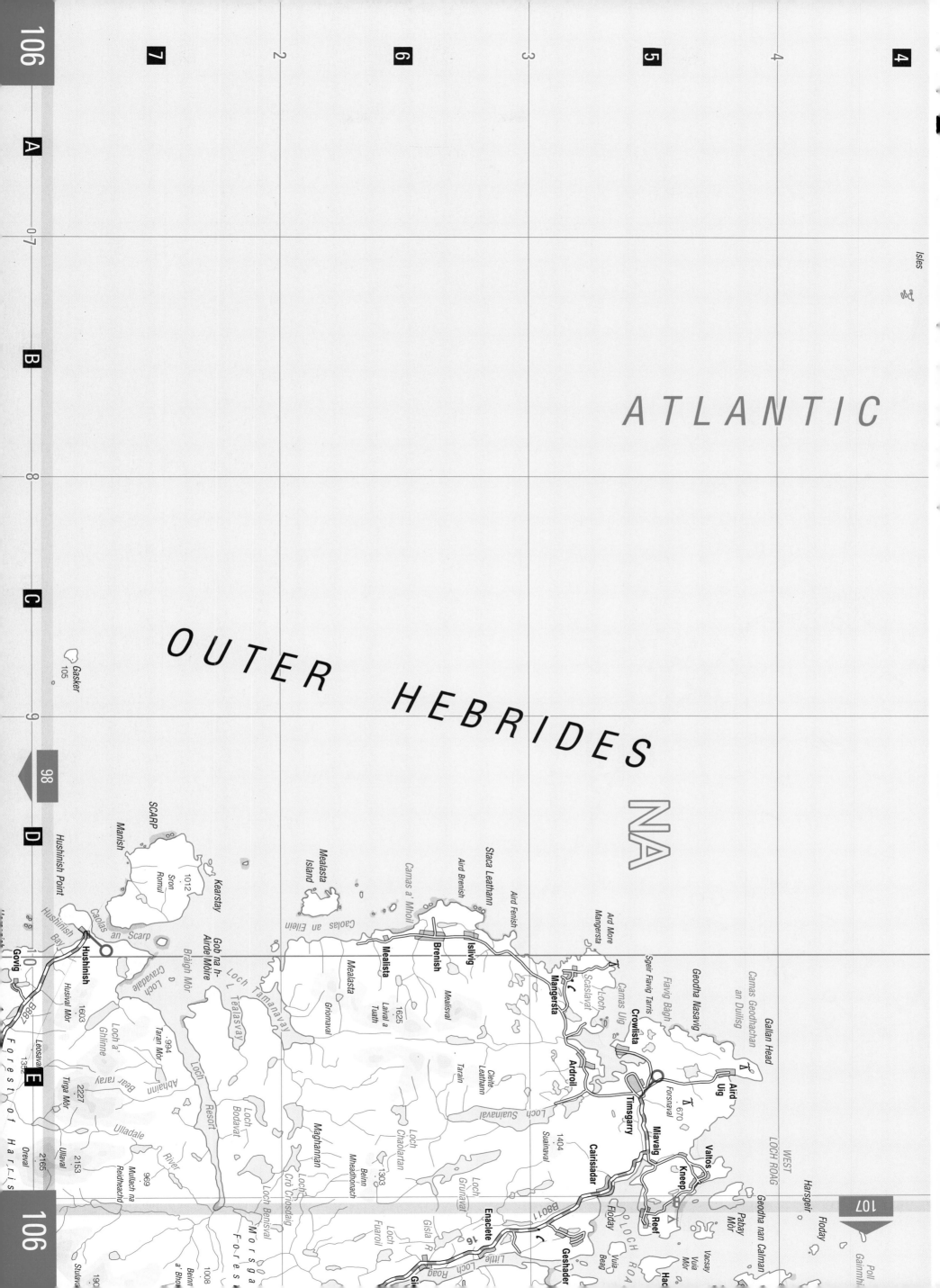

ATLANTIC

OUTER HEBRIDES

NA

Isles

Gasker
105

SCARP

Manish

Sron
Romul

1012

Hushinish Point

Hushinish Bay

Caolas an Scarp

Hushinish

Husival Mor

1603

Kearstay

Braigh Mor

Loch
Cravadale

Aird Moire

Gob na h-

L. Tealasvay

Loch Tamanavay

Loch

Resort

Mealasta
Island

Mealasta

Griomaval

Staca Leathann

Aird Brenish

Camas a' Mhoil

Caolas an Eilean

Aird Fenish

Islivig

Brenish

Mealisval

1625

Laival a
Tuath

Tarain

Cleite
Leathann

Mangersta

Ard More
Mangersta

Loch
Scaslavat

Camas Uig

Sgeir Fiavig Tarris

Fiavig Bagh

Crowlista

Geodha Nasavig

Camas Geodhachan
an Duilisg

Gallan Head

WEST LOCH ROAG

Hargeir

Floday

Poll Gainmhi

Geodha nan Calman

Pabay
Mor

Vacsay

Vuia
Mor

Ardroil

Timsgarry

Miavaig

Aird
Uig

Forsnaval

670

1404

Valtos

Kneep

Floday

Reef

LOCH ROAG

Vuia
Beag

Ha

Cairisiadar

Beinn
Mheadhonach

1303

Loch
Chabliartan

1404

Suainaval

Loch Suainaval

Loch Grunavat

Gisla R

Enaclete

16

Geshader

Gi

Little Loch Roag

Maghannan

2153
Ullaval

Ulladale

969
Mullach na
Reidheachd

Loch
Cro Criostaig

Loch
Beinisval

Morsga

Forest

Loch
Fuaroil

Loch
Fuaran

1008

Beinn
a' Bhon

Stulava

190

2165
Oreval

2227
Tirga Mor

994
Taran Mor

Beat raray

Loch Bodavat

Loch a'
Ghlinne

Loch
Abhainn

135
Leosaval

Govig

B887

Forest of Harris

98

107

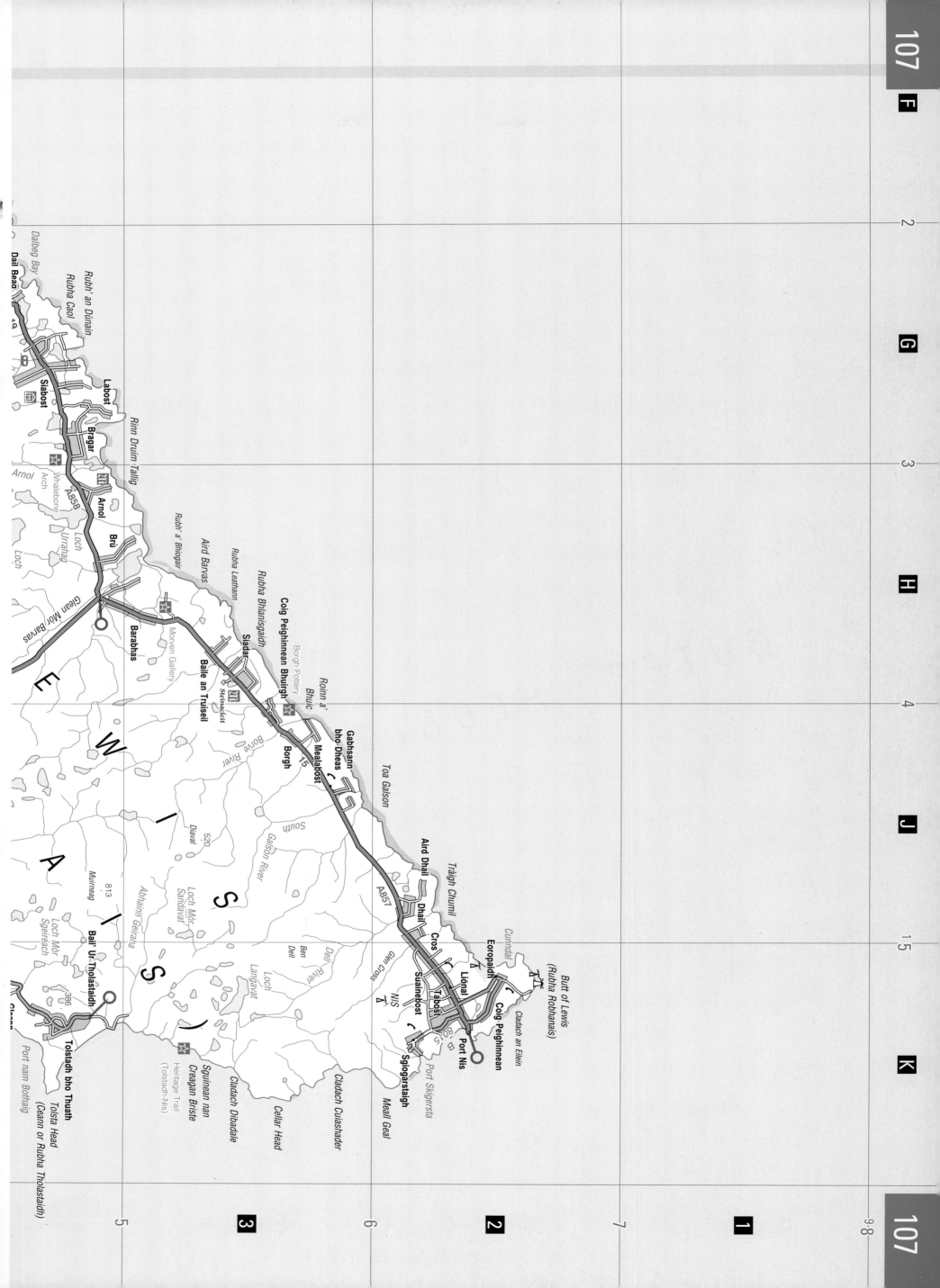

Dail Beag
Dalbeg Bay
Rubh' an Dùnain
Rubha Caol
Labost
Siabost
Bragar
Arnol
Whalebone Arch
Arnol
Brù
A858
Loch Uirahag
Barabhas
Rinn Druim Tallig
Glean Mòr Barvas
E
W
I
A
I
S
S
Loch
Loch
Rubh' a' Bhiogair
Aird Barvas
Rubha Leathann
Morven Gallery
Rubha Bhlanisgaidh
Coig Peighinnean Bhuirgh
Siada
Baile an Truiseil
Steinacleit
Borgh Pottery
Roinn a' Bhuic
Gabhsann bho Dheas
Mealabost
Borgh
15
Toa Galson
Galson River
South
Diaval
520
Murneag
813
Bail' Ur-Tholastaidh
386
Loch Mòr Sgeireach
Abhainn Ghrana
Loch Mòr Sandavat
Ben Dell
Dell River
Loch Langavat
Glen Cross
NIS
NIS
Aird Dhail
Dhail
Cros
Suaineabost
Tabost
Liònal
Eoropaidh
Coig Peighinnean
Cuundal
Cladach an Eilein
Butt of Lewis
(Rubha Robhanais)
Traigh Chumil
Toistadh bho Thuath
Tolsta Head
(Ceann or Rubha Tholastaidh)
Port nam Bothaig
Heritage Trail
(Tolstadh-Nis)
Sguinean nan Creagan Briste
Cladach Dibadale
Cellar Head
Cladach Cuiashader
Meall Geal
Sgiogarstaigh
Port Skigersta
Port Nis
B895
Sguineal

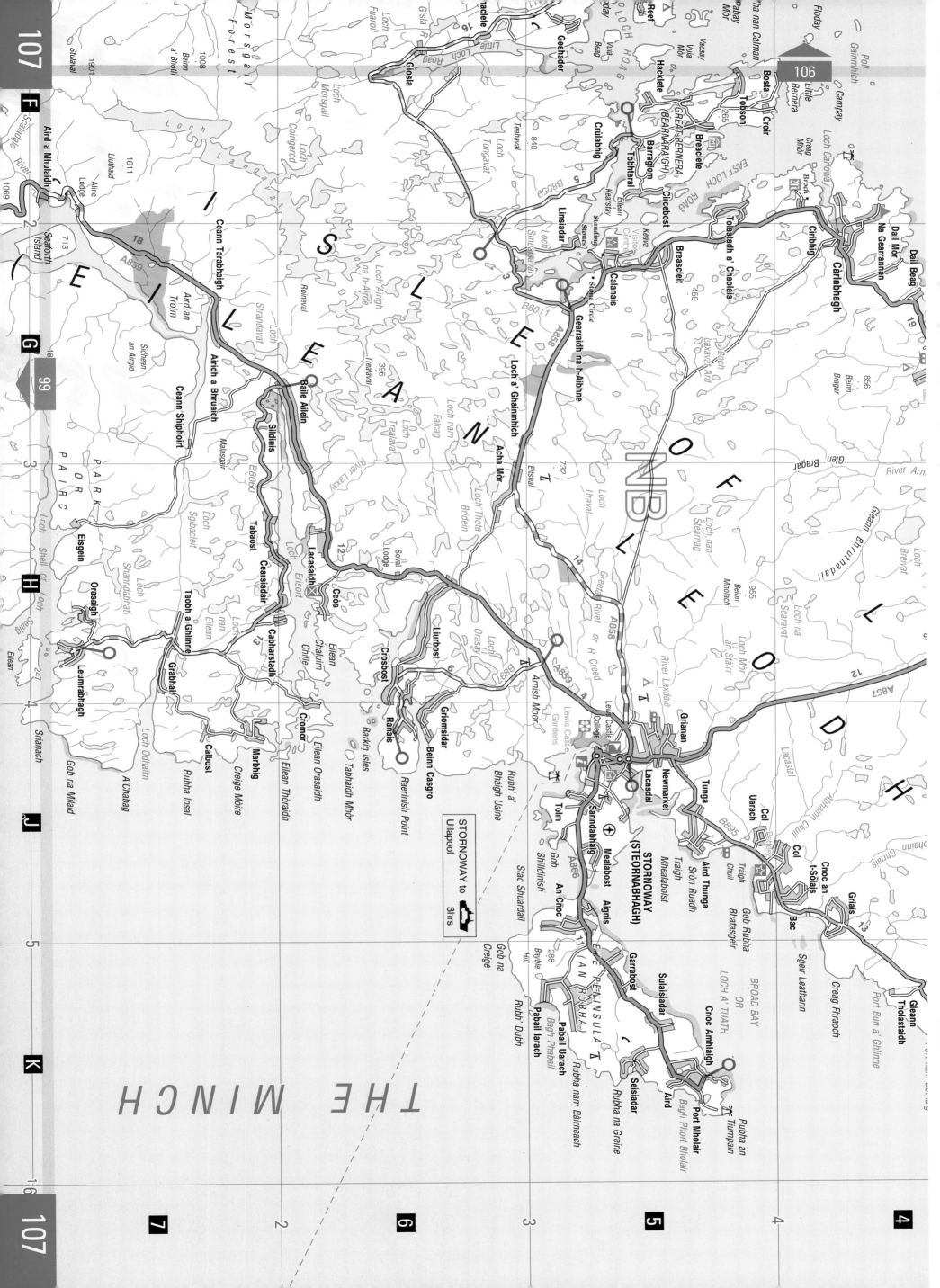

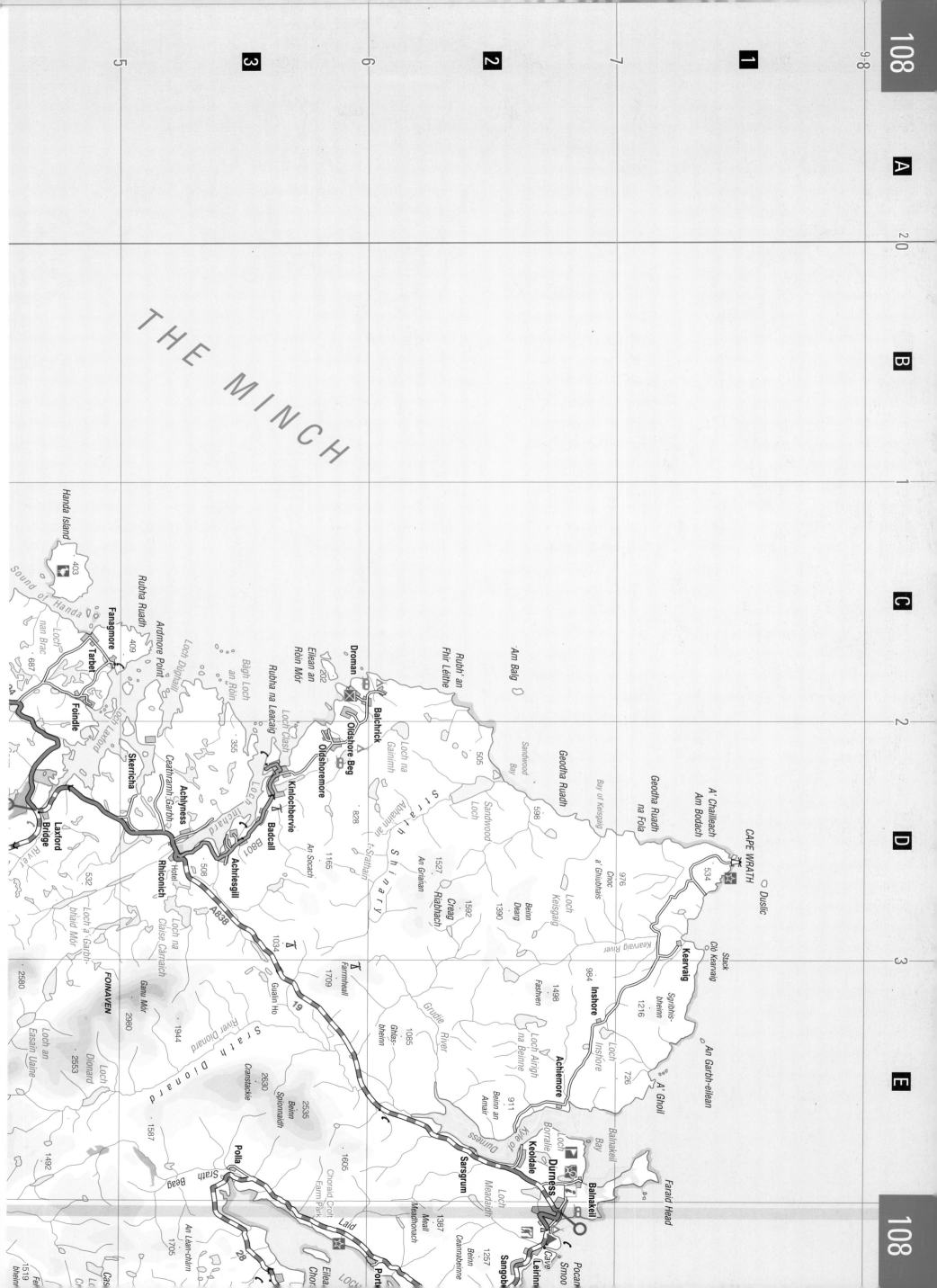

THE MINCH

CAPE WRATH

Handa Island

Sound of Handa

Fanagmore
Tarbet
Foindle
Laxford Bridge
Rhiconich
Achriesgill
Achlyness
Skerricha
FONAVEN
Polla
Laid
Portn

Rubha Ruadh
Ardmore Point
Ceathramh Garbh
Droman
Oldshoremore
Oldshore Beg
Balchrick
Kinlochbervie
Badcall
Eilean an Róin Mór
Rubha na Leacaig

Sandwood Bay
An Balg
Rubh' an Fhir Léithe
Loch na Gainimh
Sandwood Loch

Geodha Ruadh
Geodha Ruadh na Fola
A' Chailleach
An Bodach
Duslic
Stack
Clò Kearvaig
Kearvaig

Loch Keisgaig
Bay of Keisgaig
Cnoc a' Ghiubhais
Loch Inshore
Inshore
An Garbh-eilean
A' Gholl
Faraid Head

Achiemore
Durness
Keoldale
Balnakeil
Sangobeg
Sangomore
Smoo
Cave

Loch Meadaidh
Sarsgrum

Beinn an Amair
Beinn Spionnaidh
Cranstackie
Ganu Mór
Meall Meadhonach
Ceannabeinne

River Dionard
Strath Dionard
Strath Beag
Grudie River
Loch Airigh na Beinne
Kyle of Durness

Beinn Dearg
Fashven
Ghlas-bheinn
Creag Riabhach
An Grianan
An Socach
Farmheall
Gualin Ho
Strath Shinary
Abhainn an t-Strath

403
687
409
202
355
828
505
598
976
534
726
1216
984
1498
911
1085
1257
1387
1390
1592
1527
1165
1034
1709
1944
2980
2535
2630
2553
2580
1587
1492
1605
1519
1705

A838
B801
A894
19
28

Loch Laxford
Loch Dughaill
Loch Inchard
Loch Clash
Bàgh Loch an Róin
Loch na Claise Carnaich
Loch a' Garbh-bhaid Mòr
Loch an Easain Uaine
Loch Dionard
Kearvaig River

Chorad Croft Farm Park
Eilean Choraidh

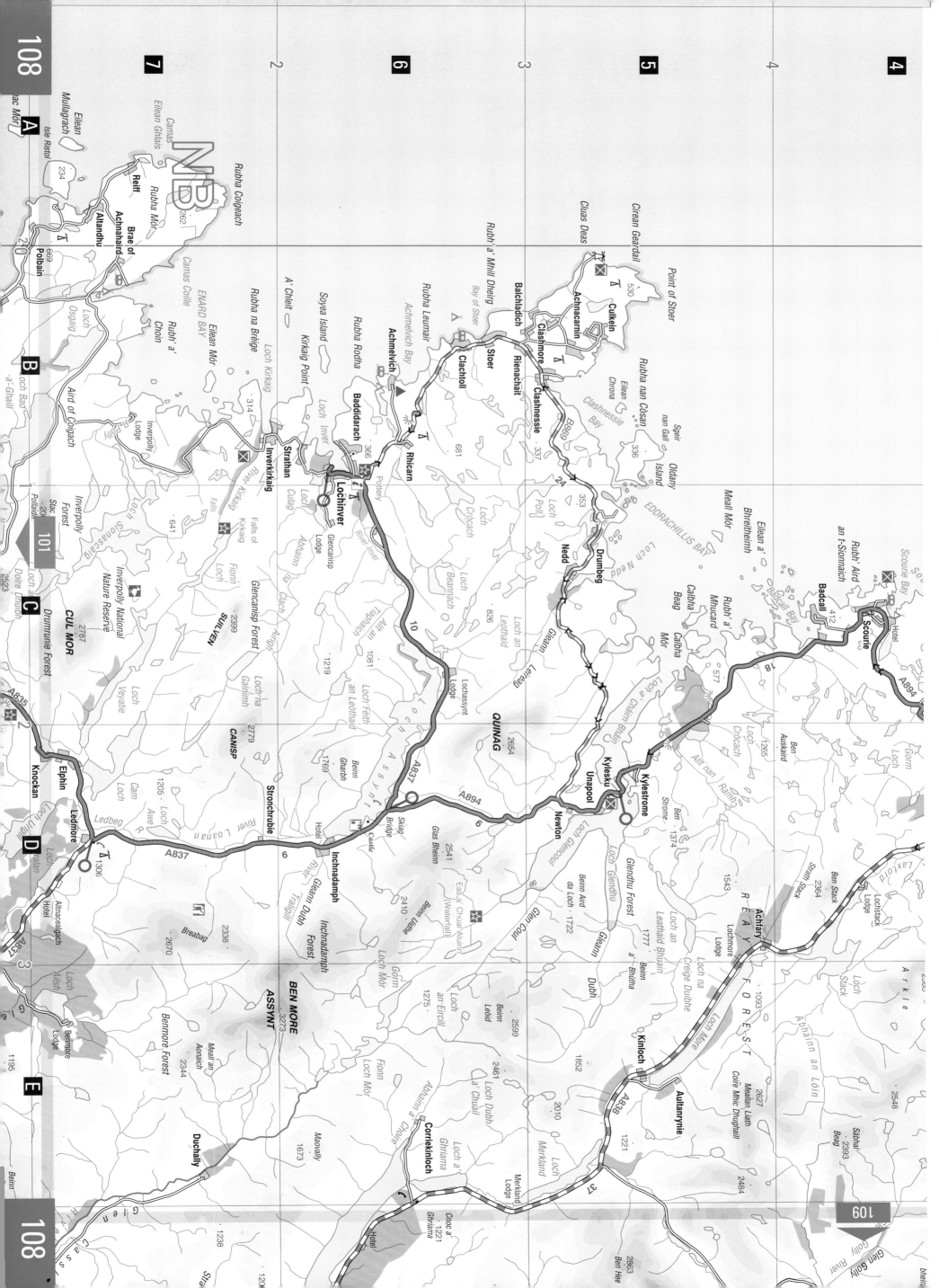

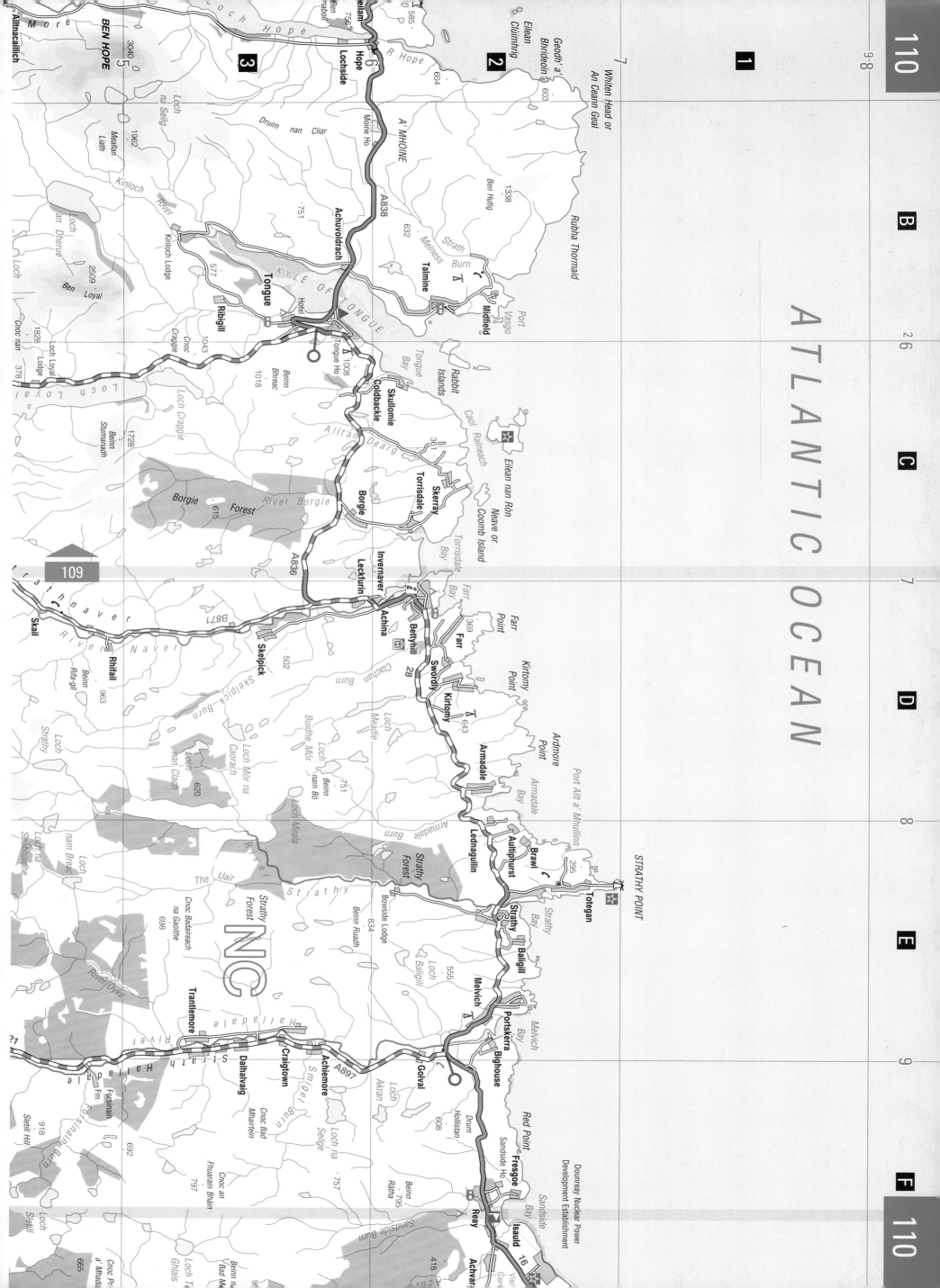

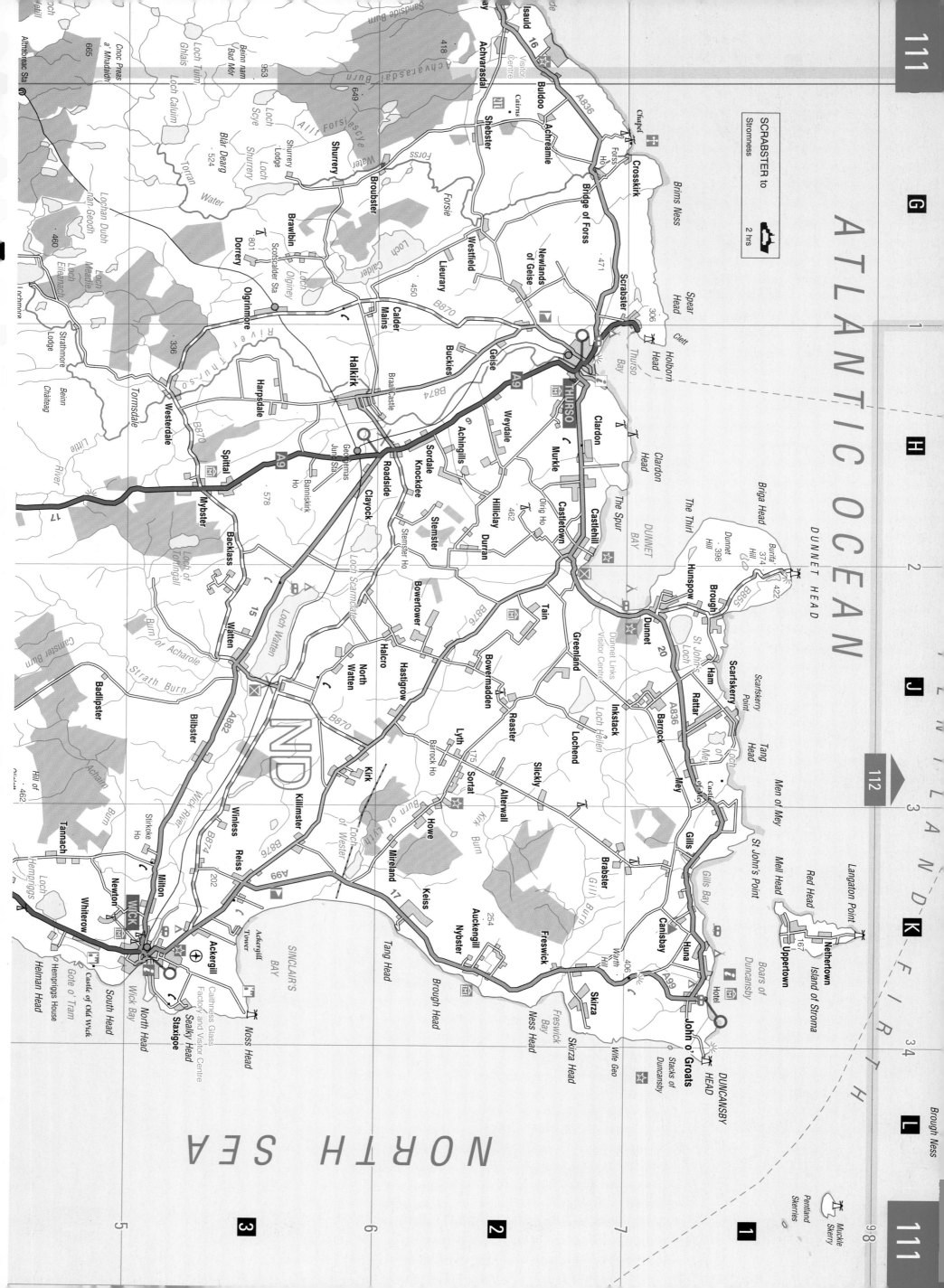

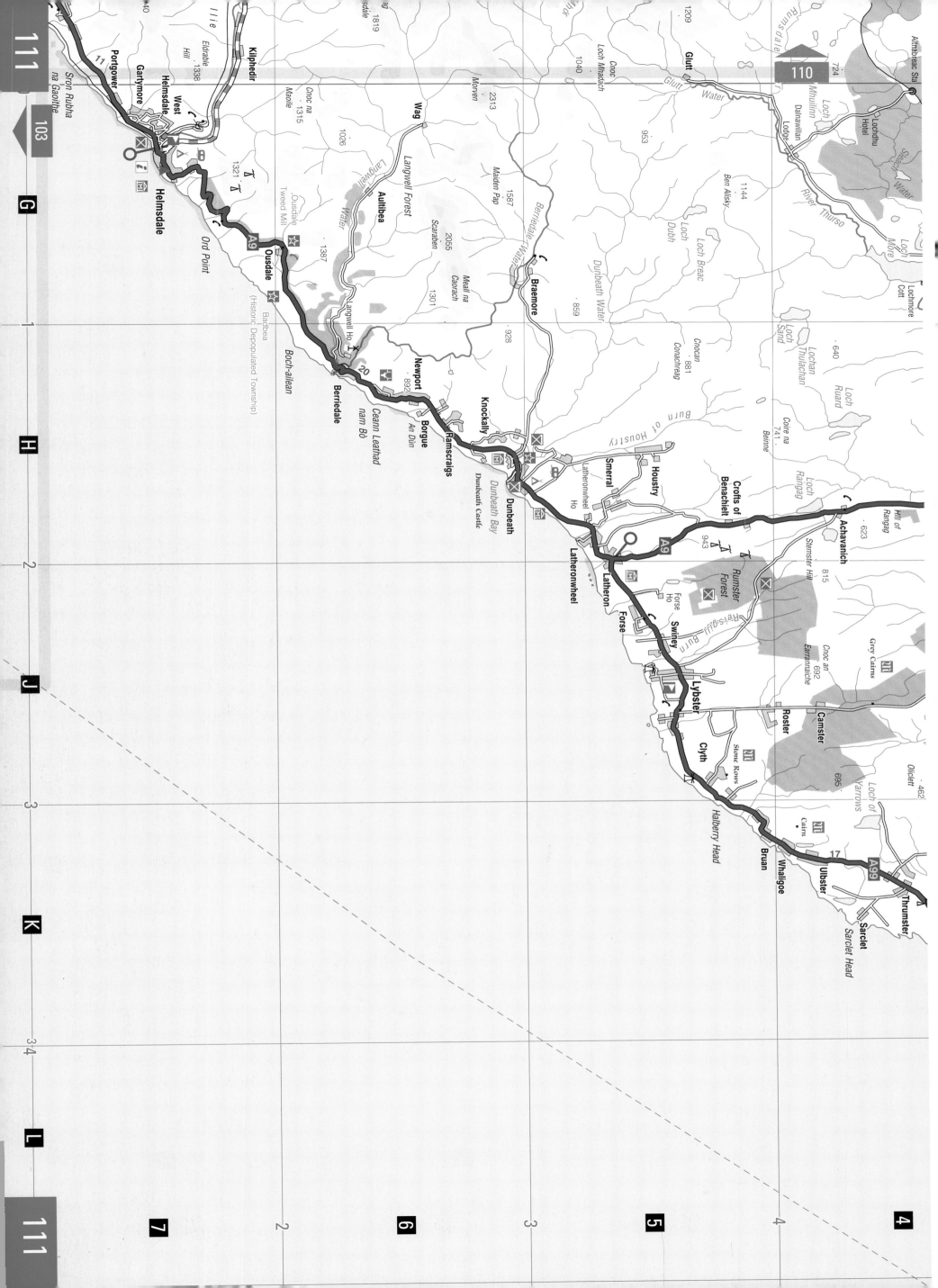

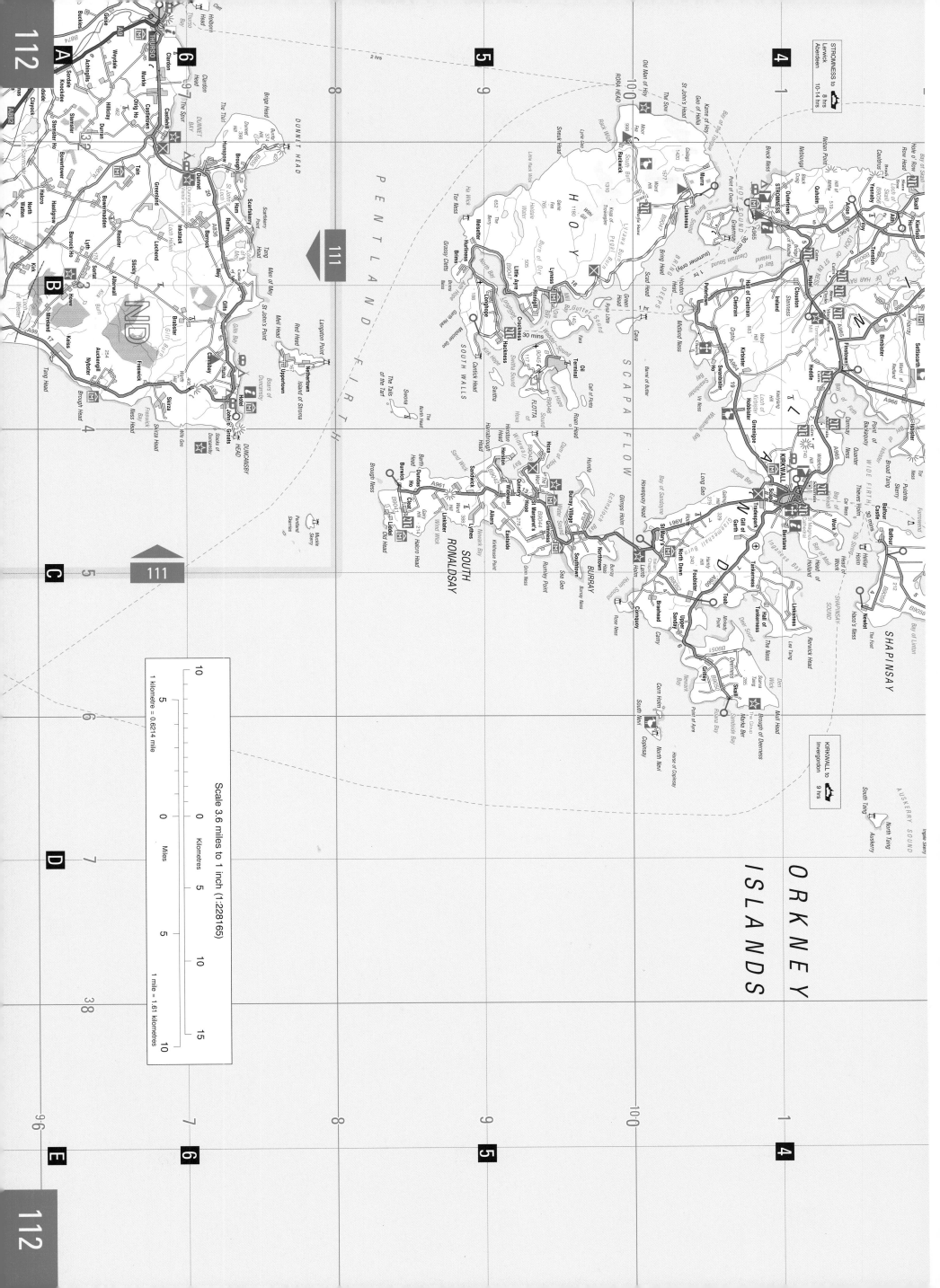

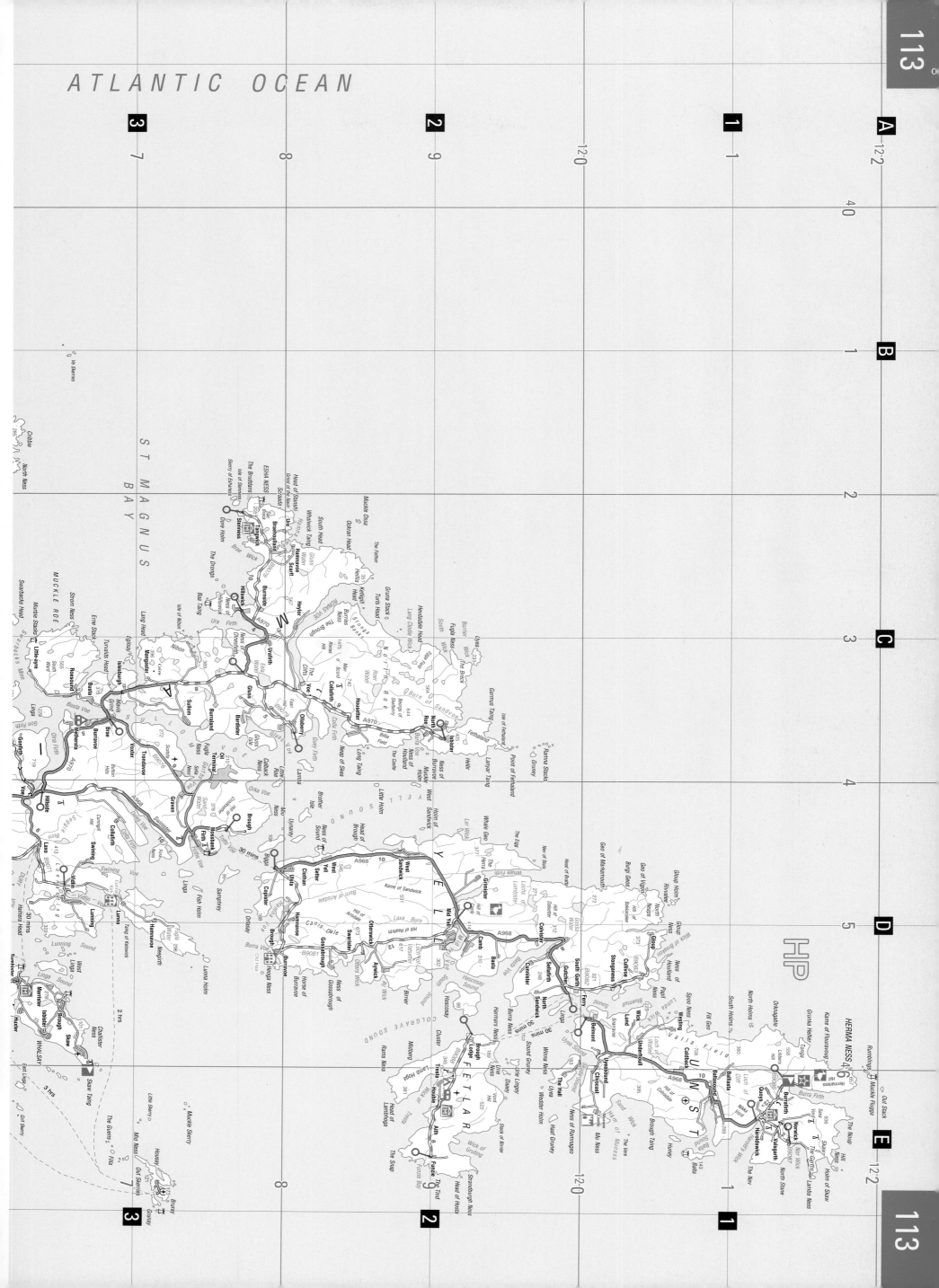

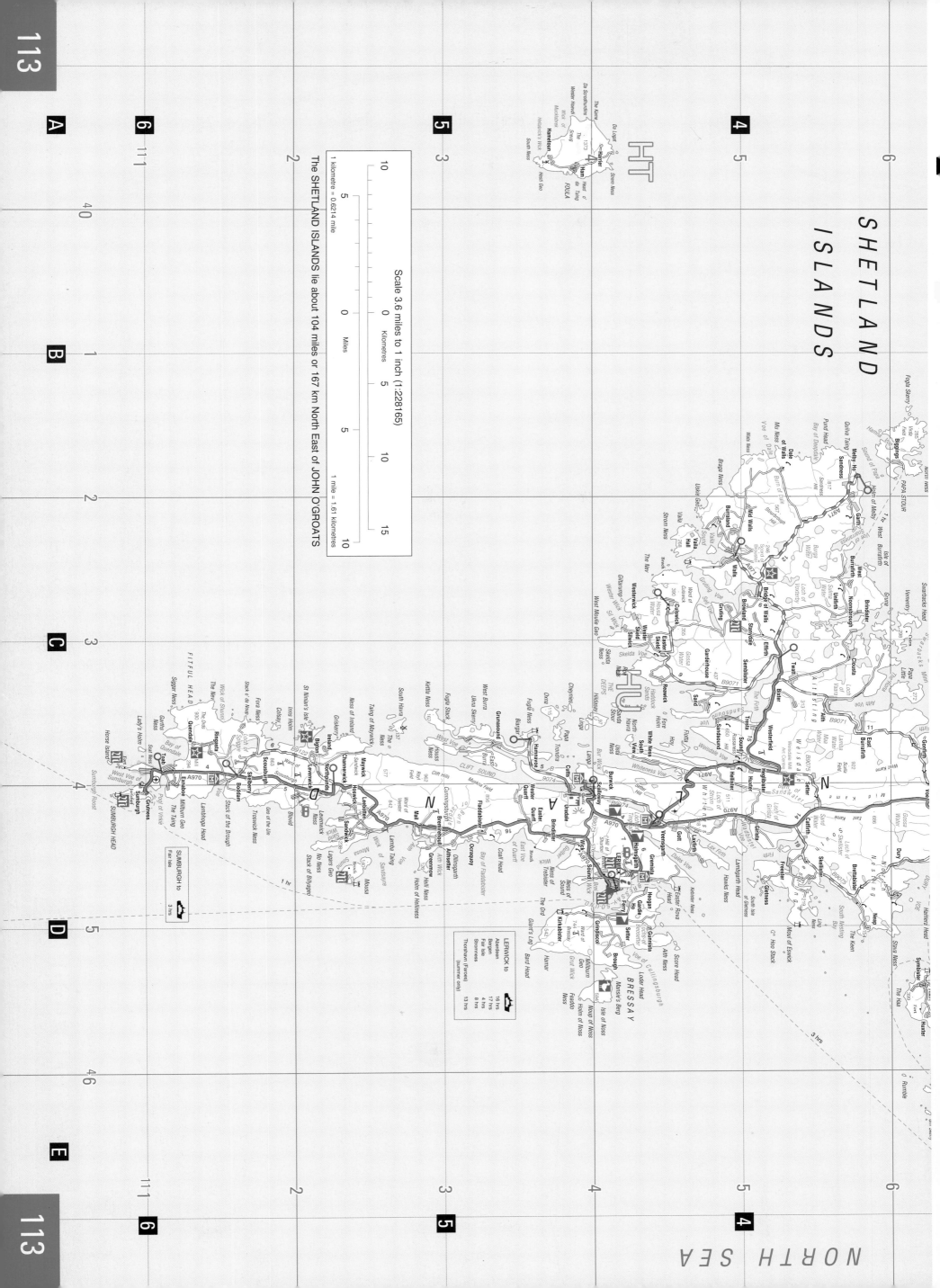

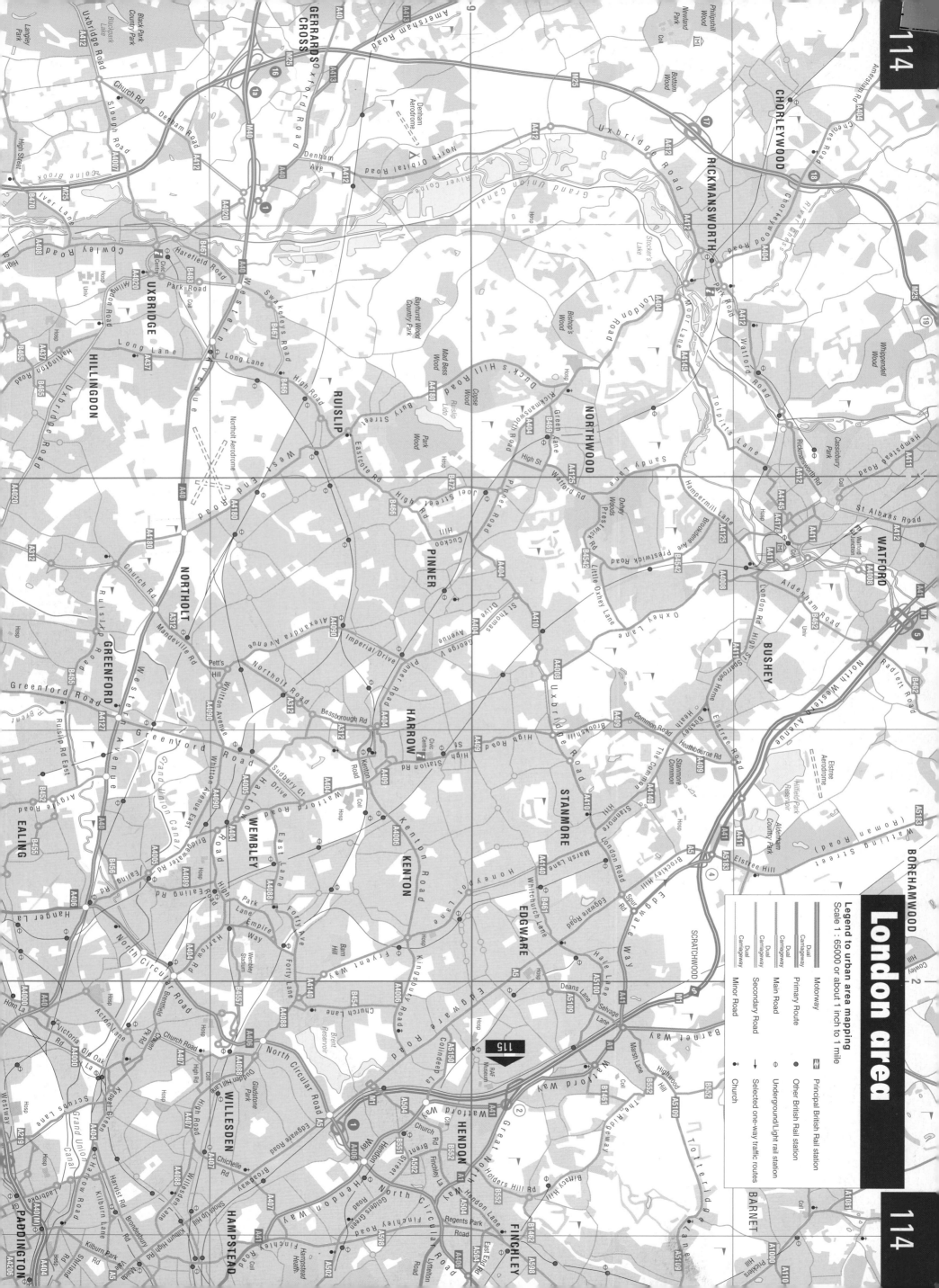

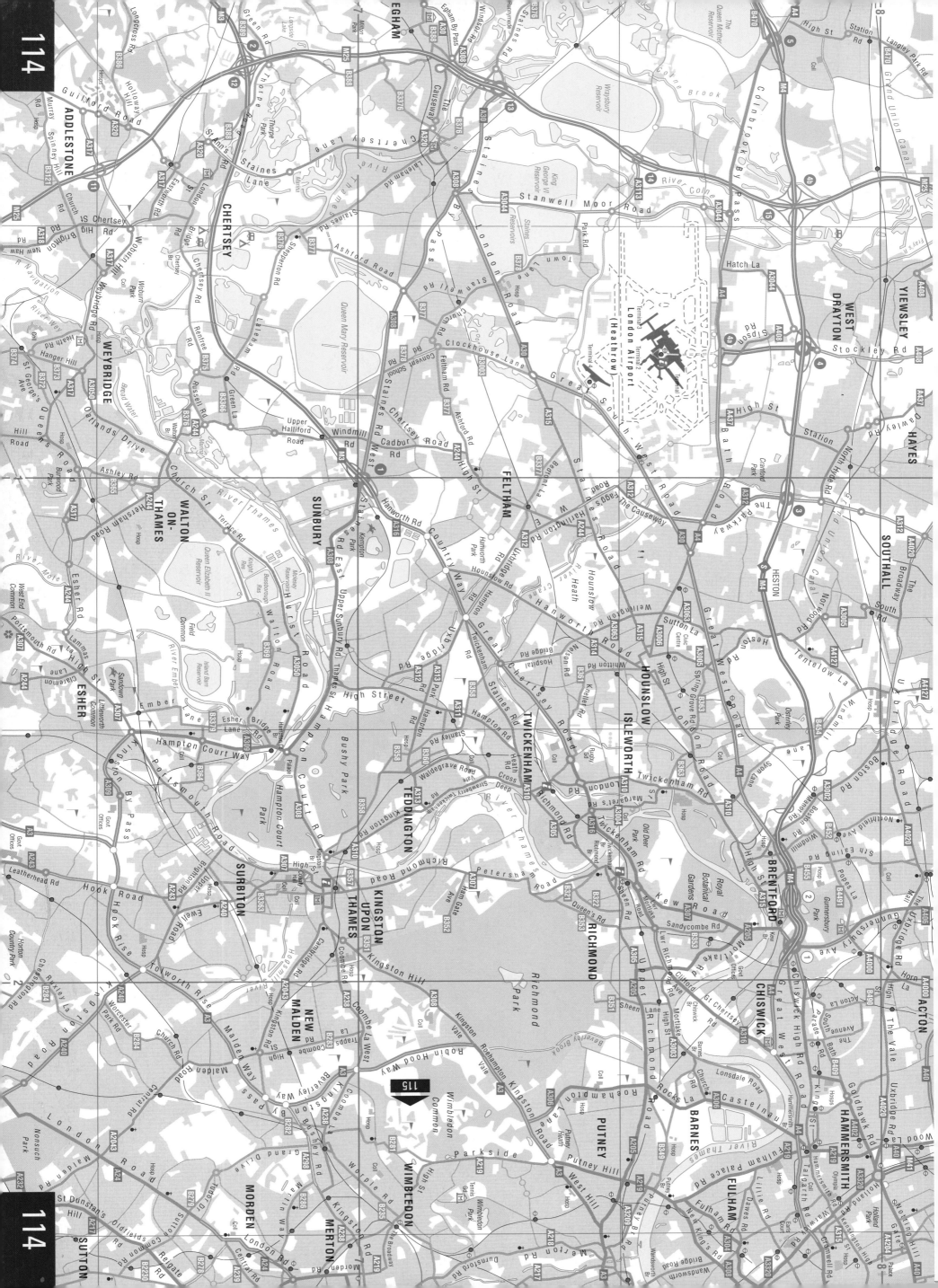

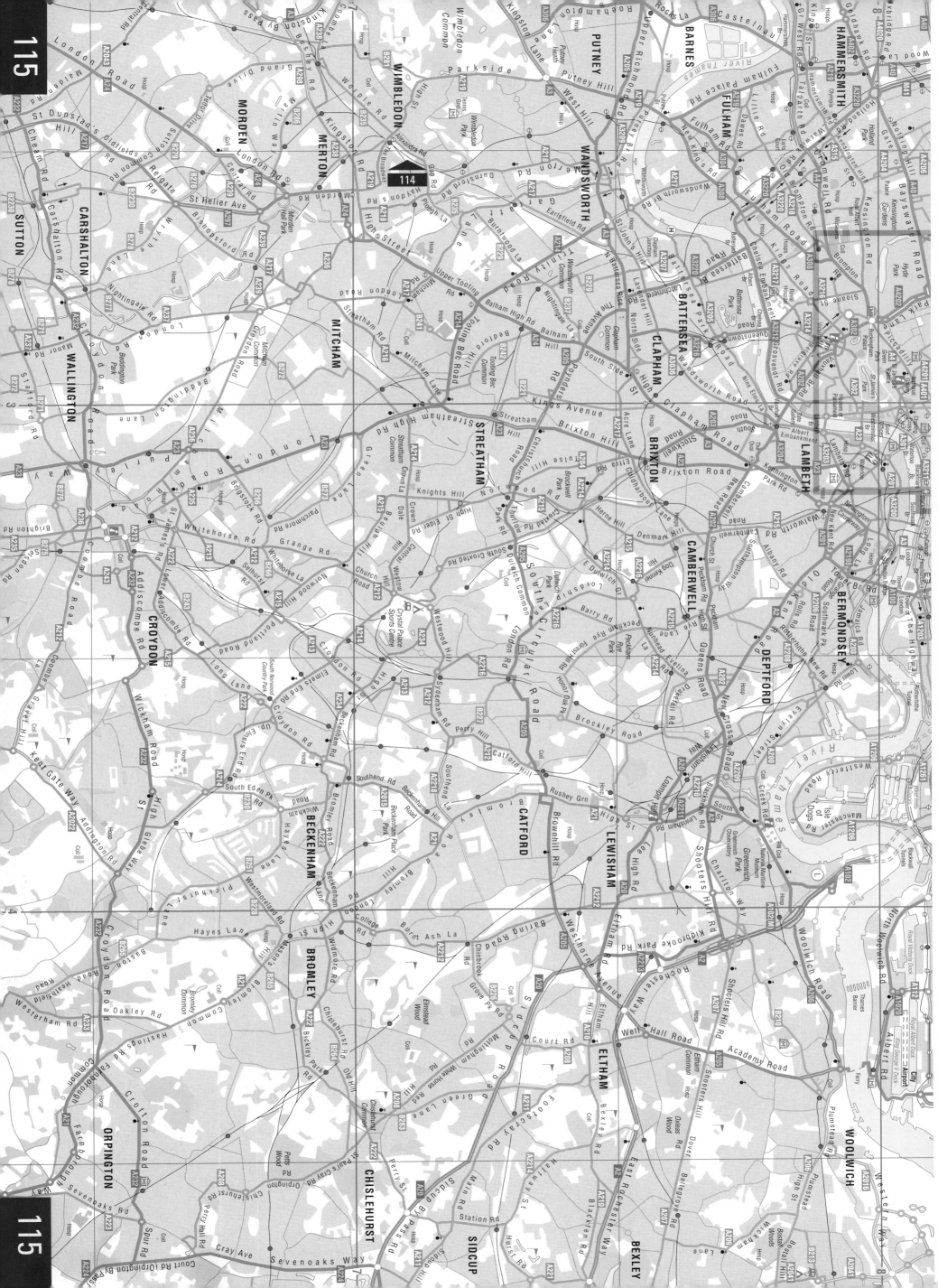

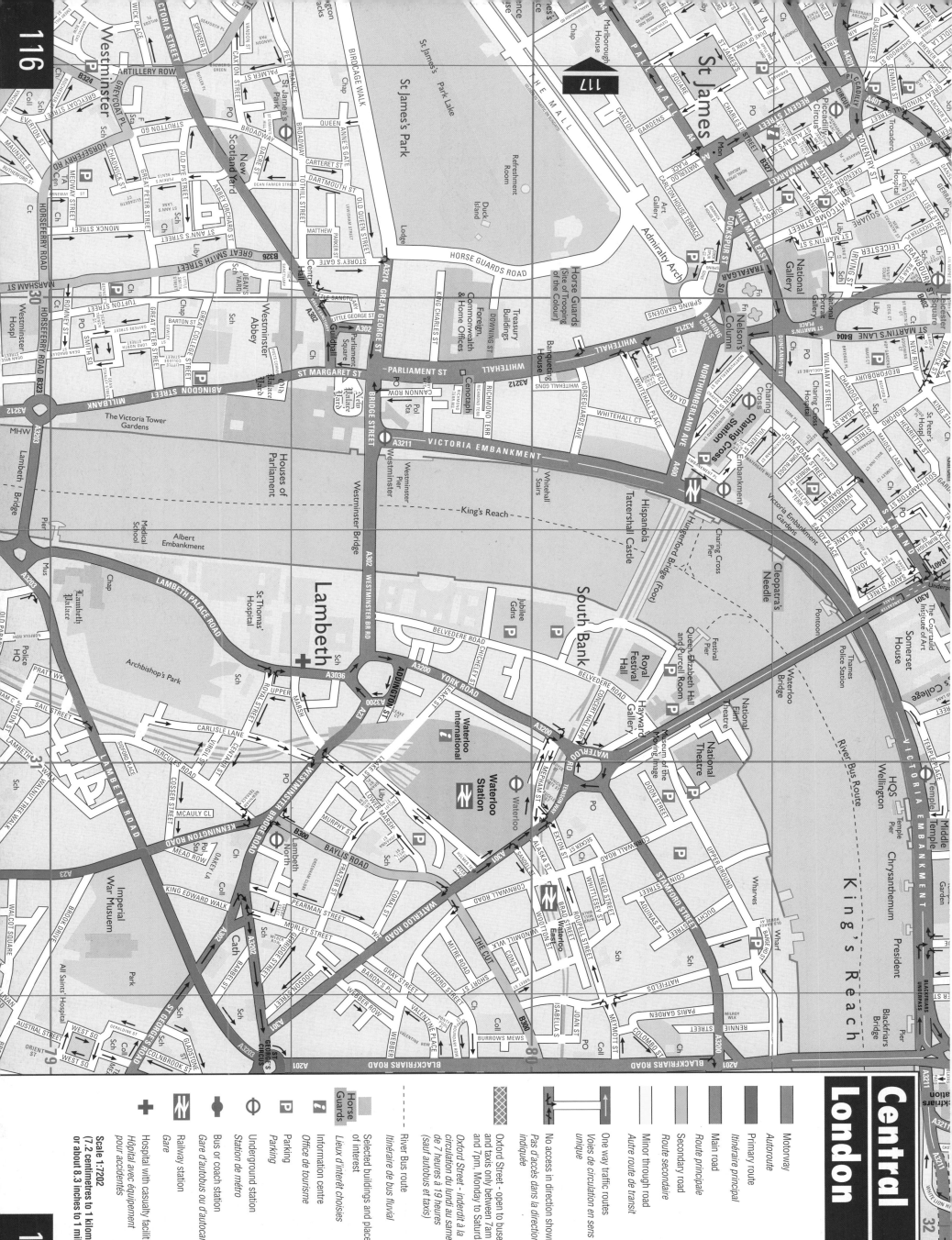

Westminster

St James

St James's Park

Lambeth

South Bank

King's Reach

Central London

Scale 1:7202
(7.2 centimetres to 1 kilometre
or about 8.3 inches to 1 mile.)

Motorway
Autoroute

Main road
Route principale

Primary route
Itinéraire principal

Secondary road
Route secondaire

Minor through road
Autre route de transit

One way traffic routes
Voies de circulation en sens
unique

No access in direction shown
Pas d'accès dans la direction
indiquée

Oxford Street - open to buses
and taxis only between 7am
and 7pm, Monday to Saturday
Oxford Street - interdit à la
circulation du lundi au samedi,
de 7 heures à 19 heures
(sauf autobus et taxis)

River Bus route
Itinéraire de bus fluvial

Selected buildings and places
of interest
Lieux d'intérêt choisies

Information centre
Office de tourisme

Parking
Parking

Bus or coach station
Gare d'autobus ou d'autocar

Underground station
Station de métro

Railway station
Gare

Hospital with casualty facilities
Hôpital avec équipement
pour accidents

Horse Guards

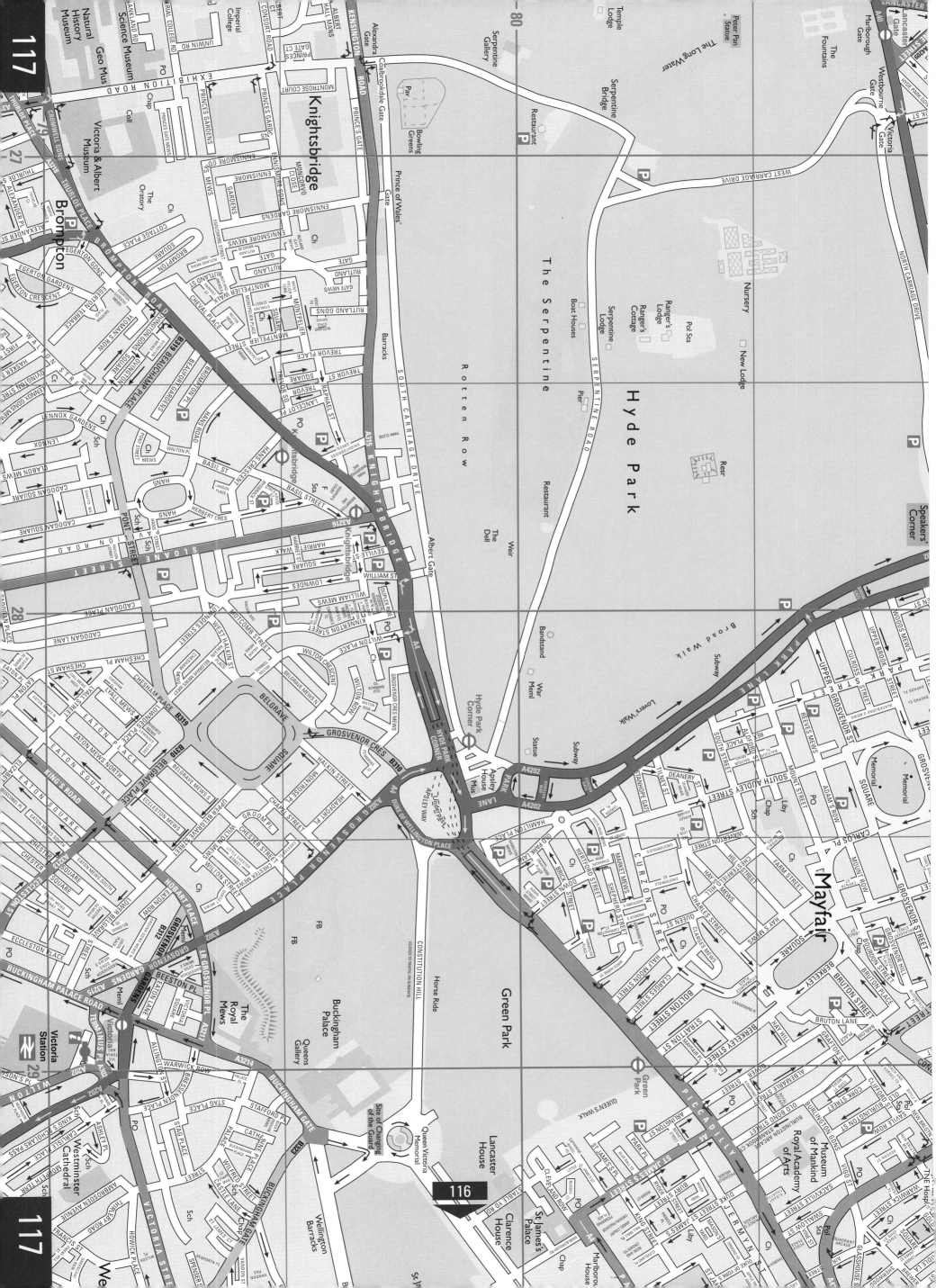

Town plans

Aberdeen

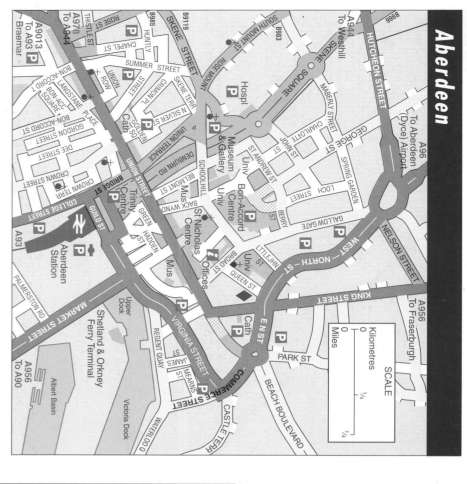

Bath

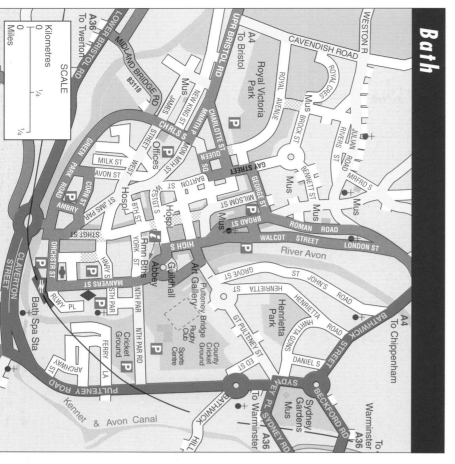

Birmingham

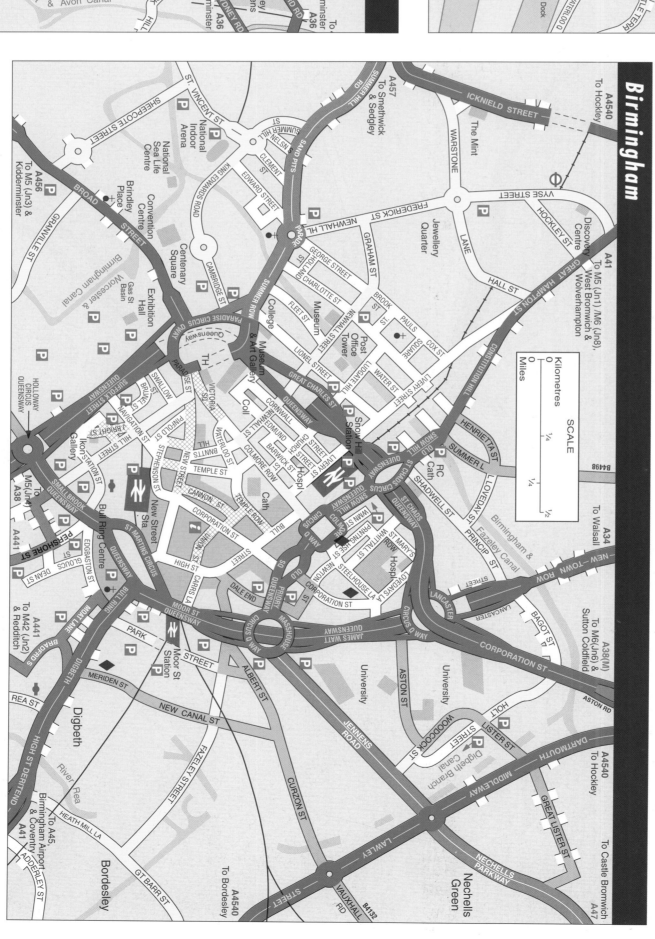

Legend

- Motorway / Autoroute
- Primary route / Itinéraire principal
- Main road / Route principale
- Secondary road / Route secondaire
- Minor through road / Autre route de transit

- Pedestrian area / Zone piétonnière
- Principal shopping centre / Centre commercial
- Main police station / Commissariat de police
- Motorway junction / Échangeur d'autoroute
- Important building / Édifice important

- TH Town Hall / Hôtel de ville
- Railway station / Gare
- Underground/metro station / Station de métro
- Information Centre, all year / Office de tourisme, ouvert toute l'année
- Information Centre, seasonal / Office de tourisme, ouvert en saison

- Church / Église
- Parking / Parking
- Information building / Office de tourisme
- Bus/coach station / Gare d'autobus/d'autocar

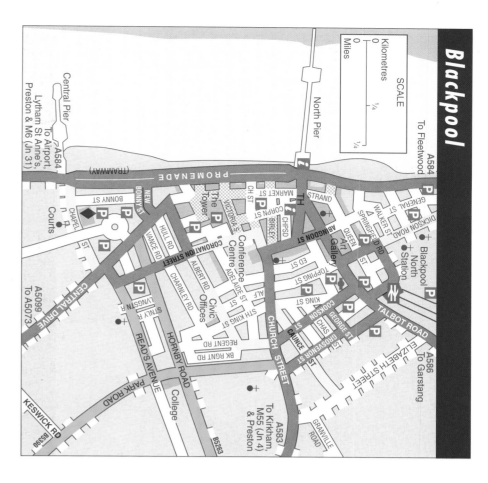

Blackpool

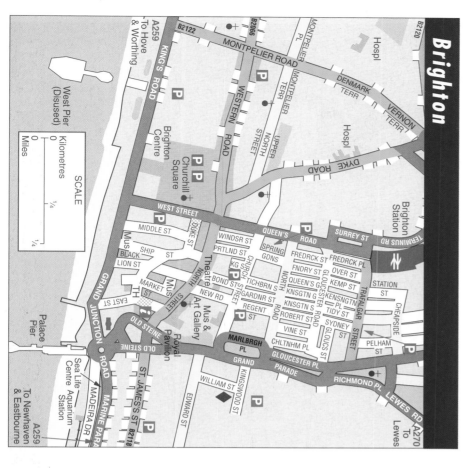

Brighton

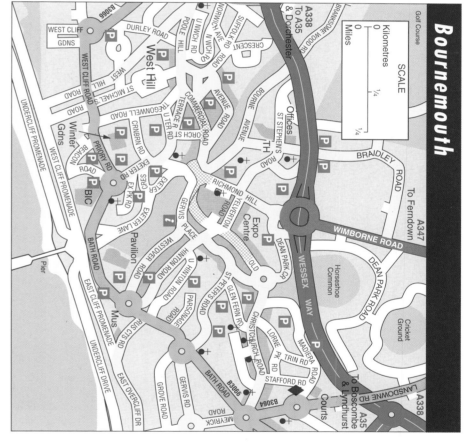

Bournemouth

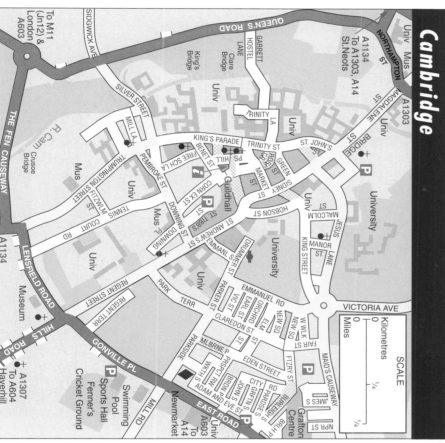

Cambridge

Bradford

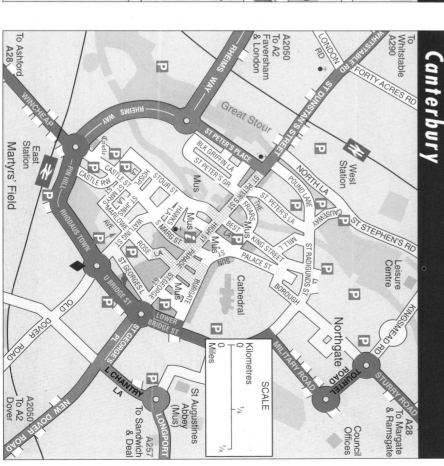

Canterbury